Reliability and Validity in Neuropsychological Assessment

Critical Issues in Neuropsychology

ASSESSMENT ISSUES IN CHILD NEUROPSYCHOLOGY
Edited by Michael G. Tramontana and Stephen R. Hooper

BRAIN ORGANIZATION OF LANGUAGE AND COGNITIVE PROCESSES
Edited by Alfredo Ardila and Feggy Ostrosky-Solis

HANDBOOK OF CLINICAL CHILD NEUROPSYCHOLOGY
Edited by Cecil R. Reynolds and Elaine Fletcher-Janzen

MEDICAL NEUROPSYCHOLOGY: The Impact of Disease on Behavior
Edited by Ralph E. Tarter, David H. Van Thiel, and Kathleen L. Edwards

NEUROPSYCHOLOGICAL FUNCTION AND BRAIN IMAGING
Edited by Erin D. Bigler, Ronald A. Yeo, and Eric Turkheimer

NEUROPSYCHOLOGY, NEUROPSYCHIATRY, AND BEHAVIORAL NEUROLOGY
R. Joseph

RELIABILITY AND VALIDITY IN NEUROPSYCHOLOGICAL ASSESSMENT
Michael D. Franzen

Reliability and Validity in Neuropsychological Assessment

Michael D. Franzen

*West Virginia University School of Medicine
and West Virginia University
Morgantown, West Virginia*

With Contributions by

Douglas E. Robbins

*Lakeshore Rehabilitation Complex
Birmingham, Alabama*

and

Robert F. Sawicki

*Lake Erie Institute of Rehabilitation
Erie, Pennsylvania*

Plenum Press • New York and London

Library of Congress Cataloging in Publication Data

Franzen, Michael D., 1954–
    Reliability and validity in neuropsychological assessment.

    (Critical issues in neuropsychology)
    Bibliography: p.
    Includes index.
    1. Neuropsychological tests — Evaluation. 2. Neuropsychological tests — Validity. I.
Robbins, Douglas E. II. Sawicki, Robert F. III. Title. IV. Series.
    [DNLM: 1. Neuropsychological Tests. 2. Neuropsychology. WL 103 F837r]
    RC386.6.N48F73   1989   152   88-35666
    ISBN 0-306-43065-7

© 1989 Plenum Press, New York
A Division of Plenum Publishing Corporation
233 Spring Street, New York, N.Y. 10013

Printed in the United States of America

Preface

Clinical neuropsychology has its origins in the medical field. The earliest practitioners were physicians who were interested in the location of lesions in patients who exhibited behavioral abnormalities or deficits. Paul Broca and Karl Wernicke are exemplars. Later, psychologists entered the field and brought with them a quantitative approach to observing and assessing behavior. Hence, the methods of assessment and interpretation moved from liance on subjective, internal, informal norms of "correct" behavior to reliance on quantitative, objective, formal norms based on the measurement of the same functions in numerous nonimpaired individuals. However, its production of a number was not sufficient for an assessment technique to be considered part of a standardized procedure. The number must possess certain characteristics; it must be stable under unchanging conditions, and it must be meaningfully related to some criterion.

In order to evaluate the degree to which the numbers produced by assessment possessed these characteristics of stability and meaningfulness, or of reliability and validity, experimental and mathematical methods were applied that had been developed in other areas of psychometrics (literally, the measurement of psychological functions). But because clinical neuropsychology still remained at least partly a medical endeavor, it was somewhat slower than some areas of psychological measurement to evaluate its instruments by psychometric methods. There were even some individuals who totally eschewed the use of assessment methods that produced numbers. That is not the case today. The practitioners who are most highly identified with psychometric methods are those clinical neuropsychologists who use a battery approach to assessment. But even those individuals who use a flexible approach, sometimes called a *process approach*, rely on smaller tests that produce numbers. It is difficult to find a contemporary clinical neuropsychologist who does not use at least a few standardized tests in evaluating a patient. The evaluation of the psychometric properties of clinical neuropsychological assessment instruments has assumed a prominent position and a higher priority than it held previously.

The Book of Psalms tells us that there is nothing new under the sun. This observation appears to be true of clinical neuropsychological assessment. Many of the instruments in current use have been with us for a while. Even the newer instruments have had previous incarnations as instruments designed to measure some other function or as subjective qualitative assessment techniques. Unfortunately, this means that many of these instruments have not been adequately evaluated by the methods of modern psychometric theory.

The psychometric evaluation of assessment instruments is a continual activity. This is true, first of all, because psychometric theoreticians keep producing innovations. Second, the psychometric properties of the instruments depend on the characteristics of the subject populations. As individuals change or as different emphases develop for a population, the instruments need to be reevaluated. This book should be seen as a takeoff point rather than as a summation point.

The purpose of this book is not to indict certain assessment instruments or to champion other instruments. Instead, the purpose is to identify areas of needed research. Recommendations regarding clinical use are made in certain cases; however, if we were to use only those instruments that have been completely evaluated and found to be completely satisfactory, our repertoire of assessment techniques would be very small indeed. This last statement is not meant to be a justification for the use of incompletely evaluated instruments or a justification for the use of instruments that have been evaluated and found to lack reasonable reliability or found to generate no valid interpretations. We have an obligation to choose the best instrument or to develop a better one. Some instruments may be useful in some situations and useless in others. We should use the results of research to guide our choice of assessment instruments.

It is hoped that the use of this book will alert the clinical researcher to the need to conduct basic research into the psychometric properties of neuropsychological instruments. It is further hoped that clinicians will use the book to make decisions regarding the use of instruments for particular patients in particular situations. It is also hoped that students will be able to use this book to learn about instruments or to generate ideas for thesis or dissertation research.

Acknowledgments

Even a book this small requires that the contributions of others be recognized. First, I'm grateful for the contributions of the coauthors of some of the chapters, D. E. Robbins and R. F. Sawicki. My thanks to the editor, Eliot Werner, who showed patience in waiting for the manuscript. I'd like to acknowledge C. J. Golden for his suggestion that the book be written in the first place. M. R. Lovell provided both intellectual stimulation and personal support. I'd like to thank S. Henderson for having typed the references on weekends and in the evenings. Finally, I'm grateful to Deb for showing patience and forbearance during the long stretches of time during which I worked on this book rather than doing other things.

Contents

Chapter 1

Preliminary Measurement Considerations in Clinical
    Neuropsychological Assessment 1

Chapter 2

General and Theoretical Considerations in the Assessment of
    Reliability 7

Item Response Theory 8
Generalizability Theory 10
Concluding Remarks 13

Chapter 3

Practical and Methodological Considerations Regarding
    Reliability 15

Statistical Methodology in Reliability Measurement 17
Design Methodology in Reliability Measurement 20
Interpretation of Reliability Information 25
Item Response Theory 27

Chapter 4

Elemental Considerations in Validity 29

The Nature of Validity 31
Validity and Nonneurological Variables 34
Concluding Comments 35

Chapter 5

Validity as Applied to Neuropsychological Assessment 37
with Robert F. Sawicki

Types of Validity 37
Validity: Basic Definitions 38
    Content Validity 38
    Criterion Validity 41
    Construct Validity 45
Threats to Test Validity 49
    Threats to Internal Validity 50
    Threats to External Validity 50
Conclusions 50

Chapter 6

The Wechsler Adult Intelligence Scale–Revised 53

Normative Information 54
Reliability 54
Validity 58
Conclusions 59

Chapter 7

The Wechsler Intelligence Scale for Children–Revised 61

Reliability 61
Validity 65
    Construct Validity 67
Conclusions 72

Chapter 8

Tests of General Intelligence 73

Goodenough–Harris Drawing Test 73
The Leiter International Performance Scale 75
The Mill Hill Vocabulary Test 76
The Pictorial Test of Intelligence 76
Peabody Picture Vocabulary Test–Revised 77
The Queensland Test 78
The Quick Test 79
Raven's Progressive Matrices 81

Stanford–Binet Intelligence Scale 86
Slosson Intelligence Test 87
The Shipley–Hartford Scale 88

Chapter 9

The Halstead–Reitan Neuropsychological Battery 91
   with Douglas E. Robbins

Normative Data 93
   Age Effects 94
   Effect of Education 95
   Effect of Sex 95
Reliability 95
   Test–Retest 96
   Internal Consistency 97
Validity 98
   Concurrent Validity 98
   Discriminative Validity 99
Differentiation between Psychiatric and Neurological Presentations 101
   Pseudoneurological Studies 102
   Detection of Faking 102
   Statistical and Actuarial Models 103
   Concurrent-Discriminative Studies 103
   Factor-Analytic Studies 106
Summary 107

Chapter 10

The Luria–Nebraska Neuropsychological Battery 109
Reliability 112
Validity 113
Luria–Nebraska Neuropsychological Battery Form II 118

Chapter 11

Benton's Neuropsychological Assessment 121
Right–Left Orientation 122
Serial Digit Learning 123
Facial Recognition 123
Judgment of Line Orientation 125
Visual Form Discrimination 126
Pantomime Recognition 128

Tactile Form Perception 129
Finger Localization 130
Phoneme Discrimination 131
Three-Dimensional Block Construction 131
Motor Impersistence 133
The Benton Visual Retention Test 134
    Reliability 135
    Validity 136
The Sentence Repetition Test 138

Chapter 12

The Minnesota Multiphasic Personality Inventory 139

with Douglas E. Robbins

Reliability 140
Validity 141
    Localizationalist Paradigm 141
    Differential Performance Paradigm 142
    Neuropsychological Functioning as a Means of Defining Group
        Inclusion 147
Addenda 150
Conclusions 151

Chapter 13

The Rorschach Inkblots 153

with Douglas E. Robbins

Normative Data 154
Reliability 155
Validity 156
Organic Signs 158
    Piotrowski Signs 158
    Hughes Signs 159
    Dorken and Kral Signs 159
    Aita, Reitan, and Ruth Signs 159
    Evans and Marmorston Signs 159
Normative Data for the Sign Systems 160
Reliability Studies 160
Validity of the Sign Systems 161
    Construct Validity 161
Conclusions 162

Chapter 14

The Wechsler Memory Scale 165

Normative Data 165
Reliability 166
Validity 171
The WMS as a Measure of Short-Term Verbal Memory 174
Attempts at Improving the WMS 175
  Russell's Revision of the WMS 176
Conclusions 179
Wechsler Memory Scale–Revised 180
  Normative Information 180
  Reliability 181
  Validity 182
  Criticisms 183
  Conclusions 183

Chapter 15

Tests of Memory 185

Memory for Designs Test 185
Paired Associates 187
Trigrams 188
Word Span 189
The Rey Auditory-Verbal Learning Test 190
Digit Span 193
Kimura's Recurring Figures Test 194
Knox's Cube Test 195
Block Tapping Test 197

Chapter 16

Tests of Verbal Functions 201

Use of Objects 201
Object-Naming Tests 202
Word Association Procedures 202
The Token Test 203
The New Word Learning Test 206
Boston Naming Test 207

Chapter 17

Tests of Visual Functions 209

The Rey–Osterreith Complex Figure Test 209
The Ishihara Color Blind Test 210
Meaningful Pictures 211
Stick Construction 211
The Minnesota Paper Form Board 212
Figure–Ground Tests 212
Hooper Visual Organization Test 213
Satz Block Rotation Test 215
    Reliability 216
    Validity 216
The Minnesota Percepto-Diagnostic Test 219
    Reliability 220
    Validity 221

Chapter 18

Tests of Higher Cognitive Functions 225

The Porteus Maze 225
Elithorn's Perceptual Maze 227
Verbal Concept Attainment Test 230
Weigl Color–Form Sorting Test 231
Wisconsin Card Sorting Test 232

Chapter 19

Screening Devices 237

The Bender–Gestalt Visual Motor Integration Test 237
    Normative Data 238
    Reliability 238
    Validity 241
Clinical Tests of the Sensorium 246
The Neuropsychological Impairment Screen 247
Personal Orientation Test 249
The Stroop Word–Color Test 249
    Reliability 250
    Validity 251
    Conclusions 251

Chapter 20

Tests of Achievement and Aptitude 253
The General Aptitude Test Battery 253
The McCarthy Scales of Children's Abilities 254
The Peabody Individual Achievement Test 255
The Wide Range Achievement Test 258

References 261

Index 299

Preliminary Measurement Considerations in Clinical Neuropsychological Assessment

As its name implies, clinical neuropsychology draws from more than just one discipline. From examining only the name, we get a somewhat simplified view of the different disciplines from which clinical neuropsychology draws. More than just simply neurology and more than just simply psychology comprise modern clinical neuropsychological practice. Current influences include behavioral therapy and assessment, internal medicine, rehabilitation, endocrinology, aphasiology, and public health, among others. Partly because of the wide divergence of sources for clinical neuropsychology, there is a wide variety of assessment techniques and instruments. The assessment methods involve everything from behavioral observation to timed pencil-and-paper tests. Many of the older assessment methods in clinical neuropsychology were derived from behavioral neurology and the medical model. These assessment instruments tend to be qualitative in nature and are scored largely on the basis of informal internal norms. Lately, there has been some activity aimed at standardizing these assessment procedures so that their use results in quantitative indices. In this way, many of the qualitative assessment procedures have become amenable to numerical analysis.

During World War II, many experimental psychologists were pressed into service as part of the war effort. These psychologists formed one of the first substantial groups of what have come to be known as *clinical psychologists*. Clinical psychology was in existence as a possibility previously, but it was at this time that the expansion and increase of clinical psychological activities accelerated. These wartime psychologists had been trained in laboratories and in the experimental method. Their conceptions of measurement had been formed largely by current psychometric theory. These psychologists brought their psychometric and experimental traditions to the clinical settings in which they found themselves or else adopted clinical techniques to their experimental methods. For example, A. L. Benton's early publications were on the use of the Rorschach to detect malingering by experimentally manipulating the administration instructions (Benton, 1945). Many of the patients in these clinical settings were soldiers who had suffered some form of brain impairment. It was this situation that was probably most responsible for the growth of psychometric and experimental influences on clinical neuropsychological assessment.

Today, clinical neuropsychological assessment has developed into something much broader and more sophisticated than what it was. There have also been developments in psychometric theory. Although classical test theory remains a primary influence on our conceptions of reliability and validity, psychometric theory is no longer associated just with classical test theory. There have been developments in measurement to include different forms of scaling, nonparametric as well as parametric statistics, and different theoretical conceptions of the process of measurement. As in any relationship between theory and practice, the movement from the theoretical side to the practical side has been somewhat slow. However, as clinical neuropsychology becomes more aligned with the scientific field of psychology and psychological training in contrast to its early background in the medical field, more clinical neuropsychologists will receive at least part of their training from psychometricians and measurement theoreticians. This last process will increase the quantitative sophistication of neuropsychological assessment.

We are not yet at the point where clinical neuropsychological assessment has become a field in which theory, science, and practice are successfully melded. Even where there are associations between theory and practice, the overlap may be minor. Many of the applications of psychometric theory to the evaluation of neuropsychological assessment instruments have been only in the area of classical test theory. However, we are seeing more applications of modern psychometric theory to the evaluation of neuropsychological assessment instruments. One example is the use of item response theory to evaluate the Knox Cube Test. More important, we are seeing a rational approach to evaluating neuropsychological assessment instruments. Not all "types" of reliability or validity need to be evaluated for each evaluation instrument. The choice of a design or paradigm within which to evaluate a neuropsychological assessment instrument should be as carefully pondered as the choice of an instrument for a particular clinical question.

There is not a hegemony of measurement theory in clinical neuropsychological assessment, and perhaps such a hegemony is not necessary. There are several different types of assessment and there are several different types of measurement strategies. These types of assessment use standardized tests to differing degrees. There are also differences in the extent to which parametric statistics have been used in analyses of the data resulting from the use of the assessment types. For example, many of the assessment strategies used by individuals who rely heavily on the clinical intuitive method associated with the behavioral neurology tradition result in qualitative information that is binary: impaired or normal. The original intent of gathering this type of information was to uncover behavioral deficits that had a strict correspondence with localized lesions. Of course, not much in the way of statistical analyses is possible with this type of qualitative information. However, some assessment instruments sum the number of qualitative signs in order to produce a number that is amenable to statistical manipulation and analysis. The Benton Visual Retention Test is an example of such a test, and there is the additional possibility of performing a qualitative analysis on the type of error exhibited by the subject.

Other assessment instruments rely on the production of numbers related to summed errors over a set of homogeneous items. This approach is seen in the psychometric tradition represented most directly in neuropsychology by the work of Ralph Reitan. Here, the number is thought to represent the placement of an index along a continuum of skill. Higher numbers indicate that the person has a larger amount of skill (or, depending on the scaling direction, has committed a larger number of errors and therefore has a smaller amount of skill) than an individual who has produced a smaller score. The same rationale has been used in the development of many smaller tests of specific neuropsychological functions. The advantage of the battery approach is that it allows an analysis of the profile and multivariate relations among the shorter tests that comprise the battery. Additionally, because the tests in the battery have been normed on the same population, comparisons across subtest performances can be meaningfully interpreted.

A final approach is one that is unique and still somewhat controversial: the measurement strategy used in the Luria–Nebraska Neuropsychological Battery. Although the LNNB was originally discussed as an attempt to use Luria's qualitative method in a standard psychometric framework, it became apparent that an even more different measurement strategy was possible. The scale scores of the LNNB are derived by summing qualitative errors and transformations of qualitatively different tasks into a set of single scores. The scales were originally headed by the names of the processes that were central to the various tasks, but the names were later removed in favor of numbering the scales. The scale scores do not represent homogeneous skills; instead, they can be used to make probabilistic statements about extratest behavior. The interpretation of the LNNB can be conducted by first examining scale elevations, then examining scale profiles, and then by conducting a qualitative analysis of individual item performance.

Perhaps some of these distinctions can be clarified by reference to a classification of measurement theories. Michell (1986) discussed three different theories of measurement with reference to acceptable statistics: representational theory, operational theory, and classical theory (not to be confused with classical test theory). At the risk of oversimplifying Michell's discussion, representational theory can be described as the use of numbers to represent the empirical relations between the objects of measurement. Operational theory views measurement as an operation that produces numbers. Classical theory views measurement as the assessment of quantity. Here, numbers are not necessarily assigned; instead, numerical relations are discovered.

In terms of these theories, the psychometric tradition can be seen to be embedded in the representational theory. The process of measurement results in numbers that reflect or represent a level of skill (or some other construct) that can be related to a level of some other skill when both skills are measured along the same scale. Or, alternately, the first number can be correlated with a number reflective of some other property, such as the degree of self-report anxiety. Representational theory applies only to single test scores. When the battery is interpreted on the basis of profiles, the applicable body of thought is classical theory. In profile interpretation, one goal is to uncover the numerical relations among the subtests as well as between the subtest profiles and external indices such as the diagnostic group or indices of extratest behavior.

The measurement and production of numbers involved in summing qualitative signs are associated with operational theory. The operation of challenging the subject to perform certain behaviors and then summing the successes results in a number that does not necessarily reflect a skill, but that can be analyzed by means of statistical manipulations. The operational theory of measurement is also implicit in the use of the behavioral assessment techniques that have been applied mainly to the assessment of the functional levels of skill in neuropsychologically impaired individuals involved in a rehabilitation program. The score on a test of cooking behaviors is not interpreted as representing cooking skill *per se*. Rather, the score is thought to be related to overall success in performing chains of behaviors embedded in some aspect of independent functioning.

The measurement theory implicit in the LNNB appears to be a combination of operational theory and classical theory. The overlap with operational theory is apparent from the discussion above regarding the summing of qualitative signs. The relation to classical theory results from the lack of reliance on a definite construct that homogeneously underlies the procedure and from the use of profile and multivariate strategies for interpretation. Elevations on certain scales in conjunction with lower scores on other scales are thought to be associated with certain diagnoses.

Despite the heterogeneity of underlying measurement theories, there is a common link across many neuropsychological assessment strategies. That link is the production of numbers. The numbers open the possibility of mathematically analyzing the data and investigating the characteristics of the instruments in an empirical and systematic fashion. Not all neuropsychological assessment strategies can be evaluated in this manner. Notable exceptions are the interview and the history. However, for those assessment strategies for which numerical analysis is appropriate, it is important to conduct those analyses in order to better understand the instruments, and ultimately to better understand brain–behavior relations and our patients. The utility and accuracy of information and interpretations derived from the interview and history need to be evaluated as well; however, the methods used to evaluate them are markedly different from those methods used to evaluate the quantitative assessment methods.

A few words may be said here about the intended purpose of this book. This book is not intended as a step-by-step manual by which a person can engage in investigations of the reliability and validity of neuropsychological assessment instruments. Instead, the book is intended to highlight pertinent issues and to alert clinical researchers and clinicians to issues that need to be dealt with when they are researching or evaluating neuropsychological instruments.

The discussions rely to some extent on prior knowledge of psychometric theory and methods. It is assumed that the reader has some familiarity with factor analysis. Of course, it is also assumed that the reader has some familiarity with neuropsychological assessment. To that extent, the book reflects certain biases regarding what basic knowledge is required of the modern clinical neuropsychologist. It is true that the use of standardized psychometric instruments is not preferred over the use of instruments that require intuitive interpretation or instruments that are scored qualitatively. It is also true that not only psychometrically standardized instruments and interpretation systems have a place in clinical neuropsychological assessment. Qualitative methods are necessary and complementary to psychometric methods. However, the psychometric methods are essential components of neuropsychological assessment.

Some statements regarding the choice of instruments reviewed in the second part of the book are also necessary. The instruments were chosen on the basis of a few principles. First, the procedures must constitute part of contemporary clinical neuropsychological practice. Second, they must be amenable to empirical, quantitative investigation. Third, there must be published research evaluating their psychometric properties. In the library research for this book, it is possible that certain instruments favored by other clinical neuropsychologists have been overlooked. Undoubtedly, these omissions will be identified in the written reviews of the book; such is the nature of public scrutiny, and the final step in the scientific method is public scrutiny and debate. However, not all readers will be able to publish their opinions, and of these individuals, personal communication is requested.

Another limitation on the instruments chosen for this book involves the traditional conception of neuropsychological assessment. Many instruments used by clinical neuropsychologists who are interested in ecological issues and in the treatment of brain-impaired individuals are not represented here. As more clinical neuropsychologists become interested in these areas, we may see a shift toward the use of other instruments and the development of new instruments to measure variables, such as aspects of interpersonal behavior, that are not typically and traditionally seen as being in the purview of clinical neuropsychologists. This shift would be welcomed as the role of the clinical neuropsychologist changes from that of a consultant to surgeons to that of a treating professional responsible for certain aspects of a patient's overall health care. Unfortunately, at the present time, there is not sufficient material to allow including those instruments in this book. Exceptions exist for those instruments that have a long history of use by clinical neuropsychologists, such as the Minnesota Multiphasic Personality Inventory (MMPI). Therefore, there are reviews of the use of the Rorschach and the MMPI in the second part of the book. However, reviews of other instruments will have to wait until their frequency of use in clinical neuropsychological practice increases sufficiently to justify their inclusion.

2

General and Theoretical Considerations in the Assessment of Reliability

The term *reliability* is often used to describe the temporal stability of a set of measurement procedures. Other frequent uses of the term are related to internal consistency and agreement among different users of the procedures. These different usages all relate to a single concept, namely, the estimation of the influence of error on the scores resulting from the use of the test or set of procedures. A perfectly reliable test is a test that measures without error. Error-free measurement is a practical impossibility. Instead, it is an ideal to which test authors and developers attempt approximations. As well as being an impossible ideal to attain in a practical sense, reliability is also an impossible concept to evaluate directly. All of the methods and designs discussed in the next chapter are able only to estimate the reliability of the test. As will be seen in the more complete discussion in the next chapter, the methods and designs are attempts to estimate the degree of error that influences test scores by systematically varying the possible sources of error. The success of the endeavor is related to the quality of the methods and designs and to the ability of the researcher to comprehensively describe the possible sources of error.

The purpose of this chapter is to consider the concept of *reliability* itself. The most common form of reliability evaluation involves obtaining test scores on two occasions, under two conditions, or from two examiners, and correlating the two sets of scores. The correlation coefficients describe the extent of covariation between the two sets of scores, and the square of the coefficient describes the amount of shared variance. All of the usual methods and designs used to estimate reliability are based in classical test theory and depend on this theory for their assumptions. The major assumption is that the observed score is composed of a true score term and an error score term, and furthermore, that the error term values are independent of each other and normally distributed. More recent developments in test theory, such as Rasch model measurement and generalizability theory, have different assumptions and require a substantial rethinking of the notion of error-free measurement.

ITEM RESPONSE THEORY

Perhaps the earliest form of item response theory was contained in Frederick Lord's dissertation that was later published in monograph form as "A Theory of Test Scores" (1952). In that book, Lord described his dissatisfaction with classical test theory, particularly in regard to its assumptions. Lord demonstrated that, when the assumptions are made to fit the test-taking situation, rather than the other way around, there are startling implications for the relation of ability to the distribution of test scores and error terms. In particular, Lord felt that it could not be assumed that the relation of ability to the distribution of scores was linear, nor could it be assumed that errors were independent of true score. There has been much controversy regarding whether item response theory or classical test theory best fits the specifics of most test situations. We will not attempt to resolve this controversy. However, by surveying some of the advances in item response theory, we find some implications for clinical neuropsychological assessment, particularly in the way in which we regard reliability.

One of the most important differences between classical test theory and item response theory lies in their respective focus for analysis. Classical test theory uses test scores as the unit of analysis. Test scores are usually an arithmetic sum or average or some weighted sum of component items. The focus of item response theory is the item itself. Clinical neuropsychological assessment is a mixed breed of psychological assessment traditions. The influential assessment methods have included the qualitative analysis of discrete performance on individual tasks, as exemplified by the behavioral neurology tradition, as well as the quantitative analysis of test scores, as exemplified by the psychometric traditions used by R. M. Reitan and others. However, most evaluations of the reliability of neuropsychological assessment procedures have been limited to applications of the classical test theory to summative test scores. This is true even of the qualitative assessment procedures, in which the subject's performances on various procedures are summed into a single score. Even where psychometric methods are used, item response theory allows one to evaluate the single items that are the focus of the response pattern analysis that takes place following interpretation of the summative score.

Classical test theory is the ascendant form of psychometric theory taught in graduate psychology programs. Most clinical neuropsychologists are familiar with classical test theory. Item response theory is less well known among general psychologists (that is, among nonpsychometricians), and a brief overview is appropriate. Contrary to the usual assumption that ability has a linear relation to test score, Lord (1952) gave a mathematical proof that the relation was actually curvilinear. In subsequent publications, Lord refined his notions. An excellent discussion of current thought on the topic can be found in Lord (1980). Other relevant publications at a level appropriate for clinical neuropsychologists include Baker (1985), Hambleton (1983), and Andrich (1988).

Aside from the level of ability of the subject in performing the skill under consideration, item response theory posits three influences on item score values: the guessing parameter (the probability that a subject completely lacking in the skill will answer correctly), the item difficulty parameter (the level of skill where the item has .5 discrimination), and the item discrimination parameter (the probability of a correct response at a given level of difficulty). In graphing the relations among these variables, we obtain the item characteristic curve (ICC). The ICC is the cumulative or additive shape of the various logistic functions that describe the relations among the variables for differing levels of ability.

Perhaps the most common model used in practical applications of item response theory is the one-parameter logistic or Rasch model. The multiple application of the Rasch model is due, in part, to the work of Wright (e.g., Wright, 1977). It is also due to the model's relative simplicity. Only one parameter is allowed (or assumed) to vary, namely, item difficulty. The two-parameter normal-ogive model allows items to vary along two dimensions: difficulty and discrimination. Finally, the three-parameter model, which adds the dimension of variability in guessing, is perhaps a more complete model, but it is also a more complex model, and computer programs using it to analyze data are not readily available.

Item response theory's advantage of focusing on the level of the item as the unit of analysis has already been mentioned. There are other advantages, depending on the appropriateness of item response theory to a given data set. First, if a model is accurately specified for a population, the parameters estimated from various samples drawn from that population will be linearly related. This characteristic is known as *invariance of the item parameters*. A second advantage is known as *invariance of ability parameters*. Even if the estimation of the parameters has been based on two subjects' performance on two different items, the ability parameters can be compared across the two individuals, assuming that the two items measure the same dimension of ability. A third advantage is perhaps the most important for clinical neuropsychology. It is related to the fact that item response theory allows estimates of the precision of measurement or the degree of error for different levels of ability.

In clinical neuropsychological assessment, the ability of the subjects varies greatly. There are some conditions, such as advanced dementia, in which there are generally uniform and severe decrements in performance. There are also conditions, such as those that may result from infiltrative tumor or cerebral vascular accidents, in which a decrement in a single skill may be present alongside normal or even superior performance in another skill. Additionally, neuropsychological skills may be conceptualized as existing along a continuum of level of performance. An adequate test should contain items that differ in difficulty, so that it will detect the early signs of degenerative disorders or document the incremental improvements following injury and treatment. Historically, clinical neuropsychological assessment did not need to attend to these considerations. The main questions were related to the diagnosis of organicity or, in more sophisticated settings, to the localization of the lesion. Answering these questions required little in the way of reliability assessment. The items were usually scored as correct or incorrect. If a given item was performed incorrectly, organicity was diagnosed. If a given item was failed and another item was passed, localization was suggested. Now clinical neuropsychologists are asked to measure the level of skill in order to help predict behavior in an open environment, or they are asked to measure changes in skill level over time, and clinical neuropsychological assessment instruments need to be evaluated for differing levels of accuracy at differing levels of skill.

Weiss (1985) discussed some of the implications of item response theory for clinical assessment conducted by computer. An important current concern of clinical neuropsychological assessment is accurately determining the levels of ability across different skills. Doing so may require uneconomical uses of both the examiner's and the patient's time. Additionally, increasing the time required for an assessment may decrease the motivation of a subject to comply with the test procedures. Adaptive testing—that is, testing that conforms in the order of the presentation of items—is one method of reducing the amount of time needed to assess an individual. Item response theory will allow the construction of computer programs that evaluate subjects, choosing the order of presentation on the basis of the accuracy of the subject's responses to past items.

GENERALIZABILITY THEORY

Generalizability theory is concerned with the systematic description of sources of variance that impact on the reliability and validity of measures. The original statement of this set of concepts can be found in Cronbach, Rajaratnam, and Gleser (1963). Generalizability theory was proposed to overcome objections to what were seen as shortcomings in classical test theory. As noted above, classical test theory assumes that the act of measurement results in obtaining a true score combined with an error term, and that one of the goals of statistical analysis of the obtained scores is to estimate the amount of variance associated with error or uncontrolled factors. The methods involved in this estimation process required that observations be obtained under equivalent conditions (e.g., the same test administered twice or parallel forms administered to the same subjects). The shortcomings of classical theory were most apparent in direct behavioral observation, where exactly the same conditions were unlikely to be found in different measurement situations.

Cronbach *et al.* (1963) examined the reasons for reliability estimation in order to determine whether some alternate to classical theory existed for behavioral observations. They decided that the reason an investigator estimates the reliability of a measure is to facilitate generalization from the measure to some other set of conditions. Estimating test–retest reliability is a method of determining the extent to which one can generalize from the scores obtained in one temporal condition to the scores likely to be obtained in another temporal condition. Similarly, we are interested in interrater reliability because we wish to know the extent to which we can generalize from the scores obtained by one rater to the scores obtained by another rater. Because the apparent *raison d'être* of reliability studies was to estimate the degree of generalizability possible, Cronbach *et al.* (1963) decided that a more useful form of analysis would focus on generalizability. The approach taken by these authors involves a systematic manipulation of the variables thought to impinge on generalizability and a measurement of the effects of such manipulations on values of the test scores.

The advances allowed by generalizability theory included the capacity to test the statistical significance of the effects of undesirable sources of variance. These advances can most clearly be seen in the later book by Cronbach, Gleser, Nanda, and Rajaratnam (1972). The overall idea was to systematically vary the sources of "error" and thus to allow the researcher to partial out the sources of variance in a factorial design. Cronbach *et al.* (1972) examined the forms of reliability and validity and subsequently relabeled the forms as universes of generalizability.

Here, the value of a score is determined by the conditions under which the score is obtained. There is no single set of conditions, known as *facets* in generalizability theory, that needs to be considered in the evaluation of every assessment instrument. Instead, the researcher is responsible for determining the sufficiency and appropriateness of each set of facets. Some examples of facets are observers, items, test forms, time, and contexts. The researcher also specifies the universe to which he or she wishes to generalize. The universe contains the various levels of the facets to which the assessment instrument will be applied. For example, a neuropsychological assessment instrument may not have alternate forms and may be used in psychiatric and neurologic populations, may require active participation by the examiner so that the examiner's behavior is part of the eliciting stimuli for the test, and may be designed to be used to measure change across time. In this case, the relevant facets include observers, occasions, and the two populations, but not parallel forms.

The basic requirements of generalizability theory are that the universe be described unambiguously, that a person's score in one condition be independent of whether the person has been observed in another condition, and that the scores be on an interval level. Neither the content of the universe nor the statistical properties of the scores within conditions have any bearing on the use of generalizability theory. The analysis results in the computation of a generalizability coefficient, which is the squared coefficient of correlation between the observed score and the universe score. The universe score may be defined as the mean score over all relevant observations. Two types of error are possible under generalizability theory: the first type includes all components of variance; the second type includes only those components that are considered extraneous and whose influence is undesirable to the researcher in that situation.

Generalizability theory provides an experimental design for the evaluation of assessment procedures. When the analysis uncovers statistical significance associated with a certain dimension, it is possible that there will be inaccuracies in generalizing across that dimension. In a G (generalizability) study, the statistical significance of the interaction between two independent variables indicates that generalizability over one dimension in the interaction is variable for different levels of the second dimension. In a D (decision) study, the statistical significance of the interaction between two independent variables indicates that predictions made regarding the effects of manipulating the first variable are variables for different levels of the second variable. This conclusion may seem confusing at first, but it is actually consistent with the way in which statistically significant interaction terms are interpreted in normal factorial designs. The difference is that now there are implications either for the reliability of an instrument or for the validity of the inferences drawn from the use of the instrument. This discussion has concentrated on the evaluation of single scores; however, it should be pointed out that Cronbach *et al.* (1972) provided methods for applying their strategies to composite scores and multiscore tests.

Generalizability theory considers both reliability and validity and can be seen to provide a general model for the evaluation of both in a single conceptual scheme. Broadly speaking, a G study involves recording data that will allow estimates of the components of variance relevant to the use of a given measurement strategy. A D study involves recording data that will outline the limits of validity of certain conclusions or decisions based on the use of the instrument. The analogue of a G study is a reliability investigation, and the analogue of a D study is a validity investigation.

In order to use generalizability theory, we must consider which facets are important in clinical neuropsychological assessment. There is no easy answer to this question. The important facets vary for each instrument and for each use to which the instrument is put. Many clinical neuropsychological assessment instruments involve a considerable amount of interactive behavior between the examiner and the subject. For those instruments, the observer is an important facet. For neuropsychological assessment instruments for which it is important to measure change over time, the facet of occasion is important. For those instruments that are used to assess the level of skill along a continuum or in different diagnostic groups, the facet of population is important.

CONCLUDING REMARKS

Although the concept of *reliability* is often taught to psychologists in training as if it were a clearly defined concept with standard measurement procedures, *reliability* is actually a somewhat slippery concept that needs to be carefully conceptualized. Furthermore, the empirical estimation of reliability requires planning and active decision-making. With the exception of the Knox Cube Test, the estimation of the reliability of clinical neuropsychological assessment instruments has been based on classical test theory. This tendency is consistent with trends in general psychological assessment, but it may be insufficient to provide the information required to choose an instrument for a particular situation.

The degree of reliability is likely to vary at the different levels of skill of the individual. One way to deal with this variability is through the use of local norms (Elliott & Bretzing, 1980). However, this procedure is costly and time-consuming and does not allow an estimation of the amount of variability associated with different populations or different geographical locations. On the other hand, the use of item response theory allows the estimation of reliability at different levels of skill with the use of a single experimental sample, and the use of generalizability theory allows an estimation of the amount of variance associated with attempts to generalize across different populations.

Another benefit of item response theory is the ability to estimate reliability for a single item. This fact is very important for clinical neuropsychology because here interpretation is often based on a consideration of performance on individual items. This is true both of assessment instruments that have been designed by traditional psychometric construction methods of homogeneous content and varying difficulty level, such as the Wechsler intelligence scales, and of instruments that have been designed by less traditional construction methods, such as the Luria–Nebraska, where items are grouped into scales on the basis of shared central skill areas. In the first case, interpretation might be based partly on the point at which the performance of the subject starts to fail. In the second case, interpretation might be more directly based on a comparison of failed and passed items.

The benefits of the use of generalizability theory are partly related to the fact that it allows the researcher to take measurement error out of the realm of the ineffable and imprecisely estimable and to place it squarely in the arena of manipulatable and observable phenomena. The use of generalizability theory also causes clinical neuropsychologists to be more conservative in their interpretation of instrument evaluation results and to be more cautious in their predictions to situations outside the research setting.

None of the above statements are intended to argue for the replacement of traditional reliability estimation methods by either item response theory or generalizability theory. Instead, the argument is for the inclusion of both of these newer methods with the older methods. Because reliability is abstract, we can understand it better and more completely through the use of multiple estimation strategies. This book contains test reviews and critiques that focus mainly on the evaluation of reliability and validity as traditionally conceptualized. These reviews offer one way of understanding the numbers that result from the use of the measurement strategies. The innovative strategies discussed in this chapter represent different approaches that provide complementary ways of understanding the numbers, and that will ultimately increase our understanding of our patients.

Practical and Methodological Considerations Regarding Reliability

Reliability refers to some form of consistency or stability in the values of the scores that an instrument elicits. Reliability has different manifestations or different methods of evaluation. We can speak of split-half reliability, test–retest reliability, or alternate-forms reliability. Although these types of reliability require different methods of measurement, they are all ways of indexing the amount of variance in a test that is the result of error in measurement. Thus, reliability measurement is an attempt to estimate the percentage of error variance (Anastasi, 1982).

Another commonality of these forms of reliability is that they all involve the computation of a measure of association, agreement, or concordance. In split-half reliability, a computation relates the score from one half of the test to the score from the other half. In the test–retest method, the score on one occasion is related to the score on another occasion. This chapter considers the concept of *reliability* in the context of the statistical computations used to estimate a measure of reliability, as well as the forms of reliability and their related methodologies.

First, it is necessary to examine some of the broader issues that arise in the discussion of reliability. The conceptualization of reliability as the estimate of error in measurement is formulated from classical test theory. A given score is thought to consist of two parts: the true score and the error. The true score is the actual value of a given individual on the construct if it were to be measured completely accurately by the test. The error is the value of the extraneous influences on the measurement process.

For example, an individual may receive a score of 96 on a test that measures mathematical ability. This individual's true score might actually be 97. However, because the individual had not had much sleep the night before, the score was lowered by 2 points. Because the individual guessed correctly on a couple of items, the score was raised by 4 points. Because the test did not assess all areas of mathematical ability equally and instead was loaded more highly on an ability (say, trigonometry) with which the individual was not very familiar, his or her score was lowered by another 3 points. The individual then ends up with a measured score of 96. The error component of the observed score may be comprised of more than one influence. In addition, these influences may either lower or raise the observed score.

All of the above fluctuations in score are subsumed under the rubric *error*. The error portion of the measured score contains all of those influences that cause the measured score to deviate from the true score. In general, reliability estimates are attempts to measure the proportion of variance that is due to these extraneous, usually unstable influences. Reliability may therefore be thought of as the degree to which a measurement instrument is able to consistently elicit a stable score from an individual. An important consequence of this definition is that reliability is not binary; rather, it is continuous. A test is not reliable or unreliable, but it can possess a low or high degree of reliability.

Two different forms of error can lower the reliability of a test (Carmines & Zeller, 1979). Random errors are those extraneous influences that fluctuate over different occasions. An example of random error in neuropsychological testing is the influence of the time of day. As another example, the performance of a child tested at school is likely to be different on a Monday morning and on a Friday afternoon.

Nonrandom error is the result of those influences that systematically affect the observed score. Nonrandom error always raises or lowers the observed score to the same extent. For example, an individual's scores on the Wechsler Adult Intelligence Scale–Revised (WAIS-R) may be consistently lower than her or his scores on the WAIS. Because of nonrandom error, one of these forms may be over- or underestimating this person's IQ.

The concept of *reliability* poses some special problems for neuropsychological assessment instruments. We would not always expect an individual's score on a neuropsychological examination to remain stable. For example, one would not expect stable scores in the serial testing of an individual who had recently suffered a blow to the head. On the contrary, one would expect that the scores would improve over time as, for example, the edema subsided and as the individual learned to compensate for impaired abilities. The important consideration is that, for reliable scores, we would not expect the values to change in the absence of outside influences.

Brown (1970) defined *reliability* as the ratio of true variance in test scores to the total variance. This definition is from the psychometric tradition. It will help us determine an appropriate statistical format for the evaluation of reliability. In a behavioral sense, *reliability* can be defined as the ability of a test to elicit a stable performance from the subject in the absence of outside influences. This definition can help us to conceptualize the observable referents of reliability.

STATISTICAL METHODOLOGY IN RELIABILITY MEASUREMENT

Let us now turn to a discussion of the different statistical methods of measuring reliability. Generally speaking, reliability is measured by computing some form of a correlation coefficient, usually a Pearson product–moment coefficient. Some readers will recognize that, given our definition of reliability as the consistency of scores, an appropriate statistical model might be some form of analysis of variance. After all, the analysis of variance is well suited to determining the differences in two sets of observations. However, the analysis of variance actually tests for the difference between the means of the two groups of observations. It would be possible for the individual scores to change drastically without affecting the analysis of variance as long as the group means remained relatively unchanged.

Using the correlation coefficient as the index of reliability helps us to address some of these problems. The correlation coefficient examines the extent to which the two sets of observations vary together. That is, a correlation coefficient keeps intact the differences between two paired observations instead of combining them in some group statistic. But the correlation coefficient does not reflect the difference in the value level of the observations. For example, if we take a set of observations and add 20 points to each and then correlate the second (created) set with the original set, we obtain a perfect correlation coefficient of 1.0.

The use of a correlation coefficient, therefore, is not perfect either. However, it is preferable to the use of the analysis of variance. One reason for this preference is that the correlation coefficient provides an index of the stability of the position of the observation in the distribution of scores. Second, its focus is on the individual observation instead of on the group mean. If there is a question regarding changes in level from one set of observations to the second, an analysis of variance (or in some cases, the use of a chi square or other nonparametric statistic) can be performed in addition to a calculation of the correlation coefficient, or else a simple examination of the group means may help to answer questions related to level. In fact, the optimum reliability evaluation may include both correlational procedures and analysis-of-variance procedures.

There is more than one correlation coefficient, and the choice of which one to use must be made on the basis of the characteristics of the data (Carroll, 1961). The most popular coefficient is the well-known Pearson product–moment correlation coefficient. The Pearson product–moment coeffi-

cient is computed by first calculating standardized deviation scores for each
of the observations and then summing the cross-products of the deviation
scores and dividing by the number of observations. This algorithm results
in a number that ranges from 1.0 to -1.0. A zero value indicates that there
is no linear relation between the two sets of observations. A value of 1.0
indicates that, as the values in one set increase, the values in the other set
increase accordingly. A value of -1.0 indicates that, as the values in one
set increase, the values in the other set decrease. The assumptions of the
Pearson product–moment coefficient include:

1. The relationship between the two sets of observations is linear.
2. The error terms are uncorrelated.
3. The error terms are normally distributed with a mean of zero.
4. The independent variable is uncorrelated with the error term.

The Pearson product–moment coefficient is relatively robust to violations
of some of its assumptions, such as normality and equal-interval measurement (Havlicek & Peterson, 1977). However, violations of the other assumptions sometimes result in an inflation of the value of the coefficient.
Therefore, it is best to use the Pearson product–moment coefficient when
one is relatively sure that the assumptions are met.

In addition, the Pearson product–moment coefficient is most accurate
when the data it describes are continuous, are of interval level, and have
reasonable variability. The use of the Pearson product–moment coefficient
with categorical data results in an overestimation of the correlation between
the two variables under consideration. The fewer the categories, the larger
the overestimation. The use of the Pearson product–moment coefficient with
data with restricted range presents the other side of the problem. Restriction
of range (or lack of variability) results in attenuation of the value of the
correlation coefficient.

When the data to be correlated are dichotomous, it is better to calculate
the phi coefficient, which is computed on the basis of the information contained in a 2 × 2 contingency table constructed from the two levels of each
of the variables. Phi can be computed from the entries in a 2 × 2 contingency
table as follows:

$$\text{Phi} = \frac{(bc - ad)}{(a + b)(c + d)(a + c)(b + d)} \tag{1}$$

where a is the entry in the upper left cell of a 2 × 2 contingency table, b is
the entry in the upper right cell, c is the entry in the lower left cell, and d
is the entry in the lower right cell (Hays, 1973).

When the data to be correlated are dichotomous in one set of observations and are continuous in the other, then the point-biserial coefficient

should be used. Both the phi coefficient and the point-biserial coefficient are versions of the product–moment coefficient, which can be used when the characteristics of the data do not match the assumptions of the Pearson product–moment, but for which it is necessary to obtain an estimate of the product–moment coefficient (Nunnally, 1978). An extension of the point-biserial coefficient is the tetrachoric correlation. This coefficient is computed when both variables are dichotomous but the researcher is interested in an estimate of what the product–moment correlation would be if the variables were continuous.

The next two indices to be discussed (Spearman's rank-order coefficient and Kendall's tau) are not, strictly speaking, correlation coefficients. They are actually descriptors of the extent to which the data tend toward monotonicity as well as of the direction of the relationship between the two sets of data (Hays, 1973). *Monotonicity* refers to the degree to which the observations on two variables are similarly ranked. A monotone-increasing relationship is one in which an increase in one variable is accompanied by an increase in the other. A monotone-decreasing relationship is one in which increases in one variable are accompanied by decreases in the other. Monotonic relationships are not necessarily linear. Therefore, these two statistics are also applied in those cases where the relationship between the two variables cannot be assumed to be linear.

The Spearman rank coefficient is calculated by treating the rank orderings as numbers and calculating the correlation between these two ranks, for example, between the rank of Subject A at Time 1 and again at Time 2. Under conditions of a bivariate normal distribution, the Spearman rank-order coefficient can be used as an estimate of the Pearson product–moment coefficient. However, in those cases, it is more convenient to calculate the product–moment coefficient.

The Kendall tau is calculated by first counting the number of times the pairs invert, that is, the number of times when that rank order of the two observations is not the same in the two sets of observations. This information is then used in the following formula:

$$\text{Tau} = \frac{2(C - D)}{n(n - 1)} \tag{2}$$

where C is the number of concordant pairs, D is the number of discordant pairs, and n is the sample size. The Kendall tau may be interpreted as a proportion of agreements to disagreements in the two rank orders. Neither Spearman's rank coefficient nor Kendall's tau provides all of the information that the Pearson product–moment coefficient can provide. For example, they cannot quantify the shared variance of the two sets of data. However, they can be quite useful as estimates of the similarity of the distributions of two sets of observations (Liebetrau, 1983). Both Spearman's rank-order coefficient and Kendall's tau compare the rank order of observations. They are useful when the data do not achieve interval level but are at ordinal level.

In some instances, the data to be correlated are subjective judgments. This can be the case in neuropsychological assessment when the end point of a procedure is the decision by a human judge to assign a category to the performance of a person. In these instances, a measure of agreement is needed in order to evaluate the consistency of the results of the procedure. Cohen's kappa may be quite useful in these instances. Cohen's kappa is a measure of agreement between two judgments that is corrected for chance agreements due to the limitations of the number of possible categories (Cohen, 1960). Kappa has been subsequently weighted to reflect the seriousness or degree of disagreement involved (Cohen, 1968). It has also been expanded to provide a measure of agreement among multiple raters (Conger, 1980).

There are several statistical methods of evaluating reliability. The choice of method must be based on the characteristics of the data involved. There must be a fit between the characteristics of the data and the assumptions of the statistical procedure. When evaluating studies that assess the reliability of neuropsychological instruments, it is important to consider the appropriateness of the statistic used in the study.

Many of the statistics used in the measurement of reliability have tests of significance associated with them. These are usually tests of the significance of the difference of the obtained coefficient from zero. The significance level of a correlation coefficient increases as a function of the sample size and as a function of the magnitude of the coefficient. With a sufficiently large sample, even a small correlation coefficient is statistically significant. This is an important point to remember. It is not enough for a reliability coefficient to be statistically significant; it must also be at least moderate-sized.

DESIGN METHODOLOGY IN RELIABILITY MEASUREMENT

Let us now turn to the different methods of estimating the stability of neuropsychological assessment instruments. *Reliability* is a single term used to describe the stability and consistency of an instrument in different settings. However, there are different ways of looking at reliability, including alternate forms, test–retest, and internal consistency reliability. Remember that reliability measurement is an attempt to estimate true variance in a test instrument; it seeks to exclude error variance. There are different methods of estimating reliability depending on the type of error variance to be excluded. Any condition that is irrelevant to the purpose of the test represents error variance.

Test–retest reliability is one of the most widely used methods of assessing the stability (reliability) of a test. In this method, the same test is given to the same individuals on two different occasions. A correlation coefficient is then computed to relate the sets of scores obtained on the two occasions. Assuming that the test measures a stable construct, we would want a correlation coefficient that approaches a value of 1. Achieving a coefficient of 1 is impossible because of practical considerations such as the instability of measurement and the influence of extraneous factors on the score, as well as because of statistical considerations such as regression toward the mean, in which extreme scores on the first test occasion regress toward the group mean on the second occasion (Nesselroade, Stigler, & Baltes, 1980). However, the more closely the correlation coefficient approximates a value of 1, the more reliable we say the test is. Correlation coefficients computed under these conditions are sometimes referred to as *coefficients of stability*. The higher the coefficients of stability are, the less a test is affected by conditions of the test situation or by those conditions of the testee's internal state that are irrelevant to the purposes of measurement.

Of course, some assessment instruments measure constructs that may not be stable themselves. In those cases, the computation of the reliability coefficient is affected by both measurement error and the instability of the construct. Heise (1969) proposed a procedure by which the effects of measurement error and of instability of the construct can be separated. The basic method involves measurement on at least three occasions instead of on only two occasions. By means of path analysis, two coefficients can be computed. The first coefficient estimates the reliability of the test, and the second coefficient estimates the reliability of the construct. The use of this procedure requires that the measurement errors not be serially correlated and that the value of the score not be influenced by an unmeasured variable during the course of the design. If these requirements cannot be met, a somewhat more complicated procedure, involving measurement on four different occasions, is recommended.

The amount of time that elapses between test occasions has an effect on the value of the coefficient of stability. Even on very stable measures, the value of the coefficient decreases with the passage of time. Therefore, when reporting the test–retest reliability, it is important to report the length of time involved in the procedure.

When assessing test–retest reliability, it is important to consider the effects of practice on the score obtained from the second test session. Practice effects may be a problem particularly when it is assumed that different individuals are affected differently by practice. If the effect of practice were to raise everyone's score by the same amount, the correlation coefficient would be unaffected. However, it is more likely that individuals are affected by practice in different degrees. Therefore, practice effects are an almost ubiquitous problem in test–retest situations. (Of course, measuring reliability by means of an analysis of variance would be sensitive even to uniform practice effects.)

Another method of assessing reliability is to compute what are known as *coefficients of equivalence*. A test samples from the universe of available items associated with a given construct. A second test, called a *parallel* or *alternate form*, could be composed of other items from the same universe. This second test could be very useful for serial testing where practice effects reduce the usefulness of consecutive testing with the original form.

The existence of alternate forms raises the question of whether the forms are actually equivalent. Stated in the terms introduced above, the question becomes: How stable are the scores obtained across forms? The method of assessing this type of reliability involves administering both forms of the test to the same individuals and computing a coefficient of equivalence. It is important that the administration of the two forms be separated by a minimum amount of time. When a period of time intervenes, the computed coefficient reflects test–retest reliability as well as equivalence reliability. This confusion results in an underestimation of the degree of equivalence between the two forms. It is not possible to administer the two forms simultaneously. However, the time that separates the two administrations should ideally be as short a period as possible when one wishes to obtain the highest estimate of equivalence reliability between the two tests. In order to estimate the influence of the time interval on the coefficient of equivalence, it is important to report the time period that intervenes between the two test occasions.

Alternate forms are very useful in serial testing, particularly when there is reason to suspect that practice effects are substantial. For example, when charting the course of recovery from an acute brain trauma, one would want to know the degree of recovery of function apart from the learning curve that would be demonstrated under the influence of practice effects.

An important point needs to be raised here. In order for the coefficient of equivalence to be reasonably interpreted, the two forms must have the same format, level of difficulty, length, and psychometric properties (Brown, 1970). Differences in these dimensions result in an attenuation of the value of the correlation coefficient. The coefficient of equivalence is usually a correlation coefficient, which is a way of describing the degree to which two sets of observations vary together. The scores from the two tests should therefore covary in a linear fashion. This is a necessary but insufficient condition for an assessment of equivalence, as the other dimensions mentioned above must also be considered.

The third method of estimating reliability is the method of split halves. This method is applicable to those tests that assume unidimensionality of the construct being measured by the test; if the test is multidimensional, the method is applied to a unidimensional subscale. (We will continue our discussion with reference to a test, with the understanding that the discussion also applies to a unidimensional scale.) As might be gathered from its name, the split-half method splits the test in half and correlates the score from one half of the test with the score from the other half. The test is administered in the usual way, and the split is performed afterward.

For obvious reasons, the split-half method cannot be used on speeded tests. It provides meaningful information on those tests that are composed of items of approximate equal difficulty and that are assumed to tap a single construct. The two most common ways of performing the split half are either actually to split the test in the middle or to perform an odd-even split, in which the sum of the odd items is correlated with the sum of the even items. However, any split of the items into two halves is possible. Different ways of splitting the test result in different values for the coefficient. Consequently, in an assessment of reliability, the researcher must accurately report which method was used to split the items.

The use of the split-half method raises a special problem. The reliability of a test depends partly on its length. When other factors are kept equal, the reliability of a test increases with its length (Anastasi, 1982). Splitting a test in half underestimates the reliability of the test with the original length. By using the Spearman–Brown formula, we can extrapolate from the obtained reliability coefficient to a prediction of what the value would be for the original length of the test. Neuropsychological tests such as the Tactual Performance Test and the Stroop Word–Color Test cannot be meaningfully evaluated by means of the split-half method.

The internal consistency method is a related method of estimating reliability. This method assesses the internal structure of the test, as does the split-half method, but it does not require that the test be split. As a result, the obtained coefficient is unique. The internal consistency coefficient is sensitive to two types of influences: content sampling of the test and the homogeneity of the construct being assessed. *Content sampling* refers to the thoroughness with which a test samples from the domain of the construct under question. For example, in order for us to say that it has adequate content sampling, a memory test may need to assess verbal memory, visual memory, tactile memory, memory with and without interference, immediate and delayed memory, and associational and contextual memory.

The homogeneity of the construct being assessed is a matter that is largely out of the control of the evaluator. One cannot increase the homogeneity of the construct of memory. As discussed above, memory has several components that may be independent of each other. For example, following closed-head trauma, one individual may exhibit deficits in recent memory but not in long-term memory. The internal consistency of a memory test can therefore be assumed to be low. However, one can group the items into relatively homogeneous scales and then assess the internal consistency of those scales. To extend our memory example, we would group the intermediate memory items together, the visual memory items together, and the tactile memory items together, and we would assess the internal consistency of these groups of items. The important point to remember here is that one needs to consider the theoretical underpinnings of the construct assessed by a test before deciding that the internal consistency reliability should have a high numerical value.

An early method of assessing the internal consistency of a test is a series of formulas developed by Kuder and Richardson (1937). Their best known formula is K-R 20. This formula provides an estimate of internal consistency for a scale of dichotomous items. An important assumption of this method is that all subjects attempt each of the items.

One of the most popular methods of assessing the internal consistency of a test is Cronbach's alpha (Cronbach, 1951). Cronbach's alpha is equivalent to the average split-half consistency coefficient for all possible divisions of the test into halves. In addition, Cronbach's alpha is a lower bound estimate of the reliability of a test. It is equal to the reliability only if all of the items are exactly equivalent (Novick & Lewis, 1967). Nunnally (1978) suggested that Cronbach's alpha may be interpreted as the expected correlation between a test and a hypothetical alternative form. All of these interpretations have in common the general notion that Cronbach's alpha is an index of the internal consistency of a test.

Far from being a fully examined concept, internal consistency estimates still occupy the time and thoughts of statistical researchers. The main question addresses the issue of the greatest lower bounds for reliability estimates. Bentler and Woodward (1980) suggested that a coefficient derived from commonalities of test parts provides the greatest lower bound. Cronbach (1988) suggested that their method capitalizes on chance relations in small samples and that constrained trace factor analysis (the method suggested by Bentler and Woodward) be used only on large samples with independent items.

The reader will remember that the internal consistency of a test is affected by the adequacy of the items in sampling from the domain of the construct. There are two ways in which this sampling may be less than adequate. First, the items may not measure the construct with equal precision, and second, the items may measure more than one construct. Factor analysis of the test can address both of these issues. Factor analysis of a test results in items being grouped into factors on the basis of the patterns of variance exhibited in the data. It therefore gives an indication of the homogeneity of the construct measured by the test. It also gives a numerical value to the relationship between an item and a factor. This number, called a *factor loading*, describes the extent to which an item measures the construct represented by the factor.

Two statistics have been proposed to represent the internal consistency reliability of a test when factor analysis is used. The first, called *coefficient theta*, is used in principal components analysis and can be interpreted as a form of Cronbach's coefficient alpha. Coefficient theta is an estimate of the maximum value of alpha (Greene & Carmines, 1980). The second statistic, called *coefficient omega,* is used in common factor analysis and can also be interpreted as a form of alpha. However, omega provides an estimate of the internal consistency reliability averaged across all of the common factors that arise in the analysis.

Clinical neuropsychological assessment instruments sometimes rely on a consideration of profiles in interpreting the results. For those multiscale instruments of which this is true, it may be important to have some estimate of the reliability of the profile. Conger and Lipshitz (1973) and Conger (1974) have provided some formulas for this purpose. These formulas have not been used in evaluating clinical neuropsychological instruments with the exception of the Wechsler Intelligence Scale for Children–Revised (which see). However, this is an important area that needs to be addressed.

Still another form of reliability refers to the stability of test scores obtained across examiners. There are two concepts involved in the determination of the stability of scores across raters. *Rater reliability* refers to the stability of the position of individuals in their respective distributions. Therefore, rater reliability is most appropriately measured by some form of a correlation coefficient. *Rater agreement* refers to the extent to which there is stability in the actual scores assigned to individuals. Both rater reliability and rater agreement are important in those cases in which the score of an individual is not arrived at totally objectively but is instead determined by some judgment on the part of the examiner. There are several measures of rater agreement, and the choice of one depends on the scaling characteristics of the ratings, the number of scoring categories possible, and the way in which agreement and disagreement are defined (Tinsley & Weiss, 1975). Additionally, Zwick (1988) recommended assessing the marginal homogeneity of the raters. If the raters have similar marginals, the use of a coefficient derived by Scott (1955) is suggested instead.

INTERPRETATION OF RELIABILITY INFORMATION

When choosing a test, it is important to evaluate it on the basis of its psychometric properties, including its reliability. Therefore, it is important to consider the meaning of the reliability coefficient in relation to the test. The type and degree of reliability expected are based on a careful consideration of the purpose of the test as well as on a careful consideration of the construct that the test purports to measure. Most neuropsychological tests seek to measure basic brain abilities. Therefore, most neuropsychological test procedures could be expected to exhibit a large degree of test–retest reliability. However, the degree of internal consistency reliability varies with the theoretical homogeneity of the construct measured by the test.

The magnitude of the reliability coefficient depends partly on the characteristics of the sample for which the coefficient is calculated. If the sample from which the coefficient is derived has limited variability, the coefficient will be attenuated because of the effects of the restriction of range. A sample that has a wide range of abilities associated with the construct will exhibit greater reliability than will a more homogeneous sample.

In addition, reliability is influenced by other characteristics of the group. The result of this influence is the existence of different reliability estimates for different groups. Therefore, it is important to examine the reliability estimate for the group relevant to the assessment at hand.

Adequate reliability is important if one is to interpret the score as reflecting an accurate measurement of the targeted construct. Another concept in the interpretation of reliability involves the standard error of measurement. *Reliability* refers to the stability of scores. *Standard error of measurement* refers to the significance of the differences between scores. Thus, it is affected by both the stability and the accuracy of the measurement. It can be used to interpret scores only from one individual, not across individuals. The standard error of measurement is calculated by means of the formula

$$SE_{\text{meas}} = SD_t(1 - r_{tt}) \tag{3}$$

where SD_t is the standard deviation of the test score and r_{tt} is the reliability of the test. By adding the standard error of measurement to the obtained score at one end and subtracting it at the other end, one can generate a confidence interval. The true score will be in this interval 68% of the time. As the standard deviation increases or the reliability decreases, the standard error of measurement increases.

The interpretation of score differences for the same individual is another important issue. One may wish to know whether the difference between an individual's score on the WAIS-R Performance scale is significantly different from that same individual's score on the WAIS-R Verbal scale. The statistic that can answer that question, the standard error of the difference, can be calculated by the use of either the standard error of measurement of the two scales or the reliability of the two scales. In the first formula, the standard error of differences between the two scales is expressed as the square root of the sum of the squared standard error of measurement for each of the two scales:

$$SE_{\text{diff}} = SE^2_{\text{meas }1} + SE^2_{\text{meas }2} \tag{4}$$

In the second formula, the standard error of differences is expressed as

$$SE_{\text{diff}} = SD(2 - r_{11} - r_{22}) \tag{5}$$

where *SD* is the standard deviation of the two scales (this formula applies only when the scales are made comparable by standardization) and r_{11} and r_{22} are the reliabilities for the respective scales.

By now the importance of reliability assessment has become apparent. Most generally speaking, the reliability coefficient associated with a given test gives us an estimate of the precision with which measurement is conducted by means of that test. It allows us to estimate the value of the true score by partialing out the influence of error. There are different methods of assessing reliability. Each one attempts to partial out the influence of a different type of error. Test–retest reliability attempts to partial out the error associated with transient situational variables. Internal consistency reliability attempts to partial out the influence of error due to imperfect content-sampling and content homogeneity. Alternate-form reliability attempts to partial out the influence of error due to imperfect content sampling. Scorer reliability attempts to partial out the influence of interscorer differences. In each of these cases, the estimation of the true score depends on the removal of the effect of an error source from the observed score. Because the estimation of the true score proceeds indirectly, it is important to make sure that all possible sources of error for a particular test have been identified. For example, if one wanted to assess an ability that was presumed to be relatively stable, one would choose a test that demonstrated adequate test–retest reliability. If the test could be scored completely objectively, one would not need to assess interscorer reliability. The assessment and use of reliability must be done with reference to the theoretical underpinnings of the test and the match of those underpinnings with the assumptions and information consequences of the methodology used.

Reliability refers to several different types of stability, such as temporal stability, equivalence stability, and internal stability. Each type of reliability estimation is an attempt to assess the accuracy of the measurement. As can be inferred from our discussion, reliability is never precisely measured; it can only be estimated. In order to give the most accurate estimate of the accuracy of the measurement, it is therefore necessary to obtain as many types of reliability estimation as are theoretically and practically possible with the particular instrument under question (Fiske, 1971).

ITEM RESPONSE THEORY

In the previous chapter, we discussed some of the theoretical implications of item response theory. We will now consider some of its practical applications in clinical neuropsychology.

In recent years, a new and exciting development has occurred in the psychometric evaluation of assessment procedures. This development is alternately referred to as the *Rasch model*, the *latent trait model*, or *item response theory*. Until now, most of the adherents of item response theory (IRT) have been mathematical psychometricians. This is true because of the complexity of the mathematics involved and the speed at which the area has developed, necessitating that interested persons keep abreast of a burgeoning body of highly complicated and sometimes contradictory mathematical material just to be conversant with the field, let alone to understand the material well enough to use it sensibly (Hambleton & Cook, 1977).

Recently, with the advent of programs that can be used to analyze data from tests using IRT, with the slowly growing consensus on the applicability of IRT to certain types of test data, and with the organizing of workshops and conferences dealing with the topic, IRT has started to trickle down into the armamentarium of methods used by psychologists to assess tests.

IRT assumes that the performance of a subject on a test can be partly predicted by the abilities or traits of the subject. These traits cannot be directly measured—hence the title *latent trait*. The emphasis of IRT is on the item. Rather than evaluating the summed score of the items that make up a test, each of the items is evaluated. Earlier, it was stated that classical test theory stipulates that the score on an item is composed of the true score and error. IRT stipulates that the latent response to an item is composed of two values: (1) the product of the latent trait times its correlation between the latent trait and the latent response and (2) the error component, which has a mean of zero and a distribution that is constant for all values of the latent trait (Bejar, 1983). IRT attempts to estimate the item's characteristic curve, which is determined by three parameters: the difficulty of the item, the ability of the subject, and the discrimination of the item. It is possible to hold constant any of those three parameters and to estimate the value of the third. It is this flexibility that gives IRT its wide applicability (Lord, 1980).

The first applications of IRT have been to achievement testing in the primary schools. However, it is easy to see that applications to ability and achievement testing in neuropsychological assessment are a logical extension. Item response theory does not require that all items be given to each subject, which is one of the requirements that limit classical theory. Therefore, IRT is well suited to the evaluation of an instrument in which the ceiling and floor specifications limit the number of items administered to each subject, such as the Stanford–Binet and the WAIS-R. Additionally, with IRT, it is possible to perform an assessment of equivalent forms that is much more fine-grained than that allowed by the current methods. It not only assesses the equivalence of test scores but also assesses the equivalence of items' difficulty and discrimination. Until now, there have been no published reports of the use of IRT to evaluate neuropsychological assessment techniques. However, it is only a matter of time before IRT will be applied to neuropsychological data in an attempt to further understand the psychometric properties of neuropsychological instruments.

4

Elemental Considerations in Validity

Validity is a term that is often invoked in decisions to use neuropsychological tests. Unfortunately, the context of this use is usually negative; a test is disparaged as being invalid. The use of the term implies that a test can be determined to be either valid or invalid. Of course, most clinical neuropsychologists agree that a test that is "valid" for one population may be "invalid" for another population. If this is true, can a test ever be evaluated as universally valid or invalid? A second question relates to how we evaluate a test as valid or invalid. This is a question of both method (How do we evaluate a test?) and of epistemology (How do we know what we know?). Although method may be discussed separately from epistemology, the obverse is not necessarily true. That is, how we know something is highly related to how we investigate that something. This chapter discusses general issues in the relation between epistemology and method, and the following chapter discusses the methodological issues more directly.

Historically, validity in clinical neuropsychological research has involved either the demonstration that scores derived from a test can accurately separate brain-impaired individuals from nonimpaired individuals or the demonstration of a statistical relation between scores on a neuropsychological test and the results of a medical neurodiagnostic procedure such as postmortem surgical investigations or CT scans. We say that we know the validity of a test by systematic, empirical investigation. Limiting neuropsychological validity studies to these variables was the result of the questions posed to the neuropsychologist in the clinical setting. Clinical neuropsychological assessment did not have its own canon of methods or its own set of mature scientific principles. To a large extent, clinical neuropsychology still doesn't have these. However, along with the development of clinical neuropsychology as a form of behavioral science with unique training requirements and professional identity has come a growth in methods that, although not unique in principle, are unique in application.

These developments have made necessary the examination of the concepts of both *reliability* and *validity* as applied to clinical neuropsychological assessment. The methods for investigating these concepts are formed partly by the nascent body of neuropsychological assumptions and principles and partly by the changing questions that are posed to the neuropsychologist in the clinical setting. Instead of being asked to localize the site of a lesion, clinical neuropsychologists are being asked to predict the limits of the behavior of a patient in the open environment or to determine whether a substantial change in skill level has occurred as the result of applications of a rehabilitation strategy.

Earlier, we stated that we know the validity of a test by empirical observations. However, there is a leap that needs to be made before we can make statements regarding the validity of a test. That leap is from the specific results of a particular procedure to statements regarding the test used as part of the procedure. The investigation is actually an evaluation of the conclusions drawn from the use of the test. These conclusions may relate to localization issues or to prediction issues, but they always depend on the procedure used and the context in which the procedures are used. These issues are usually discussed in terms of internal and external validity, and they are applied to the interpretations of the results of empirical investigations. Threats to internal validity are offered by those events or processes that present doubt about the reasonableness of the conclusions drawn. Threats to external validity are offered by those events or processes that present doubt about the generalizability of the results to other populations. These terms may be easily applied to the investigations of neuropsychological tests and may also be appropriate to discussions of the conclusions drawn from the use of these tests in a clinical situation. It may be misleading to speak of a test as valid or invalid when our research actually investigates specific hypotheses.

There is yet another consideration linking validity to method. In discussing personality constructs, Fiske (1973) argued that there was too much variance in the results when constructs are measured by different methods. Instead, Fiske proposed that the unit of analysis be the construct–operation unit. Huba and Hamilton (1976) replied that there was too much convergence among the data to support such a notion. Even though different instruments give slightly different results, they seem to share a central construct, as demonstrated by covariation among the instruments. Huba and Hamilton implicitly suggested that the best way to measure a construct is through multi-operationalization; however, they did not suggest a way to concatenate the data into a single index. Fiske (1976) replied that the presence of even small variations in relations among different methods of measuring constructs indicates the need to include the method as an integral part of the measuring unit.

Not all of these arguments may be applied to clinical neuropsychological assessment; however, parts of the arguments are very pertinent to the present discussion. Clinicians are familiar with the pattern of results when a patient performs well on a test of verbal memory but not on a test of visual memory. Alternately, the patient may perform well on a test of recognition memory, but not on a test of free recall. When these results occur, clinical neuropsychologists do not generally throw up their hands and conclude that the results are due to method variance but that the construct is singular. Instead, more than one construct is used to explain the pattern of results.

Clinical neuropsychologists often attempt to delineate the actual skill or ability that is deficient by presenting a task to a patient under different conditions. A useful method for conceptualizing this set of relations is to consider aspects of the stimulus (e.g., the sensory modality used and the potency of the stimulus compared to other stimuli in the environment), aspects of the processing required to perform the task (mental arithmetic vs. the use of paper-and-pencil or verbal encoding vs. abstract visual encoding), and aspects of the response (motoric, verbal, and recognition). In this way, we arrive at an assessment of the ability of the individual to copy abstract line drawings and not an assessment of the construct of construction apraxia. The construct–operation unit may be specified by means of the three aspects of the behavior requested: stimulus, processing, and response. We can then aim our validity investigations at the evaluation of the conclusions drawn from the results of a specific test procedure.

It is still important to consider the underlying central trait, that is, memory. The trait may help us to generate hypotheses that can then be tested with data. For example, knowing that spatial skills are related to certain types of mathematical skills allows us to generate some hypotheses regarding performance on mathematical tasks when a subject demonstrates spatial manipulation deficits. One of the tasks is to determine the conditions and subjects for which the relations occur or do not occur. By focusing on the construct–operation unit, we do not as easily commit the error of assuming that the traits measured are singular. By focusing on the construct–operation unit, we can remain close to the behavioral data and can use a more parsimonious set of cognitive constructs.

THE NATURE OF VALIDITY

In the area of general psychological research, there is an unsettled debate about whether validation is tripartite or unitary. Cronbach and Meehl (1955) suggested that validity is composed of three varieties: criterion-related (comprising both predictive and concurrent validity), content validity, and construct validity. Other theorists, such as Landy (1986), have suggested that validity has a unitarian nature. In this view, validation is a multidimensional activity by which the type of validity is determined by the inference attempted. Landy suggested that validation be viewed as hypothesis testing. Taking this suggestion a step further, one concentrates on evaluating the validity of the inference rather that on the validity of the test.

Discussions of the validity of a test may be clarified by considering the conditions, populations, and types of generalization that form the parameters of the inference. Instead of stating that a given test is valid, we should state instead that it is valid (or invalid) for drawing certain conclusions when it is administered to a certain individual in a certain setting. Doing so helps to make it clear that validity has as its central concern the evaluation of hypotheses formed by attempts to generalize past the test situation.

Some people draw distinctions between constructs (such as reasoning ability) and observable facts (such as the accuracy of an individual's attempt to solve some problem). The construct helps us to make predictions beyond the individual, the setting, and the observed behavior by hypothesizing a central commonality. In this way, we reduce the uncertainty of each new clinical question by pointing out the similarities with other previously answered questions. Concentrating on the observable fact allows us greater accuracy in predicting a specific outcome. There is an obvious trade-off in this situation: the greater the extent to which constructs are used, the greater the generality of the predictions made. On the other hand, the obverse is true of the reliance on observable facts: the greater the extent to which the predictions are restricted to observable facts, the more accurately can predictions be made in a given situation. The distinction is not just semantic, for the clinician is faced with a decision that has implications for the eventual validity of inferences.

There is no single answer to the question of how extensive the level of abstraction should be in naming the skills evaluated by clinical neuropsychological methods. In one sense, the task is completed during the assessment when the clinician gathers data from extratest sources, that is, clinical and collateral interviews, behavioral observations, and reviews of previous test results. The limits of the inferences drawn regarding the visual-spatial skills of a subject as determined by a test score are partly determined by data regarding the performance of the subject on real-life tasks that require visual-spatial skills. Unfortunately, the strategy of allowing all of the limitations of generalizability to be described by extratest data removes the process from quantification and public observation. A preferable strategy is to limit the description of the construct being assessed to the most basic level of behavioral description that can still allow generalizability to other situations but not to other skills. As a result, the inferences remain in the public scrutiny of the community of clinicians and researchers. The inferences can then be quantified and empirically evaluated.

For example, a test of visual-spatial skills may require the subject to reproduce a simple abstract line drawing after having viewed the test stimulus for 10 seconds. Because the task requires memory, motor skills, and visual-spatial perception, it would be misleading to label the test as purely an index of visual-spatial constructional skills. Performance on the test may not generalize to situations in which memory is not required. Although it may seem more cumbersome to describe the test as assessing visual-spatial motor-reproduction skills for which short-term memory is required, it is less cumbersome than the theoretical excess baggage required to explain discrepancies in performance between a situation that requires memory and a situation that does not require memory. The clinician can identify which skill component of the construct–operation unit is actually deficient by comparing the results of the application of various construct–operation units (tests or procedures) that vary only slightly in the content of their components. This method is similar both to Luria's method of qualifying the symptom and to Teuber's concept of double discrimination. However, in order to show the similarity to double discrimination, the goal of assessment must be changed from physical localization to functional localization. For example, if a patient performs poorly on a test of visual-recognition memory but performs adequately on tests of verbal recognition and verbal free recall, we might hypothesize that some aspect of visual encoding is impaired.

Limiting construct descriptions to the lowest possible level of necessary abstraction has its roots in the concept of face validity and has implications for both construct and content validity. A prerequisite for naming a test as an index of a given neuropsychological skill is that the test appear to tap the construct of interest. A test of visual-spatial constructional skills should contain tasks that require the subject to perform using those skills or else that require the performance of skills highly related to the construct of interest, for example, drawing to command.

We return now to a consideration of the construct–operation unit. As an abstract entity, the construct is not actually measurable. When we specify the construct–operation unit, we provide both an abstract definition of the skill and a public observational system for assessing that skill. The validity of the inferences drawn from test scores is related to the similarity of the method to the demands of the environment in the performance of the behavioral products of the skill. Memory tests generally assess the skill of an individual in receiving, encoding, and retrieving discrete bits of information in a relatively distraction-free environment. Those particular conditions are rarely met in the free environment. As a result, predictions from test scores may be inaccurate (that is, may have limited validity) in describing the performance of the subject in everyday memory tasks. By concentrating on the construct–operation unit, we explicitly accept the theoretical considerations underlying the use of the test, namely, that memory performance differs under differing levels of distraction. We may wish to devise and use two tests, one with and one without distraction methods. When we desire to make predictions to extratest behavior, we would choose the test with the method that best approximates the conditions under which the subject is expected to perform. Or conversely, we may specify the environmental limitations and conditions under which performance of the central task is expected, for example, telling the subject to learn new material under minimal distraction.

VALIDITY AND NONNEUROLOGICAL VARIABLES

There is always a problem with omitting variables. When we omit relevant variables in our research, we consign to error variance those sources of variance that might otherwise be explained systematically. Clinical neuropsychological assessment tends to look at the score derived from a test and the possible membership in a certain class, such as a diagnostic subgroup. In doing so, it ignores the context of the evaluation, the demographic characteristics of the subject, the learning history of the subject, and the influence of conative variables such as level of motivation or affective state. This occurs even though theory states that these variables are important. The role of these variables is relegated to the domain of clinical inference, intuition, or decision. The price we pay for this omission ranges from unfortunate (in the form of lowered validity coefficients) to inexcusable (in the form of misleading information resulting in disservice to the patient). These variables can be theoretically argued to have import in the decisions regarding the validity of inferences drawn from test scores; however, in reality, the import of these variables is an empirical question yet to be answered.

At this point in the development of clinical neuropsychological assessment as a scientific endeavor, it may not be possible to directly specify the effects of nonneurological variables on assessment results. It is still necessary to attempt to delineate these effects. We are evaluating the validity of inferences drawn from test results. Therefore, we need to rule out the extraneous effects of conative variables, or else we need to make some statements regarding the likely effects of these variables. Table 4-1 describes a model for determining the possible relevant variables. The variables are divided into three major classes: examiner variables, contextual variables, and subject variables.

The effect of these variables may be different for different levels of other variables in the model. That is, the variables may have moderating effects on each other. An obvious example would be the gender of the examiner, which may have different effects, depending on the gender of the subject and the learning history of the subject. Again, these are all empirical questions that need to be addressed if we are to increase the validity of the inferences drawn from our test results. It is likely that there are other vari-

TABLE 4-1. Variables Affecting Test Results

Situation	Subject	Examiner
Setting	Gender	Gender
Reason for assessment	History	Voice inflection
(perceived, objective,	IQ	Level of skill and experience
rationale provided)	Occupation	
Forensic	Reaction to examiner	
For child: School versus		
medical setting		

ables that need to be placed on the table. More conceptual work as well as empirical work must be done.

Fiske (1978) observed that most psychologists recognize (or pay lip service to) the importance of the person–situation interaction. His comments were made in the context of discussing personality assessment, but some of the same considerations apply to clinical neuropsychological assessment. It is not sufficient to state that anxiety plays a role in the assessment of memory functions or that forensic settings affect test results. It would be better, instead, to make the person–situation interaction the focus of our investigations. By stating and experimentally controlling the situations in which assessment takes place, we bring the moderating influence of these situations into the arena of public scrutiny, and the result is greater agreement regarding the confirmation or disconfirmation of the inferences drawn.

Every person is different. Each of us has different levels of skills as the result of genetic heterogeneity, different learning histories, and differing current states. However, faced with these differences, we should not throw up our hands at the insurmountability of the task. As Fiske (1978) recommended, it would be more productive to attempt to determine whether any regularities exist in the phenomenon under study and to uncover the conditions in which these regularities exist.

CONCLUDING COMMENTS

Validity is a term that is better applied to inferences than to tests. We can know little about the validity of a test, but we can know the accuracy of the hypotheses and inferences associated with its use. It may be difficult to change the language of a profession, but doing so could have beneficial effects on our use of test instruments. When we focus on the validity of inferences, we draw attention to the construct–operation unit. In essence, we become more behavior-minded; our conclusions are limited by the characteristics of the observed data rather than by references to categorical abstracts. We also become more aware of the nonneurological variables impinging on test performance. Much work needs to be done. A fact that should cheer us and increase our motivation is that much work has already been done. We know some of the basics regarding the different performance by diagnostic groups on certain tests. We now need to determine the basics regarding performance that differs because of other variables.

Validity as Applied to Neuropsychological Assessment

with Robert F. Sawicki

The concept of test validity basically corresponds to the question of whether a test or an assessment procedure supplies the kind of information intended by the test's designer. This issue is very important because the test scores in and of themselves are meaningless unless they refer to a defined realm of observable phenomena. In clinical psychology, the consequences of interest may be a particular personality style or behavioral disorder. For clinical neuropsychology, the consequences of interest may range from whether brain impairment exists to the implications of the test results for adaptive behavior with regard to the type of brain impairment that is identified. Before going on to describe some particular issues that affect the validity of neuropsychological tests, we review general applicable concepts of validity and threats to validity.

TYPES OF VALIDITY

Recent texts reinterpret validity as "validation"; that is, the issue of interest is not only what a test measures, but also what a test's strengths and weaknesses are in terms of particular subjects, particular interpretive questions, and particular settings. Answers to these questions may be found in various sources: the test manual, test reviews, general test standards, and published research. Throughout this book, the reviews of neuropsychological assessment instruments use the test manuals as sources as well as the publicly available research data from the literature and, in some cases, from conference presentations or directly from the researcher. Validity is not a unitary construct, nor is it a construct that can be readily and permanently decided by a single piece of research. Additionally, test validity is something about which clinical neuropsychologists sometimes disagree.

We will not attempt to resolve the issues of disagreement. We will attempt to enlarge the discussion of validity by including issues of contextual and comparative quality as discussed by Cronbach (1984). We will also attempt to keep the discussion focused on a very important central point: tests are not valid or invalid, but inferences drawn from test results can be described as valid or invalid.

VALIDITY: BASIC DEFINITIONS

Validity may be defined in an empirical sense as a statistical relation between the results of a particular procedure and a characteristic of interest, that is, between a contrived procedure and other independently observed events (Anastasi, 1982; Nunnally, 1978). These relations may be defined in terms of the content of a test, in terms of related criteria, and in terms of underlying constructs. All of these can be qualified in terms of contextual variables and subject variables.

Content Validity

Content validity is the degree to which a test adequately samples from the domain of interest. For example, if a test is intended to be sensitive to the global aspects of memory dysfunction, there need to be sufficiently representative tasks that access the construct defining "global memory processes" as understood by the test developer. Therefore, it is important that the developer describe the definition of the construct fairly completely, so that discussions in the literature can focus on the theoretical adequacy of the definition, rather than on content validity. In our example of a test of memory, if the test designer subscribed to the Atkinson and Schriffin (1968) model of memory, the content of the test would optimally include tasks that demonstrate the acquisition of information at the sensory level, decay from short-term storage, decay from long-term storage, and the effects of rehearsal and interference.

The process of content validation begins when the initial test items or procedures are selected during the design of an instrument. Careful selection and design in the initial stages will help to ease the task of later validation. Most arguments used to support content validation are theoretical and logical. Content validation may be most easily evaluated or demonstrated when the procedure is an operational version of a well-defined theory or a component of a theory. A "table of specifications" (Hopkins & Antes, 1978) that demonstrates the translation of theory into test items will further facilitate the demonstration of content validity.

A table of specifications can be described as a two-dimensional matrix in which one dimension represents the skills or traits of interest and the

TABLE 5-1. *Specifications for the Luria–Nebraska Neuropsychological Battery: Visual Processes Scale*

	Task	
Function	Simple	Complex
Visually mediated recognition	Items 86, 87	Items 88, 89
Figure–ground perception		Items 90, 91
Spatially mediated perception	Items 94, 95, 96	
Mental imagery		Items 97, 99

other dimension represents the behavior characteristic of the interest areas. This diagram can be used to determine the number of items that ought to be assigned to a given topic area as well as the type of item (e.g., timed vs. untimed or spoken vs. written) that ought to be included. With the use of these guides, a neuropsychological battery can be expected to include diverse and apparently unrelated items, whereas a test of language comprehension should contain items that are more consistent with each other.

As an example, Table 5-1 demonstrates a table of specifications for the Visual Processes Scale of the Luria–Nebraska Neuropsychological Battery (LNNB). This table has been greatly simplified for descriptive purposes. The functions described here could also be further specified as visual recognition of objects, visual recognition of line drawings, visually mediated inferential reasoning, and so on, and topic areas could be weighted according to their perceived theoretical importance (20% of the items could be selected to represent operations based on mental rotations).

Items are usually derived by a variety of methods, ranging from examples of behavior that are directly stated in the theoretical model (e.g., the expectation of increased skin conductance as anxiety increases) to the selection of items by expert judges. In terms of neuropsychological procedures, the sensory modality (visual, auditory, or tactile) through which a stimulus item is presented and the likely internal processes used to achieve a solution (rote vs. reasoned) are all important to content validity as well as to construct validity. The pertinent issue is the likely generalizability (Nunnally, 1978) of the information derived from an item and, consequently, the likely generalizability of the test as a whole. In dealing with content validity, the test designer must be aware of the trade-off between lack of specificity or insufficient sampling of the domain and tedious redundancy that does not usefully articulate the characteristic of interest.

The success with which a test designer resolves this trade-off balance is an issue for later validational research. Later investigators may propose a contrasting theory or may propose a different set of items as better translating the initially proposed theory. When tests are shown to have limited content validity, the issue raised is insufficient generalizability to the purported domain of interest. The causes of limited content validity are usually incomplete understanding of the underlying theory, lack of a guiding theory, or a tendency to assume greater generalized interpretations of item performance at the time of construction. One's intent may be to design a widely applicable neuropsychological screening test, but the items may all require that the subject copy simple geometric designs. There is a large subset of brain-impaired subjects (e.g., subjects with specific impairments in language skills) for whom performance on such a test will not be diagnostically useful.

Face validity is often erroneously used as a synonym for *content validity*. However, a more accurate description of the relation between content validity and face validity is that face validity is a category of content validity. *Face validity* refers primarily to the perceptions of the examinee. The subject forms some conclusions regarding what the test is measuring on the basis of the content or language of the test procedures. In more ambiguous test situations (for example, personality evaluation), the examinee's assumptions about the nature of the test may be widely disparate from the examiner's intent. Face validity becomes an important concern to the extent that the perceptions of the examinee affect his or her performance on the test; the result may be confounds with the intended measurement purpose of the test. An examinee is more likely to participate in an assessment that uses procedures that appear to provide information that will answer his or her concerns.

Face validity can also affect the decision-making process of potential users of the test. The astute clinician will ultimately choose tests on the basis of the available empirical literature, but the original decision to investigate the utility of a test may be influenced by the "look" of a test. Face validity may also influence later empirical validation work by researchers other than the test designer. Subsequent investigators may assume different intents for the items or test scales based on their interpretation of the intent of an item or the meaning of a scale name. Some of the these problems can be avoided by including in the manual a specific discussion of the theoretical background of a test as well as a discussion of particular item and scale intents. The manual can also describe the scale titles as somewhat arbitrary labels and give titles that have readily shared meanings in the community of test researchers and consumers. This last point is not always possible because there is no standard dictionary of neuropsychological terms. Even if such a dictionary existed, there would not be universal acceptance of the definitions, given the diverse theoretical, epistemological, and procedural backgrounds of the group of individuals who constitute the practitioners of clinical neuropsychology.

It is advisable to give titles that have a relatively large amount of acceptance and agreement among clinical neuropsychologists. It is further advisable to give names to the scales and to the skill areas purported to be measured that reflect behavioral descriptions rather than unobservable constructs. For example, a test might be described as a test of memory, but it would be more accurate to describe the scales and procedures as being measures of new learning, immediate recall, or delayed recall. From the above discussion, it can be seen that, although face validity does not play a direct role in the empirical definition of a test, it does play a mediating role in the understanding and evaluation of the test data.

Content validity plays a large role in the development of a test. Most of the evaluative processes involved in investigating content validity are based on logial considerations. Nunnally (1978) suggested a few ways in which content validity can be evaluated. For example, if a scale is thought to measure a single construct, the items can reasonably be expected to demonstrate a fair amount of internal consistency, a relation that can be empirically evaluated. For those constructs thought to be affected by experience, content validity can be evaluated by demonstrating improved performance following a training procedure. Content validity can also be evaluated by comparing performance on the test in question with performance on other tests thought to tap the same or similar constructs. Anastasi (1982) suggested a qualitative method of checking content validity by having subjects think out loud during the testing. Of course, this suggestion has limited utility for assessing brain-impaired populations.

Still another method of assessing content validity is to conduct an error analysis. When persons of similar brain dysfunction fail an item, a review of their error patterns for signs of consistency may suggest how the brain dysfunction translates into behavior. For example, failures during the block design subtest of the WAIS-R that are due to the individual's breaking the external configuration of the target design have been related to right cerebral dysfunction (Kaplan, 1983).

The demonstration of content validation is limited by the extent to which extraneous factors affect test performance. The relative contributions of motivation, academic experience, prior intellectual resources, socioeconomic status, sex, and psychological status must be understood before an accurate assessment of content relevance and generalizability can be conducted. Differences in timing procedures, administration instructions, or scoring procedures may cause relations with external criteria to vary considerably. Clinical education optimally emphasizes the role of these variables in the process of measurement, but it is wise for both researchers and clinicians to be mindful of the need to minimize the effect of the variables on the derived score.

Criterion Validity

Anastasi (1982) described criterion-validating procedures as those that demonstrate a test's effectiveness in a given context. Criterion validity is commonly expressed as the correlation between a test score and some external variable, which may be another test that is assumed to measure the same characteristic of interest or future behavior that is assumed to demonstrate the characteristic of interest. In the former case, one usually speaks of concurrent validity, as allied behavior is measured at the same time. In the latter case, one usually speaks of predictive validity, as performance on the test being evaluated is used to temporally predict the criterion, whether it is diagnostic group membership or behavioral change.

Although the information is rarely offered in test manuals, a validity coefficient may be computed as the correlation between the score achieved on a particular test and some criterion variable. For example, one may correlate the relation between a score on the Category Test (Reitan & Wolfson, 1985) and a dummy-coded variable indicating diagnostic group (i.e., 1 = normal, 2 = brain-impaired). In this case, a significant positive relation would indicate that a high score on the Category Test was associated with a subject's membership in the brain-impaired diagnostic group. Assignment to the diagnostic group would have to be made on the basis of external, independent criteria, such as a neurological evaluation, the results of neuroradiological evaluation, or previous history.

The validity coefficient can be negatively affected by the degree of homogeneity of the sample. This can occur both numerically and conceptually. Numerically, the magnitude of the correlation coefficient decreases as the overall sample becomes more similar in test scores because of the restriction of range. Conceptually, a high validity coefficient might be associated with a particular type of brain impairment, but not with others. Validity coefficients can also be affected by gender, level of education, age, and so on. This is important information for determining the utility of the instrument; however, it can be disheartening when it is not intended by the test author.

The relation between a validity coefficient and decision theory is important in deciding the significance of the validity coefficient. Decision theory, as applied to tests, is a mathematical operationalization of the decision-making process. Early models of the theory were based on the net improvement in accuracy over the base rate (the natural frequency of occurrence of a given phenomenon) that one could gain at various levels of validity. Applications to psychological instruments were developed by Cronbach and Gleser (1965). We may see the application of the theory in the following example: If we were to identify all persons as brain-impaired, even a test with a perfect validity coefficient ($r = 1.0$) would not contribute additional information to the decision. On the other hand, if we knew ahead of time that approximately 70% of the people referred for neuropsychological evaluation were brain-impaired, that same test with the perfect validity coefficient would improve our accuracy by approximately 16%. If the prior base rate were 20%, the same test would improve our accuracy by 80%. As a rule of thumb, a base rate of 50% optimizes the utility of an instrument. As the likelihood of seeing a condition becomes more rare, the utility of an instrument in terms of improving on the base rate decreases. The cost–benefit ratio of developing and applying an instrument for rare conditions is low. It might be more useful to learn the qualitative and historical symptoms of the disorder and to assess for them rather than to develop a specific identification instrument. Tables for computing the relation between base rate and validity coefficients for specific decision levels can be found in Taylor and Russell (1939).

An elaborate alternative to computing a validity coefficient is a research design sometimes referred to as the *method of contrasted groups* (Anastasi, 1982). Here, the researcher evaluates the results of testing two groups that are assumed to be different on the criterion that is of interest. For example, persons with no known brain impairment and persons with known brain impairment are both administered the Luria–Nebraska Neuropsychological Battery. The scores are then compared by some statistical method. A traditional method of comparing test performance has been to test for the significance of the difference between mean scores for the two groups. Unfortunately, the two groups may contain members whose scores lie in the region of overlapping distributions of the two groups. An alternate and preferable method begins with a use of the statistical technique known as *discriminant function analysis*. The results of such an analysis produce a linear composite that may be used to demonstrate maximal separation between the two diagnostic groups. The weightings derived from this analysis may then be used to assign the subjects statistically to "predicted" groups. Predicted group membership is then compared with actual group membership, and an accuracy rate, or "hit rate," is computed. The latter part of this analysis is referred to as *classification analysis*.

Although many examples of this set of procedures may be found in even a quick review of current journals, misapplications of the procedures are common. In applying such a design, two major points should be kept in mind. First, the discriminant function analysis and the classification analysis are separate procedures. The discriminant analysis identifies those variables that significantly contribute to the function that statistically separates the groups of interest, and the classification analysis applies an equation based on those significant variables in order to predict group membership. Optimally, applying the equation to the group on which it was derived should result in a relatively high hit rate. Second, demonstrating a significant hit rate in such a derivation sample is only the first step in determining predictive validity. It is not until the derived equation can significantly predict group membership in a second, or cross-validation, sample that predictive validity can be said to have been demonstrated for that set of test procedures.

The use of such a design is a sophisticated demonstration and is open to many sources of contamination. One of the major sources is sample representativeness. If the procedure being evaluated is intended to have broad applications rather than to demonstrate the presence of a particular type of brain impairment, and if the effects of ancillary subject characteristics are to be ruled out, both the diagnostic subgroup characteristic of brain impairment and the diagnostic subgroup characteristic of "normality" ought to be as heterogeneous as possible. To the extent that they are not heterogeneous, the generalizability of the validating investigations needs to be clearly defined. Additionally, the usual subject-matching procedures in the contrasting-groups methodology ought to be observed just as they would be in any clinical research.

The hit rate itself may be contaminated. Willis (1984) demonstrated that the meaning of a given rate of accuracy may be inflated if one does not take into account the prior probabilities of group membership (the base rate). Thus, when one is comparing two diagnostic groups, 50% accuracy is not the correct point for chance assignment if prior membership is 70% and 30% for the two groups.

Concurrent validity of neuropsychological tests is a bit more complex than is a similar analysis of general psychological measures. Although neuropsychological tests may be related to other tests that purport to measure similar brain functions, concurrent neurophysiological measures (i.e., a CT scan, an EEG, an MRI, and an rCBF) can also provide a major source of validation. The cost of such a validational exercise may be prohibitive even if it is rewarding. In reviewing such demonstrations, we must consider several issues. First, what is being demonstrated? Although the CT scan may be accurate in detecting acute subdural hemorrhage, it is significantly less accurate in detecting subtle, residual subcortical changes that may leave an individual profoundly perseverative or memory-impaired. The individual may look impaired on the neuropsychological test but not on the CT scan. If one wishes to demonstrate the general utility of the neuropsychological measure, a series of both physiological and behavioral measures may be a more accurate set of criteria.

Second, what is the population to which the measures will be applied? Although severely impaired individuals may be more likely to present classically demonstrable physiological findings, unless such individuals are the intended population such criterion-validational exercises are likely to be inappropriate because of their limited generalizability. In those cases, it may be necessary to use some other forms of criteria.

Third, how will the instrument be used in clinical settings? Physiological criteria may be useful for instruments that will be used primarily for diagnostic or localization purposes. On the other hand, behavioral measures may be more appropriate for instruments that are intended to provide information for intervention programs or to document the course of recovery. Clinical neuropsychologists are often in the uncomfortable situation of having to make statements regarding the behavior of an individual in the free environment based on test data. The field is in need of instruments that have been validated against behavioral criteria.

Generally speaking, greater numbers of criteria and greater degrees of heterogeneity in the sample used in the validation of an instrument will enhance the clarity with which the utility of a test can be defined. In validating an instrument, it is important to remember that the identification of the populations, the context, and the questions for which a particular instrument is inappropriate is just as important as the identification of the populations, the context, and the questions for which an instrument is appropriate.

Construct Validity

Construct validity was conceptually introduced in Cronbach and Meehl (1955). Construct validity can be described as that aspect of the validation process that attempts to demonstrate the dimensions or traits that the test was designed to measure. Construct validation is an ongoing process. It runs through the demonstration of content and criterion validity and, in addition, is built from exploratory and confirmatory hypothesis-testing of the procedure of interest. The goal of construct validation is to build a nomothetic net or inferential definition of the characteristics that a test seeks to measure. In many ways, the process of construct validation returns the investigators to the beginning of the design of the instrument because the relation between the test and its underlying theory is constantly at issue.

To return to a point made earlier (in the discussion of criterion validity), devising demonstrations of what a test does measure as well as what it does not measure is a crucial aspect of examining the validity of the inferences drawn regarding a particular test. The results of such demonstrations help us to understand how a particular pattern of behaviors occurred during a test as well as to define how a test may be improved. This latter point is often ignored during the construction of test procedures. No instrument or procedure should be assumed to be completely finished at the time that it is introduced. Instead, we should expect that, as investigations of the technique refine our understanding of that technique, and as knowledge in the area of brain–behavior relations grows, the technique itself, if viable, will evolve. This is not to give permission to test authors to publish incompletely specified or incompletely investigated new tests. Test authors have ethical imperatives to publish only test materials that have met minimum guidelines as specified in the American Psychological Association standards (American Educational Research Association, American Psychological Association, & National Council on Measurement in Education, 1985).

There are several common ways to investigate the construct validity of a test. The most basic research method is theory testing. By using a theory or a set of alternative theories of brain–behavior relations, one may test hypotheses regarding test performance following definable brain injuries. In this way, one would expect the items of a test that tap functions attributed to the damaged area to show the most frequent failures, and the items tapping functions not usually attributed to the damaged area to be relatively error-free. At a simpler level, performance on a test thought to be sensitive to brain dysfunction should be able to discriminate brain-impaired individuals from non-brain-impaired individuals. The scores on such a test should vary with the degree of brain compromise or cognitive inefficiency. Therefore, psychiatrically impaired persons, especially those individuals with major psychiatric disorders, might also be expected to show varying degrees of impaired performance on the test.

Serial testing during recovery from brain injury can also provide a useful test of construct validity. For example, knowing that edema is more likely to cause general impairment during the first few weeks after brain injury, one may expect more impaired test performance early in the course of recovery, with improvement in test performance following expected recovery time lines. Similarly, as compensatory skills are taught in rehabilitation programs or as the individual learns to compensate for the deficits with feedback from the environment, one may see significant changes in some functional areas. Using the logic of Finger and Stein (1982), one might also expect that the most severely and directly damaged functions would show deficits more impervious to recovery. This latter point is especially true if very fine component skills are assessed with the instrument.

An alternate approach to construct validation focuses on predictions regarding performance on other tests that are postulated to measure the same traits as the original test or other tests that measure underlying traits. In this fashion, one might expect that a measure of a certain cognitive skill would show moderate correlations with measures of general intelligence, little or no relation to a measure of trait anxiety, and a strong correlation with an instrument purported to measure the same cognitive skill. As noted earlier, an important aspect of these validational investigations is the degree to which the investigator accurately understands the intent of a test and the theory underlying the test.

Campbell and Fiske (1959) operationalized this design into a model that evaluates a measurement technique in terms of discriminant and convergent validity. Discriminant validity is defined by relations with tests assumed to be unrelated to the test of interest. One expects divergent coefficients to be nonsignificant or very low. Convergent validity is demonstrated by positive significant correlations with tests thought to measure the same or a similar construct. Furthermore, higher correlations are expected between two procedures that use the same methodology instead of different methodologies (e.g., behavioral observation vs. self-report). This method of analysis is usually identified as the *multitrait–multimethod matrix*.

With such an analysis, the postulated underlying trait dimension is measured by a variety of procedures, including the test under consideration, that use both the same and different methodologies. At the same time, those methodologies are used to measure a different trait. In this way, the traits are crossed with the methods. The intercorrelations among these measures constitute the multitrait–multimethod matrix. The results thought to support the instrument under evaluation include a pattern of positive correlations with other tests measuring the same trait and low to zero correlations with instruments measuring the unrelated traits.

Jackson (1969) criticized the multitrait–multimethod design and offered an alternative. The majority of Jackson's criticisms focus on the issue that Campbell and Fiske's method compares individual correlations without examining the overall structure of the relations. This is an important point because the pattern of correlations may be affected by the way in which variance is distributed in measuring the traits under consideration.

In order to obviate these concerns, Jackson (1969) suggested that a factor analysis of the monomethod matrix be conducted. During such an analysis, the correlation matrix is first orthogonalized and submitted to a principal-components analysis, followed by a varimax rotation. The number of factors is set to equal the number of postulated underlying traits. Although Jackson's suggestion offers some advantages, it may be of limited use in cases in which relations exist among the traits under consideration, as in the neuropsychological assessment of many interrelated cognitive skills. Secondarily, when the monomethod matrix is used, the influence of different measurement methods may not be examined. Cole, Howard, and Maxwell (1981) investigated the result of using a mono-operationalization of constructs and reported that the overall effect is to spuriously deflate validity coefficients. Therefore, the two methods (i.e., Campbell and Fiske's and Jackson's) may be seen as complementary. In a rigorous attempt at construct validation, it is useful to apply both.

Cole (1987) also criticized the multitrait–multimethod matrix in general and suggested an alternative. Some of Cole's criticisms parallel Jackson's criticisms. That is, Cole noted that there are no specific guidelines for the evaluation of the size of the resulting zero-order correlation coefficients. Additionally, Cole stated that the collection of multiple measures of multiple constructs is an endeavor that is extremely expensive in clinical settings and that is therefore rarely done. Finally, Cole noted that the multitrait–multimethod matrix is sensitive to the presence of correlated errors. The errors may be correlated because of a similarity in the time of day at which certain aspects of the assessments are conducted or because of certain of the instruments being administered by the same person.

Cole suggested instead the use of confirmatory factor analysis to analyze the data and investigate discriminant and convergent validity. Confirmatory factor analysis allows for a statistical test of the hypothesis, unlike examination of the multitrait–multimethod matrix, which allows for only a description of the relations among variables. Confirmatory factor analysis can also test for the presence of correlated errors and can control for their effects. Finally, the use of confirmatory factor analysis allows the clinical researcher to analyze less costly data sets by allowing the use of monotrait–monomethod data sets (for the evaluation of factorial validity), monotrait–multimethod data sets (for the evaluation of convergent validity), and multitrait–monomethod data sets (for the evaluation of discriminant validity), as well as the analysis of multitrait–multimethod data sets (for the evaluation of both discriminant and convergent validity).

The drawbacks of confirmatory factor analysis are related to its requirements. Usually, a very large data set is necessary for confirmatory factor analysis. In addition, complete data sets are required for each subject. Confirmatory factor analysis cannot handle missing data. The data set must also be multivariate normal; failure to meet this requirement will affect the results of the test of significance considerably. Finally, the covariance matrix must contain multiple measures of each construct. Another requirement of confirmatory factor analysis can be seen as a benefit; that is, the factor structure must be specified before analysis, and therefore, the researcher must more fully consider the implications of the chosen data analysis before analyzing the data.

Exploratory factor analysis provides another way to examine construct validity. As before, the investigator starts from the theory underlying the test or from an alternative theory thought to explain test performance. This type of factoring can be seen to be a rudimentary version of confirmatory factor analysis, as opposed to exploratory factor analysis, which makes relatively few assumptions regarding the underlying structure of a set of data.

For example, in the validational work with the Luria–Nebraska Neuropsychological Battery (LNNB), predictions were made from Luria's theory regarding the likely number of dimensions that would underlie a given LNNB subscale. These predictions were based on operational definitions of conceptually similar tasks that represented a given component function. Oblique rotations were initially selected because factors were assumed to be interrelated. In many cases, the assumptions from the theory were confirmed (for a review see Golden, Hammeke, Purisch, Berg, Moses, Newlin, Wilkening, & Puente, 1982d).

Exploratory factor analyses may also be used to develop support for conclusions regarding the construct validity of a test. A test composed of a variety of subscales may be reduced to factorially simple dimensions. Once the factors have been identified, a linear-weighted composite (a factor score) may be used to determine the relative contribution of a given factor to the specified test performance. The factorial validity coefficient of a test may then be computed by correlating test scores with the factor score (Anastasi, 1982). For example, if a motor speed factor were identified, the relative contribution of motor speed to test performance could be computed.

Marker variables can also be used in factor-analytic construct validation. A marker variable is usually a descriptive rather than a conceptual measure. Its meaning is relatively better understood than that of the test procedure being evaluated. Age, gender, education, and IQ are common marker variables; however, the scores generated by accepted neuropsychological measures may also be included as markers. When reviewing the results of such a factoring procedure, the researcher looks for factors on which the marker variables are significantly loaded. Consideration of the meaning of the marker variables contributes to an understanding of the construct meaning of the tests of interest that also load on that factor.

Serial factor analyses with the same sample or across independent samples demonstrate the stability of a test's underlying dimensions across time or across samples. Although temporally stable results may be less desirable for those measures thought to be sensitive to the current neuropsychological status of an individual, the latter method (independent samples) is highly desirable for those techniques that are not intended to be impairment-specific.

A final method that may be used in construct validation is also useful for refining a measure. The method of examining the homogeneity of a scale was previously discussed in the context of evaluating the reliability of a test. On scales that are assumed to measure a general underlying dimension, especially scales that use a sum across items to derive the score, the correlation of individual item scores with the total scale score may be used to identify items that are less likely to be related to the underlying trait. As an example, let us consider a 15-item scale intended to measure perceptual constancy, for which the test's author intended to sum the individual item scores to produce a single score that would represent an individual's degree of perceptual constancy. Correlations between the items and the total scale score would indicate the degree to which each item is related to the trait as measured by the instrument. Items whose scores are low would be candidates for revision, which could improve the overall validity of the homogeneous scale. Yet another consideration is the application of this procedure to the contrasted-groups design in order to evaluate the extent to which the trait is homogeneous across the intended subject pools (Anastasi, 1982).

THREATS TO TEST VALIDITY

The factors that compromise the internal and external validity of a research design (Campbell & Stanley, 1963; Cook & Campbell, 1979) also provide a typology of internal and external threats to the validity of a neuropsychological measurement instrument. Threats to internal validity reflect design contamination that limits conclusions about treatment effects, and threats to external validity reflect limitations on generalizability. In terms of neuropsychological assessment, the following threats are likely to negatively affect the content validity and construct validity of an instrument.

Threats to Internal Validity

The threats to internal validity are:

1. *History.* The uncontrolled effects of educational level, premorbid intellectual resources, age, handedness, gender, or socioeconomic status.

2. *Test interval.* In neuropsychological batteries or procedures that are administered across successive days, the uncontrolled effects of fatigue, changes in level of consciousness, or changes in the level of motivation.

3. *Testing effects.* The uncontrolled effects of exposure to or practice on instruments without parallel forms that are used serially to monitor recovery.

4. *Instrumentation.* An inexact manifestation of the concepts in methods because of an incomplete comprehension of the underlying theory; the use of procedures that are unclear in intent; and the use of procedures that are strongly affected by irrelevant testing or patient characteristics.

5. *Statistical artifacts.* The application of norms that are derived from extreme or inappropriately homogeneous samples, the result being either a masking or a potentiation of the effects of impairment.

6. *Ceiling effects.* The application of procedures that do not allow for the normal variability in a normal population, that is, procedures that are intrinsically too easy or too difficult, irrespective of the effects of impairment.

Threats to External Validity

The threats to external validity are:

1. *Interactive effects.* Lack of attention to the effects of medication, surgery, or other diagnostic procedures on performance.

2. *Multiple procedure effects.* Lack of attention to the effects of the sequence of assessment procedures on performance.

3. *Reactive effects.* Lack of attention to patient–examiner interpersonal effects on performance, especially in light of the fact that many neuropsychological assessment procedures require active cooperation for maximal interpretability.

CONCLUSIONS

From the preceding information, one may conclude that Cronbach's (1984) redefinition of test validation as test evaluation is a sensible approach that neatly captures the meaning of *validity*. As a result of many studies in a variety of conditions, a procedure can be defined in terms of the populations about whom it is maximally informative, the conditions under which it is maximally applicable, and the decisions to which it is maximally applicable, and the decisions to which it is maximally contributory. Although it may be easy to become lost in the excitement of investigating a new instrument or of investigating new uses for an old instrument, it is important to remember that the ultimate purpose of validating a test is to inform the clinician or the consumer about the kinds of decisions that may be made, based on the results of the procedure in question.

The ultimate evaluative-validational demonstration of a test is its clinical utility. Tests survive to the extent that they provide information that is useful in the individual case as well as on the average. The various forms of validation are markers that indicate to a clinician the relative importance of a pattern of performance and the likelihood that a given pattern of performance is diagnostically or predictively contributory.

6

The Wechsler Adult Intelligence Scale–Revised

The Wechsler Adult Intelligence Scale–Revised (WAIS-R; Wechsler, 1981) is, as its name implies, a revised form of the Wechsler Adult Intelligence Scale, which was published in 1955. There were two main reasons for the revised version. First, some of the items on the WAIS had become dated, and the outdated items were replaced with more contemporary items. There was also some attempt to make the test more culture-fair by including items related to black people and black history. Whether these attempts succeeded is an empirical question. Second, with the passage of three decades, the norms for the WAIS were unlikely to describe deviation intelligence. Scores could be interpreted as deviation IQs from the original sample, not from the general contemporary population.

The structure of the WAIS was maintained in the WAIS-R. There are 11 subtests, each of which is purported to measure components of intelligence. These 11 subtests are grouped under two general headings: the Information, Digit Span, Vocabulary, Arithmetic, Comprehension, and Similarities subtests are included in Verbal IQ (VIQ), and the Picture Completion, Picture Arrangement, Block Design, Object Assembly, and Digit Symbol subtests are included in Performance IQ (PIQ). All of the subtests are included in Full Scale IQ (FSIQ). Interpretation can take place at the level of the subtest scores, the PIQ and VIQ scores, or the FSIQ scores. Although the WAIS and the WAIS-R appear similar in content, structure, and procedure, there are important differences in the scores obtained from the two tests. Wechsler (1981), Lippold and Claiborn (1983), and Smith (1983) have all reported that use of the WAIS-R results in significantly lower estimates of IQ than does use of the WAIS.   .

NORMATIVE INFORMATION

The WAIS-R was normed on a sample of 1,880 individuals in the United States who were between the ages of 16 and 74. By the use of information contained in the 1970 U.S. Census, the sample was stratified into groups on the basis of sex, age, race, geographic location, occupation, education, and urban versus rural residence. Raw scores on the WAIS-R are converted to scale scores by comparing the performance of the subject with the performance of the normative sample. The subtest scale scores have a mean of 10 and a standard deviation of 3. By examining the conversion tables for the age groups, one can see that it is mainly decrements in Performance subtests that make the age norms necessary. Although scale scores are available for the different age groups, the determination of IQ is made by obtaining scale scores based on the performance of the normative sample as a whole. It is when the subtest scale scores are summed that the age norms are used in the determination of IQ. IQ scores have a mean of 100 and a standard deviation of 15.

RELIABILITY

The scoring reliability of the WAIS-R was evaluated in a study reported by Ryan, Prifitera, and Powers (1983). In this study, 19 Ph.D. psychologists and 20 psychology graduate students scored two WAIS-R protocols that had been obtained from vocational counseling clients. The consequent IQ scores varied as much as 8 points across scorers. The variability in the scores of the two groups (Ph.D.s vs. students) was approximately equal, except in the case of the PIQ, where the Ph.D.s had a larger variance in scores that was statistically significant for both of the protocols. The results of this study underline the necessity of strict adherence to the standardized scoring system when using the WAIS-R.

The manual for the WAIS-R (Wechsler, 1981) gives split-half reliability information for each of the subtests except for the speeded subtest of Digit Symbol and the power subtest of Digit Span. In both of these cases, the test-retest reliability is reported. Reliability information is given for each of the nine age groups and is then averaged, by means of Fisher's r-to-z transformation, to yield a reliability coefficient averaged across the age groups. The reliability coefficients for the IQ scores were obtained by a methodology for computing the reliability of a composite group of tests. The split-half reliability coefficients are corrected for the length of the tests by use of the Spearman-Brown formula, but no information is given regarding the nature of the split. The reliability coefficients range from .68 for Object Assembly to .96 for Vocabulary. The reliability coefficients for the IQ scores are .97

for VIQ, .93 for PIQ, and .97 for FSIQ. It is important to remember that the IQ reliability coefficients are estimates based on composite scores.

Test–retest reliability is presented for each of subtests as well as for IQ scores. The test–retest values were computed from the results of two administrations to a group of 71 subjects between the ages of 25 and 34 years and a sample of 48 subjects between the ages of 45 and 54 years. The intertest intervals ranged from 2 to 7 weeks. The test–retest reliability coefficients ranged from .69 for Digit Symbol in the 25- to 34-year-old group to .94 for Information in the 45- to 54-year-old group. The IQ test–retest coefficients were substantially high, the lowest being .89 for the PIQ in the 35- to 44-year-old group and the highest being .97 for verbal IQ in the 45- to 54-year-old group. There was no test for the difference in level across the two test sessions. This is a potentially important issue as studies have indicated that, at least for the WAIS, there are substantial gains in IQ scores across time even in the presence of significant correlation coefficients (Catron & Thompson, 1979; Matarazzo, Carmody, & Jacobs, 1980).

The manual also presents information regarding the standard error of measurement for each of the subtest scores and the IQ scores for the nine age groups. These values are then averaged to provide an estimate of the overall standard error of measurement. The values are presented as scaled-score units. These values range from .61 for Vocabulary to 1.54 for Object Assembly. The standard error of measurement values for the IQ scores are 2.74 for the VIQ, 4.14 for the PIQ, and 2.53 for the FSIQ. Naglieri (1982) presented values for confidence limits for the IQ scores. However, there is a problem with the values reported in the manual and by Naglieri. There are three formulas for the computation of the standard error of measurement. The formula used in the manual provides an estimate of the amount of error variance in the score and does not provide confidence boundaries for the scores, as the manual incorrectly states. Knight (1983) presented the values computed from the formula, which allow an interpretation of the confidence boundaries.

The manual provides a table of the minimum value required for the significance of differences between the scale scores and between the IQ scores. Many people erroneously interpret a statistically significant difference between PIQ and VIQ as a clinically significant one. This is an especially important issue when the VIQ-PIQ split is used to generate hypotheses about the presence of organicity. For example, according to the manual, a VIQ-PIQ split of 12.04 is statistically significant at the .05 level for the 16- to-17-year-old group. However, Knight (1983) reported that over 25% of the normative sample in that age group exceeded that difference. Clearly, a difference of that magnitude cannot be clinically significant. Grossman (1983) also examined the prevalence of different magnitudes of VIQ-PIQ splits in the normative sample for the WAIS-R. He reported that 10% of the normative sample, averaged across age groups, had a VIQ-PIQ split of at least

18 points. The normative sample was chosen partly on the basis of a negative history of neurological impairment. The large percentage of subjects manifesting reliably large VIQ-PIQ splits argues against the use of the split to diagnose organicity.

An important distinction must be made among the reliability, the abnormality, and the validity of the VIQ-PIQ split. *Reliability of the split* refers to a computation that denotes the probability that a split of a certain magnitude will occur as the result of error of measurement. *Abnormality of the split* refers to the observed percentage of subjects manifesting a split of a certain magnitude. *Validity of the split* refers to the clinical meaning of a split of a certain magnitude. Ryan (1984) calculated values for the abnormality of VIQ-PIQ differences in the normative sample. Associated with each difference value is a probability level that can be interpreted as the proportion of subjects who exhibit that magnitude of difference. Ryan reported that a difference of 28 points could be found in 1% of the normative sample. The fact that a split of that magnitude could occur in normal subjects emphasizes the need for an empirical evaluation of the validity of the VIQ-PIQ split.

In order to assess the validity of the VIQ-PIQ split in neuropsychological diagnosis, Bornstein (1983b) examined the VIQ-PIQ split in patients with unilateral and bilateral cerebral dysfunction using a sample of 89 patients. Of these patients, 20 had left-hemisphere dysfunction, 24 had right-hemisphere dysfunction, and 45 had bilateral dysfunction as determined by neurodiagnostic techniques. It was found that the left-hemisphere patients had significantly lower VIQ than PIQ; however, the mean difference was only 4.9 points. Similarly, the right-hemisphere patients had significantly lower PIQ than VIQ, but the mean difference was 10.7 points. Most tellingly, the bilaterally dysfunctional patients had significantly lower PIQ than VIQ, and the mean difference was 7.8 points. It appears that cerebral dysfunction may have effects on the VIQ-PIQ split, but the absence of a control group in this study lessens our confidence in such a conclusion. However, the results of this study in conjunction with the examination of the VIQ-PIQ data in the WAIS-R normative sample emphasize the tenuous nature of performing a neuropsychological diagnosis using WAIS-R data only.

Some authors have suggested that the VIQ-PIQ split in unilateral lesions is differential by sex. McClone (1978, 1979) presented data and Inglis and Lawson (1981) provided a literature review that seem to support this idea. However, a report by Bornstein (1984) concludes that sex does not make a difference in the validity of this split. Snow, Freedman, and Ford (1986) reviewed published studies that evaluated the possibility of differential laterality results in WAIS and Wechsler–Bellevue scores for males and females. They concluded that the effect of sex was nonrobust and might therefore be a reflection of a relation between sex and other variables, such as education level. Sundet (1986) examined VIQ-PIQ differences in 83 subjects with unilateral brain impairment. When the magnitude of the split was used, only 70% of the subjects were correctly classified as left- or right-hemisphere-impaired. Female subjects were not found to be any more or less lateralized than male subjects. The argument is far from settled, and researchers will need to take sex into account when planning the design and executing the statistical analysis of a future study to examine this idea.

The WAIS-R may be valuable in providing collateral evidence of the existence of lateralized deficits once the existence of cerebral dysfunction has already been determined. The differences in VIQ-PIQ splits for the unilaterally damaged subjects in the above study conform to the expectations derived from the widely held assumption that verbal abilities are largely mediated by the dominant hemisphere, whereas spatial tasks are largely mediated by the nondominant hemisphere. In order to investigate the possibility that a more empirically derived indicator of lateralized deficits may result in more useful neuropsychological information, Lawson, Inglis, and Stroud (1983) performed a principal-components factor analysis of the WAIS-R normative data. They derived a solution with two factors, the first of which they interpreted as general intelligence, and the second of which they interpreted as laterality. These authors then derived a weighted-sum method of combining subtest scale scores into a single laterality index. They then used a formula for computing the reliability of a composite score from the reliabilities of the constituent scale scores and reported an average split-half reliability of .78 for their laterality index. A test–retest coefficient was similarly derived from the data contained in the WAIS-R manual and reported an average value of .79. A very important point needs to be made here. The values for reliability reported by Lawson et al. (1983) were derived from a sample of normal subjects. These authors contended that their index is valid only for unilaterally damaged males, although no data are presented to substantiate that claim. The laterality index appears to be a good idea, but much more work, including an investigation of the reliability and validity of the index in the population for which it is intended, is needed before it can be recommended for clinical use.

Pattern analysis, or an examination of the scatter of scores among the subtests of the WAIS-R, is often recommended as an interpretive strategy. The rationale is based on the discovery of statistically significant differences among the subtest scale scores by use of the confidence boundaries published in the manual. Silverstein (1982a) pointed out that the published confidence boundaries are based on differences that compare only two subtests at a time. However, interpretation is based on a comparison of all of the subtests. The experiment-wide error in this case is likely to increase the probability of a Type I error. Instead, Silverstein recommended that the Bonferroni approximate correction for experiment-wide error be made. Unfortunately, even with this correction, the problem of the clinical interpretation of statistically significant differences remains, as discussed in the case of the VIQ-

PIQ split above. What is needed is an empirical investigation of the meaning of these differences.

VALIDITY

The factor structure of the WAIS-R is an important issue in the evaluation of the construct validity of the instrument as well as an important issue in the interpretation of the test results. Silverstein (1982b) conducted a principal-factor analysis on the standardization data from the normative sample as reported in the manual. The number of factors was determined by Kaiser's rule of latent roots >1.0 and the parallel analysis method (Franzen & Golden, 1984a). Silverstein then compared the similarity of the factor solutions for the nine age groups and for the WAIS and WAIS-R standardization data by using the coefficient of congruence. Unfortunately, this descriptive statistic is highly influenced by the number of variables that have the same algebraic sign in their factor loadings. Because of the characteristics of the data, the resulting coefficient of congruence is highly inflated and is misleading to interpret. However, by visual inspection of the averaged factor loadings, we can see that there is some similarity between the solutions for the WAIS and for the WAIS-R.

Parker (1983) performed factor analysis on the standardization data from the manual. The method used was a principal-factor analysis with varimax rotation. The number of factors extracted was stopped after two, three, and four factors in order to afford comparison with earlier studies that had reported those numbers of factors when analyzing WAIS data. Except for the method of determining the number of factors, this study is identical to that of Silverstein (1982b), even using the same subjects. However, because Parker reported the results separately for the age groups, the study is of interest to us. The analyses were conducted separately for each of the nine age groups in the normative sample. Parker concluded that the three-factor solution reported for the WAIS is also tenable for the WAIS-R, and that this solution is stable across the age groups. This solution consists of verbal comprehension, perceptual organization, and freedom from distraction. There was no test performed to compare the appropriateness of one solution to another. Instead, the factor solutions were visually inspected. Using a similar methodology, Atkinson and Cyr (1984) reached a similar conclusion from a sample of 114 psychiatric inpatients.

Ryan, Rosenberg, and DeWolfe (1984a) reported an attempt to replicate the results of the factor analysis performed by Silverstein (1982b) in a sample of 85 VA vocational-counseling clients. The authors used a principal-factor analysis with varimax rotation. They did not report what criterion they used to terminate the extraction of factors. They interpreted the two resulting factors as verbal concentration and perceptual organization similar to the earlier solution. They then used the coefficient of congruence to determine the similarity of the factor structures. Unfortunately, the use of the coefficient of congruence was inappropriate. The coefficient of congruence is inflated when many of the factor loadings of the variables have the same algebraic sign (Levine, 1977). In examining the table of factor loadings reported by Ryan et al. (1984a), we see that they all have the same algebraic sign, so that the results of this comparison are highly suspect. Gorsuch (1974) warned against the use of the coefficient of congruence when comparing the results of factor analyses unless only the factor loadings are known. In this case, the authors would have been better advised to use the salient variable similarity index (Cattell, 1949; Cattell, Balcar, Horn, & Nesselroade, 1969). The distribution of the coefficient of congruence is unknown, so it is difficult to agree with the conclusion of these researchers that the factor loadings agree at more than a chance level.

A methodological improvement over the Parker (1983) study would involve a rigorous statistical comparison of the various solutions. O'Grady (1983) performed a maximum-likelihood–confirmatory-factor analysis on the nine age groups in the normative sample. Oblique and orthogonal one-, two-, and three-factor solution were compared with the null model of no common factors by the use of an index of fit expressed as a chi square. In each case, there were no significant differences between the fit afforded by the null model and the fit afforded by the model being tested. The important implication is that none of the solved factor models account for the relations among the subtests better than the other models examined. O'Grady (1983) suggested that the single model be adopted for the sake of parsimony. However, the possibility that a five- or six-factor model may account for the data better cannot be ruled out by this study. It seems safe to say that the factor structure of the WAIS-R remains an empirical question.

Blaha and Wallbrown (1982) reported the results of a hierarchical factor analysis of the standardization data reported in the WAIS-R manual. They concluded that the structure of the WAIS-R is composed of a general intelligence factor that includes two factors. The two secondary factors appeared to be similar to the verbal comprehension and the perceptual organization factors found in previous research.

CONCLUSIONS

The WAIS-R is a nearly ubiquitous instrument in clinical evaluation settings. Its reliability has been relatively well investigated, although its reliability still needs to be examined in special populations such as epileptic subjects, the learning-disabled, and the elderly. But it is the validity of the instrument that is most in need of evaluation. The WAIS-R and its predecessors, the WAIS and the Wechsler–Bellevue, have become the standard criterion against which other tests of intelligence are evaluated on their concurrent validity. This information alone does not allow us conclusions regarding the construct validity of the WAIS-R.

The utility of the WAIS-R in neuropsychological evaluation is also a matter of debate. The simplest solution would to be use the WAIS-R as an index of academically related intellectual skills without invoking diagnostic interpretation strategies. Attempts to use the WAIS-R may have results similar to the attempts to use the WAIS, such as that of Strauss and Brandt (1986), who found that the WAIS was unable to identify subjects with Huntington's disease.

Patterns of performance on the WAIS, such as the use of hold–don't-hold scales, have also been suggested, most notably by Fuld (1983), who suggested that a certain pattern of subscale scores could help identify the central cholinergic deficiency thought to be responsible for the memory deficits found in Alzheimer's disease. Tuokko and Crockett (1987) did not find this pattern in healthy elderly people. However, both Filley, Kobayashi, and Heaton (1987) and Heinrichs and Celinski (1987) have reported results that suggest that this pattern is not specific to an etiology of cholinergic deficiency; it may also be found in patients with closed-head injury or other brain impairments. Russell (1987) suggested strategies for interpreting the WAIS in a neuropsychological setting. However, many of these suggestions are in need of rigorous experimental evaluation and, further, may not apply to WAIS-R results.

The manual for the WAIS-R mentions correlational studies that have related the WAIS and the Wechsler–Bellevue to other psychometric measures of intelligence; it then goes on to state that similar conclusions can be drawn regarding the WAIS-R. This is a dangerous suggestion. What is needed is direct empirical evidence regarding the WAIS–R that impinges directly on the issue of validity. This evidence could come from discriminant-convergent validity methodologies, predictive validity methodologies, or concurrent validity correlational methodologies.

The Wechsler Intelligence Scale for Children–Revised

The Wechsler Intelligence Scale for Children–Revised (WISC-R, Wechsler, 1974) is, as its name suggests, a revised and updated version of the WISC, which was first published in 1949. It attempts to measure intelligence by assessing 10 abilities. (Actually, there are 12 with the supplementary Digit Span and Mazes subtests.) Its scoring procedure eventuates in a scaled score for each of the subtests. These scores have a mean of 10 and a standard deviation of 3. The scaled scores are combined to produce scores for Verbal IQ (VIQ), Performance IQ (PIQ), and Full Scale IQ (FSIQ). The IQ scores have a mean of 100 and a standard deviation of 15.

In revising the WISC, some items that were thought to be ambiguous or culturally loaded were eliminated, new items were devised to replace them, and a few more items were added to increase the reliability of the test. The WISC-R was normed on a stratified sample that was designed to be representative of the U.S. population with regard to age, sex, race, geographic location, occupation of household head, and urban versus rural residence (Wechsler, 1974). There were 2,200 children in the normative sample ranging in age from 6.5 to 16.5 years old. These children were divided into 11 age groups for the purpose of deriving the scaled scores.

RELIABILITY

The scorer reliability of the WISC-R was assessed by Bradley, Hanna, and Lucas (1980). These authors constructed two WISC-R protocols for two hypothetical 10-year-old females whose intended IQ was 110. One of the protocols was constructed without ambiguous responses or administration errors. The other protocol was constructed with ambiguous responses, errors with regard to starting and stopping points, and a few highly unusual responses. These protocols were given to 63 members of the National Association of School Psychologists, who were then asked to score the protocols. Although the manner in which the data are presented does not allow us to estimate the amount of variance that was due to scorer error, the standard deviation of the IQ scores for each of the protocols is presented. The standard deviation can be used as an estimate of the variability among the scorers. The standard deviation for FSIQ for the difficult protocol is 4.3; the standard deviation for FSIQ for the easy protocol is 2.9. These values indicate that, even with unambiguous responses rated by trained test administrators, there will still be some variability in test scores that is attributable to the scorer.

Split-half reliability coefficients were computed for all of the subtests except the power test of Digit Span and the speeded test of Coding. The manual reports that an odd-even split was used for most of the subtests, but it does not identify these subtests, nor does it say what method was used in the other cases. The Digit Span and Coding reliability estimates were based on test–retest values for 50 children in each of the age groups. The reliability coefficients were computed separately for each of the 11 age groups. The reliability coefficients for the IQ scores were computed by means of a formula for composite scores. Overall reliability coefficients were computed by averaging the values for each of the age groups by means of an r-to-z transformation. The reliability coefficients range from .73 for Picture Arrangement to .86 for Vocabulary. The reliability coefficient for VIQ is .94, for PIQ it is .90, and for FSIQ it is .96. Dean (1977b) reported split-half reliability coefficients for a sample of behavior-disordered male children that are very similar to the values reported in the manual, indicating that these coefficients have some degree of stability in a sample of "nonnormal" children.

The reliability of the WISC-R with special populations needs to be addressed because the original reliability estimates were derived on normal populations. Hirshoren, Kavale, Hurley, and Hunt (1977) investigated the internal consistency reliability of the performance IQ of the WISC-R for a sample of children who had been deaf before language acquisition. This is an interesting study because it not only provides information on the WISC-R in a special population, but it also allows us to examine the reliability of the part of the WISC-R that supposedly measures intelligence without the influence of language in a sample that has less language ability than the normative sample. Reliability estimates for the sample of deaf children were computed by the use of Cronbach's coefficient alpha. The reliability coefficients for the Performance subtests were not significantly different from the values reported in the manual, with the exception of the Picture Arrangement, for which the reliability estimates for the deaf sample were significantly higher than the value reported in the manual. The overall reliability of the Performance IQ score was equal to that reported in the manual.

The test–retest reliability for the scores was also computed and reported in the manual. A total of 303 children spread across three age groups were retested after an interval of approximately 1 month. Once again, the subtest scores were combined, so that composite reliability estimates were computed for the IQ scores. The reliability coefficients were corrected for the variability of the norm groups. All of the corrected scores for the age groups were averaged by use of the r-to-z transformation. These values ranged from .65 for Mazes to .88 for Information. The average corrected reliability estimates for the IQ scores were .93 for the VIQ, .90 for the PIQ, and .95 for the FSIQ. There were no tests for the difference in absolute level over time.

Vance, Blixt, Ellis, and Bebell (1981) investigated the test–retest stability on a sample of 75 learning-disabled and retarded children. The intertest interval was 2 years. Because reliability deteriorates over time, these values were likely to be lower than those reported in the manual, which had an intertest interval of 1 month. Correlation coefficients were computed for each of the subtest scores as well as for the IQ scores. Additionally, t tests were performed to assess the change in the absolute value of the scores. The correlation coefficients for the Verbal subtests ranged from .63 for Similarities to .80 for Digit Span. The correlation coefficients for the Performance subtests ranged from .59 for Picture Completion to .80 for Object Assembly. The correlation coefficients for the IQ scores were higher; .80 for the VIQ, .91 for the PIQ, and .88 for the FSIQ.

Despite the significant positive correlations between Time 1 and Time 2, there were significant differences in absolute level for five of the subtests: there were significant decreases for Similarities, Vocabulary, Digit Span, and Block Design, and there was a significant increase in the scores for Picture Arrangement. There was also a significant decrease in Verbal IQ. An important caveat needs to be issued before these results can be interpreted. All of the subjects in this study were students who had abnormal conditions that might impede their development. IQ scores are deviation scores for certain age groups. Therefore, decreases in IQ for these groups may reflect the fact that, while their cohorts are developing normally, these subjects are developing more slowly or are remaining static in their ability levels. The plausibility of this explanation is increased by the pattern of significant changes. Three of the four significant decreases were in Verbal subtests, and the only IQ score to change was Verbal IQ. It is the verbal abilities in which we would not expect the subjects to keep pace with their cohorts. Although this hypothesis may help to explain these differences, the results of the study imply that changes in level may occur in WISC-R scores over time. Evidence to support this hypothesis must come from empirical studies of other populations.

The standard error of measurement values was computed for each of the subtests. However, as discussed in the chapter on the WAIS-R, the formula used by the manual results in an estimate of the variance attributable to error rather than in confidence boundaries for the test scores. The magnitude of the determination of the significance-of-difference scores between subtest scores and between IQ scores is also given. The danger of interpreting these statistically significant differences as clinically significant parallels the danger in the same kind of interpretation of scores on the WAIS-R. The reader is referred to that section for a more thorough discussion of the issue.

There are actually three levels on which to evaluate the split between the VIQ and the PIQ. The manual deals with the reliability of the split, or the probability that the magnitude of the split did not occur by chance. The second level involves the abnormality of the magnitude of the split, or the proportion of the subjects tested who exhibited that magnitude of split. In reviewing the relevant research, Berk (1982) stated that abnormal splits are about twice the size of reliable splits at the same probability levels. That is, if a split of 10 points is reliable at the .05 level, a split of 20 points is probably abnormal at the .05 level. The last level is the validity of the split. This consideration can be restated as a question: What is the clinical significance of a 10-point split? Kaufman (1979) stated that there may be many reasons for a VIQ-PIQ split, and it is up to the clinician to determine the reason in each case. In reviewing the research, Berk (1982) concluded that the validity of the VIQ-PIQ split in the WISC-R is yet to be determined and recommended against its use in a clinical setting.

Often, interpretation of the WISC-R depends on an examination of the pattern among the scale scores or among the IQ scores. This is especially true of the use of the WISC-R in neuropsychological assessment. As a result, the reliability of the pattern of scores needs to be assessed if we are to be confident of such interpretations. Assessing the reliability of the univariate scales is insufficient for this purpose because it fails to take the multivariate structure of patterns into account.

Conger, Conger, Farrell, and Ward (1979) examined the profile reliability of the WISC-R across the age groups of the normative sample. They found that, although the factor structure of the WISC-R appeared to be relatively invariant across age, the salience of those factors changed across age. By assessing the reliability of various types of profile analysis, they were able to recommend the following strategies for profile analysis: comparison of IQ scores, comparison of the VIQ with the PIQ, and comparison of individual scale scores with the average of all scale scores. These profile strategies possess sufficient reliability to recommend their use. The next step would be to assess the validity of these strategies and to discover the clinical meaning of differences in these profiles.

Dean (1977) examined the relationship of various suggested interpretive pattern strategies by using a sample of 41 Caucasian male children who had been referred for psychological evaluation because of their manifestation of behavior disorders. With the exception of the rule that emotionally disturbed children demonstrate Picture Arrangement scores that are greater than their Picture Completion scores, and Object Assembly Scores that are greater than their Coding scores, each by 3 scaled score points, the examined rules demonstrated reasonable accuracy in classifying the children as emotionally disturbed. The interpretation of this study is hampered by its design. No normal children were included in the study; therefore, we do not know how accurate these rules are in classifying children in general. However, this is the type of study that needs to be done in order to assess the clinical utility of profile analysis.

Intercorrelations among the subtests were computed separately for each of the age groups and are reported in the manual. These values were then averaged by means of an r-to-z transformation. In addition, the manual presents information regarding the correlation of each subtest with the relevant IQ scores, which are corrected for membership in the composite that comprises the IQ score. The subtests are moderately correlated with each other.

VALIDITY

The manual reports that concurrent validity of the WISC-R was assessed by correlation with three other tests of intelligence: the Wechsler Preschool and Primary Scale of Intelligence (WPPSI), the Stanford–Binet Intelligence Scale (using the 1972 norms), and the Wechsler Adult Intelligence Scale (WAIS). The WISC-R–WPPSI correlation study used 50 children who were 6 years old. The two tests were administered in counterbalanced order with an intertest interval of between 1 and 3 weeks. The VIQ and the PIQ both correlated .80, and the FSIQ correlated .82.

For the study that examined the relationship between the WISC-R and the WAIS, 40 children aged 16 years, 11 months were used. Once again, the tests were administered in counterbalanced fashion with an intertest interval of 1–3 weeks. The VIQ correlated .96, the PIQ correlated .83, and the FSIQ correlated .95.

The study reported in the manual that examined the relation of the WISC-R to the Stanford–Binet used a sample of children that was divided into four age groups. There were 33 children from the WISC-R–WPPSI study who were also administered the Stanford–Binet. Additionally, 29 children aged 9.5, 27 children aged 12.5, and 29 children aged 16.5 were administered the WISC-R and the Stanford–Binet in counterbalanced fashion. These age-related correlations were averaged by means of the r-to-z transformation. The WISC-R VIQ correlated .71 with the Stanford–Binet IQ. The corresponding correlation for the PIQ was .60, and for the FSIQ, the value was .73.

White (1979) reported a study in which the WISC-R, the Wide Range Achievement Test (WRAT), and the Goodenough–Harris Draw-a-Man test were intercorrelated in a sample of 30 children, 20 of whom had been referred for diagnosis of learning problems, and 10 of whom were the children of friends of the researcher. Moderately high correlations between the WISC-R IQ scores and the WRAT and Draw-a-Man scores were obtained, whereas only moderate correlations were obtained between the WISC-R subscales and the WRAT and Draw-a-Man scores. These findings indicate moderate support of the WISC-R IQ scores as a predictor of academic achievement, as well as support of the WISC-R IQ scores as agreeing with the Draw-a-Man IQ estimates.

Other studies offer moderate support for the concurrent validity of the WISC-R. Wickoff (1979) reported that the IQ scores of the WISC-R correlated moderately with the Peabody Individual Achievement Test (PIAT) in a sample of children referred for an evaluation of learning problems. The VIQ was correlated best with the PIAT scores, followed by the FSIQ and the PIQ. The correlation values ranged from .40 to .78. Brooks (1977) examined the relationship between the WISC-R and the WRAT and Stanford–Binet in a sample of 30 children. The WISC-R correlated .95 with the Stanford–Binet. The correlations between the WISC-R and WRAT scores were more modest: .76 for the Arithmetic scale, .65 for the Spelling scale, and .06 for the Reading scale. Kaufman and Van Hagen (1977) examined the relationship between WISC-R and Stanford-Binet IQs in a sample of 45 retarded children. They reported correlations of .73 for the VIQ, .65 for the PIQ, and .82 for the FSIQ.

One method of assessing the validity of the WISC-R is to evaluate how well scores from the WISC-R can predict academic performance. Schwarting and Schwarting (1977) assessed the relationship between the WISC-R and the WRAT in a sample of 282 children who had been referred for evaluation because of suspected learning problems. The subjects were divided into two age groups of 6–11 and 12–16 years. Particularly for the older group, the WISC-R PIQ did not correlate well with the WRAT scores. However, for the VIQ and the FSIQ, the correlations were moderate, ranging from .56 to .75. Hartlage and Steele (1977) reported moderate correlations between WISC-R IQ scores and WRAT scores in a sample of 36 children. All of the correlations were significant; they were as low as .36. Hale (1978) reported the results of an investigation into the ability of the WISC-R to predict WRAT scores in a group of 155 schoolchildren. When all three of the WISC-R subscores were entered into a multiple-regression formula to predict each of the three WRAT scale scores, only the VIQ was found to significantly, independently predict the Reading and Arithmetic scores of the WRAT.

The information gathered from the studies discussed above points out the significant relation between the WISC-R and measures of academic achievement. The important point to remember is that, although significant, the relationships are moderate; often, only 10% of the variance is shared by the tests. This result may be construed as acceptable, as there are other variables that impinge on academic achievement; however, it is important to determine what makes up the variance in the IQ tests that is not shared by tests of academic achievement. The much higher correlations with the Stanford–Binet argue for the validity of the WISC-R, but we are faced with correlating a test said to measure IQ with a test that is also said to measure IQ. What is really needed is a study that correlates WISC-R IQ with real IQ, whatever that may be. Because IQ is traditionally measured by the use of the tests, such a study is not foreseeable until some basic work has been done on the theoretical definition of IQ.

Construct Validity

Kaufman (1975a) investigated the factor structure of the WISC-R by performing several factor analyses on the normative data published in the manual. For each of the 11 age groups, a principal-components factor analysis with varimax rotation was performed, as well as principal-factors factor analysis with varimax, oblimin, and biquartimin rotations of two-, three-, four-, and five-factor solutions. No statistical analysis of the different solutions was performed. However, the appearance of the WISC three (interpretable) factor solution was fairly consistent across age groups. These three factors are usually interpreted as verbal comprehension, perceptual organization, and freedom from distractibility.

A corollary question involves the factor structure of the WISC-R in a sample of children who are not free from neurological impairment. This is especially appropriate because an instrument like the WISC-R is more likely to be used to evaluate a child for whom there is suspicion of impairment than it is to be used to provide an assessment of a child for whom there is no suspicion of impairment. Richards, Fowler, Berent, and Boll (1980) examined the factor structure of the WISC-R by using a sample of 113 epileptic children aged 6–12 years old and a sample of 124 epileptic children aged 12–16 years old. These authors used maximum-likelihood factor analysis with oblimin rotation. For both groups, the solved-factor structure consisted of a Verbal Comprehension factor and a Perceptual Organization factor. For the older group, the third factor was interpreted as Freedom from Distractibility.

Groff and Hubble (1982) examined the factor structure of low-IQ children in two age groups. The first group consisted of 107 children between the ages of 9 and 11 years with an average FSIQ of 70.4. The second group consisted of 78 children between the ages of 14 and 16 years with an average FSIQ of 66.5. Principal-factor analysis was performed on the data. The method of rotation was not reported. Three, four, and five factors were examined, and the three-factor solution was chosen as the clearest explanation of the data, although the criterion for deciding this point was not given. The three factors for both of the groups were interpreted as Verbal

Comprehension, Perceptual Organization, and Freedom from Distractibility. Although the factors were consistent across the two groups, the Distractibility factor accounted for 14% of the shared variance in the older sample and for 20% of the shared variance in the younger sample. Apparently, the importance of the factors is sensitive to age.

Another study investigated the factor structure of the WISC-R in low-IQ children, this time in 80 retardates between the ages of 6 and 16 who had an average IQ of 58.1. Van Hagen and Kaufman (1975) conducted principal-components factor analysis with varimax rotation of factors with a minimum eigenvalue of 1.0, principal-factor analysis with varimax rotation of two-, three-, four-, and five-factor solutions, and principal-factor analysis with oblimax and biquartimin rotations of two-, three-, four-, and five-factor solutions. They reported that the three-factor solution, as determined in the factor analysis of the standardization sample, was fairly stable across factor-analytic methods in this sample of retardates with a few exceptions: the Verbal Comprehension factor for the standardization sample had greater agreement with the retardates' Freedom-from-Distractibility factor and the retardates' Freedom-from-Distractibility factor had greater agreement with the standardization sample's factor of the same name than did either of the other factors with their namesakes. This finding indicates that there are differences in the factor structure of the WISC-R for retardates in spite of the seeming similarities to each other. An important clinical consequence is a more cautious interpretation of the WISC-R for retardates.

Silverstein (1982b) performed correlated multiple-group-components factor analysis on the standardization data for 7.5-, 10.5-, and 13.5-year-old age groups and compared the two- and three-factor solutions. He found that the two-factor solution was at least as accurate as the three-factor solution in describing the data.

Wallbrown, Blaha, Wallbrown, and Engin (1975) performed a hierarchical factor analysis of the normative data from the WISC-R manual. They interpreted a general intelligence factor that was composed of a verbal-educational factor and a spatial-perceptual factor. This solution was stable across age groups, as determined by a visual inspection of the factor loadings. The differences between the solution in this study and the solution in the Kaufman (1975a) study can be attributed to the different factor-analytic techniques. Hierarchical factor analysis assumes a general factor with component factors. Principal-components factor analysis assumes that a few factors will explain the variance in the data. It is interesting to note the similarities in the solutions. Both of the studies conclude that a verbal and a spatial factor are involved in the WISC-R.

Interpretation of the factors is necessary to the clinical utility of the scores. Kaufman (1975a) recommended that the scale scores of the subtests that comprise the factor scores for a given subject be changed to percentile scores and then be translated into IQ scores through the use of a table found in the WISC-R manual that gives percentile equivalents of IQ scores. Noting that the table gives IQ equivalents only in 5-point increments, Sobotka and Black (1978) presented tables that allow a quick transformation of the scale scores of the three factors into IQ scores for use in clinical interpretation. These authors stated that interpretation then follows the usual procedure for IQ scores. However, these resultant factor "IQ" scores have unknown psychometric properties. Nothing is known of their internal consistency or stability. Gutkin (1978) presented a method for a linear combination of subtest scale scores into IQ scores for the factor scales, as well as a table of reliable differences between the scores. Gutkin (1979) then extended these tables to provide separate estimates of the values for each of the age groups. However, aside from their computed composite reliabilities, little is known about the psychometric properties of these scores. Little is known of the validity or meaning of either the Sobotka and Black (1978) or the Gutkin (1978) factor "IQs."

Grossman and Johnson (1982) reported that the Verbal Comprehension and the Freedom-from-Distractibility factors significantly predicted wide-range achievement test (WRAT) scores in a multiple-regression formula, but that the Perceptual-Organization factor did not. Squared multiple-correlation coefficients indicated that, although the relationships were significant, they accounted for only 25%–36% of the variance in the WRAT scores. More needs to be known about these factor scales before they can be recommended for clinical use.

The factor analysis studies have produced results that are similar to the rational structure of the WISC-R. This similarity can be construed as support for the construct validity of the WISC-R. It is necessary also to provide external evidence of the construct validity of the WISC-R. The correlational studies of the WISC-R with the WPPSI, the WAIS, and the Stanford–Binet are only preliminary steps in this direction. What is needed is evidence that IQ scores as determined by the WISC-R are indeed related to intelligence.

There is evidence to suggest that performance on the WISC-R is related to other factors in addition to intelligence. Brannigan and Ash (1977) classified 73 children (out of a sample of 100) as either extreme impulsives or extreme reflectives and then compared the WISC-R scores of the two groups. The reflective subjects were found to have significantly superior performance on the VIQ, the PIQ, and the FSIQ.

Another variable that is often thought to have an effect on performance on the WISC-R is race. One of the purposes behind revising the WISC was the minimization of racial bias in the test. Race is a heated issue in our society, and the arguments regarding it are often more emotional than rational. Sometimes, although rarely, the proponents are able to agree on basic facts. One of those facts is that black children perform more poorly on the WISC-R than do Caucasian children. The divergence of opinion and the genesis of irrationality occur when the reason for this difference in performance is proposed. Some people declare that the WISC-R is a culture-fair instrument and that the difference in performance reflects a genetic difference in ability. Other people declare that the difference in performance reflects the bias of the test, that is, that the WISC-R measures abilities and information to which Caucasian children are more likely to be exposed.

According to an extensive review by Sattler and Gwynne (1982b), there is no evidence that the race of the examiner influences performance on the WISC-R. The more pressing question is whether the test itself is sensitive to race. As might be expected in a case such as this, there are studies that purport to present evidence for both of the competing viewpoints. Vance and Engin (1978) administered the WISC-R to 154 black children. Because there were significant differences between the scale scores, the authors concluded that the WISC-R is a valid instrument for the assessment of black children. It is difficult, if not impossible, to agree with the conclusions of these authors. There is no evaluation of the validity of the WISC-R, nor is there even a comparison of the performance of the black children to the performance of Caucasian children.

Mishra (1983) examined the predictive validity of the WISC-R IQ and factor scores in relation to Wide Range Achievement Test scores of 64 Mexican-American children. There were small and insignificant correlations between the WISC-R factor scores and the WRAT scores, indicating a limited predictive validity of the WISC-R factor scores for this sample of Mexican-American children. There were significant but moderate correlations between the IQ scores and the WRAT scores, indicating some predictive validity of these measures for the achievement of these children.

Munford, Meyerowitz, and Munford (1980) looked at the difference between WISC and WISC-R scores of Caucasian children and then compared these results to those of an earlier study that had examined the same differences in black children. They reported that, whereas there were no differences between WISC and WISC-R scores for the Caucasian children, the black children performed significantly worse on the WISC-R than they did on the WISC. Although this evidence is suggestive, two obstacles block the interpretation of this study. First, the study that examined Caucasian children used only 20 subjects, as did the study that examined black children. The Caucasian children also performed more poorly on the WISC-R, but their differences did not reach significance. Second, the conclusions would be stronger if the data had been analyzed as part of the same design.

Mishra (1982) examined the performance on three of the WISC-R subtests (Information, Similarities, and Vocabulary) by 40 Caucasian and 40 Navaho children. Differences in performance across individual items were assessed by the use of a log-linear transformation of the data and the maximum-likelihood-ratio chi square. Mishra concluded that 15 of the items evoked performance differences attributable to race. There was no evaluation of performance differences on scale scores, which is another pertinent method of examining this question. However, it is likely that such a difference may exist.

In what is probably methodologically the best of the studies investigating this question, Oakland and Feigenbaum (1979) evaluated the internal consistency, the item difficulty, the item–total correlations, correlation with the California Achievement Test (CAT), and the factor structure of the WISC-R in subjects who were stratified by race (Caucasian, black, and Mexican-American), family size, family structure, socioeconomic status, urban versus rural residence, age, health, and birth order. The analysis for internal consistency, item–total correlations, and concurrent validity (CAT scores prediction) was performed by correlating the values for the subtests for one group with the values for another group. The analysis for item difficulty involved an analysis of variance in which the groups were the independent variables and the item difficulty indices were the dependent measures. The factor analyses were evaluated by correlating varimax loadings on the first principal component and by similarly correlating both of the solved factors after rerotation of one solution to maximize the contiguity between the two vectors. The results indicated that the internal consistency values, the item–total correlations, and the factor structures were relatively unaffected by the independent variables. However, there were differences in item difficulty indices and concurrent validity that were due to the independent variables, indicating differential sensitivity of the WISC-R to race.

The use of the WISC-R to evaluate the presence of brain impairment is a speculative endeavor. Certainly, because of the WISC-R's omnipresence in child clinical settings, any validated use would be extremely welcome. Tramontana and Boyd (1986) evaluated the concurrent validity of the WISC-R in screening for neuropsychological abnormalities in a sample of 90 psychiatric patients with a mean age of 92.8 months. All of the patients were administered the WISC-R, the Aphasia Screening Test, and the age-appropriate form of the Halstead–Reitan or the Luria–Nebraska Neuropsychological batteries. When the results of the neuropsychological batteries were used to classify the subjects as 41 impaired and 49 nonimpaired individuals, there were significant differences on all WISC-R subscale scores except Objects Assembly. When the WISC-R and the Aphasia Screening Test scores were used as predictors in a discriminant function analysis, 91.1% of the subjects were correctly classified. However, the ratio of predictors to subjects was extremely low, limiting the potential generality of the results. In cross-validating the discriminant function with a sample of 84 psychiatric subjects, Boyd and Tramontana (1987) obtained a correct classification rate of 79.3%.

Because the results of the above investigations may suggest that the relation between performances on the WISC-R and on the Halstead–Reitan and Luria–Nebraska batteries may be influenced by shared variance in the skills tapped, it is important to delineate the amount of overlap between the

WISC-R and the neuropsychological measures. Sweet, Carr, Rosini, and Kaspar (1986) administered the WISC-R and the child's revision of the LNNB (LNNB-C) to a sample of 32 psychiatric patients, 28 brain-impaired patients, and 32 normal subjects between the ages of 8 and 12. There were significant correlations between the WISC-R and the LNNB-C measures only in the brain-impaired sample, a finding indicating that the information derived from the WISC-R may not be redundant with the LNNB-C, but that both may be influenced by brain impairment.

CONCLUSIONS

The WISC-R is an instrument for which reliability has been fairly well assessed. The reliability still needs to be assessed in certain populations, such as epileptic children or psychiatric inpatients, but these are minor points in comparison to the reliability assessment already performed. The major issue in the evaluation of the WISC-R is the determination of its validity. There have been no attempts to evaluate the discriminant and convergent validity of the instrument, such as might be done with the Fiske–Campbell methodology, nor have there been sufficient studies of the predictive validity of the WISC-R. Despite the lack of content validity studies, the WISC-R has become the criterion against which the validity of other tests of intelligence are being measured. This fact should not signal our unconditional acceptance of the WISC-R; instead, it should alert us to the paucity of other instruments available to measure intelligence. A particularly important issue for neuropsychologists is the validity of the WISC-R in making diagnoses regarding organic impairment in the child. The WISC-R is most appropriately used as a measure of the child's current IQ.

8

Tests of General Intelligence

GOODENOUGH–HARRIS DRAWING TEST

The Goodenough–Harris Drawing Test has its origins in the Goodenough Draw-a-Man Test, which was developed in 1926. It was revised by Harris in 1963. It requires the subject to draw a man. Alternate forms include instructions for the subject to draw a woman or to draw himself or herself. It is scored on the basis of 73 items related to the detail, the proportion, and the position of the drawing. The result of this scoring procedure is known as the Point Scale. There is also a set of quality scores, which are determined by comparison with a set of 12 drawings said to represent different levels of conceptual maturation. The Quality Scale can be transformed into IQ estimates. The Goodenough–Harris can be administered to either a group or an individual. Age-related norms are available for individuals between the ages of 5 and 15. The score values are normally distributed and increase with age (Scott, 1981).

Harris (1963) found that girls and boys performed differently on the woman and the man forms of the test and consequently provided separate tables for transforming the raw scores into standardized scores. He reported that correlations between the standardized woman and man forms were .76 for boys, .77 for girls, and .75 for both sexes combined. These findings were replicated by McGilligan, Yater, and Hulsing (1971). Harris (1963) further reported that the Point Scale correlates about .80 with the Quality Scale, a finding indicating that time may be saved by scoring only the procedurely easier Quality Scale. However, research investigating the respective accuracy of each scale in estimating IQ has not provided such positive results.

On the basis of a review of 19 studies, Scott (1981) reported that interscorer reliability coefficients range from .80 to .96, with values for the Point Scale being somewhat higher than for the Quality Scale. However, the absolute level of scores was significantly different for the scorers, a finding indicating that mean scores should be computed from the use of multiple scorers or that a study should use only a single scorer in order to measure change. Naglieri and Maxwell (1981) reported an interscorer reliability coefficient of .94 for a sample of 60 children between the ages of 6 and 8. The rescoring of the same protocols by a single scorer resulted in coefficients of .75–.99 (Dunn, 1967; Levy, 1971; Yater, Barclay, & McGilligan, 1969); however, the differences in mean levels were not significant.

In the original study, the test–retest reliability values ranged from .68 for a 3-month interval to .91 for a 1-week interval (Harris, 1963). In later studies, the test–retest reliability coefficients ranged from .53 to .87 for the Point Scale for intervals of either 2 or 3 weeks in samples of 4- to 8-year-old children. A single study investigated the test–retest reliability of the Quality Scale and reported a coefficient of .73 for a sample of 10- to 13-year-old subjects, with a 4-month interval (Struempfer, 1971).

Harris (1963) reviewed several studies that investigated the criterion-related validity of the Harris–Goodenough by correlating its results with those of the Stanford–Binet, the Porteus Maze, Raven's Progressive Matrices, and the Primary Mental Abilities Test. The results were disappointing: the correlation coefficients ranged from .17 to .72, and most coefficients lay in the lower ranges. Joesting and Joesting (1972) found a correlation of .45 between the Goodenough–Harris and the Quick Test in a sample of 44 children ranging in age from 6 to 13. Naglieri and Maxwell (1981) reported that use of the Goodenough–Harris results in significantly lower IQs than does use of the WISC-R. The results of the Goodenough–Harris have correlated approximately .29 with measures of academic achievement (Dudek, Goldeberg, Lester, & Harris, 1969; Pihl & Nimrod, 1976). Scott (1981) reviewed 10 studies that used a multiple-regression methodology to determine the incremental validity of the Goodenough–Harris in predicting academic achievement in conjunction with other variables that are commonly used for that purpose. In each case, the Goodenough–Harris scores did not contribute enough independent variance to remain in the final equation.

One study attempted to validate the diagnostic validity of the Goodenough–Harris in classifying 48 subjects into the four groups: paranoid schizophrenic, schizophrenic but nonparanoid, neurological, and normal controls (Watson, Felling, & Maceachern, 1967). These authors used seven different scoring systems but did not find acceptable accuracy for any of them.

In conclusion, although the Goodenough–Harris appears to demonstrate adequate reliability, it has not demonstrated adequate validity even for the population for which it was intended. It is possible that it demonstrates validity in neuropsychological populations, but that is an empirical question that has not yet been adequately addressed. Further information regarding the equivalence of the group and individual form is needed.

THE LEITER INTERNATIONAL PERFORMANCE SCALE

The Leiter International Performance Scale (LIPS) is a nonverbal instrument that seeks to provide an estimate of the intelligence of an individual. As such, it has the potential of providing an assessment not only of congenitally impaired individuals but also of individuals with acquired receptive aphasia. It has two sections, which have split-half reliabilities of .89 and .75 (Arthur, 1949). In an sample of mentally retarded children, it had a test–retest reliability of .91 (Sharp, 1958). In a sample of language-impaired children, it had a test–retest reliability of .86. Black (1973a) administered the LIPS to a group of 100 children who had either acquired or developmental aphasia. With a 6-month interval, there was a .92 correlation between the scores obtained on the two occasions. The scores increased an average of 1 point, which was not statistically significant.

In evaluating the concurrent validity of the LIPS, Birch, Stuckless, and Birch (1963) reported correlations of .75 with the Stanford–Binet and .74 with the WISC in a sample of deaf children. Beverly and Bensberg (1952) reported a correlation of .62 between the LIPS and the Stanford–Binet with retarded children. Bensberg and Sloan (1951) reported a correlation of .75 with the Stanford–Binet in a sample of brain-impaired children. Black (1973a) reported a correlation of .55 with the Peabody Picture Vocabulary Test (PPVT) in a sample of 100 aphasic children. There was a statistically significant difference between the IQs provided by the PPVT and the IQs provided by the LIPS: the LIPS provided higher IQs.

White, Lynch, and Hayden (1978) administered the LIPS to 6 aphasic and 6 matched-control adult subjects. The scores obtained were comparable across the two groups. There was no attempt to investigate the validity of the IQs. Ratcliffe and Ratcliffe (1979) reviewed over 15 studies that had investigated the validity of the LIPS. They reported a median correlation with other tests of intelligence of .70 and concluded that the LIPS was an accurate measure except in cases of average intelligence.

Reeve, French, and Hunter (1983) administered the LIPS, the Stanford–Binet, and the Metropolitan Achievement Test (MAT) to 25 male and 35 female Caucasian kindergarten students. The LIPS and the Stanford–Binet were administered in counterbalance order with a 10-day interval. The MAT was administered 6 months later. The authors reported Kuder–Richardson 20 values of .81 for the LIPS and .89 for the Stanford–Binet. The Spearman–Brown prophecy formula resulted in values of .89 for the LIPS and .94 for the Stanford–Binet. The correlation between the two tests of intelligence was .70; the LIPS produced a nonsignificantly lower IQ by 1 point. The Stanford–Binet correlated .77 with the MAT, and the LIPS correlated .61 with the MAT.

More work needs to be done in the evaluation of this instrument in adult language-impaired or non-English-language populations.

THE MILL HILL VOCABULARY TEST

The Mill Hill Vocabulary Test is a paper-and-pencil measure of the ability of an individual to provide definitions for words. The original scoring of the test provides grade equivalents and percentile scores. These were converted into deviation IQ scores by Peck (1970). Impaired performance on this test has been associated with left-hemisphere lesions (Costa & Vaughan, 1962). Farley (1969) reported that the two subtests of the Mill Hill may result in different estimates of intelligence. There are no reports on the reliability of this instrument.

THE PICTORIAL TEST OF INTELLIGENCE

The Pictorial Test of Intelligence (PTI; French, 1964) is a test that assesses intelligence in children without requiring a verbal response. It was standardized for children between the ages of 3 and 8. The manual reports test–retest reliability coefficients of .69 with an average interval of 55 months. Bonfield (1972) evaluated the stability of the PTI in a sample of 46 subjects who were residents of a state facility for the retarded. With approximately an 18-month interval, the overall correlation was .80; there was a nonsignificant 14-point increase in scores across time. When the subjects were divided into high-IQ (between 55 and 83) and low-IQ (between 40 and 55) groups, the high-IQ group had a correlation of .92, and the low-IQ group had a correlation of .50, indicating differences in stability across the range of ability.

Elliott (1969) investigated the concurrent validity of the PTI in a group of 12 female and 18 male 7- to 14-year-olds. The mental age scores of the PTI correlated .79 with the Wide Range Achievement Test (WRAT) Reading Scale and .73 with the WRAT Arithmetic Scale. The PTI subtests correlated with the WRAT in the range of .09–.04. Coop, Eckel, and Stuck (1975) investigated the concurrent validity of the PTI in a sample of 46 children with cerebral palsy. All of the subjects were between the ages of 4 and 7. The PTI correlated .83 with the PPVT, .88 with the Columbia Mental Maturity Scale, and .76 with the Achievement Rating Scale.

Sawyer, Stanley, and Watson (1979) examined the construct validity of the PTI by factor-analyzing the subtest scores of 52 kindergarten and 38 second-grade children. Using principal-factors factor analysis, these authors found significant overlap among the subtests and a single factor solution. They suggested that the overall score and not the subtests be interpreted.

PEABODY PICTURE VOCABULARY TEST–REVISED

The Peabody Picture Vocabulary Test–Revised (PPVT-R; Dunn & Dunn, 1981) is an updated version of the original PPVT, which was published in 1959. It provides an estimate of intelligence by assessing the size of an individual's vocabulary. It can be quite a useful test in a neuropsychological setting because no verbal response is required of the subject. All that is needed is a yes or no signal, which can be arranged to allow for the deficits of the individuals. The current version is administered in two alternate forms. The alternate forms were constructed with the use of the Rasch–Wright Latent Trait Item Analysis model. With the use of this statistical model, a growth curve for hearing vocabulary was estimated, and items for the two forms were chosen to fit similar locations on the curve, in this way maximizing the degree of item equivalence before the final test was fully constructed.

The PPVT-R was normed on a sample of 4,200 subjects, who were stratified to conform to the demographic characteristics of the 1970 U.S. Census. There were 100 females and 100 males in each of the children's age groups. The age groups were formed every 6 months, from age 2 to age 8, and every 12 months from age 8 to age 18. Additionally, there were 828 adult subjects between the ages of 19 and 4.

The manual reports split-half reliability values for the various age groups. These values were calculated with the use of the Wright–Rasch model in order to correct for the fact that not all items were administered to all subjects. Correct responses between the basal and the ceiling items for each subject were divided into odd- and even-numbered items, and W-ability scores were calculated for each split and then correlated with each other. These values were then corrected for length by use of the Spearman–Brown formula. For the child sample, the median values were .80 for Form L and .81 for Form M. For the adult sample, split-half reliabilities were calculated only for Form L and only for the adults as a group, rather than by age. The split-half reliability coefficient for the adult sample was .82.

A subsample of the children's normative group (n = 962) was given both forms of the PPVT-R, and alternate-form reliability was assessed. For raw scores, the coefficient was .82. For standard scores, the value was .79.

Test–retest reliability was assessed in a sample of 962 children, who were tested with intervals that ranged from 9 to 31 days. For raw scores, the coefficient had a value of .78. For standard scores, the coefficient had a value of .77.

Evidence for validity in the manual (Dunn & Dunn, 1981) is only theoretical, stating that vocabulary is usually a good estimate of intelligence and citing a few validity studies that had been conducted with the original PPVT.

Alternate-form reliability was assessed by Stoner (1981), who examined the reliability in a sample of 39 male and 40 female Head Start children. The children ranged in age from 3 years, 9 months to 6 years, 3 months. The correlation coefficient was .79. However, the standard score equivalents were significantly higher for Form M (93) than they were for Form L (89). The difference between the levels of scores was not examined in the manual, and these results therefore represent important findings. Tillinghast, Morrow, and Uhlig (1983) administered both forms of the PPVT-R to 120 children in Grades 4, 5, and 6. They reported an alternate-form reliability coefficient of .76. Eight days later, they administered both forms to the same children, but in reversed order, and found a reliability coefficient of .87. McCallum and Bracken (1981) reported alternate-form reliability coefficients ranging from .74 to .86 for black and Caucasian preschool children. In mentally retarded subjects, alternate-form reliability values ranged from .66 to .70 (Bracken & Prassee, 1981). Obviously, the value of the reliability coefficients varies with the characteristics of the sample.

Test–retest reliability has also been evaluated, also only in samples of children. Scruggs, Mastropieri, and Argulewicz (1983) examined the stability of PPVT-R scores in extremely small samples of Anglo children ($n = 7$), Mexican-American children ($n = 22$), and native American children ($n = 27$) on Form L over a 9-month interval. The rank value correlation was used because of the sample size. The values were .71 for the Anglos, .90 for the Mexican-Americans, and .74 for the native Americans. The total sample coefficient was .90.

An attempt at validation of the PPVT-R was reported by Quattrochi and Golden (1983), who correlated the PPVT-R with the scales of the children's form of the Luria–Nebraska Neuropsychological Battery. They found only a small correlation with the Receptive Speech Scale, although they had predicted a large value. The PPVT-R also had small correlations with the Visual, Arithmetic, Memory, and Intellectual Processes scales, indicating a confused picture regarding the construct validity of the PPVT-R.

In neuropsychological practice, none of this research has been conducted on adult subjects. Much more information about both the reliability and the validity is needed before this instrument can be recommended for clinical neuropsychological practice.

THE QUEENSLAND TEST

The Queensland Test (McElwain, Kearney, & Ord, n.d.) is a combination of five subtests that require no verbal interaction for their administration. Three of the tasks (the Knox Cube Test, the bead-threading task from the Stanford–Binet, and Koh's Block Design Test) are borrowed from other tests. Thus, this test holds at least as much promise as its component tests; however, research regarding the tests collected as a battery is sparse, to say the least. Cartan (1971) administered the Queensland Test, the Stanford–

Binet, and the WISC to a group of 10 boys with a mean IQ of 57. She found rank difference correlations of .85 between the Queensland Test and the FSIQ of the WISC. The rank difference correlation between the Stanford–Binet and the Queensland Test was not significant. In the same study, a group (an unspecified number) of adult males (mean age = 24) was administered the Queensland and the WAIS. The rank difference correlation was .87.

Because of its lack of reliance on language for its administration, the Queensland has potential for use with neuropsychologically impaired subjects. However, much more information regarding its reliability and its validity is needed before it can be recommended for clinical use.

THE QUICK TEST

The Quick Test is meant to be a rapid-estimation procedure for intelligence. In it, an individual is shown a series of cards on which four pictures are printed. The examiner says a word, and the subject is to point to the picture that best illustrates the word. There are three alternate forms, and the test's authors recommend combining the three forms in order to increase the accuracy and reliability of the test when sufficient time is available.

Normative data (circa 1960) is available on 458 nonimpaired subjects. The subjects were stratified according to demographic information from the 1950 U.S. Census. There were 23 subjects in each of the age groups from ages 2, 3, and 4 years, and then for every academic year from kindergarten to the senior year in high school. Unfortunately, the ages of about one half of these subjects were not recorded. Normative data are also available for 90 adult subjects between the ages of 24 and 45, and for 20 superior subjects at the 12th-grade level (top 10% of their class) and 20 subjects in their first and second years of college who scored in the 90th percentile on the Ohio State Psychological Examination. The normative data are published in the provisional manual (Ammons & Ammons, 1962). A list of published and unpublished research using the Quick Test is available in Ammons and Ammons (1979a,b).

The provisional manual also provides alternate-forms reliability information based on a subsample of 40 of the preschool subjects. The mean correlation of the three forms was .61. Other mean correlations among the three forms range from .96 for subjects between Grades 2 and 12 to .60 in a sample of seventh-graders. Rotatori (1978) evaluated the test–retest reliability in a sample of 50 retarded children between the ages of 6 and 16. With a 1-week interval, the reliability coefficients were .98 for the female subjects and .87 for the male subjects. The overall reliability coefficient was .92. Vance, Blixt, and Ellis (1980) reported that Forms 1 and 3 correlated .97 in a sample of 44 children who were receiving special-education services.

There was a slight nonsignificant increase in scores across the interval. Abidin and Byrne (1967) administered all three forms to 32 adult organic subjects and 32 psychiatric inpatient subjects and reported overall correlations of .81 for Forms 1 and 2, .77 for Forms 1 and 3, and .84 for Forms 2 and 3. The correlations were slightly higher for the organic subjects than for the psychiatric subjects. There were significant differences between Forms 1 and 3 and Forms 1 and 2 for the organic subjects and between Forms 1 and 2 and Forms 1 and 3 for the psychiatric subjects. Joesting (1975) administered all three forms to 26 male and 31 female college students. There was no attempt to counterbalance or to investigate order effects. The correlations ranged from .55 to .80.

Ammons and Ammons (1962) attempted to investigate the concurrent validity by correlating the Quick Test with the Full Range Picture Vocabulary Test. In the various subsamples of the normative subjects, the correlations ranged from .13 to .97. Other investigations have reported that the Quick Test correlated .68 with the Shipley Institute of Living Scale (Martin, Blair, & Vickers, 1979), .70 with the WISC-R FSIQ in Caucasian adolescents referred for court-ordered evaluation (Paramesh, 1982), and .50 with the WISC FSIQ in a sample of 40 retarded children (Lamp & Barclay, 1967). In each of these cases, there were significant differences in IQ values between the two tests used, calling into question the accuracy of using the Quick Test to estimate IQ. These results were supported by Abidin and Byrne (1967), who found significant differences between the two tests, and by Ciula and Cody (1978) and Law, Price, and Herbert (1981), who found systematic, but not significant, differences. Traub and Spruill (1982) concluded that the Quick Test was most inaccurate in the superior range of intelligence. DeFilippis and Fulmer (1980) reported that the relation between the Quick Test and the WISC-R varies both with level of IQ and with age. In their study of 99 students, the Quick Test tended to underestimate the WISC-R IQs of the high-IQ first- and fourth-grade students and to overestimate the WISC-R IQs of the lower-IQ fourth-graders and all of the seventh-graders.

Husband and DeCato (1982) reported a correlation of .89 between WAIS IQs and Quick Test IQs in a sample of 40 subjects in a prison hospital; the differences between the two tests were not significant. Nicholson (1977) reported correlations ranging from .39 to .79 between subtests of the WISC-R and the Quick Test in a sample of 62 children between the ages of 6 years and 13 years, 11 months. These subjects had been referred for evaluation because of low achievement in school. All of the forms of the Quick Test were administered, and the result was the generation of 182 correlation coefficients; many of these correlations might have been due to chance relations. Levine (1971) tested 50 subjects, aged 60–100, and found a correlation of .91 between the Quick Test and the WAIS FSIQ; the Quick Test resulted in significantly higher IQ values.

Predictive validity was investigated by O'Malley and Bachman (1976), who used the test records of 2,213 students in Michigan. The Quick Test correlated .37 with grades achieved in the same year as the testing, .33 with grades achieved 3 years following testing, and − .03 with hourly wages earned 8 years after testing. In order to investigate the incremental validity of the Quick Test, the ability to predict WAIS IQs in 31 psychiatric inpatients was compared to psychiatrists' estimates of IQ. The Quick Test was found to be a more accurate predictor, although still inaccurate (Templer & Tarter, 1973). The use of psychiatrists' estimates is a questionable comparison procedure, as almost any test procedure is likely to be more accurate than the estimate of a group of professionals who do not have experience in standardized testing.

Orpen (1974) reported that the Quick Test is susceptible to instructional set. In this study the Quick Test was administered to 126 "Coloured" male pupils from South Africa who were in their last year of high school and 135 "Coloured" male pupils in their second year of high school. The subjects were randomly assigned to one of three groups: a group that was told that the Quick Test was a measure of achievement, a group that was told that the Quick Test was a measure of intelligence, and a final group that received the standard instructions. The subjects in the two special-instruction groups scored significantly higher than the subjects who received standard instructions, a finding underlining the need for carefully adhering to standardized administration.

The data suggest that the alternate forms of the Quick Test may, in fact, provide estimates of IQ differently for different populations, and this possibility needs to be better documented. More information is needed regarding the test–retest reliability of the test. Additionally, the Quick Test does not appear to be an accurate estimator of WAIS and WISC IQs. For these reasons, the Quick Test probably should not be used to evaluate IQ except when time is extremely limited and only a rough estimate is needed. The provisional manual is now 24 years old and is in need of replacement.

RAVEN'S PROGRESSIVE MATRICES

Raven's Progressive Matrices is intended to be a test of nonverbal intelligence. It consists of a series of increasingly difficult patterns with a piece missing. At the bottom of the stimuli is a set of six alternative pieces, one of which correctly completes the design. The test exists in three forms, Standard, Colored (intended mainly for children), and Advanced. Because it requires accurate perception of spatial relations, it can also be seen to be a test of visual-spatial integrity. The manual (Raven, Court, & Raven, 1977) states that the test measures a person's ability to think clearly, irrespective of past experiences or present ability for verbal communication. It is stated to be standardized for subjects between the ages of 6 and 65.

The manual presents information regarding the reliability of the instrument in a wide range of subjects. In keeping with the multicultural applications of a test of nonverbal intelligence, the reliability of the instrument has been assessed in non-English-speaking populations. Internal-consistency reliability was assessed in a sample of 727 Greek school-aged children. The correlation coefficient had a value of .60 for the 6-year-old subjects and of .98 for the 12-year-old subjects. The modal value was .90. The split-half reliability in a sample of Yugoslavian teenagers (unspecified age range and sample size) was .96. An assessment of the 1-year test–retest reliability in Congoese schoolchildren resulted in a correlation coefficient of .55. Information regarding the differences in absolute level was not reported.

The Colored Matrices have been recommended for young children, mental defectives, and older people. A group of 291 children was tested on the Colored Matrices in 1948 in order to provide normative information presented in the form of percentiles. Fifty-eight of those children were retested after an unspecified interval; the result was a correlation coefficient of .60 for the 6.5-year-old subjects and of .80 for the 9.5-year-old subjects. A sample of 25 normal children and 29 emotionally disturbed children was tested three times with an interval of 3 months. For the normal subjects, the correlations between Times 1 and 2 was .89, between Times 1 and 3 was .86, and between Times 2 and 3 was .90. For the disturbed subjects, the correlations between Times 1 and 2 was .92, between Times 2 and 3 was .85, and between Times 2 and 3 was .92.

The manual also presents limited information regarding the validity of the instrument. Its criterion validity was assessed by correlating the matrices with intelligence test scores (the name of the intelligence test is not stated). For children, the correlation coefficients ranged from .54 to .86. For adults, the correlation coefficients ranged from .75 to .85. In children, the matrices correlated with scores from the California Achievement Tests in the range of .26–.61, and with school grades in the range of .20–.60. The manual states that the matrices correlate .70 with later school grades, but it does not specify the sample composition, the time interval, or the measure of achievement. Content validity was assessed by calculating the biserial item–total correlation; the result was a mean value of .52. A factor analysis extracted a single factor that the test's authors interpreted as g-factor intelligence. Although the report does not give enough information to allow an evaluation of the appropriateness of this conclusion, later studies have resulted in data that indicate that the initial conclusions were drawn from faulty methodology.

For example, Dolke (1976) performed a principal-components factor analysis with varimax rotation on the data from 521 Indian subjects. Extracting factors until the residual was not significantly different from zero resulted in a solution of five factors, none of which were interpreted as g.

Dillon, Pohlmann, and Lohman (1981) hypothesized that the single-factor solution was an artifact of the dichotomous scoring method, and that the factor therefore actually represented a level of difficulty rather than a common construct. They therefore performed a factor analysis on the phi/phi coefficients derived from the item data. Using a principal-components factor analysis with varimax rotation, they derived two factors, one of which they interpreted as pattern addition–pattern subtraction and the other as pattern progression.

Dolke (1976) reported the results of an investigation into the psychometric properties of the Raven's Progressive Matrices in a sample of Indian subjects. The total sample for all of the data analyses involved 521 normal male subjects with a mean age of 42 years. In order to reveal the discriminability of the individual items, a random sample of 370 subjects was drawn from the larger sample. The highest and lowest scoring 27% of this subsample were formed into two groups. Then, a discrimination index was calculated based on the biserial correlation between group membership and score on the item. Conventional methodology labels a value of .35 as acceptable. Only 47 of the total 60 items demonstrated values greater than .35. Next, Dolke examined the sequence of items to see if their level of difficulty increased with their serial position in the test. Calculating the percentage of subjects passing each item, he found generally increasing difficulty, but with reversals in the sequence. A probit analysis conducted on the scores of all 521 subjects indicated that the level of difficulty did not proceed uniformly; instead, there was a discontinuous pattern with reversals, as well as a tendency for difficult items to be bunched in the middle of the sequence. In addition, the distance (measured in increments of difficulty) between the items was not well spaced.

Hall (1957) also reported an uneven progression of level of difficulty in his sample of 82 U.S. subjects, as did Bromley (1953) in his sample of 35 British subjects. Johnson and Oxiel (1970) examined the item difficulty in a sample of 100 male nonparanoid chronic schizophrenics and 100 paranoid chronic schizophrenics and found no differences between the two samples, although as a whole there was an uneven series of item difficulties. These results indicate that a different sequence of the items may result in a more precise instrument.

An unspecified subsample of the subjects was retested after a 6-week interval; the result was a correlation of .80. An odd-even split of the items produced a Kuder–Richardson (K-R) 20 value of .67 and a Spearman–Brown value of .73. Hall (1957) found a higher K-R 20 value of .86. Finally, Dolke administered the General Aptitude Test Battery (GATB) to another unspecified subsample to obtain a correlation of .55 between the GATB IQ score and the score from Raven's Progressive Matrices. Hall found that Raven's Progressive Matrices correlated .72 with the WAIS FSIQ, .58 with the VIQ, and .71 with the PIQ.

   The construct validity of Raven's Progressive Matrices has been examined. The result has been data that call into question whether the test
actually is a measure of nonverbal intelligence. Bock (1973) argued that
because Raven's stimuli have the *a priori* easily verbalized descriptors of
shading, shape, and size, the test is actually one of verbal abilities. He
performed a factor analysis on the Raven's and the Tests of Primary Mental
Abilities and found that the Raven's loaded heavily on the extracted verbal
factor. Burke and Bingham (1969) administered the Raven's, the WAIS, and
the Army General Classification Test to 91 male VA inpatient subjects. When
principal-components factor analysis with varimax rotation was used, the
Raven's loaded highly on the verbal factor. Urmer, Morris, and Wendland
(1960) compared 20 nonneurological patients with 20 cardiovascular-acci-
dent (CVA) patients and found significant differences in Raven's scores even
when WAIS IQ was partialed out in an analysis of covariance. However,
these results are difficult to interpret precisely because the CVA patients
had a wide variety of location of lesions. After reviewing four studies investigating the Colored Matrices, Sigmon (1983) concluded that there were
inadequate normative data, and additionally, that boys tend to perform better
than girls.
   A possible problem of Raven's Progressive Matrices is that the alternate
answers are arranged in a horizontal line, which may influence the performance of individuals with unilateral neglect or visual hemifield deficits. Gainotti, D'Erme, Villa, and Caltagirone (1986) produced a form of the Raven's
in which the alternatives are arranged in a vertical line; there were no differences in performance between the left-hemisphere- and right-hemisphere-
lesioned subjects. However, the aphasic subjects performed significantly
more poorly than the nonaphasic left-hemisphere-lesioned subjects, a finding
indicating again that verbal skills may play a role in successful performance
on Raven's Progressive Matrices.
   Other studies have tried to investigate whether Raven's Progressive
Matrices can be used to lateralize neurological impairment. Archibald, Wepman, and Jones (1967) tested 39 left-hemisphere and 29 right-hemisphere
subjects using the Colored Matrices. They reported that the left-hemisphere
subjects performed more poorly, but only at the $p < .06$ level of significance.
Campbell and Oxbury (1976) tested stroke patients at 3 weeks and 6 months
following stroke. Of all of the comparisons performed, only the right-hemisphere patients with unilateral neglect were significantly worse than the
right-hemisphere patients without neglect. All of the patients improved over
time. Colonna and Faglioni (1966), Costa and Vaughan (1962), DeRenzi and
Faglioni (1965), and Zaidel, Zaidel, and Sperry (1981) concluded that performance on Raven's Progressive Matrices cannot be used to lateralize brain
impairment. In a rigorous examination of the laterality question, Denes,
Semenza, Stoppa, and Gradenigo (1978) evaluated 42 subjects with unilateral
damage. In order to rule out the effects of contracoup, they used only sub-

jects with ischemic cerebrovascular pathology. They also matched their subjects on the degree of their sensorimotor and visual field defects. The subjects were tested at admission and again 2 months later. All of the subjects improved over time, but there were no differences between the left- and the right-lateralized subjects.

In studies that concluded that lateralization is possible, Arrigoni and DeRenzi (1964) concluded that left-hemisphere subjects performed more poorly, but Piercy and Smith (1962) and Miceli, Caltagirone, Gainotti, Masullo, and Silvero (1981) concluded that right-hemisphere subjects performed more poorly. Basso, DeRenzi, Faglioni, Scotti, and Spinnler (1973) investigated Raven's Progressive Matrices performance in 159 subjects with unilateral brain impairment and 55 control subjects. The brain-impaired subjects were subdivided on the basis of the presence or absence of visual field defects, and the left-hemisphere-impaired subjects were further subdivided into aphasics and nonaphasics. As a whole, the brain-impaired subjects performed significantly more poorly than the control subjects. Out of all of the possible pairwise comparisons of the subgroups with the control subjects, only the right-hemisphere subjects with visual field defects and the aphasic subjects performed significantly more poorly than the control subjects. The right-lateralized subjects performed more poorly, although not significantly so, than did the left-lateralized subjects. The role of unilateral visual neglect was examined by Colombo, DeRenzi, and Faglioni (1976), who reported that these patients tended to choose alternatives from the side of the response sheet homolateral to their injured hemisphere, regardless of the correctness of the response chosen.

Zaidel and Sperry (1973) reported the results of an innovative technique to examine the laterality of Raven's Progressive Matrices. They examined seven commissurotomy patients between 2.5 and 7 years postsurgery. They reduced the number of responses possible from six to three. Although they allowed the subjects to view the stimuli, the possible responses were behind a screen and could be felt by only one hand at a time. The use of the left hand always resulted in a better performance, a finding indicating that Raven's may be a right-hemisphere task. However, the results are clouded by the presence of additional damage in the subjects secondary to epilepsy, the extremely small sample size, and the presence of a ventricular-jugular shunt in one subject.

Given the studies described, it is safer to conclude that the Raven's can not be easily lateralized. The results of Zaidel and Sperry indicate that this is an area that may bear fruit with the application of more creative methodology.

Costa (1976) argued that the reason that a clear consensus on laterality has not been reached is that the laterality and the locus of the lesion affect performance on the three subsets of the Raven's differently. This approach makes sense, as the summing of item scores often results in loss of information. Whether this approach will bear experimental fruit remains to be seen, but it does offer promise for future research.

In an examination of the concurrent validity of Raven's Progressive Matrices, Bolin (1955) administered the test to 76 college juniors and found a .65 correlation with the Otis Gamma Mental Ability Test, a .48 correlation with the American Council on Education Psychological Qualifying Exam total score, .29 with the linguistic portion of the same test, and .59 with the quantitative portion of the same test.

Raven's Progressive Matrices have readily recognizable advantages in testing language-impaired individuals. Brown and McMullen (1982) modified the administration of the test to allow movement-impaired subjects to indicate their responses by simple eye movements, further increasing the test's applicability.

STANFORD–BINET INTELLIGENCE SCALE

The Stanford–Binet Intelligence Scale (S-B) has one of the oldest histories of any standardized test in current use in the United States. It is based on A. Binet's pioneering work in measuring the aptitude of French children for school and on Louis Terman's adaptation of that work for children in the United States. Because of the test's venerable history, it is surprising that the reliability of the current form of the S-B has not been evaluated and that the validity of the S-B has been meagerly evaluated. The manual (Terman & Merrill, 1972) reports that internal consistency has been evaluated only for the 1960 revision of the S-B, and not for the 1972 renorming. The mean biserial correlation for each subtest is .67 for subjects between the ages of 6 and 14 years and .61 for subjects between the ages of 2.5 and 5 years. The new norms were generated from an administration of the S-B to approximately 150 subjects in each of 21 age groups. The manual states that attempts were made to stratify the sample in terms of the demographic composition of the United States, but these attempts are not described. The safest conclusion to be drawn is that the reliability of the S-B needs to be more fully evaluated.

There are three abbreviated forms that serve as approximations of alternate forms. Bloom, Klee, and Raskin (1977) administered the Stanford–Binet to 50 children with developmental disabilities. These authors found fairly high correlations between the full form and the abbreviated form (.99, .98, and .92). However, all of the abbreviated forms tended to underestimate the IQ derived from the full-length form. As many as 34% of the subjects had discrepancies of 5 points or more between their full-length Stanford–Binet IQ and their abbreviated-form IQs. The results of this study indicate that the short forms should not be considered alternate forms. Further, when an IQ score is desired, it would be better to administer the entire test.

Most studies of the S-B have been mainly of the concurrent validity of the instrument; these studies have used a correlational design. For example, Harper and Tanners (1972) correlated the S-B with the French Pictorial Test of Intelligence in a sample of 40 physically handicapped children, reporting a value of .79. Sewell (1977) administered the Stanford–Binet and the WPPSI to 35 black children from a lower-SES background. He found correlations of .75 with the Verbal IQ score of the WPPSI, .70 with the Performance IQ, and .71 with the Full Scale IQ. In a test of the difference in absolute level, the WPPSI provided significantly greater IQ scores than did the Stanford–Binet. Davis (1975) found a correlation of .91 between the Stanford–Binet and the General Cognitive Index of the McCarthy scales in a sample of low-IQ kindergarten children. On the other hand, Harrison and Wiebe (1977) reported a correlation of only .45 between the same two tests in a sample of average-IQ preschool children. Apparently, the accuracy of the Stanford–Binet is different at different levels of ability.

An examination of the predictive validity of the S-B found that it was more accurate in predicting WISC scores after a period of 3 years than was the WPPSI (Crockett, Rardin, & Pasework, 1975).

Brossard, Reynolds, and Gutkin (1980) investigated the question of whether the Stanford–Binet had differential validity as a function of race. They administered the Stanford–Binet and the Wide Range Achievement Test (WRAT) to 60 white children and 60 black children. They used the Stanford–Binet IQ scores to predict scores on the three WRAT subtests, separately by sex, and then tested for the significance of differences between the two races. There were no significant differences due to race.

Although the Stanford–Binet is an often-used instrument for both clinical and research purposes, there is much that can be done to evaluate the instrument. In particular, studies of the reliability of the test are much needed. The test appears to have reasonable concurrent validity, but the construct and predictive validity of the test can be further evaluated.

SLOSSON INTELLIGENCE TEST

The Slosson Intelligence Test is a short, easily administered test of intellectual ability that is derived from the Stanford–Binet. It is stated to be appropriate for individuals 1 month and older. It can be administered by people with average intelligence with a minimal amount of training. Its items appear to tap verbal comprehension and production, arithmetic reasoning, verbal-auditory memory, and general fund of knowledge. The reliability of the Slosson has not been evaluated.

There has been some research investigating the concurrent validity of the Slosson. The manual for the Slosson (Slosson, 1963) reports two studies that compare it to the WAIS and the WISC. However, these two studies used only 10 subjects (WAIS) and 15 subjects (WISC). More research is obviously needed. Stewart and Jones (1976) reviewed research correlating the Slosson with the Stanford–Binet and reported that most correlation coefficient values were in the .90s. This is not surprising, as the Slosson is based on the Stanford–Binet. A more relevant research design would be to relate the Slosson to other tests of intelligence. Covin (1977) reviewed four studies that compared the Slosson with the WISC and the WAIS; the samples were larger than those used in the manual. Covin found a range of correlation coefficients from .49 to .6. She then reported the results of her own study, which investigated the relationship between the Slosson and the WISC in 50 children who had been referred for psychoeducational assessment. She found moderate correlations between the Slosson and the WISC IQs for black students and somewhat higher correlation values for Caucasian students. The overall trend was for the Slosson to be more highly related to the VIQ than to the PIQ or the FSIQ.

Lowrance and Anderson (1979) also compared the Slosson with the WISC-R in school-aged children. The subjects were 34 females and 35 males between the ages of 6 and 13. The authors reported a correlation of .79 with the PIQ and of .92 with the VIQ. The Slosson tended to provide higher estimates of IQ than did the WISC-R at the upper ranges of this distribution and lower estimates of IQ at the lower end of the distribution. Martin *et al.* (1979) correlated the Slosson with the California Short Form Test of Mental Maturity ($r = .73$) and with the Shipley Institute of Living Scale ($r = .69$) in a sample of 50 college students. These studies of the concurrent validity of the Slosson are helpful but are insufficient to determine the validity of the instrument. Needed are studies of the test's construct validity and predictive validity, as well as studies of all forms of its reliability.

THE SHIPLEY–HARTFORD SCALE

The Shipley–Hartford Scale was originally designed as a measure of mental deterioration in psychiatric patients (Pollock, 1942). It is a brief instrument that can be administered individually or in groups. It consists of two parts. The first part is a measure of vocabulary, and the second part is a measure of abstraction skills. The comparison between the two scores is said to demonstrate the amount of deterioration that has occurred. The Shipley–Hartford has recently aroused interest as a screening instrument in the determination of general intellectual level. There are no reports of evaluations of any form of reliability.

The Shipley–Hartford has been evaluated only in terms of its concurrent validity. Prado and Taub (1966) investigated its accuracy in estimating IQ scores derived from either an abbreviated form of the WAIS or the Stanford–Binet in a sample of 59 psychiatric patients in a VA hospital and a second group of 55 employees of a state hospital. These authors reported that the Shipley–Hartford showed better agreement in individuals with above-average IQ. Black (1974) reported similar findings in a sample of 40 subjects with penetrating head wounds. Again, the Shipley–Hartford predicted WAIS scores more accurately in above-average IQ subjects. Interestingly, the IQ scores derived from the two instruments agreed within 3 points in only 33% of the subjects. The two instruments agreed within 12 points in 80% of the subjects. Bartz (1968) reported that the Shipley–Hartford was a better predictor of WAIS IQ scores than was the Army Beta Test, although the overall correlation between Full Scale IQ values was only .73.

The Halstead–Reitan Neuropsychological Battery

with Douglas E. Robbins

The Halstead–Reitan Neuropsychological Battery is one of the most widely used instruments for the assessment of brain dysfunction. This set of clinical procedures was originally developed and validated by Ward Halstead and was later extended and modified by Ralph Reitan. There is general agreement that the Halstead–Reitan battery is a highly reliable, valid, and widely used assessment of brain dysfunction (Hevern, 1980), although there is limited empirical information about its reliability. The original Halstead–Reitan battery consisted of the following seven tests, which were selected for their ability to discriminate between patients with frontal lobe lesions and patients with other lesions or normal subjects (Halstead, 1947; Reitan & Davison, 1974): (1) the Category Test; (2) the Tactual Performance Test (a modification of the Seguin–Goddard Form Board); (3) the Rhythm Test (which originally appeared in the Seashore Measures of Musical Talent); (4) the Speech Sounds Perception Test; (5) the Finger Oscillation Test (Finger Tapping Test); (6) the Critical Flicker Fusion Test; and (7) the Time Sense Test. The Flicker Fusion Test and the Time Sense Test are not typically included in current modifications of the Halstead–Reitan battery as they have not been shown to reliably differentiate neurologically impaired subjects from unimpaired subjects (Boll, 1981; Russell, Neuringer, & Goldstein, 1970). The five remaining tests produce seven individual scores, three scores (total time, memory, and location) being derived from the Tactual Performance Test (TPT). These scores are used to calculate an Impairment Index, which represents the proportion of the patient's scores that fall within the impaired range. An Impairment Index of .5 is considered the cutoff for overall performance within the impaired range. The conversion procedure for calculating the Impairment Index is illustrated in Table 9-1. Impairment Indexes are computed only for the adult battery, as similar cutoff scores are not available for the intermediate or the young children's batteries. Table 9-2

TABLE 9-1. Halstead Impairment Index

Number of tests in impaired range	Impairment index
0	.0
1	.1
2	.3
3	.4
4	.6
5	.7
6	.9
7	1.0

provides the cutoff scores for the seven tests contributing to the Impairment Index for the adult neuropsychological battery (based on Halstead's original norms).

Although the Impairment Index has proved to be a clinically useful measure, it is important to note that diagnostic conclusions regarding the simple presence or absence of brain damage that are based on this measure have been found to be less accurate than those obtained by clinical judgment based on tests, interviews, and medical history (Tsushima & Wedding, 1979).

In addition to the tests listed above, many clinicians augment this core battery with tests of verbal and visuospatial memory (e.g., Dodrill, 1978, 1979; Matarazzo, Wiens, Matarazzo, & Goldstein, 1974; Russell, 1980); perceptual integrity (e.g., Reitan, 1966; Russell et al., 1970); and motor performance (e.g., Harley, Leuthold, Matthews, & Bergs, 1980; Matthews & Haaland, 1979). In addition to the original tests comprising the Halstead battery, Reitan has included several additional procedures: the Wechsler Adult Intelligence Scale, an aphasia and sensory-perceptual battery, the Trail Making Test, and a measure of grip strength. The Minnesota Multi-

TABLE 9-2. Halstead Cutoff Scores That Contribute to the Halstead Impairment Index

Test	Impaired range
Category Test	>50 errors
Tactual Performance Test	
Total time	>15.6 min
Memory	<6
Localization	<5
Seashore Rhythm Test (rank score)	>5
Speech Sounds Perception Test	>7
Finger Oscillation Test (dominant hand)	<50

phasic Personality Inventory (MMPI) is also routinely used as a measure of the patient's emotional state and response to her or his current psychological-medical situation. It should be noted that the titles "Halstead–Reitan Neuro-psychological Battery" and "Halstead–Reitan Battery and Allied Procedures" refer to three separate test batteries (adult, intermediate, and young children). The adult battery, the Halstead Neuropsychological Test Battery and Allied Procedures, is used for persons 15 years old and older. The procedures for children aged 9–15 is the Halstead Neuropsychological Test Battery for Children and Allied Procedures. The battery for children aged 5–9 is the Reitan Indiana Neuropsychological Test Battery for Children. Each of these batteries includes a minimum of 14 separate tests and 26 variables, as well as an aphasia and constructional praxis test of 31 separate items (Boll, 1981).

NORMATIVE DATA

Table 9-3 provides a listing of cutoff scores for the Halstead–Reitan battery and many of its commonly used augmentative procedures. The norms for this table were adopted from Halstead (1947), Reitan (n.d.), Russell *et al.* (1970), and Golden (1977, 1978a).

TABLE 9-3. *Ranges for Brain-Injured Performance on the Halstead–Reitan Battery*

Test	Impaired range
Aphasia exam	>6 points or 72 errors
Category Test	>50 errors
Finger Agnosia	>2 errors
Finger Tapping Test (dominant)	<51 taps
Finger Tapping Test (nondominant)	<46 taps
Fingertip Number Writing	>3 errors
Grip Strength (dominant)	<40 kg
Grip Strength (nondominant)	<35 kg
Impairment Index	>.4
Rhythm Test	>4 errors
Speech Sounds Perception Test	>7 errors
Suppressions (all modalities)	>0
Tactile Form Recognition	>0 errors
Tactual Performance Test	
Total time	>942 seconds
Memory	<6 correct
Location	<5 correct
Trail-Making Test (Part A)	>39 seconds
Trail-Making Test (Part B)	>91 seconds

Although the research literature in general is supportive of the Halstead–Reitan, it is important to note that the original norms for this battery (see Boll, 1981) were not well founded. It is questionable whether the 29 subjects that were used as normals in this research were appropriate. For example, 10 of the subjects were diagnosed as having "minor" psychiatric problems, 1 subject was awaiting criminal sentencing (either life imprisonment or execution) at the time of testing, and 4 subjects were awaiting lobotomies because of aberrant behavior. In spite of these criticisms, the Halstead–Reitan battery has proved to be quite robust in its ability to assess brain impairment.

For those reasons, recent publications have sought to provide more comprehensive normative information. Bornstein (1986c) presented normative information on the differences between left- and right-sided performance on the Grooved Pegboard, the Smedley dynamometer, and the Finger Tapping Test. Bornstein (1986a) examined the cutoff scores in relation to performance by 365 normal subjects and found that between 15% and 80% of the subjects would have been misclassified as impaired. Fromm-Auch and Yeudall (1983) presented normative data based on a sample of 193 normal adult subjects. Steinmeyer (1986) reviewed the available normative data and calculated metanorms for the Halstead–Reitan.

Age Effects

The restricted age range of the normative group for the Halstead–Reitan merits serious concern. The subjects ranged from 14 to 50 years of age; the average age was 28.3. However, as noted by Lewinsohn (1973), Prigatano and Parsons (1976), and Bak and Greene (1980), performance on most of the subtests decreases with age. As a result, spuriously elevated Impairment Indices and erroneous diagnostic conclusions may be reached with older adults (e.g., see Ehrfurth & Lezak, 1982; Price, Fein, & Feinberg, 1979). In general, the research literature indicates that tests that are more complex measures of cognitive skills show stronger age effects than measures of specific motor or sensory skill (Fitzhugh, Fitzhugh, & Reitan, 1964; Golden & Schlutter, 1978; Reed & Reitan, 1963; Reitan, 1967). Older subjects tend to demonstrate greater deficits on tasks requiring immediate adaptive ability, and to excel on tasks requiring the recall of stored information or previous experience. Age-related norms have been established in an attempt to rectify this problem. Pauker (1977), for example, supplied means and standard deviations for five age levels (for subjects between the ages of 19 and 76) for the seven commonly used Halstead–Reitan scores plus the Impairment Index. WAIS Full Scale IQ is used as a covariate. Harley et al. (1980) provided t-score conversions, derived from a veteran population, for five age ranges from 55 to 79. In their posthumous publication of Halstead's gerontological data, Schludermann, Schludermann, Merryman, and Brown

(1983) provided an excellent review of the neuropsychological changes associated with aging.

Effect of Education

The patient's educational level has also been found to be a confounding variable in performance on the Halstead–Reitan battery (Finlayson, Johnson, & Reitan, 1977). Well-educated subjects with neurological deficits may obtain relatively high scores, whereas less educated, neurologically intact subjects may obtain low scores indicative of brain impairment. Vega and Parsons (1967) reported that the Speech Sounds Perception Test and the Seashore Rhythm Test are most susceptible to this effect. Finlayson et al. (1977), however, found that education was a confounding variable across all of the Halstead–Reitan subtests.

Effect of Sex

Sexual differences have been reported on the Halstead–Reitan battery. For example, in a study using a matched-subjects design for a sample of 47 nonneurological subjects and a sample of 47 neurological patients, Dodrill (1979) found that males obtained significantly higher scores on tasks containing a strong motor and/or spatial component (e.g., Finger Tapping; dynamometer; and Wechsler Memory Scale, Visual Reproduction). On the WAIS, females performed better on the Digit Symbol subtest, whereas males performed better on the Arithmetic, Picture Completion, and Block Design subtests. No significant differences were noted on the WAIS summary measures (Verbal IQ, Performance IQ, and Full Scale IQ). In their evaluation of the Finger Tapping Test, the Form Board, and the State–Trait Anxiety Test, King, Hannay, Masek, and Burns (1978) found a sex effect on the Finger Tapping Test: females performed slower. In females, trait anxiety was also found to be negatively correlated with finger-tapping performance and to be positively correlated with the time used to complete the Form Board.

RELIABILITY

Only a limited number of reliability studies have been reported that have assessed the Halstead–Reitan battery in its entirety. The focus of the majority of this research has been test–retest reliability. Typically, research in this area has involved calculating the traditional psychometric index of reliability, that is, Pearson's coefficient of correlation (r).

Test–Retest

Investigators have generally reported significant correlations (Dodrill & Troupin, 1975; Klonoff, Fibiger, & Hutton, 1970; Matarazzo et al., 1974; Matarazzo, Matarazzo, Wiens, Gallo, & Klonoff, 1976) in studies assessing the test–retest reliability of the Halstead–Reitan. Klonoff et al. (1970), for example, demonstrated test–retest correlations for the complete battery that ranged from .87 on Part B of the Trail Making Test to .59 on the Localization component of the TPT. Research has also been reported, however, that indicates that the more complex measures on the Halstead–Reitan battery are subject to statistically and clinically significant practice effects. Findings reported by Dodrill and Troupin (1975) suggest that the Category Test, the Tactual Performance Test (TPT) Location, and the Impairment Index are most sensitive to practice effects. Dodrill and Troupin reported that, in a study using serial testing of a group of chronic epileptics, the subjects' performance improved (e.g., there was a 10-point gain on the second administration of the Category Test. The mean score on the Category Test improved another 10 points for the epileptic subjects by the fourth testing. Significant improvement, as noted above, was also noted on the Location score of the Tactual Performance Test. Overall score improvements made by the chronic epileptics lowered the average Impairment Index from .60 to .45 by the fourth administration.

In a test–retest study (20 weeks apart) of 29 healthy young males, Matarazzo et al. (1974) obtained results consistent with Dodrill and Troupin's findings (1975) regarding the Category Test and the TPT Location score. However, Matarazzo et al. (1974) interpreted the results of this study as supporting the reliability of the Halstead–Reitan battery. In their discussion of this research, these authors made an important distinction between psychometric and clinical reliability. For example, whereas a Pearson test–retest coefficient of reliability of .08 (p not significant) was obtained for the Halstead Impairment Index, perfect clinical reliability was demonstrated in terms of correctly classifying all 29 subjects as being "normal" on both test and retest. The results of this study were extended by the addition of a comparison group of 16 older subjects with cerebrovascular disease (Matarazzo et al., 1974), and later by the addition of a sample of 35 chronic schizophrenic patients and a sample of 15 organic patients who had undergone endarterectomy (Matarazzo et al., 1976). As noted in Table 9-4 (and in Matarazzo et al., 1976), significant differences exist across samples in terms of age, education, IQ, and intertest interval.

As noted previously, a high degree of clinical as well as psychometric reliability for most of the tests comprising the Halstead–Reitan battery was reported by Matarazzo et al. (1976). The results of these studies were extended further by comparing the performance of a drug-free alcoholic sample (n = 91) with a nonalcoholic medical inpatient sample (n = 20) (Eckardt &

TABLE 9-4. Age, Education, and IQ Characteristics of Subjects in Test–Retest Samples

	Healthy normal males	Chronic schizo-phrenic patients	Carotid endar-terectomy patients	Cerebro-vascular disease patients
Mean age	24	47	62	60
Mean education	14	10	9	11
Mean				
Full scale IQ	118	101	99	116
Verbal IQ	116	102	101	108
Performance IQ	118	99	97	122
Intertest interval (weeks)	20	52	20	12

Matarazzo, 1981). The drug-free alcoholic group was evaluated within 7 days of their last drink, and again 17 days later. The nonalcoholic medical inpatient group was reported to be similar in terms of education, age, and socioeconomic characteristics. This group was reevaluated 2–3 weeks after the first administration. Both groups were judged to be stable neuropsychologically. Significant Pearson's coefficients of correlation between test–retest scores were obtained. An evaluation of the stability in the binary classification scheme (abnormal versus normal), however, revealed less than desirable clinical reliability.

In evaluating the research literature as a whole, it would appear that mildly to moderately impaired persons with stable brain conditions are likely to have test–retest reliabilities that are different from those of normal or severely impaired subjects. The performance of normal subjects, for example, may be more subject to the relative ceiling effects of these test instruments. Severely impaired subjects would be expected to demonstrate a reduced capacity for new learning and therefore would not demonstrate significant practice effects. Conversely, patients with stabilized, mildly to moderately impaired brain functions may demonstrate changes in scores as a function of practice effects. Clinicians should be sensitive to these findings when evaluating changes in test performance in patients of varying levels of ability.

Internal Consistency

Aside from the test–retest studies discussed above, other measures of the reliability of the Halstead–Reitan battery as a whole are lacking. Similarly, relatively few studies have been conducted to assess the reliability of the individual instruments. Shaw (1966) reported a split-half reliability on the Category Test of .98, while Bornstein (1983b) has reported split-half reliability coefficients of .74 and .77 for two different combinations of items from the Seashore Rhythm Test.

VALIDITY

Although a pathognomic approach was used in the development of many of the tests comprising the Halstead–Reitan battery, no major studies have addressed the issue of content validity *per se*. Validational research has traditionally focused on discriminative validity. Several studies are identified in the following review as evidence of the concurrent validity of the Halstead–Reitan. Although the research cited does provide support for this measure of validity, the original focus of these studies was more typically concerned with the comparative effectiveness of different neuropsychological instruments and their ability to assess or differentiate between different neuropsychological conditions. Predictive validity studies have not been a major focus of neuropsychological research except in attempts to relate performance on neuropsychological tests to future adaptive functioning (e.g., McSweeny, Grant, Heaton, Prigatano, & Adams, 1985). Traditionally, neuropsychological testing has been used primarily to describe a patient's relative strengths and weaknesses, relating patterns of the patient's neuropsychological deficits to either known neuropathological disease processes or concomitant behavioral manifestations. Also, few incremental and factorial studies have been performed. Again, the studies reviewed that addressed the issue of incremental validity (see Goldstein & Shelly, 1984) have been the result of research focused on the discriminative ability of the Halstead–Reitan versus another neuropsychological procedure. Finally, in the present review, the only reference that was found to a factor-analytic design using only the subtests of the Halstead–Reitan as variables was Halstead's early work (1947) leading to his four-factor theory of "biological intelligence."

Concurrent Validity

Attempts have been made to establish the validity of the Halstead–Reitan by correlating test findings with certain neuropathological conditions associated with cerebral dysfunction. For example, Matthews and Booker (1972) demonstrated that a relation exists between the size of the ventricles and performance on neuropsychological tests. This relation became evident, however, only when the extremes of the distribution (subjects with the largest ventricles and subjects with the smallest ventricles) were compared.

In a subgroup of the patients used in the above study, 15 cases with the largest right- over left-ventricle measurement ratios and 15 cases with the largest left- over right-ventricle measurement ratios were compared. Although not statistically significant, a consistent relation was noted between ventricular dilation and lateralized neuropsychological deficits.

In contrast to the above research, Klove (1959a, 1963) has attempted to demonstrate the unique contribution that neuropsychology—and more specifically, the Halstead–Reitan—has made to the neurodiagnostic process. For example, Klove (1959) demonstrated that this battery is sensitive to behavioral deficits related to impaired brain functions in brain-damaged patients who have either a normal or an abnormal EEG. Klove (1963) also cited research that illustrates that patients with severely abnormal EEGs tend to be more neuropsychologically impaired than patients with normal EEGs. Finally, Klove (1963) demonstrated that brain-damaged patients may be correctly identified on the Halsted–Reitan independent of the patients' performance on neurological examination.

Filskov and Goldstein (1974) evaluated the diagnostic validity of the Halstead–Reitan battery in comparison with such medical procedures as the brain scan, cerebral-blood-flow studies, the EEG, the angiogram, the pneumoencephalogram, and the X ray. These procedures were compared in terms of their hit rates for a sample of 89 patients with confirmed diagnoses of seizure disorder, neoplasms, degenerative neurological disease, subdural hematoma, cerebrovascular accident, specific cerebrovascular disease, and arteriosclerotic cerebrovascular disease. Overall, the Halstead–Reitan battery was found to be superior to these medical procedures in terms of the identification, lateralization, and determination of the neuropathological process (100%, 89%, and 85% correct, respectively).

In a somewhat different approach, Swiercinsky and Leigh (1979) used CT scans as the criterion for determining the presence or absence of brain impairment, as well as the lateralization of the deficit, in a sample of 62 patients. Clinical decisions based on the results of neuropsychological testing (essentially the Halstead–Reitan battery) were found to agree with the criterion measure more often than did conclusions based on electroencephalographic results, routine neurological examination, and the results of the Russell *et al.* (1970) neuropsychological keys.

Discriminative Validity

There are many reports demonstrating the effectiveness of the Halstead–Reitan battery in discriminating a variety of neurological conditions (e.g., Klove, 1974; Wheeler, Burke, & Reitan, 1963). There does, however, appear to be a significant amount of variability in terms of the reported effectiveness of this battery in diagnosising the presence, the lateralization, and the localization of brain dysfunction. Wheeler *et al.* (1963), for example, reported an average lateralization classification rate of 93.56%, whereas Swiercinsky and Warnock (1977) reported lateralization classification rates of only 42.7% when the Russell *et al.* (1970) neuropsychological keys were used, 51.9% when key variables in a discriminant function were used, and only 56.9% when a maximum set of variables in a discriminant function were used.

An initial validiation of the test procedures comprising the Halstead battery was reported by Reitan in 1955. This study presented a cross-validation of Halstead's work. An excellent and more current review of the validity of the Halstead–Reitan can be found in Halgrim Klove's "Validation Studies in Adult Clinical Neuropsychology" (1974). To summarize these reviews, the tests comprising the Halstead–Reitan battery have generally been found to be sensitive to the effects of neurological impairment. In a study using 50 pairs of subjects (brain-damaged and non-brain-damaged), Reitan (1955c) found, with the exception of two measures based on the critical-flicker-fusion test, significant differences between the two groups on all instruments. Comparable results were reported by Vega and Parsons (1967) in their cross-validation study. Studies using populations from different geographical areas (i.e., the Midwest, an Eastern metropolitan area [New York City], the Southwest, and Norway) have produced similar findings (e.g., Chapman & Wolff, 1959; Vega & Parsons, 1967; Klove, 1974). Support for the statistical and clinical validity and utility of these procedures has also been reported by other researchers (Goldstein, Deysach, & Kleinknecht, 1973; Klonoff et al., 1970; Matthews, Shaw, & Klove, 1966; Schreiber, Goldman, Kleinman, Goldfader, & Snow, 1976) in a variety of geographical and neuropsychological settings.

Using a discriminant function technique, Wheeler et al. (1963) reported prediction rates ranging from 90.7% to 98.8% correct for a group of 140 subjects assigned to groups with: (1) no cerebral damage; (2) left cerebral damage; (3) right cerebral damage; and (4) diffuse cerebral damage. The subjects were assigned to these groups based on "independent neurological criterion information." Wheeler and Reitan (1963) attempted to cross-validate these results by using the discriminative weights derived in the above study in an evaluation of a sample of 304 subjects. A 10%–20% reduction in accuracy was obtained for all comparisons, except for the right-damage versus the bilateral-damage groups, where the discrimination was essentially no better than chance. These results may be attributable, in part, to the fact that the neurological evidence used for group inclusion was not as distinct in the cross-validation study.

The diagnostic accuracy of the Halstead–Reitan battery would appear to be a function of, among other things, the disease process being assessed and the area of the cortex involved. Reitan (1955c) and Klove (1974), for example, have shown that different performance patterns exist in patients with left- and right-hemisphere lesions. It is clear that, in such cases, the sensory examination contributes significantly to the discriminatory power of the Halstead–Reitan battery. Wheeler and Reitan (1963) and Schreiber et al. (1976), for example, have reported that, without the sensory examination, right–left-hemisphere differences are not identified with sufficient consistency to warrant basing clinical decisions regarding lesion localization on the Halstead–Reitan test scores alone. Goldstein and Shelly (1973) found that the presence of suppressions (i.e., extinction and unilateral inattention) is the single best discriminator of left- and right-hemisphere lesions. Lateralized motor and tactile recognition dysfunctions also appear to be good lateralization indicators.

To summarize, there is evidence that the Halstead–Reitan battery can predict, to a high degree, right- versus left-hemispheric involvement (Reitan, 1955b, 1966); focal diffuse or bilateral focal damage (Reitan, 1959); lobular localization (Reitan, 1966); static versus rapidly growing lesions (Fitzhugh, Fitzhugh, & Reitan, 1961); and the disease process, including cerebrovascular disease, neoplasm, trauma, or degenerative disease (Reitan, 1966). In general, the diagnostic accuracy would appear to be greatest in cases involving primary and secondary functional systems. Whereas lesions of the sensorimotor area of the brain, for example, localize quite reliably, lesions of the tertiary areas of the brain show less localization. A more comprehensive review of the lateralization, localization, and process literature may be found in Parsons (1970).

DIFFERENTIATION BETWEEN PSYCHIATRIC AND NEUROLOGICAL PRESENTATIONS

Watson, Thomas, Anderson, and Felling (1968) attempted to differentate patients diagnosed as schizophrenic from those diagnosed as "organics" by (1) assessing the *statistical* differences in the performance of these two groups vs. (2) a "clinical" evaluation of the test data. Neither the statistical analysis nor the clinical evaluation of the test protocols succeeded in differentiating the two groups. Klove (1974) criticized this study on methodological grounds for failing to provide appropriate evaluations before classifying a subject as "organic" or schizophrenic. The confounding influence of medication effects and prior electroconvulsive treatment (ECT) treatments also limits the conclusions that we can draw from this study.

Lacks, Colbert, Harrow, and Levine (1970), in a study of 64 male patients (predominantly veterans), found the Bender–Gestalt to provide greater predictive accuracy in differentiating between organic and nonorganic patients (schizophrenics and general medical patients) than did the Halstead–Reitan. Unfortunately, the authors did not separate the hit rates for the two groups composing the nonorganic group. Similarly, there is no evidence that any medical or testing evaluations were conducted to rule out the existence of neurological deficits in the schizophrenic group. This is especially important given the chronicity of the schizophrenic group (their mean length of hospitalization was 36.7 months). Finally, from the brief description of

Lacks *et al.*, it would appear that the organic group was comprised primarily of individuals who presented with diffuse brain damage (e.g., encephalitis or Pick's disease) and whose clinical presentation most likely had a psychiatric overlay.

In contrast to the above research, Golden (1977), in a study using a mixed psychiatric and brain-injured sample of 116 patients, found the Halstead–Reitan battery 90% effective in identification and localization, according to a discriminant function analysis. See Watson, Thomas, Felling, and Andersen (1969), Klonoff *et al.* (1970), Barnes and Lucas (1974), and Malec (1978) for additional research in this area.

The research literature indicates that the predictive accuracy of making a differential diagnosis of "organic" versus "schizophrenic" is contingent on whether chronic or acute populations are evaluated. Neuropsychological instruments in general have been found to be more accurate in differentiating acutely psychotic patients from neurologically impaired subjects. The predictive accuracy is typically lower for psychiatric patients than for normal subjects. For example, Wheeler *et al.* (1963) found the Category Test to be the test most sensitive (in the Halstead–Reitan) to the presence of brain dysfunction, with a hit rate of nearly 90% in differentiating brain-injured and normal subjects. However, even after raising the cutoff point for the Category Test from 51 to 64 errors, Golden (1978a) was able to obtain only a 70% hit rate when using an acute schizophrenic control group.

In addition to chronicity (as discussed above), several other variables may account for the results obtained in the study of psychiatric and neurologically impaired subjects. The selection of the tests from the Halstead–Reitan battery, for example, may be quite variable. Different base rates for different disorders may exist from study to study. Similarly, medication effects are rarely controlled. Finally, the process of patient selection and the method of test analysis may create a confounding variable.

Pseudoneurological Studies

Matthews *et al.* (1966) compared the performance of 32 patients with unequivocal evidence of brain damage with that of 32 patients who presented symptoms strongly suggestive of organic brain damage (e.g., headache, nausea, paresthesia, motor weakness, and gait disturbance), but who, upon extensive neurological and medical examination, revealed negative results. The subjects were matched for age, sex, and years of education. Even though the groups were deliberately composed to attenuate rather than to maximize differences in performance, a number of significant differences were found by the authors.

Detection of Faking

Goebel (1983) obtained a hit rate of 94.4% in the blind interpretation of neuropsychological test data from a sample of brain-impaired patients (*n* =

46) and a group of nonimpaired subjects who were instructed to fake brain damage (*n* = 149). Heaton, Smith, Lehman, and Vogt (1978) correctly classified 100% of a sample of 16 volunteer malingerers from a group of 16 head-trauma patients via a discriminant function. The diagnostic accuracies of 10 neuropsychologists who interpreted the test data blind, however, ranged from chance-level prediction to about 20% better than chance. Overall, these results indicate that the Halstead–Reitan battery is sensitive to the effects of faking brain damage.

Statistical and Actuarial Models

Several studies have been conducted to assess automated interpretations of the Halstead–Reitan as opposed to clinical interpretation. Heaton, Grant, Anthony, and Lehman (1981) compared interpretations by two relatively experienced clinicians with those generated by the Key Approach to the semiautomated interpretation of the Halstead–Reitan battery (Russell *et al.*, 1970) for accuracy of classification along the dimensions of presence, chronicity, and laterality of brain damage. Although the ratings of severity were highly correlated (*r* = .95), the clinicians made significantly more accurate classifications of both the presence and the laterality of brain damage. Neither the Key Approach nor the clinicians were able to predict chronicity better than base rate.

Anthony, Heaton, and Lehman (1980) investigated the diagnostic effectiveness of automated interpretations by comparing the Key Approach (Russell *et al.*, 1970) and a Fortran IV program called BRAIN 1, which was devised to simulate clinical inference. The prediction rates for both programs surpassed chance levels but were lower than had been predicted by their authors. Both programs failed to provide clinically useful predictions of localization or recency of damage. For a further discussion of the controversy over the clinical utility of statistical and actuarial models in predicting brain damage, see Swiercinsky and Warnock (1977), Anthony *et al.* (1980), and Wedding (1983).

Concurrent-Discriminative Studies

Several reported studies have compared the discriminative validity of the Halstead–Reitan to that of the Luria–Nebraska Neuropsychological Battery (LNNB). Kane, Sweet, Golden, Parsons, and Moses (1981) compared the differences in accuracy of these two batteries in discriminating a heterogeneous group of neurological patients (*n* = 23) from a mixed group of psychiatric patients (*n* = 22). Two expert clinical neuropsychologists were used as raters in the study, one of whom administered the Halstead–Reitan battery, and one of whom administered the LNNB. The results of this study revealed a nonsignificant tendency for the Halstead–Reitan rater to correctly identify a higher percentage of the psychiatric patients (86% vs. 77%). The LNNB rater identified a greater percentage of the brain-damaged patients (87% vs. 70%). This latter difference was reported as being statistically significant. Overall hit rates of 78% and 82% were obtained for the Halstead–Reitan and the LNNB, respectively. The two raters were found to agree with each other's classifications in 82% of the cases.

Similar results were reported by Golden, Kane, Sweet, Moses, Cardellino, Templeton, Vicente, and Graber (1981b), in which a discriminant analysis found the Halstead–Reitan and the LNNB equally effective in identifying brain damge, with hit rates over 85%. In this study, 30 patients diagnosed as schizophrenic, 48 as brain-damaged, and 30 as normal were used. No significant differences in age or education existed in the three groups. The patients diagnosed as schizophrenic had been evaluated with a CT scan to rule out the existence of structural changes indicative of organicity. The brain-damaged patients had confirmed evidence of organicity as evidenced by CT scan, angiogram, EEG, or history of a coma of at least 24 hours' duration following head trauma. The Halstead–Reitan yielded a hit rate of 90% in the neurological group and 84% in the control group; the overall hit rate was 86%. The LNNB classified 87% of the neurological patients and 88% of the controls; the overall hit rate was 88%. Complete agreement between the batteries was obtained in 89% of the cases. Hit rates for the schizophrenic patients were similar for both batteries (23/30 for the Halstead–Reitan, and 24/30 for the LNNB). Using a combination of all 14 LNNB scales through multiple regression analysis, Golden et al. attempted to predict 14 Halstead variables. Predictions of the LNNB scale scores were made by the Halstead–Reitan in a similar manner. The multiple Rs for the Halstead tests ranged from .71 to .96. The multiple Rs for the LNNB scores ranged from .77 to .94.

These results also support the concurrent validity of these instruments. For an excellent overview of the Halstead–Reitan, as well as a discussion of the relationship between this instrument and the LNNB, see Incagnoli, Goldstein, and Golden (1986). Diamant (1981) also reported that the Halstead–Reitan battery and Luria's Neuropsychological Investigation (LNI) (see Christensen, 1979) generated comparable conclusions concerning the presence of brain dysfunction, its lateralization, and its localization in a sample of 31 psychiatric inpatients suspected of having brain dysfunction.

It has been argued that the high correlations reported between various neuropsychological measures such as the Halstead–Reitan and the LNNB have been attributed to the confounding effects of intelligence, and that, when one partials out the effect of intelligence, these correlations are substantially reduced (Chelune, 1982). Golden, Gustavson, and Ariel's response (1982b) to this criticism emphasizes the importance of partialing out the effects of education when interpreting neuropsychological test data (as a control for premorbid level of functioning) but argues against the partialing out of postmorbid intelligence, as postmorbid measures of intelligence may reflect the effects of brain damage (the very thing that neuropsychological batteries attempt to assess).

In their reviews of the literature on the Halstead–Reitan, Parsons and Prigatano (1978) and Hevern (1980) concluded that at least five variables may moderate the outcomes of past validational studies: the age of the subjects, possible different educational levels, gender performance differences, different levels of socioeconomic status, and inexperienced or poorly trained examiners. An additional moderator variable that should be considered in this area of research is the criteria used to define brain dysfunction (e.g., the use of different medical testing procedures such as the CT scan, EEG tracings, studies of regional cerebral blood flow, and physical neurological findings).

Klesges, Fisher, Pheley, Boschee, and Vasey (1984), in a study that addresses many of these methological shortcomings, conducted a validational study of the Halstead–Reitan with a sample of 224 subjects (83 normal and 141 brain-damaged) who did not differ in age, education, sex, and SES. All the subjects were assessed by trained examiners. Brain damage was determined by a CT-scan evaluation that was read independently by both a radiologist and a neurologist and by at least one additional diagnostic evaluation (i.e., a pneumoencephalogram, an angiogram, or an EEG). Both procedures had to agree on the presence, absence, and site of the dysfunction. The brain-damaged sample was evaluated approximately 9 months after injury (median = 9.18; SD = 80.9) and consisted of subjects with heterogeneous injuries: occlusions (n = 26), tumors (n = 22), hematomas (n = 18), contusions (n = 16), and aneurysms (n = 12). In this study, an overall correct classification rate of 64% was achieved (67% of all normals and 62% of all brain-damaged subjects). These results are disappointing because the base rate for brain damage in this study was 63% (141 of 224 subjects). The most correctly classified group was left-hemisphere-damaged subjects (71%), whereas subjects with diffuse damage were classified correctly 33% of the time. When those subjects with diffuse brain damage were excluded from the statistical analyses, the overall correct classification rate increased to 66%. The authors noted that, when only left- versus right-hemisphere cases were compared (as in other reported validational studies—e.g., Wheeler *et al.*, 1963), the classification rate improved to 81%. In terms of localization, 60% of left anterior injuries, 65% of right anterior injuries, 50% of posterior left injuries, and 37% of posterior right injuries were correctly classified via a discriminant function. The overall correct classification rate for this sample was 55%. When normals were excluded from the analysis (as in other studies—e.g., Klove, 1974), correct classification improved to 71%.

It should be noted that, in the Klesges *et al.* (1984) study, the classification rates for lateralization and localization noted earlier were significantly lower than those reported in other published studies on the Halstead–

Reitan (Boll, 1981). However, as illustrated above, with the exclusion of certain groups (i.e., normals and those subjects with diffuse brain damage), the classification rates compared favorably with those in other studies of the Halstead–Reitan. The marginal rate of discrimination between neurologically impaired and normal subjects deserves additional comment. One hypothesis proposed by Klesges *et al.* (1984) for this finding was related to the fact that the "normal" group used in this study consisted of subjects who had initially been referred for testing because they were suspected of having "some type of problem." When a similar group of normal subjects was used by Swiercinsky and Warnock (1977), disappointing discrimination rates were obtained. However, in contrast, Matthews *et al.* (1966) reported that "pseudoneurological" subjects were successfully discriminated from subjects with definitive brain damage. A more plausible explanation for the results noted in the Klesges *et al.* (1984) study may have to do with the sensitivity of neuropsychological test procedures, such as the Halstead–Reitan, and their ability to assess subtle changes in brain function following an insult or a disease process. Neurodiagnostic medical procedures such as the CT scan may prove to be inadequate as criterion measures in this area of research.

Factor-Analytic Studies

To date, no major factor-analytic studies have been performed using only the subtests of the Halstead–Reitan. However, it was based on a factor analysis of 13 tests developed in Halstead's laboratory, that Halstead proposed his concept of "biological intelligence." Halstead (1947) summarized his four-factor theory of biological intelligence as follows:

1. A central integrative field factor C. This factor represents the organized experience of the individual. It is the ground function of the "familiar" in which the psychologically "new" is tested and incorporated. It is the region of coalescence of learning and adaptive intelligence. Some of its parameters are probably reflected in measurements of psychometric intelligence, which yield an intelligence quotient.
2. An abstraction factor A. This factor concerns basic capacity to group to a criterion as in the elaboration of categories and involves the comprehension of the central similarities and differences. It is the fundamental growth principle of the ego.
3. A power factor P. This factor reflects the undistorted power factor of the brain. It operates to counterbalance or regulate the affective forces and thus frees the growth principle of the ego for further ego differentiation.
4. A directional factor D. This factor constitutes the medium through which the process factors, noted here, are exteriorized in any given moment. On the motor side, it specifies the "final common pathway," while on the sensory side, it specifies the avenue or modality of experience. (p. 147)

Royce, Yeudall, and Bock (1976) performed a factor analysis of the data obtained from 176 patients with heterogeneous brain impairment. Unfortunately (for our purposes), the results are clouded because the researchers included 21 other variables of cognitive test data along with the 15 Halstead–Reitan variables. Newby, Hallenbeck, and Embretson (1983) performed a confirmatory factor analysis on data from 497 subjects. The variables were a modified Halstead–Reitan battery. The confirmatory factor analysis sought to determine which of four models provided the best fit with the data. The four models included Royce's model of the structure of intellect (eight first-order factors and three second-order factors), Swiercinsky's model of nine factors, Lezak's model of a two-factor (verbal and nonverbal) structure, and Luria's model of 10 intercorrelated factors. None of the models fit the data adequately, although three of the models provided a fit somewhat better than chance. We are still in need of a major factor-analytic study of the Halstead–Reitan.

SUMMARY

There is considerable disagreement in the literature about which tests in the Halstead–Reitan are the best predictors of cerebral dysfunction. Klove (1963), for example, reported that the best predictors of brain damage were the Category Test, the TPT (Time, Memory, and Location), the Rhythm Test, the Speech Sounds Perception Test, and the Time Sense Test. Swiercinsky and Warnock (1977), however, found the Finger-Tapping test scores for the dominant and nondominant hands, TPT left-hand time, Trails A, and Tactile Dysfunction (hand and face) to be the best predictor variables. The order effects of testing also need to be addressed. Further research in these areas is not only warranted but is imperative if the Halstead–Reitan is to continue to be one of the neuropsychologist's most utilized neuropsychological instruments.

10

The Luria–Nebraska Neuropsychological Battery

The Luria–Nebraska Neuropsychological Battery (LNNB) is an attempt to provide a comprehensive neuropsychological assessment technique that combines features of Alexandr Luria's neuropsychological theory of brain organization and function with the North American psychometric tradition. Administration of the LNNB can be learned in approximately 1–2 weeks. However, interpretation is extremely complex, relying on complicated notions of test theory as well as on an understanding of the neuropsychological theory of Alexandr Luria. Although the items in the LNNB are based on actual procedures used by Luria and published by Anne Lise-Christensen (1979), the LNNB should not be confused with Luria's Neuropsychological Investigation or with Lurian methodology.

The LNNB is divided into 11 subscales: Motor, Tactile, Rhythm, Visual Processes, Receptive Speech, Expressive Speech, Reading, Writing, Arithmetic, Memory, and Intellectual Processes. (Form II of the LNNB has 12 subscales, with the addition of an Intermediate Memory scale.) Consistent with Lurian theory, none of the items are presumed to measure only a single function. Therefore, in more recent versions of the test, the names of the scales have been dropped in favor of numbers. However, the items in Scale C1, for example (formerly the Motor scale), measure mainly motor functions.

Lurian theory specifies that observable behaviors are the result of combinations of molecular skills and that the successful performance of a behavior depends on cooperation among several brain areas. These brain areas are linked in a functional chain that eventuates in the behavior. Therefore, according to Lurian theory, there is no such thing as a pure point-to-point localization of molar skills as measured by overt tasks. Failure to perform a given task successfully can be the result of an impairment in any of the component molecular (nonobservable) skills that comprise the functional chain. By comparing performance across similar items that differ in their single-task requirements, we can isolate the dysfunctional unit.

The LNNB material consists of several visual stimuli and a set of audiotaped rhythm and pitch stimuli. In addition, the examiner provides a few common items (a rubber band, a key, a nickel, a protractor, a rubber eraser, and a large paper clip) for use in the tactile and visual recognition items. The procedures are interactive: the examiner gives verbal instructions and then observes and, in some cases, times the responses of the subject. The test is portable and can be performed at the bedside. Forms I and II of the LNNB are intended to be used with subjects over the age of 15. The LNNB can be used with most levels of neuropsychological functioning, although the reliability of the test is attenuated in the normal range of ability. Because of ceiling effects, the accuracy of the LNNB is limited in the superior range of functioning.

The test answer protocol also contains instructions for the administration of each item. There is also a patient response booklet in which the subject can write and draw when items require these activities.

All of the scales are presented as standardized t scores with a mean of 50 and a standard deviation of 10. Interpretation is conducted partly by comparing the scale score with the critical level. The critical level is individually determined through a regression formula that uses the subject's age and level of education. Scale scores that exceed the critical level can, in general, be viewed as reflecting impaired performance. However, there are several other interpretive strategies that increase the accuracy of the instrument: an examination of the scatter of the scores, an examination of the factor-analytic derived scales, an examination of the empirically derived localization scores, an item analysis, a pattern analysis, and consideration of the qualitative aspects of performance.

The LNNB is administered in a one-to-one setting with the examiner and the subject sitting across from each other at a desk. The test can be administered by a B.A.-level technician who has received training specific to the LNNB. The manual states that most experienced test technicians can learn to administer the battery in 30–40 hours of training. Most of the items involve a straightforward administration technique. However, some of the items require behavioral skills that will need practice before they can be successfully completed. For example, in the expressive speech section, the subject is asked to give a spontaneous speech about the conflict between the generations. The examiner is expected to record the time that elapses before the response begins and then to count the number of words produced in the first 5 seconds following the initiation of the response. This procedure necessitates the simultaneous recording of time latency and frequency, a task that requires practice.

Each item is given a score of 0, 1, or 2, where 0 corresponds to a normal performance, 1 corresponds to a borderline performance, and 2 corresponds to an impaired performance. The manual contains explicit rules for the assignment of item scores. The item scores are then summed to provide scale raw scores, which are translated to standardized t scores with a mean of 50 and a standard deviation of 10 points. Besides the original 11 clinical scales, there are a Right and Left sensorimotor scale, and a Pathognomonic scale. The Right and Left scales can be used to help lateralize the area of dysfunction. The Pathognomonic scale is composed of the items that best differentiated between neurological and psychiatric subjects. Recent work has developed two additional scales, which are comprised of items drawn from items on the original clinical scales (Sawicki & Golden, 1984b). These scales can provide useful information about the recency of the injury, the severity of the impairment, and the degree of the predictable compensation. Moses (1985) subsequently presented data regarding the relation of these two scales to neurological status.

In addition, items can be summed to provide factor scale scores and localization scale scores, which are also standardized t scores. The factor scales were derived from separate principal-components factor analyses for each of the clinical scales. The localization scales were empirically derived from an examination of those items that are able to discriminate groups of subjects with localizable deficits.

There are several steps in interpretation. The first step involves calculating the critical level, which is the score beyond which the obtained scores represent impaired performance (Golden, Hammeke, & Purish, 1980b). The critical level is 1 standard deviation above the average scale score expected from a person with a given age and level of educational attainment. The critical level is determined by substituting values for age and education in a regression formula that was empirically derived. In this way, interpretation is more individualized than would be the case with absolute cutoff points. The critical level can be adjusted to reflect the amount of scatter in the scale scores. If there is more than 30 points' difference between the highest and the lowest scale score, the critical level can be lowered to 25 points above the lowest scale score (Moses, Golden, Ariel, & Gustavson, 1983a).

Interpretation of the LNNB occurs at five levels. First, the clinical scales are examined for a determination of which are above the critical level. Next, the scatter among scale scores is examined. The localization scales are also examined against the critical level, as are the factor-analytic scales, although there are no rules regarding the interpretation of scatter on these two sets of scales. Next, performance on items across scales is examined to reveal whether any patterns consistent with neuropsychological theory exist. Last, the qualitative aspects of performance are examined. Although interpretation can be terminated at any level (and should be terminated early by inexperienced examiners), the battery gives the most amount of information and the most accurate information when the five interpretive steps are followed (Golden, Ariel, Wilkening, McKay, & MacInnes, 1982c).

RELIABILITY

Golden, Berg, and Graber (1982a) evaluated the test–retest reliability of the LNNB in a study of 27 patients who had diagnoses of static injuries. These individuals were tested twice; the average test–retest interval was 167 days. The resulting correlation coefficients ranged from .77 for the Right Hemisphere scale to .96 for the Arithmetic scale. These results were subsequently replicated by Plaisted and Golden (1982), who used 30 psychiatric subjects.

Interscorer reliability was evaluated on a sample of five patients. For each patient, a different pair of examiners scored the responses while simultaneously observing the patient. The agreement between raters ranged from 92% agreement for one patient to 98% for another patient. Overall, there was a 95% agreement rate (Golden, Hammeke, & Purish, 1979). These percentages may be inflated because approximately two thirds of the items are trichotomously scored and the remaining one third of the items are dichotomously scored.

Bach, Harowski, Kirby, Peterson, and Schulein (1981) addressed the deficiencies of the above study by evaluating the interrater agreement on a sample of borderline performances by two subjects and five raters. Bach *et al.* used Cohen's kappa as an uninflated measure of agreement and reported values ranging from .79 to 1.00. The subjects used in this study were normal confederates who were instructed how to respond to the items so as to produce borderline performance on a random set of items. The identities of the items that had been performed in a borderline manner were unknown to the examiners.

In order to evaluate and extend these findings, Moses and Schrefft (1985) used two examiners to evaluate 16 neurological patients, 15 psychiatric subjects, 3 subjects with a history of substance abuse, and 2 normal medical patients (a total of 36 subjects). The authors found that the correlation coefficients for the summary score ranged from .97 for the Intellectual Processes scale to .99 for the Receptive Speech scale, with mean differences in total scores of 1.47 and 0.00 *t*-score points, respectively. The localization scales' correlation coefficients ranged from .96 to .99. The authors also evaluated the agreement on decisions regarding whether the scales exceeded critical level. Agreement levels ranged from 33/36 for the Receptive Speech scale and the Writing scale to 36/36 for the Expressive Speech, Tactile, Arithmetic, and Intellectual Processes scales. Analyses of the same data using the chi square and Kendall's tau resulted in similar results. In examining agreement on individual item scores, the authors found complete agreement on 95.71%, disagreement of 1 point value on 3.5%, and disagreement of 2 points on 0.78% of the individual item scores.

Under Lurian theory, the battery was constructed so that the scales are not completely homogeneous. Therefore, one would expect moderate degrees of internal consistency in the scales. Golden, Fross, and Graber (1981a) evaluated the split-half reliability of the clinical scales using an odd–even split in a sample of 338 patients. The sample constituted 74 normal controls, 83 psychiatric patients, and 181 neurological patients. The split-half reliability correlation coefficients ranged from a high of .95 for the Reading scale to a low of .89 for the Memory scale. Once again, these values may have been inflated by the restricted range of the scoring procedure. However, the values do represent acceptable degrees of consistency.

The internal consistency reliability of the summary, localization, and factor-analytic scales was evaluated for a heterogeneous group of subjects by Moses, Johnson, and Lewis (1983b). These evaluations were also conducted separately for a sample of 451 brain-impaired, 414 schizophrenic, 128 mixed psychiatric, and 108 normal subjects. The values for the normal subjects ranged from .54 to .78, and for the remaining subjects, they ranged from .83 to .93. The relatively lower values for the normal subjects were probably due to restriction of range in those subjects and underline the problems encountered in using the LNNB to describe neuropsychological functioning in normal subjects.

Internal consistency reliability was again evaluated for the summary and for localization in a sample of 451 brain-damaged subjects, 414 schizophrenic subjects, 128 subjects with mixed psychiatric diagnoses, and 108 normals (Maruish, Sawicki, Franzen, & Golden, 1985). With the use of Cronbach's coefficient alpha, which is a conservative estimate of internal consistency reliability, the values were moderately high. In the brain-damaged subjects, the values ranged from .93 (for three of the scales) to .84 (for four of the scales). For the schizophrenic subjects, the values ranged from .93 (for three of the scales) to .83. For the mixed psychiatric subjects, the values ranged from .92 to .82. For the normal subjects the values ranged from .54 to .78.

VALIDITY

The original attempts to provide validational evidence for the LNNB focused on its accuracy in discriminating neurological patients from normal subjects. Hammeke, Golden, and Purish (1978) reported that all of the summary scales were successful in discriminating brain-damaged from normal subjects at the .001 level of significance. Other studies have investigated the discriminative ability of the LNNB for elderly subjects (Spitzform, 1982), for psychiatric populations (Golden, Graber, Moses, & Zatz, 1980a; Golden,

MacInnes, Ariel, Ruedrich, Chu, Coffman, Graber, & Bloch, 1982d; Puente, Heidelberg-Sanders, & Lund, 1982; Shelley & Goldstein, 1983), for alcoholics (Chmielewski & Golden, 1980), and for epileptics (Berg & Golden, 1981). It should be mentioned that later research by Herman and Melyn (1985) indicated that the success of the LNNB in discriminating epileptic subjects from control subjects may have been partly due to the use of severely affected inpatient epileptics, and that with outpatient epileptics, the LNNB is no better than the Halstead–Reitan or other neuropsychological instruments. These studies have reported varying levels of success, but they generally support the utility of the LNNB in discriminating brain-impaired subjects from normal subjects.

A difficult question in neuropsychological assessment is the differential diagnosis of patients who present ambiguous or inconclusive symptoms and who consequently represent difficult diagnostic problems. Using the rule of classifying as impaired those subjects who have three or more clinical scales above critical level, Malloy and Webster (1981) found 80% agreement between the LNNB and noninvasive neurodiagnostic techniques in subjects with mild cortical impairment.

In order to evaluate the validity of the LNNB as a technique for measuring specific neuropsychological tasks, a series of factor analyses were undertaken. The several studies that were conducted present general support for this idea, but too little is known about the temporal stability of these scales to allow them to be recommended for clinical use in retest situations (Golden et al., 1982d).

The concurrent validity of the LNNB has been assessed by correlating its results with that of the Halstead–Reitan Neuropsychological Battery, with encouraging results. Golden et al. (1981b) reported that, when the summary scores of the LNNB were correlated with the summary scores of the Halstead–Reitan, the minimum value was .71. Chelune (1982) objected that the large correlations may have been due to shared overlap of the two batteries with the Wechsler Adult Intelligence Scale (WAIS). Golden et al. (1982b) responded to this criticism with a conceptual argument, namely, that postmorbid IQ will reflect brain impairment. Golden et al. (1982b) then partialed out level of education as an estimate of premorbid IQ and still found moderate correlations between the two batteries. Shelley and Goldstein (1982) reported that, in a sample of 137 subjects, correlations between the LNNB and the Halstead–Reitan scores ranged from .60 to .96. They also conducted a factor analysis and found that both batteries contributed substantially to the extracted three-factor solution, a finding indicating shared sensitivity to the same neuropsychological variables.

Another factor to consider is whether the use of the LNNB and the Halstead–Reitan results in a similar classification of subjects. Golden et al. (1980a) found that a discriminant function analysis of the two batteries resulted in approximately 85% accurate classification for each. Goldstein and

Shelley (1984) reported similar rates of accuracy in diagnosis for the two batteries, as did Kane, Parsons, and Goldstein (1985). Berg, Bolter, Ch'ien, Williams, Lancaster, and Cummings (1984) reported that the LNNB and the Halstead–Reitan had equivalent diagnostic accuracy in the assessment of idiopathic epileptics.

Other attempts to evaluate the concurrent validity of the LNNB have correlated the results of the Peabody Individual Achievement Test with appropriate scales of the LNNB in 100 neurological, psychiatric, and normal subjects, with acceptable results (Gillen, Ginn, Strider, Kreuch, & Golden, 1983).

Evaluation of the construct validity of the individual scales has been conducted on a limited basis. Moses (1984a,b) examined the relationship of LNNB results in subjects with and without sensorimotor deficits and with and without forms of cognitive impairment. He reported that the Motor, Tactile, Receptive Speech, Pathognomonic, and Left and Right Sensorimotor scales were able to discriminate the four groups of subjects formed by crossing the two conditions of sensorimotor and cognitive deficits. This finding lends limited support to the construct validity of these particular scales.

Prifitera and Ryan (1982) compared the performance of the LNNB Memory scale with other memory assessment techniques. Larrabee et al. (1985) examined the construct validity of the Memory factor scales. They found that the two LNNB Memory factor scales loaded highly on the factor on which the Benton Visual Retention Test and portions of the Wechsler Memory Scales also loaded. However, they concluded that there may not be much clinical utility in the Memory factor scales because of item heterogeneity and short scale length. Prifitera and Ryan (1981) compared the LNNB Intellectual Processes scale with the WAIS. Pheley and Klesges (1986) evaluated the relation of the LNNB Memory scale score to various laboratory memory tasks. They found a correlation between the LNNB and the laboratory tasks of paired associates and face–name association but not the laboratory tasks of digit span and trigrams with distraction. The lack of a significant correlation may have been due to the small sample size and the restricted range of scores. These studies represent a start on the necessary task of evaluating the specific concurrent validity of the components. However, more research needs to be done before definite conclusions can be reached.

Studies evaluating the accuracy of the localization scales of the LNNB have been conducted and have resulted in a generally accurate identification of the site of lesion. The use of the localization scales resulted in a 89% correct classification rate in the derivation sample and a 74% correct classification rate in the cross-validation sample (Golden, Moses, Fishburne, Engum, Lewis, Wisniewski, Conley, Berg, & Graber, 1981c). However, these results need to be replicated because of the inclusion of closed-head-injury subjects in the sample. Closed-head-injured patients may be injured in sites other than the site of the main injury because of contrecoup effects, and they may contaminate these characteristics of the experimental sample.

Like many new tests, the LNNB has been the subject of criticism. And as with many new tests, there have been replies to these criticisms in the literature. The exchange of criticisms and answers has helped to assess the limits of the utility of the LNNB. Adams (1980a) criticized the LNNB on the basis of the methodology of its development, stating that multiple t tests were an inappropriate means of deciding which items to retain in the battery. He similarly criticized the use of a small subject sample in the discriminant function analysis. Although Golden (1980) replied that the derived discriminant function had an acceptable ratio of predictors to subjects, the fact remains that the number of tested potential predictors exceeded the number from which safe conclusions can be reached, given the sample size. Golden's reply to the criticism of multiple t tests is more to the point. T tests were used in an apparent attempt to minimize the probability of Type I errors, an acceptable practice in the early stages of test development. The items have subsequently been evaluated, and this methodology has apparently had little effect on the accuracy of the battery as a whole. Adams (1980b) replied by questioning the veracity of the reports of the accuracy of the battery, calling into question the scientific honesty of the test's developers. Empirical evidence is needed to validate the relevance of these doubts.

Spiers (1981) published a few conceptual criticisms of the LNNB. He stated that the idea of a battery was antithetical to the methods of Luria, and that the availability of MMPI-like graphs on which to plot results may increase the probability that insufficiently trained psychologists will use the battery clinically. The first criticism is undeniable. The use of the name "Luria–Nebraska" is honorific because of its reliance on the contributions of Luria to the field of neuropsychology and the reliance of the battery on his theory. The second criticism is directed more at the users of the battery than at the battery itself, and it is well taken. Unless the users of the LNNB have had specific training in neuropsychological assessment, they would do better to limit themselves in interpretation.

Spiers (1982) further criticized the LNNB on the basis of the intent of the items. In the same paper, he criticized the standardized, quantified approach in general because of its reliance on average scores, which mask individual differences. Hutchinson (1984) criticized Spiers (1982) on a factual basis, stating that there are discrepancies between Spiers's reading of the manual and verbatim quotes from the manual. Hutchinson further accused Spiers of misunderstanding the intended use of the battery. Spiers (1984) replied that Hutchinson (1984) had misinterpreted his (Spiers's) statements and accused Hutchinson of misreading his article. Stambrook (1983) also criticized the LNNB in the literature; however, his article repeats concerns raised by Adams (1980a,b) and by Spiers (1981, 1982) and will therefore not be discussed here.

At least two conclusions can be drawn from this discussion. First, some of the controversy surrounding the LNNB is actually related to disagreements between the proponents of the standardized, quantified approach to neuropsychological assessment and the proponents of the intuitive, qualitative approach. Second, the controversy has degenerated into personal accusations. Theoretical arguments may be necessary in the evaluation of any assessment technique, but they are insufficient without direct empirical evidence.

The LNNB does not have a universally valid utility for all populations. The LNNB should be used with reference to the experimental literature regarding the population in question. Further, the LNNB is not totally comprehensive, as it does not assess reading comprehension or memory, other than short-term, mainly verbal memory.

Because of its reliance on Lurian theory and on Luria's emphasis on the verbal mediation of behavior, valid use of the LNNB depends largely on language skills. Crosson and Warren (1982) criticized the use of the LNNB for aphasic populations. Delis and Kaplan (1982) presented a case in which the use of only the clinical scales for an aphasic would result in a misunderstanding of the subject's deficits. Golden *et al.* (1982c) reexamined the data regarding the case reported by Delis and Kaplan and found that the LNNB had been inappropriately used, as the primary language of the subject was Spanish. Golden *et al.* (1982c) also found evidence in the subject's history of chronic alcohol abuse, a seizure disorder, bilateral atrophy, and a left temporal-parietal infarct, indicating that the conclusions of the LNNB were in closer agreement with the actual deficits of the subject than had been implied by Delis and Kaplan (1982). Despite this foray into personal aspects of the controversy, the heavy dependence on language may limit the utility of the LNNB in the language-impaired.

Because the LNNB cannot distinguish between average and superior performance, it may be inappropriate in the assessment of normal neuropsychological functioning, except to rule out the possibility of impairment. As stated earlier, the reliabilities of the scale scores are attenuated in normal subjects.

Finally, although the LNNB relies on an understanding of Lurian constructs for its most effective use, these constructs have yet to be conclusively validated. In short, despite the many studies conducted to date, because of the complexity of the battery there is still a need for more research to fully evaluate each aspect of the LNNB. For example, the construct validity of the clinical scales is in need of empirical investigation. The LNNB can be recommended for clinical use, but only in the hands of a trained psychologist who is familiar with the research regarding the question to be answered and the population from which the subject is drawn. The LNNB seems to have applicability in both research and clinical settings.

LURIA–NEBRASKA NEUROPSYCHOLOGICAL BATTERY FORM II

The Luria–Nebraska Neuropsychological Battery Form II is an attempt to provide both an alternate to Form I and some improvements over the original form. The organization of Form II is similar to the organization of Form I except that there is an additional scale: C12 (Intermediate Memory). Partly in response to criticism regarding the relation of the names of the scales to the content validity of the scales, the names have been removed and replaced with numbers, C1 through C11 for the clinical scales, S1 through S5 for the supplementary scales, L1 through L8 for the localization scales, and alphanumeric characters for the factor scales. The LNNB relies heavily on the subject's ability to comprehend verbal instructions and may therefore have limited utility in assessing subjects with receptive language impairments. However, revised administration instructions allowing for alternate response modalities extend the utility of the instrument for assessing subjects with expressive language impairments.

As in the case of Form I, Form II combines features of Alexandr Luria's theories of brain function with a standardized approach to assessment. Therefore, many of the comments made with regard to Form I also apply here and will not be repeated in great depth. For a discussion of the particulars, the reader is referred to the discussion of Form I in the earlier parts of this chapter.

Because of the heterogeneity of the scale composition, interpretation of the LNNB must not be limited to scale interpretation, although that is a necessary first step. Full interpretation must also take into account scores on the empirically derived localization scales, the factor-analytic scales, comparisons of items across scales, and a consideration of the qualitative aspects of the subject's performance. Interpretation is best left to individuals who have received specialized training in neuropsychological assessment and who are familiar with Lurian theory.

The stimulus materials for Form II are similar to those for Form I. The visual stimuli have been bound into a single booklet arranged in the chronological order required for administration, an improvement over the separately bound portions of Form I. The visual stimuli were enlarged so that subjects with poor vision would not be penalized for peripheral impairment reasons. The audiotape stimulus for the C2 (Rhythm) scale is identical to the audiotape for Form I.

In some instances, entirely new stimuli have been devised for Form II, using the same rationale as was used in devising the original items. For example, the C8 scale (Reading) shares no items across the two forms, nor does the C11 scale (Intellectual Processes). As mentioned above, the C12 scale (Intermediate Memory) is a new development in Form II, not having existed in Form I. In other instances, items were retained across the two forms, as in the case of the C2 scale (Rhythm), where 92% of the items originally appeared in Form I. The additional scale on Form II is Scale 12, which is conceived of as a measure of intermediate or delayed memory.

In the C12 (Intermediate Memory) scale, the examiner questions the subject about aspects of items that were previously given in the test. Therefore, this scale can be seen as tapping incidental memory as well as delayed memory with interference.

Because of the great similarity between the two forms of the LNNB, the information regarding administration and scoring can probably be assumed to be equivalent. Research regarding the amount of training necessary to achieve reliable scoring indicates that approximately 40 hours of training will produce adequate administration by a B.A.-level technician. The tests are administered from test protocols that contain the administration instructions as well as the basic scoring criteria. More detailed scoring instructions are contained in the manual. In addition, a patient response booklet contains space for the written and drawn responses of the subject, as well as the printed stimuli for two of the C4 scale. In both forms, scores are represented in the form of standardized t scores with a mean of 50 and a standard deviation of 10 points. A critical level is computed with a regression formula using the age and level of education of the subject as predictors.

There is a new manual to accompany Form II (Golden, Purish, & Hammeke, 1985). Actually, it is a combined manual for both forms. The new manual is substantially larger than the original manual and it includes information regarding new derived scales, such as the Impairment and Elevation scales. These scales contain items that were drawn from across the various scales, the patterns of which provide information regarding the acuteness of an injury as well as the probability that behavioral compensation will still occur. There are also a power scale and a speed scale composed of items that were hypothesized to be related to those constructs. T-score conversions are available for the Impairment and Elevation scales, based on a normative sample of approximately 800 cases. T-score conversions for the Speed and Power scales are based on a normative sample of 45 medical patients. Initial empirical studies suggest that a relatively higher Elevation scale (over the Impairment scale) is related to recency of injury and the probability of compensation, and that a relatively higher Speed scale (over the Power scale) is related to a posterior focus of the injury. More research is needed before these rules can be strongly recommended for clinical use.

Other changes in the manual include decomposing the C7 scale (Writing) into a Spelling and a Motor Writing scale. Hopefully, users of the LNNB were already making that distinction in formulating an interpretation of results, but this change helps to ensure that process. The new manual also describes the development of a set of qualitative categories that can be scored independently of the quantitative scores. These categories can be summed, and the frequency counts can be compared with the frequency of occurrence in the normative sample ($n = 48$). Because of the limited size of the normative sample, interpretation of the qualitative information is best conducted with reference to neuropsychological theory. At present, the qualitative scores have the potential to serve a useful function by helping the assessor to systematize his or her observations. In order to make the qualitative scores more useful, one would need a larger normative sample as well as a comparison sample of impaired subjects.

The expanded administration instructions in the new manual provide guides for administering the LNNB to individuals with peripheral sensory losses. The manual also contains a set of 25 cases written by James A. Moses. There are also discussions of illustrative profiles for different localizations. Although these features can be an aid in learning interpretation, they should not be used as a substitute for supervised learning experiences.

The appendices to the manual contain information regarding the factor structure of Form I, as well as item difficulty indices and information regarding mean performances for each item. Similar information regarding Form II is needed.

Form II was developed and standardized on a sample of 73 subjects who were given both forms of the test. There were no significant differences in the raw scores for any of the scales. Scale scores for Form II were then derived by regressing the raw scores for Form II against the raw scores for Form I and applying the linear solution to t-score transformations for Form II. Form II was then administered to a sample of 125 normal subjects, 140 subjects with central nervous system dysfunction, and 34 schizophrenic subjects. A MANOVA conducted on the data resulted in significant differentiation among the groups. Subsequently, Form II was administered to 100 normal subjects and 100 neurologically impaired subjects. Use of the clinical rules stated in the manual resulted in classification accuracy rates equivalent to those for Form I. Although these studies help us to evaluate the validity of Form II, much of the research originally conducted on Form I now needs to be conducted on Form II. Also needed is a separate normative sample for the derivation of t scores for Form II. Although the above-mentioned research indicates that Form I and II appear to be equivalent, a separate normative sample will help to ensure the accuracy of estimates of the precision of scores obtained by the use of Form II.

Overall, Form II of the LNNB shows promise as a clinical neuropsychological assessment instrument. The initial research supports its equivalency with Form I. There are approximately 150 published studies using the LNNB Form I. Not all of this research needs to be replicated on Form II. But the basic reliability and validity studies are in need of replication.

11

Benton's Neuropsychological Assessment

Arthur Benton has made several large contributions to the field of neuro-psychological assessment. Benton's general approach is to take laboratory tasks that had been found to be sensitive to differences in cortical integrity and to apply them in a clinical setting. Although not all of Benton's tasks actually derive from the laboratory, the construction of all of the tasks has the spirit of laboratory investigations. Additionally, the procedures are well defined and standardized. Scoring is described explicitly, and the results are summarized in a quantitative score. A third characteristic of Benton's tests is the use of norms that represent the influence of age and education. Benton is perhaps the first clinical neuropsychologist to pay more than mere lip service to the confounding effects of age and education in the assessment situation. Finally, Benton is not bound by the left-hemisphere bias of traditional neuropsychology. Many of his tests are either sensitive to the effects of right-hemisphere impairment or, as in the case of the Tactile Form Perception Test, are designed to partial out the linguistic (left-hemisphere) effects from the more purely perceptual (right-hemisphere) effects.

Benton may be the person in this country most responsible for the rise of the flexible approach to neuropsychological assessment. His tests do not constitute a battery. Instead, the tests to be used in each assessment are chosen on the basis of presenting complaints, the type of referral question, or the results of previous testing. Therefore, a different set of assessment techniques is likely to be used on each subject. The tests were not normed on the same set of normative subjects, and therefore, comparisons of scores across tests of the same individual are limited. However, the tests are extremely useful when used for the assessment of particular functions or when used in conjunction with other assessment devices.

The tests included in the Benton conglomeration are the Benton Visual Retention Test, the Multilingual Aphasia Examination and the tests of Temporal Orientation, Right–Left Orientation, and Serial Digit Learning. Benton's perceptual and motor tests include Facial Recognition, Judgment of Line Orientation, Visual Form Discrimination, Pantomine Recognition, Tactile Form Perception, Finger Localization, Phoneme Discrimination, Three Dimensional Block Construction, and Motor Impersistence. We will consider these tests singly.

RIGHT–LEFT ORIENTATION

Right–left orientation has been interpreted as being reflective of spatial impairment and as being associated with linguistic impairment. The Benton Test of Right–Left Orientation requires the patient to respond with rudimentary motor responses, a requirement that minimizes the influence of aphasic symptoms on the test results. The test consists of 20 commands, which are presented in increasing order of complexity. The first set of commands requires the patient to point to right or left parts of his or her own body. The second set of commands requires the patient to point to lateralized parts of his or her body with either the right or the left hand. The third set of commands requires the patient to point to lateralized parts of the examiner's body. Finally, the fourth set of commands requires the patient to point to lateralized parts of the examiner's body with the right or left hand.

There are alternate forms of the test. Form B is identical to Form A except that the words *right* and *left* are interchanged. The responses are scored for whether the patient uses the correctly lateralized body part or the correct body part. In addition, errors are separated on the basis of whether the command required the subject to point to his or her own body or to the body of the examiner. Formal investigations of the alternate-forms reliability of the test have not been conducted. However, because of the similarity between the two forms, equivalency can probably be safely assumed. Form R is for patients who cannot use their right hand, and Form L is for patients who cannot use their left hand. Because Forms R and L are sufficiently different, the alternate-forms reliability of these two forms needs to be investigated.

The test was normed on a sample of 234 male and female subjects who had no history of brain impairment. Statistical analyses indicated no significant differences due to age, sex, or level of education. Distributions of scores for the impaired subjects are also presented in the manual (Benton, Hamsher, Varney, & Spreen, 1983). The impaired subjects consisted of 34 patients with bilateral brain impairment, 20 patients with right-hemisphere lesions, 20 aphasic patients with left-hemisphere lesions, and 20 nonaphasic patients with left-hemisphere lesions. The interpretation of results is based on the similarity of the type of error made by the patient in reference to the normative data. Although interpretations of Forms R and L are referred to the normative data, formal evaluations of the validity of these two forms need to be conducted.

Knowledge about relations to other tests (concurrent validity) will help us to understand the nature of the deficit underlying poor performance on this test. Information regarding the internal consistency reliability and the test–retest reliability would also enhance the clinical utility of the test.

SERIAL DIGIT LEARNING

Benton's Serial Digit Learning Test is a standardized form of digit supraspan. (The reader is referred to the discussion of supraspan procedures elsewhere in this book.) One of the advances in Benton's Test of Serial Digit Learning is that normative data are available for different levels of education and for different age groups. Another advance is that scoring is sensitive to the degree of error manifested by the patient. Nearly correct responses (an error involving only 1 digit in the series) are scored 1 point, and perfectly correct responses are scored 2 points.

There are two forms of this test. Form SD9 can be given to patients between the ages of 16 and 64. Form SD8 can be given to subjects up to the age of 74. Normative data are available for 500 medical patients without a history of brain disease. The quantitative score is converted to percentiles differently for the age and the education level of the patient. There were no statistically significant differences due to sex in the normative sample. Therefore, there are no corrections for sex in the scoring procedures.

Hamsher, Benton, and Digre (1980) found that, in a sample of 100 patients with diagnosed brain impairment, use of the Serial Digit Learning Test was more likely to result in a correct diagnosis than was the use of the Digit Span subtest of the WAIS. The increase in diagnostic accuracy was greatest for subjects with bilateral lesions. The increase in diagnostic accuracy was least for patients with left-hemisphere lesions. Despite this difference in accuracy as related to laterality of the lesion, it does not appear that the Test of Serial Digit Learning would be useful in lateralizing brain lesions.

FACIAL RECOGNITION

Benton's Test of Facial Recognition is an evaluation of the patient's ability to recognize unfamiliar faces from black-and-white photographs. (The reader is referred to the discussion of other tests of familiar and unfamiliar faces elsewhere in this book.) This test has three parts. The first part requires the subject to identify the face in a stimulus photograph from a choice of six front-view photographs. The second part requires the patient to identify the person in the stimulus photograph from a series of six three-quarter-view faces, three of which are of the stimulus face. The third part requires the patient to identify the face in the stimulus photograph from a series of six photographs under different lighting conditions. Again, three of the faces are the same as the stimulus face. The test has a short and a long form. The long form differs only in having a larger number of items. The photographs are organized into a spiral-bound booklet.

The normative data are available in the manual based on a sample of 196 medical inpatients with no history of brain disease, psychiatric disorder, or childhood mental deficiency, and on a sample of 90 normal subjects. All 286 subjects were between the ages of 16 and 74. Significant differences due to age were found. Significant differences due to education were found only in the 55- to 74-year-old group. Therefore, a correction factor for age was added for the subjects in the 55- to 64-year-old and the 65- to 74-year-old groups. A correction for education was added for the same two groups.

Normative data are also available for patients between the ages of 6 and 14. These data are based on a sample of 266 schoolchildren. The IQ of all of the children was in the 85–116 range as measured by the WISC.

The relation between the short and long forms has been investigated by correlating the scores of the items in the short form with scores of all of the items. The correlation coefficient for 151 of the control subjects was .88, and the correlation coefficient was .92 for the brain-damaged subjects. Overall, a correlation coefficient of .93 was obtained for the entire sample of 336 subjects. Based on these data, short-form scores can be converted to long-form scores by the use of a table in the manual (Benton *et al.*, 1983).

After the appropriate age and education corrections have been made, the scores are converted to percentiles. Percentile conversions using age conventions are also available for the child sample.

Hamsher, Levin, and Benton (1979) investigated the performance of brain-impaired subjects on the Test of Facial Recognition. The overall sample of 286 subjects consisted of 196 controls, 23 subjects with right anterior lesions, 36 subjects with right posterior lesions, 15 nonaphasic subjects with left posterior lesions, 5 aphasic subjects without comprehension deficits but with left anterior lesions, 8 aphasic subjects without comprehension deficits but with left posterior deficits, 17 aphasic subjects with comprehension deficits and left anterior lesions, and 27 aphasic subjects with comprehension deficits and left posterior lesions. Poor performance appeared to be related to right-hemisphere lesions as well as to left-hemisphere lesions in the presence of comprehension deficits. Levin, Grossman, and Kelly (1977) found that closed-head injury was associated with poor performance on the Test of Facial Recognition only when patients had been comatose for longer than 24 hours. There were no relationships with the presence of abnormal EEGs or the presence of depressed skull fracture.

Levin and Benton (1977) investigated the performance of 44 psychiatric patients whose symptoms implied the presence of cortical impairment and found that their scores were all in the normal range, with the exception of the score of one paranoid schizophrenic. The authors therefore recommended the Test of Facial Recognition as being useful in differential diagnosis. However, these recommendations need to be tempered in light of the results of Kronfol, Hamsher, Digre, and Waziri (1978), who found that, of 18 severely depressed psychiatric inpatients, 3 performed in the impaired range.

All aspects of the reliability of this test need to be evaluated. Additionally, it would be instructive to compare the internal reliability of the short and long forms. More information is needed regarding the validity of this test in psychiatric populations. The relation of receptive aphasic symptoms to performance on the Test of Facial Recognition needs to be more clearly delineated.

JUDGMENT OF LINE ORIENTATION

The Test of Judgment of Line Orientation resulted from Benton's earlier investigations into the effects of right-hemisphere lesions on spatial orientation skills. His earlier investigations involved the tachistoscopic presentation of two lines that may or may not differ in angle. Because of the difficulty in using tachistoscopic presentation methods at the bedside, a booklet form of this procedure was devised in which the stimulus items are presented as incomplete lines in order to approximate the level of difficulty when full-length lines are presented tachistoscopically (Benton, Varney, & Hamsher, 1978).

There are two forms of the test, which actually contain the same items presented in slightly different order. There are 30 items in this test. Each item contains two lines of angles varying from the horizontal. For each item, there is also the same template stimulus of a collection of lines in an arrangement with 18-degree increments. The task presented to the patient is to identify the lines in the constant template stimulus that match the angles of the two incomplete lines.

The normative data are available in the manual based on a sample of 137 adult control subjects who ranged in age from 16 to 74. Significant differences due to age and sex were found. Therefore, corrections are suggested on the basis of these two variables. There was no systematic effect of level of education, so no corrections for this variable are suggested. However, a larger sample may result in systematic differences due to level of education, and this possibility needs to be investigated. Normative data are also available based on a sample of 221 children aged 7–14. Corrected scores are converted to percentiles for the purpose of interpretation.

The split-half reliability of Form H, corrected for attenuation, was found to be .94 in a sample of 40 subjects. The split-half reliability of Form V was found to be .89 in a sample of 124 subjects. The split-half reliability of the test (the form used was not identified) was found to be .84 in a sample of 221 children (Lindgren & Benton, 1980).

Although test–retest reliability has not been evaluated separately for the two forms, it was evaluated when first one form and then the other was administered to a sample of 37 patients. The interval varied from 6 hours to 21 days. The reliability coefficient was .90, and there were no significant differences between the two scores.

The sensitivity of the test to lateralized impairment was investigated in a sample of 50 subjects with left-hemisphere lesions and 50 subjects with right-hemisphere lesions. None of the subjects were aphasic. Although both groups contained subjects with a wide range of scores, the right-hemisphere-lesioned subjects were much more likely to perform in the impaired range. The test therefore appears to be sensitive to lateralized impairment. However, much more knowledge is needed regarding the construct validity of the test. Preliminary investigations of this type are promising. Benton *et al.* (1983) reported that, at least for children, there is a low partial correlation of this test with the Test of Facial Recognition (when age and Verbal IQ are corrected for), indicating that the two tests measure separate constructs.

VISUAL FORM DISCRIMINATION

The Test of Visual Form Discrimination is an attempt to assess the ability of a patient to perceive and recognize complex visual patterns. The test stimuli are spiral-bound in a booklet. Each item consists of a target stimulus and four choices, one of which matches the target exactly. Each stimulus consists of two major figures and a peripheral figure. Aside from the correctly matching stimulus, one of the alternate stimuli involves the rotation of a major figure, one involves the rotation of the peripheral figure, and one involves the distortion of a major figure. Qualitative information about the type of error made can be derived from this multiple-choice test.

Originally, there were 64 items in the test. A pilot study based on a sample of children (sample size unspecified) provided estimates of item difficulty. Sixteen items representing a wide range of difficulty levels were chosen to comprise the final test. The items are presented in increasing order of difficulty.

Scoring is based both on a record of the type of error and on a numerical system in which correct responses are assigned values of 2 points, peripheral errors are assigned 1 point, and the major rotations and major distortions are assigned zero points. In this way, scores are potentially sensitive to the degree of visual impairment.

The normative information is available from the manual on a sample of 85 subjects (medical inpatients and normal subjects with no history of brain disease). The subjects ranged in age from 19 to 74. There were no significant differences in performance due to age, sex, or education; therefore, no corrections were recommended. Most of the normative sample achieved nearly perfect scores.

As with the other Benton tests, interpretation is conducted by reference to the normative distribution as well as to the distribution of scores of a sample of impaired individuals. Fifty-eight patients with a diagnosis of lateralized brain dysfunction constituted the sample of impaired individuals. Of these subjects, 19 had right-hemisphere dysfunction, 23 had left-hemisphere impairment including aphasic symptoms, 9 had left-hemisphere impairment but no aphasic symptoms, and 7 had bilateral brain impairment. Although there is some overlap in the two distributions, none of the normal subjects scored below 23 points, whereas 50% of the brain-impaired subjects scored in that range. Impaired performance was therefore defined as a score lower than 24 points. When that value was used as a cutoff point, there were no false positives in the original sample, and 53% of the brain-damaged subjects were classified as presenting impaired performance.

With use of the recommended cutoff value, the manual reports a study where patients classified as presenting defective performance were examined for the impaired sample broken down by laterality of lesion, for anterior or posterior site of lesion, and (for the left-hemisphere subjects) for the presence and absence of aphasic symptoms. When the effects of laterality were investigated, 47% of the left-hemisphere subjects, 58% of the right-hemisphere subjects, and 71% of the bilateral-diffuse subjects were classified as having impaired performance. A higher percentage of left anterior (58%) than left posterior (47%) subjects were classified as impaired. However, the opposite pattern was found in the right-hemisphere subjects: 43% of the anterior subjects and 78% of the posterior subjects were classified as impaired. Left-hemisphere nonaphasic subjects (56%) were more likely to present impaired performance than were left-hemisphere aphasic subjects (43%).

Because no specific information was provided about the etiology or the degree of brain lesion on these subjects, it is difficult to interpret the construct validity of this test. Because the group of bilateral-diffuse subjects had the highest percentage of impaired individuals, it may be that the Test of Visual Form Discrimination is sensitive to a wide range of corticobehavioral skills, with a slightly higher loading on right-hemisphere skills. The degree of impairment in the bilateral-diffuse subjects may also reflect sensitivity of the test to impairment in attention and concentration, in which case one would expect closed-head-injury patients to perform poorly.

The relation between aphasic symptoms and performance on this test also needs to be better investigated. Varney (1981) reported a relation between performance on the test and alexia. However, the larger percentage of left-hemisphere nonaphasic individuals with impaired performance and the interaction of laterality with caudality represent areas where further research is needed to explain the results. Research is also needed to determine the different forms of reliability of the test.

PANTOMIME RECOGNITION

The Test of Pantomime Recognition grew out of investigations that seemed to show that some aphasic patients demonstrate an impairment in their ability to comprehend the symbolic meaning of activities. There is a long tradition of the conceptualization of aphasia as an impairment in symbolic functions, and this test was devised to allow a partial assessment of the degree to which nonlinguistic symbolic functions may be impaired in aphasics.

The test consists of 30 videotaped pantomimed activities. Although the use of the videoplayer required for this test is cumbersome and expensive, videotapes represent an important advance in the standardization of pantomime assessment techniques. The tape reduces the possibility of variability in the presentation of the stimulus items. The subject is shown the pantomime of an object's use and is then asked to choose the picture of the correct object from among four alternatives. The four alternatives are the correct object, an incorrect object drawn from the same semantic class as the correct choice, an object that would be the correct choice elsewhere in the test, and an object that is not suitable for pantomime. The subject is asked to point to the correct object; thus, the need for a linguistic response is obviated. The test is scored on the basis of the total number of correct answers, as well as the total of the different types of errors (e.g., the number of times an object from the same semantic class is chosen).

The normative information in the manual was derived from a limited sample of 30 hospitalized inpatients who did not show evidence of brain disease. Nearly all of the subjects gave perfect performances, although two of the subjects did make four errors. Data were also collected on 105 aphasic patients. Of these subjects, 30% gave perfect performances or performances with only one error. Altogether, 60% of the aphasics gave performances in the normal range. The performances of the remaining aphasics ranged down to 20 errors. Most of the errors made by the aphasics were in choosing objects from the same semantic class as the correct choice. Varney and Benton (1982) found that, in a sample of 40 aphasic patients with impaired performance on this test, 36 made the largest number of their errors in the semantic class.

Although it appears that aphasia plays a role in impaired performance on this test, investigations using brain-impaired individuals without aphasic symptoms have not been conducted. The only investigation of the construct validity of this test indicates that poor performance on this test in aphasic patients is not related to poor performance on the Block Design subtest of the WAIS.

The Test of Pantomime Recognition appears to have great promise in the clinical setting. However, a much larger normative base is required. There is no information regarding the reliability of the test. More information regarding the diagnostic validity as well as the construct validity is needed before this test can be recommended for unlimited clinical use.

TACTILE FORM PERCEPTION

Tests of sensory impairment have a long history in neuropsychology. However, in many of these tests, the assessment of tactile sensation is confounded with linguistic ability, as in the case of the naming tests or the fingertip letter-drawing tests. Benton's Test of Tactile Form Recognition requires only the skills of tactile-information processing that allow the subject to identify a line drawing of an object that is presented tactilely. Because the stimulus items are cards with geometric designs cut from sandpaper, verbal encoding is not required. However, in the case of the simple figures, such as the star and the circle, linguistic encoding is possible. The subject is told to feel the design on the card, which is kept out of sight. The subjects then identifies the object from a card that contains 12 line drawings of the figures. After one form of the test is given to one hand of the subject, the second form is given to the other hand. There is a 30-second limit for each item. Scoring is based on the total number of correct responses for each hand separately and for the two hands together. The manual encourages the examiner to record the response latency but does not provide normative data for these time scores.

The manual (Benton *et al.*, 1983) states that the two alternate forms are equal in difficulty. The alternate-forms reliability of the two was investigated by administering the two forms to a sample of 56 normal right-handed individuals. The order of the tests was counterbalanced as was the first use of either the right or the left hand. There were no significant differences due to the form of the test used, the hand used first, or the order of test administration.

Normative information is available from the manual on a sample of 90 normal subjects between the ages of 15 and 70. Because performance appeared to decrease with age and with lower levels of education, there are corrections for these variables. Further normative information has been based on data from a group of 25 subjects between the ages of 71 and 80. Spreen and Gaddes (1969) presented normative information based on the performance of 404 children between the ages of 8 and 14.

Data from a sample of 104 patients with brain dysfunction indicate that brain dysfunction is related to poor performance on this test, especially brain dysfunction that results in motor or sensory impairment. Additionally, although left-hemisphere dysfunction can result in poor performance, right-hemisphere dysfunction is more likely to result in poor performance. Bilateral brain dysfunction resulted in the highest percentage of patients with poor performance.

The Test of Tactile Form Recognition appears to be another promising tool in the assessment of spatial functions. However, more information is needed regarding its temporal reliability, its concurrent validity, and the actual construct underlying performance.

FINGER LOCALIZATION

Finger recognition is an important aspect of many different forms of neuropsychological assessment. Behavioral neurologists have long used some form of finger recognition task when assessing clients for parietal lobe damage. The Luria–Nebraska contains a finger recognition section as part of its assessment of tactile functions. Acknowledging that finger localization may have more than one component skill, Benton's Test of Finger Localization presents the stimuli in three different modalities.

The test consists of 60 items; each of the 10 fingers are touched individually two times in each of the three touches. The first touch allows visual input as well as tactile output. The second touch is done without the benefit of visual information. For the remaining 20 items, two fingers are touched simultaneously. In each case, the subject is asked to identify the fingers touched by name, by pointing, or by referring to a chart on which the fingers are assigned numbers.

Normative information is available on a sample of 104 medical inpatients who had no history of brain dysfunction or psychiatric disorder. These subjects ranged in age from 16 to 65. Sixty-two of these subjects made two or fewer errors on the test. Of the errors made by these normative subjects, 82% were on simultaneous stimulation. No significant differences were found due to age, sex, or education. The normative scores were converted into percentiles for each hand separately, as well as for the difference between the scores for the two hands.

Normative information has been provided for children based on earlier studies conducted by Benton (1955 and 1959) and Wake (1956, 1957, cited in Benton et al., 1983). In all of these cases, the section using simultaneous stimulation consisted of only 5 trials instead of 10 trials. These scores were therefore doubled so that they could be consistently prorated with the adult data. There are also normative data derived from a sample of 61 right-handed individuals with diagnosed brain dysfunction. The ages of these subjects ranged from 18 to 64.

Interpretation is suggested on the basis of patterns of scores, including such categories as left and right unilateral impairment, bilateral asymmetrical impairment and normal performance. There are different relations between different diagnostic categories and score patterns; however, the safest conclusion regarding poor performance is that the subject has some form of brain impairment. The manual suggests a relation between finger recognition scores and later reading skills in children; however, this question needs to be more thoroughly addressed.

Data are needed about the different forms of reliability, as is information regarding the validity of the different score patterns. Concurrent-validity and predictive-validity studies also need to be conducted.

PHONEME DISCRIMINATION

The manual describes this test as a brief screening measure for the assessment of phonemic decoding. The test consists of a taped set of sound pairs that the subject is asked to identify as being either the same sounds or different sounds. There are 10 single-syllable pairs and 20 two-syllable pairs, for a total of 30 items. The scoring is based on the number of correct "same" and "different" responses and the number of incorrect "same" and "different" responses. A summary score is obtained from the total number of correct responses.

Normative data are available on the scores attained by 30 inpatients who did not have signs of brain dysfunction. There was no evaluation of the effects of age, sex, or education. There is also information regarding the distribution of the scores attained by 16 nonaphasic patients with right-hemisphere lesions, as well as the distribution of the scores attained by 100 aphasic left-hemisphere-lesioned subjects. Because none of the normal subjects scored lower than 22, that value was chosen as the cutoff point. Only one of the right-hemisphere-lesioned subjects scored lower than the cutoff, but 24% of the left-hemisphere aphasic patients scored lower than the cutoff.

Because oral comprehension skills may be seen to be partially dependent on phonemic discrimination skills, this test holds much promise for the evaluation of subjects with receptive aphasic symptoms. However, more information is needed regarding the different forms of reliability, as is a more complete understanding of the relation of performance on this test to performance on other tests of receptive language skills.

THREE-DIMENSIONAL BLOCK CONSTRUCTION

Constructional apraxia is assessed in many different ways. Constructional practic skills are components of the Bender–Gestalt Visual Motor Test as well as of the Block Design subtest of the WAIS-R. Benton's test attempts to assess constructional practic skills without the confound of the fine-motor response required in drawing tests, and with a three-dimensional element not found in the Block Design test.

There are two forms of the test, each consisting of three stimuli. For each item, the subject is shown a photograph of a block model and is asked to reconstruct the model from a set of loose blocks. In an investigation of the alternate-forms reliability of this test, the test was administered to 120 subjects who were equally divided among three diagnoses (Benton *et al.*, 1983): one third of the subjects had no evidence of brain impairment, one third of the subjects had evidence of left-hemisphere dysfunction, and the remaining one third had evidence of right-hemisphere dysfunction. These subjects were divided into four groups: one half received Form A and one half received Form B; furthermore, one half received the photographic stimuli and one half received actual models of the designs from which to complete their models. There were no significant differences among the groups. This finding indicates not only that Form A and Form B are equivalent, but also that the photographic-model method is equivalent to the actual-model method of administration.

The scoring is based on the type of errors committed by the subject. The errors are classified as omissions, additions, substitutions, or displacements. Additionally, the total number of correctly placed blocks is counted, and if the subject takes more than 380 seconds to complete the test, 2 points are subtracted from her or his score.

Normative data for the block model presentation method are available on a sample of 100 medical patients with no evidence of brain impairment, as well as on a sample of 20 individuals with left-hemisphere dysfunction and a sample of 20 individuals with right-hemisphere dysfunction. Normative data are also available on the same number of similar patients who received the photographic-presentation method.

Normative data for children were taken from Spreen and Gaddes (1969). In this study, the test was administered to 259 children between the ages of 6 and 12. These scores were transformed to percentiles for the purpose of interpretation. The children's scores generally increased with age, although there was great variability within age groups. Benton *et al.* (1983) estimated that, at age 14, the children's performance would approximately equal adult performance.

Validational studies have found that the test is sensitive to brain dysfunction in general (Keller 1971, reported in Benton *et al.*, 1983). Benton (1973) found that, although about 35% of 14 right-hemisphere-lesioned subjects and about 32% of 34 left-hemisphere-lesioned subjects gave impaired performances, there was an interesting relationship of aphasic symptoms to performance. Of the 18 left-hemisphere-lesioned subjects with aphasic symptoms, 59% gave impaired performances. Of the 9 subjects with severe aphasic symptoms, 67% gave impaired performances. This relationship needs to be better elucidated in future research. Additionally, reliability information is needed.

MOTOR IMPERSISTENCE

The inability to maintain a motor activity on command has been associated with right-hemisphere disease. However, the relation is far from clear and is not universally accepted. The Test of Motor Impersistence is an attempt to provide a standardized assessment of the phenomenon. There are eight different tasks in this test, and in each case, the subject is asked to continue the activity until he or she is told to stop. The score is some variant of the time in seconds during which the behavior is persistently engaged in or the number of times the subject ceases to follow the instructions. The tasks range from telling the subject to keep her or his eyes closed (up to a limit of 20 seconds) to instructing the subject to retain central fixation during confrontation testing of visual fields.

Impersistence is scored somewhat differently for each task, and the total score for the test is the number of subtests on which impersistence is demonstrated. Normative data are available on a sample of 106 medical inpatients with no history of brain dysfunction. Based on these data, moderate impersistence is defined as defective performance on two or three subtests, and marked impersistence is defined as defective performance on four or more subtests. Normative data are also available on a sample of 140 normal children between the ages of 5 and 11 years. Because there was great variability in impersistence across the tasks in the child sample, and because the tasks sample such a wide range of motor skills, it is important that the internal consistency reliability of this test be evaluated. Other forms of reliability also need to be evaluated.

Earlier studies investigated the association between brain dysfunction and impersistence, but only the studies that used the Benton test are considered here. Levin (1973) found that 44% of patients with unilateral lesions demonstrated impersistence; however, no hemispheric differences were found. Garfield (1964) found that 68% of a sample of children with brain dysfunction exhibited impersistence on two or more tasks, but that only 3% of a sample of normal children exhibited impersistence on two or more tasks.

Benton, Garfield, and Chorini (1964) showed that, on each task of the test, mentally retarded children demonstrated a larger degree of impersistence than did normal children, a finding that was supported by Rutter, Graham, and Yule (1970). Garfield, Benton, and MacQueen (1966) compared the performance of retarded children with brain damage to that of retarded children with equivalent IQs but without other signs of brain damage; these authors found that the brain-damaged children had a greater degree of impersistence. Domrath (1966) reported that schizophrenics exhibited a greater degree of impersistence than did normals, but a smaller degree than did neurological patients. Impersistence appears to be related to mental impairment, but this relation is unclear, especially in light of the Garfield *et al.* (1966) study.

Age appears to play a role in performance on this test, and this variable needs to be better investigated. Reliability data would enhance the clinical utility of this instrument, as would a greater understanding of the test's diagnostic validity and its concurrent validity.

THE BENTON VISUAL RETENTION TEST

The Benton Visual Retention Test (BVRT) is perhaps the most famous and most frequently used of all of the assessment procedures that have come out of the Neuropsychological Laboratory at the University of Iowa. Arthur Benton's large contributions to neuropsychological assessment included his approach of adapting laboratory procedures to the purposes of clinical assessment. The BVRT involves several complex cognitive-behavioral skills and is therefore sensitive to organic impairment in these areas; visual motor construction, visual spatial perception, immediate memory, and visual conceptualization. In addition, because some of the items have verbal referents, the test also taps verbal conceptualization. However, it is not appropriate as an individual screening device.

The BVRT exists in three forms: C, D, and E. These are alternate forms, although there is evidence that Form C is a little less difficult than the other two forms under conditions of immediate recall (Benton, 1974). There are three forms of administration. In Administration A, the subject is shown the stimuli for 10 seconds and is then asked to reproduce them. In Administration B, the subject is shown the stimuli for 10 seconds and is asked to reproduce them after a delay of 5 seconds. In Administration C, the subject is allowed to copy the stimuli directly.

The manual (Benton, 1974) presents normative data for all three forms and administrations. Although it is not clear which of the alternate forms were used to yield these norms, from the alternate-forms studies it is apparent that each of the forms may be referred to the norms. Performance on the BVRT is positively correlated with IQ and negatively correlated with age. Therefore, the norms are for the expected correct responses and the expected number of errors for each of three adult age groups (15–44, 45–54, and 55–64 years) crossed with each of six IQ groups (corresponding to the diagnostic groups of very defective, defective, borderline, low average, average, and superior). In addition, norms are available for five IQ groups (high average is combined with superior) crossed with the ages of 8, 9, 10, 11, 12, and 13–14 years.

The norms for Administration B were generated from the performance of 103 medical patients who had no history of brain disease and who were between the ages of 16 and 60. On the basis of these data, the manual proposes that subtracting the number 1 from the normative scores for Administration A will provide norms for Administration B.

Norms for Administration C were derived from the test protocols of 200 medical patients with no history of brain disease. The children's norms for Administration C were obtained from the performance of 236 schoolchildren between the ages of 6 years, 6 months and 13 years, 5 months. All of these children had IQs between 85 and 115. Additionally, norms were obtained from a group of 79 children in the same age groups who had IQs higher than 115. Norms are not available for more detailed divisions by IQ value. There is no normative information for Administration D.

There is yet another alternate form of the BVRT. Form I is an attempt to remove the motor component of the BVRT in order to assess a more purely visual skill. In this form, the subject is asked to pick out the original form from a series of four alternatives (Benton, 1950; Benton, Hamsher, & Stone, 1977). Unfortunately, this form of the test may be solved by a logical strategy not related to visual memory. Blanton and Gouvier (1985) pointed out that, by simply picking the alternative that does not have the characteristics shared by the other three, one can answer all items correctly even if one has not seen the original stimulus. Therefore, when this form is used, the examiner should interview the subject afterward to see if the logical strategy was used.

Reliability

The manual (Benton, 1974) provides an estimate of the test–retest reliability of Administration A based on the equivalent-forms reliability coefficient. This value is .85, and it appears to overestimate, according to the values reported by Lezak (1982). Lezak administered Forms C and E to a small group of normal males on three occasions. The intertest intervals varied from 6 months to 1 year, and not all of the subjects received each administration. For Form E, the correlation between the first and second occasions was .50. Between the first and third occasions, the correlation was .79. For Form C, the value of the correlation between the first and second occasions was .58. Between the first and third occasions, the correlation was .60. Because Lezak (1982) did not report which administration was used, it is difficult to interpret these data. However, it does appear that the values reported in the manual may overestimate the actual value. Brasfield (1971) reported a correlation coefficient of .75 when Administration C was given twice to a group of 194 kindergarten children, with an interval of 4 months. Wahler (1956) investigated the interscorer reliability and reported that, for Form C, interscorer agreement for the total number of errors was .95.

Alternate-forms reliability has been more extensively evaluated. When the BVRT is given under Administration A, Forms D and E appear to be easier than Form C (Breidt, 1970). However, for normal children, under Administration C, Form D appears to be easier than Form C (Benton, Spreen, Fangman, & Carr, 1967). For mentally retarded children, there appear to be no differences among the forms (Brown & Rice, 1967). Although there are moderately high correlations between the different administrations of the same form, the correlations between the different administrations of the different forms tend to be low (Breidt, 1970).

Validity

The concurrent validity of the BVRT was examined by correlating the performance of 100 brain-impaired patients on Administration C of the BVRT with their performance on a three-dimensional block-construction test, a stick-construction test, and the WAIS Block Design subtest. The BVRT was found to be related to the construction tasks, but less than the construction tasks were related to each other (Benton, 1967). In the same study described above under "Reliability," Breidt (1970) correlated the BVRT with various subtests of the WAIS and reported that the higher correlations were obtained with the visual-spatial subtests of the WAIS.

Discriminative validity was examined by giving Administration A to a group of normal, organic, depressed, and schizophrenic subjects. Only the difference between the normal subjects and the depressed subjects was statistically significant, although the normal subjects performed better than each of the clinical groups (Velbrosky, 1964). Cronholm and Schalling (1963) reported that the BVRT was able to discriminate between subjects with focal brain injury and normal subjects even when the influence of IQ was statistically partialed out. Watson (1968) reported that the BVRT was able to discriminate between schizophrenic and organic subjects when neither the Bender–Gestalt nor the Memory for Designs was able to do so. Marsh and Hirsch (1982) reported that, in a sample of 100 neurological patients, the BVRT was able to correctly classify more of the subjects as impaired than was the Memory for Designs. However, the results of this investigation can not be interpreted strongly because of the lack of a control group and the high base rate (100%) of impairment. Crockett, Clark, Browning, and MacDonald (1983) found that a background interference procedure, such as that used for the Bender–Gestalt, increased the discriminative ability of the BVRT in separating psychiatric subjects from brain-damaged subjects. These authors stated that they used Form C, but they did not specify which administration was used.

Benton (1967, 1968) investigated the construct validity of the BVRT and reported that poor performance was associated with lesions in the right hemisphere. Nehil, Agathon, Greif, Delagrange, and Rondepierre (1965) reported that performance on the BVRT was associated with diagnoses as determined by EEG tracings. The manual (Benton, 1974) also suggests interpretations of qualitative aspects of performance that had been validated by Poitrenaud and Barrerre (1972). However, cross-validation of these results is necessary. Silverstein (1962, 1963) concluded that there was a complexity of factors involved in performance on the BVRT, at least for mentally retarded subjects. Larrabee, Kane, Schuck, and Francis (1985) investigated the construct validity of the BVRT by factor-analyzing the data from 102 subjects. The variables included in the analysis were the Wechsler Memory Scale (WMS) Logical Memory Score, Paired Associates, Visual Reproduction, Administration A of Form C of the BVRT, and the two-factor scales of the Luria–Nebraska Neuropsychological Battery. Two factor analyses were conducted, one using the immediate recall administration of the WMS and the second using the delayed recall of the WMS. In both cases, the BVRT loaded more heavily on a visual-perceptual motor factor and secondarily on the memory factor.

Moses (1986) performed a factor analysis of the BVRT, the BVRT–Multiple Choice Form, the Benton Visual Form Discrimination test, Digit Span, and the Rey Auditory-Verbal Learning Test in a sample of 97 VA neuropsychiatric patients. The copying and recall procedures emerged as separate factors, but the BVRT was found to have a significant loading on factors interpreted as being verbal. The exact construct measured by the BVRT needs to be specified.

There is a set of information regarding the BVRT that is unique in the area of clinical neuropsychological assessment; it regards subterfuge and dissimulation. This is a problem faced by clinical neuropsychologists who work in a forensic setting or who must evaluate individuals who might be motivated to manipulate the data. Benton and Spreen (1961) compared the performance of 48 subjects with moderate and severe brain impairment with 47 college students and 23 medical inpatients with no history of brain impairment. The brain-impaired subjects were given Administration A of Form C under normal conditions. The normal subjects were first given Administration A of Form E under normal instructions and were then given Form C with instructions to perform as if they had moderate brain damage from a car accident 3 months before. The simulators exhibited more errors overall than did the real brain-impaired subjects. Qualitatively, the simulators gave more distortions, fewer perseverations, and fewer omissions than did the brain-impaired subjects. Spreen and Benton (1963b) followed this finding with a study of the performance of subjects who were instructed to simulate moderately low IQ (the mind of a 10-year-old). The same design as above was used, with similar quantitative and qualitative results. Therefore, the BVRT is one of the few neuropsychological tests for which patterns of dissimulation are known.

THE SENTENCE REPETITION TEST

The Sentence Repetition Test (Spreen & Benton, 1963a) is a series of sentences that increase by single-syllable increments, eventuating in a final sentence of 26 syllables. The subject is asked to repeat the sentence. The score on this test is the number of syllables in the final sentence that has been accurately repeated. Spreen and Gaddes (1969) presented norms for the test for children aged 6–13. Carmichael and MacDonald (1984) subsequently published norms for children between the ages of 3 and 13, using a much larger sample than was used in Spreen and Gaddes (1969). This test has also been used as part of the Multilingual Aphasia Examination. Hinshaw, Carte, and Morrison (1986) administered the Sentence Repetition Test to a sample of 74 children who had been diagnosed as reading-disabled. The subjects were divided by median split into a group aged 6.5–8.5 and a group aged 8.5–11. All of the subjects had an IQ of at least 80 and a difference between IQ and standardized reading scores of .6 standard deviations. There was no relation between performance on the Sentence Repetition Test and performance on either the Reading Comprehension scale of the WRAT-R or the Gates–MacGinitie reading test. This finding indicates that the Sentence Repetition Test may not be related to academic aspects of reading. Relatively little is known about the reliability and validity of the Sentence Repetition Test, although Davis, Foldi, Gardner, and Zurif (1978) presented some data that suggest that the best may be useful in the diagnosis of transcortical aphasia.

The Minnesota Multiphasic Personality Inventory

with Douglas E. Robbins

The Minnesota Multiphasic Personality Inventory (MMPI) represents one of the most intensively researched instruments for personality assessment, with over 6,000 citations recorded. An extensive literature exists on the construction of the MMPI as well as related validity and reliability issues (e.g., Cottle, 1950; Dahlstrom & Welsh, 1960; Dahlstrom, Welsh & Dahlstrom, 1975; Gravitz & Gerton, 1976; Hathaway & McKinley, 1942; Hathaway & Meehl, 1951; Holzberg & Alessi, 1949; Horn, Wanberg, & Appel, 1973; Johnson, Klinger, & Williams, 1977; Kroger & Turnbull, 1975; McKinley & Hathaway, 1942, 1944; Mehlman & Rand, 1960; Ritter, 1974). For an excellent discussion of the psychometric "weaknesses" of the MMPI, the reader is referred to David Rogers's review in *The Seventh Mental Measurements Yearbook* (1972). Rogers raised several stimulating questions in this review: Does the MMPI represent a "personality inventory"? Are the MMPI scales truly "dimensional"? Is the usage of *t*-score scaling with the MMPI appropriate? Does the MMPI successfully categorize individuals into mutually exclusive nosological groups (the original intent of the test)? He also raised the issue that the MMPI was standardized on the card-sort form and was not renormed for the booklet format, even though these two forms do differ, and, finally, the issue that the MMPI was based on a geographically limited and rather atypical population, creating nongeneralizable anomalies in the scale content. Even with these criticisms, Rogers noted that the MMPI is a remarkably robust instrument that has proved to be applicable to a wide range of cultures; over 39 translations of the test existed at the time of Rogers's review.

The focus of the present review is on evaluating the existing literature regarding the use of the MMPI in neuropsychological assessment. Specifically, the MMPI has been used by researchers as an objective measure of personality for the purpose of delineating the relationship between brain function and personality. Three general research designs have been used in this endeavor. In the first design, a localizationalist approach is used in an attempt to relate differences in personality (as demonstrated on the MMPI) to specific areas of brain dysfunction. The second research design attempts to differentiate neurologically impaired subjects from some other group of subjects (e.g., schizophrenics) by identifying the differences in their response patterns. The third research design uses deficits on neuropsychological tests as a means of defining group inclusion. Those subjects whose performance falls at the brain-damaged level are compared for personality differences on the MMPI.

It is important to note that the MMPI lends itself to research of this type not only on theoretical grounds, but also by the nature of its test items and its scale composition. For example, as Lezak and Glaudin (1969) noted, among the 51 items of the 357 scored items on a short form of the MMPI (omitting scale *Si* and all items normally not scored) that are referrable to symptoms of physical disease, 26 relate to central nervous system diseases, and 8 describe problems associated with being ill. Many of the "neurological-symptom" items have double and triple MMPI scale loadings.

RELIABILITY

Although there has been some research on the development of new scales to assess neuropsychological impairment by recombining items, there have been no investigations regarding the forms of reliability of these new scales. However, because some of the research has concerned the use of the clinical scales of the MMPI, the reliability investigations for the clinical scales are relevant here. It must be noted that in none of these studies were the subjects individuals who had organic brain impairment. Dahlstrom *et al.* (1975) presented information regarding the reliability of the MMPI scales. They reviewed several studies and formulated the information into tables. Many of the reliability studies were conducted on college students. In a study using 288 male and 33 female college students, the test–retest reliability coefficients with a 1-day interval ranged from .97 for the F Scale for males to .71 for Scale 6 for females. In a sample of 42 college males and 55 college females, and with test–retest intervals of 1–2 weeks, the reliability coefficients ranged from .49 for Scale 6 in males to .92 for both the K Scale and Scale 7 in the females. In a sample of 35 male psychiatric patients and 39 female psychiatric patients, the test–retest reliability coefficients for a 1- to 2-day interval ranged from .46 for the K Scale in the males to .86 for Scale 2 in the females. Internal-consistency reliability coefficients ranged from − .05 for Scale 1 in 97 college students to .90 for Scale 1 in 220 VA patients.

VALIDITY

Localizationalist Paradigm

As noted above, researchers have speculated on the relation between personality changes and the location of the cerebral insult. Anderson and Hanvik (1950), for example, attempted to characterize the differences between patients with parietal lobe damage and those with frontal lobe damage. These authors concluded that frontal patients tend to be "accepting, non-irritable, not anxious, affable, easygoing, and possessed of a relatively low general level of aspiration" (p. 179). In contrast, parietal patients were described as having an "anxiety neurosis" personality type. Unfortunately, the differences between the MMPI profiles for these groups were not tested for statistical significance. Similarly, the groups used did not consist of pure cases of discrete lesions, as the "parietal" group contained certain patients with additional damage to the temporal and/or the occipital lobes.

Friedman (1950), whose research represents a methodological improvement over the Anderson and Hanvik (1950) study, analyzed MMPI differences in patient groups with discretely localized parietal and frontal lobe damage. Friedman's 32-item Parietal-frontal (*Pf*) scale (Dahlstrom & Welsh, 1960, p. 463) enjoyed initial success. Williams (1952) constructed a similar scale, the Caudality (*Ca*) scale, in which 40% of Friedman's scale was reproduced. Williams's 36-item scale was reported to significantly differentiate patients with parietal and temporal lesions, as a group, from those with frontal lesions (Dahlstrom & Welsh, 1960; Meier, 1969). Reitan (1976), however, reported that more recent research does not support these earlier findings.

Black (1975) and Templer and Connolly (1976) attempted to separate the associated personality variables within a laterally dichotomized (left-versus right-hemisphere) brain-damaged population, much as Anderson and Hanvik (1950) attempted to do with the anterior versus the posterior brain-damaged subjects. In Black's study, for example, differential effects were found in the two groups. On the *F, K, D, Pa, Sc,* and *Si* scales, the left-hemisphere-damaged subjects scored reliably higher ($p < .05$) than did the right-hemisphere-damaged subjects. The right-hemisphere-damaged subjects manifested few marked cognitive and sensory deficits compared to the left-hemisphere-damaged subjects.

Using the lesion localization paradigm, Vogel (1962) attempted a global study of effects on the MMPI. Vogel hypothesized that left-hemisphere-lesioned subjects would show a more pathological profile than right-hemisphere-lesioned subjects, and that subjects with parietal and temporal lobe damage would show a more pathological profile than those with frontal lobe damage. To assess personality changes, an overall index of MMPI pathology was provided by the number of *t* scores greater than 70. With this overall pathology index, neither of Vogel's hypotheses were confirmed. Vogel proposed that his second hypothesis might not have been adequately tested because of the limited number of subjects with frontal lesions and because of the use of the overall index.

Dikmen and Reitan (1974b) attempted to demonstrate personality changes as a result of different locations of brain damage (defined by conclusive medical techniques) along rostrocaudal as well as lateral dimensions. No significant differences among the MMPI scales were found, and the investigators concluded that the MMPI was a poor measure of personality changes when groups were derived according to the location of brain damage.

Consistent with the above discussion is Lezak's review of lateralization research (1983):

> The findings of investigations into the effects of lesion lateralization on MMPI performance have been variable. Studies that have found lateralization differences consistently report that patients with left hemisphere damage tend to have elevated scores on scale 2 (Depression). Scales 8 (Schizophrenia), 1 (Hypochrondriasis), and 7 (Psychasthenia) may also be higher with left-sided lesions (Black, 1975). High scale 8 scores also distinguished a group of predominantly left hemisphere damaged patients, all of whom had aphasic symptoms, from a predominantly right hemisphere damaged group without aphasic symptoms (Dikmen & Reitan, 1974b). Black interpreted the high (T-score > 70) 8–2–1 scale pattern as reflecting a tendency to catastrophic reaction in young (mean age $= 21.7 + 2.1$) missile wound patients whose injuries were predominantly on the left. Gasparrini and his colleagues pointed out that the 2–8–7 pattern of high mean scores made by their relatively young (mean age $= 36.5$) patients with left-sided lesions of mixed etiology was characteristic of a major affective disorder. The right hemisphere damaged patients in these latter two studies were comparable to the left hemisphere groups in age and etiology but, in both cases, produced essentially normal profiles. In three other studies, two involving organic populations with mixed diagnoses (Dikmen & Reitan, 1974a; Flick & Edwards, 1971), and one of patients with temporal lobe epilepsy (Meier & French, 1965), no lateralization differences were found. (p. 612)

In summary, little reproducible evidence has been generated by the localizationalist approach to the study of brain–personality relationships. The problem may be related to the different effects of lesions even within the same broad area of the brain because of differences in their etiology, the time since onset, the medical treatments, their pressure effects, and their exact location (Luria, 1966; Reitan, 1966). Finally, observed personality differences may relate more to differences in the behavioral deficits suffered by individuals than to the area of the damage.

Differential Performance Paradigm

The second approach taken to delineating the personality patterns characteristic of brain damage is comparing the performance of brain-injured subjects with that of nonneurologically impaired subjects in order to identify differentiating scales or items on the MMPI. Several different strategies have been used within this research design: (1) comparison of differences in performance across MMPI scales by brain-injured and control groups; (2) the development of organicity scales; and (3) the development of decision rules for diagnosing organicity. Similarly, in this endeavor, varying populations have been used for both brain-injured and control groups. For example, the performance of patients diagnosed as presenting with multiple sclerosis (Dahlstrom & Welsh, 1960; Gilberstadt & Farkas, 1961; Schwartz & Brown, 1973), epilepsy (Klove & Doehring, 1962; Kristianson, 1974; Matthews, Dikmen, & Harley, 1977; Meier, 1969; Small, Milstein, & Stevens, 1962; Stein, 1972), Huntington's chorea (Boll, Heaton, & Reitan, 1974; Norton, 1975), Guillain–Barre syndrome (Sziraki, 1979) has been reviewed. Similarly, brain-injured subjects have been compared with normals (Hovey, 1964), neurotics (Reitan, 1955a), schizophrenics (Ayers, Templer, & Ruff, 1975; Holland, Lowenfeld, & Wadsworth, 1975a; Markowitz, 1973; Neuringer, Dombrowski, & Goldstein, 1975; Russell, 1977; Watson, 1971), and psychiatric patients in general (Shaw & Matthews, 1965).

As noted above, a common research strategy entails comparing the performance of a brain-injured group with some other clinical control group. Although the MMPI has been found to differentiate between organic and psychiatric or normal subjects (Matthews *et al.,* 1966; Reitan, 1955a; Watson & Thomas, 1968), no profile unique to one group has emerged. For example, in the study by Reitan (1955a), a heterogeneous brain-damaged group scored higher on the *F, Pa, Pt, Sc,* and *Ma* scales of the MMPI than did the control group. The experimental subjects varied according to the type, extent, and location of the brain lesion and were matched for sex, age, and education with members of a control group that contained normal and neurotic subjects with no known brain damage. The experimental group yielded a wide range of personality profiles. In contrast to this study, Watson and Thomas (1968) compared neurological patients with schizophrenic patients on the 10 MMPI scales and found significant differences on the *Hs, D, Mf, Pt, Sc,* and *Si.* Four decision rules were developed (a strategy to be discussed in detail later) that yielded a 69% correct classification. Three validation studies yielded classification rates of 71%, 79%, and 45%. Norton and Romano (1977) conducted a cross-validation study of the Watson–Thomas rules on a sample of 14 neurological patients, 14 alcoholic patients, 14 married schizophrenic patients, 14 unmarried schizophrenic patients, and 14 patients with mixed psychiatric diagnosis who lacked neurological symptoms. These authors reported generally good levels of accuracy of classification for all except the unmarried schizophrenic patients. However, the accuracy of their classification rates may have been inflated by their use of ''pure'' cases and by the use of equal frequencies of subjects in all groups, neither of which condition is likely to occur in the clinical setting.

The most consistent finding in these studies, aside from being unable to generate a common patient profile, was that the *Sc* scale can differentiate psychotic patients from organic patients. For example, Russell (1977) found that a cutoff score of 80 on the *Sc* was sufficient to differentiate 78% of brain-damaged and schizophrenic patients (with schizophrenics obtaining higher *Sc* elevations). However, when schizophrenics comprised only half the group of patients with functional disorders, an *Sc* cutoff score of 80 resulted in a 67% correct classification.

The second approach to diagnosis with the MMPI has been to establish organicity scales that can discriminate between experimental and control groups. The major scales in this area have been suggested by Hovey (1964), Watson (1971), Shaw and Matthews (1965), and Watson and Plemel (1978). In general, the results on these scales have been highly variable, because of the use of populations that varied widely in severity, chronicity, type of injury, age, education, and duration of hospitalization (Ayers *et al.*, 1975; Holland *et al.*, 1975; Neuringer *et al.*, 1975; Pantano & Schwartz, 1978; Ruff, Ayers, & Templer, 1977; Russell, 1977; Sand, 1973; Siskind, 1976; Upper & Seeman, 1966; Zimmerman, 1965). Few studies have attempted to compare any combination of these scales on a single population to eliminate much of the interpretive problem in the current literature. The exception is the Golden, Sweet, and Osmon (1979) study, which is discussed later.

In the Hovey (1964) study the five items were chosen from the MMPI that appeared to be most able to discriminate brain-injured patients and controls. Items 10, 51, 192, and 274 are marked false, and Item 159 is marked true. The cut-off score for organicity is 4. Hovey recommended that, to minimize the possibility of false positive errors, this scale be used only when the K-scale score is 8 or above. As a group, the items consist predominantly of questions about balance and walking, eyesight, and problems with physical health in general. Using these five items, Hovey correctly classified 50% of the brain-damaged subjects; there was a 9%–18% misclassification of the normal subjects. Upper and Seeman (1966) attempted to validate Hovey's scale by using a non-brain-damaged schizophrenic control group. Similar differences between groups were found. Overall, however, the Hovey five-item scale has met with only limited success. This scale was found to be ineffective in discriminating patients with organic impairment from groups of organically intact patients with functional disorders (Dodge & Kolstoe, 1971; Maier & Abidin, 1967; Schwartz & Brown, 1973), schizophrenic patients (Watson, 1971), and normal control subjects (Weingold, Dawson, & Kael, 1965). A classification of chronic alcoholic patients by the Hovey scale was not found to bear any systematic relation to cognitive indices of organic impairment (Chaney, Erickson, & O'Leary, 1977). Jortner (1965) also reported a failure to replicate Hovey's results.

Watson (1971) abandoned his attempt to develop a profile indicative of neuropsychological impairment in favor of developing a new MMPI scale, the Schizophrenia–Organicity (*Sc-O*) scale, for differentiating brain-damaged patients from schizophrenic patients. Eighty items were initially identified and combined to form the scale. Two other scales were derived from the original 80 items by first weighting all of the items according to their power of discrimination, and then by weighting only the 30 most powerful items. Using these scales, Watson reported 85% accuracy; on cross-validation with a similar patient population, the scale yielded 76% accuracy. Holland *et al.* (1975a) also reported that the *Sc-O* Scale can discriminate brain-damaged from schizophrenic subjects. However, when the degree of emotional disturbance (as measured by the psychotic triad) was held constant statistically, the *Sc-O* scale failed to discriminate. Halperin, Neuringer, Davis, and Goldstein (1977) were unable to separate nonorganically impaired schizophrenics from organically impaired schizophrenics (as determined by the Halstead–Reitan) using Watson's *Sc-O* scale and called the validity of the scale into question.

Watson (1973) noted that the *Sc-O* Scale does not separate nonschizophrenic functional groups from organics. Therefore, he developed the Psychiatric-Organic (*P-O*) Scale. This scale consists of 56 items that were found to differentiate 40 brain-damaged subjects from a group of 60 psychiatric patients (all subjects were male veterans). The group of functionally disordered patients consisted mostly of alcoholics (35). The *P-O* scale correlates positively with age ($r = .30$). The internal consistency of the scale, as reported by Watson and Plemel (1978), was .90 for the organics, and only .68 for the controls. These authors appropriately noted that additional research is needed before one can use this scale with additional populations.

Shaw and Matthews (1965) also addressed the problem of differentiating between organic and psychiatric deficits by developing a neurological impairment scale—with two important differences. Unlike in the Watson studies, the subject-sampling procedure was designed deliberately to include "pseudoneurological" patients who were diagnosed as being psychiatric patients but who also manifested "soft" neurological symptoms. This study also differed in the procedure it used to identify the items to be included in the scale: 17 items, 5 of which are marked true (38, 47, 108, 238, and 253) and 12 of which are marked false (3, 8, 68, 171, 173, 175, 188, 190, 230, 237, 238, and 243), were chosen from only those scales that, as a whole, differentiated between the two groups (*Hy, Hs,* and *Pt*). Items on other scales that may or may not have differentiated between the groups were excluded from analysis. A cutoff score of 7 was established for the scale.

Originally, accuracies of 78% were reported. A cross-validation sample yielded 73% correct classifications, with misclassifications 33% of the time in the psychiatric group and 22% of the time in the neurological group. Again, the scale failed to meet the criterion normally expected of a clinical diagnostic device.

The final strategy within this research design entails the use of the MMPI in the development of decision rules for diagnosing organicity. In this approach, an algorithm or decision tree that uses a hierarchy of rules is used to differentiate the diagnostic categories. Major systems of this type have been proposed by Watson and Thomas (1968) and Russell (1975b, 1977). Limited success has been reported for these approaches. For example, in a study of 20 brain-damaged, 21 schizophrenic, and 24 clinically depressed subjects, Trifiletti (1982) found that Russell's MMPI key correctly identified 85% of the brain-damaged subjects and 0% of the schizophrenics, and only 33% of the depressed subjects; the overall hit rate was 68%. The difficulty in separating brain-damaged subjects from the clinically depressed subjects is not surprising, given Russell's original conceptualization of the pattern profiles of the neurologically impaired subject (i.e., such subjects present as a reactive depression on the MMPI). Overall, it must be concluded that additional cross-validation is needed for decision-tree–algorithm approach to the differential diagnosis of organicity.

Golden *et al.* (1979) compared each of the above approaches in their study of a single population consisting of 30 schizophrenic, 30 brain-injured, and 30 hospitalized normal patients. Their results indicated that the most effective diagnostic device was the use of the Sc scale alone or in conjunction with the remaining clinical scales and the F scale. None of the organic scales or keys were able to match the performance of the Sc scale alone. The result of this study does not support the existence of an unique organic profile. The study does support the effectiveness of the Sc and Pa scales in the diagnosis of brain damage. These results were identical to those reported by Russell (1977). These findings suggest that the stronger the psychosis present, the less likely it is that one is dealing with an organic brain syndrome. However, as noted by Golden *et al.*, even this limited conclusion is questionable. The Golden *et al.* study did not include individuals with brain-damage who were also psychotic. It is likely that such a group would show high elevations on the Sc, Pa, and other MMPI scales equal to those shown by the schizophrenic group without brain damage. Thus, when a diagnosis of organic brain syndrome with psychosis is considered, even the presence of psychosis cannot rule out the presence of brain damage, as it does in the Golden *et al.* study and other studies using "pure" populations.

Although the second research design (differentiating groups by their performance on the MMPI) shows that personality differences do exist between brain-damaged and non-brain-damaged psychopathological groups, it has been unable to produce clinically useful diagnostic devices, perhaps, in part, because of the large personality differences within heterogeneous brain-damaged populations (Reitan, 1955a).

The difficulty of cross-validating research in this area may also be attributable to the fact that those general pattern tendencies that characterize the responses of the neurologically impaired subject may only be an artifact of the test items and the scale composition of the MMPI. For example, a confounding factor in research of this type is that many of the "neurological-symptom" items appear on the *Sc* scale, and many have double and triple scale loadings, particularly on scales *Hs, D,* and *Hy.* As a result, non-psychiatric patients with central nervous system disease tend to have an elevated "neurotic triad" (*Hs, D,* and *Hy*) (Dikmen & Reitan, 1974b) and higher-than-average *Sc* scores. *Pt* is also among the scales most likely to be elevated in an organic population (Mack, 1979). Schwartz (1969) examined both the 1–3–9 and the 2–9 profiles in a sample of 50,000 consecutive medical outpatients. Using the 1–3–9 rules resulted in a sample of 24 subjects. Using the 2–9 rules resulted in a sample of 23 subjects. There were no differences in the independently determined degree of organic impairment between these subjects and control subjects with 1–3/3–1 profiles who were matched for age, sex, and date of clinic appointment. Additionally, only one of the 1–3–9 subjects and five of the 2–9 subjects had been diagnosed as being organically impaired. These results seriously question the accuracy of the rules.

The 2–9 and 1–3–9 scale elevations once thought to represent organic patterns have not been validated (Russell, 1977). However, Casey and Fennell (1981) reported elevations on Scales 2, 8, and 1 that characterized the MMPI profiles of traumatically injured patients; Heaton *et al.* (1978) also observed that head-injured patients tended to have elevated scores on Scales 2 and 8. In general, elevated MMPI profiles tend to be common among brain-damaged populations, a finding reflecting the relatively frequent incidence of emotional disturbance in these patients (Filskov & Leli, 1981). The tendency of *Sc* to be the highest or one of the highest scales has been noted for epileptic patients (Klove & Doehring, 1962; Meier, 1969). High scores on the neurotic triad have characterized the MMPI profiles of patients with multiple sclerosis (Dahlstrom & Welsh, 1960). Huntington's disease patients, too, have abnormally high score profiles, but these profiles are indistinguishable from the profile pattern of heterogeneous groups of brain-damaged patients (Boll *et al.,* 1974; Norton, 1975).

Thus, for brain-damaged patients, acknowledgment of specific symptoms accounts for some of the elevation of specific scales. Premorbid personality tendencies and the patient's reactions to his or her disabilities also contribute to the MMPI profile. The combination of the symptom description, the anxiety and distress occasioned by central nervous system defects, and the need for adaptive psychological measures probably accounts for the frequency with which brain-damaged patients produce neurotic profiles.

Neuropsychological Functioning as a Means of Defining Group Inclusion

The third paradigm was developed in response to the failure of the first two approaches. This paradigm assumes that behavioral deficits specifically related to a brain lesion can be used to create more exact definitions of brain-injured groups, and therefore to make more homogeneous samples possible.

As a result, a group with similar behavioral deficits can be identified. With such groupings, one need not presuppose an all-encompassing personality profile of brain damage.

In an early study by Doehring and Reitan (1960), behavioral deficits were used to define three groups of diagnoses: brain-damaged aphasic dysfunction, brain-damaged nonaphasic dysfunction, and intact neurosis. The MMPI data were assessed with an analysis of variance, but no significant differences between the groups were found on the various scales.

It was later suggested by Dikmen and Reitan (1974a) that the failure of the Doehring and Reitan (1960) study to find personality differences between the three groups was probably due to the heterogeneity of the personality deficits in the neurotic group, which masked any intergroup differences that might have existed. The method of data analysis was also cited as being a potential problem, and another analysis was performed on the data that used t ratios. When the neurotic group was eliminated, significant differences on the *Pd* and *Sc* scales were found between the two brain-damaged groups.

In a similar study, Dikmen and Reitan (1974a) successfully demonstrated personality differences within a brain-damaged population by assigning their subjects to brain-damaged aphasic and brain-damaged nonaphasic groups. These subjects were matched for age, education, and type (but not location) of lesion. The dependent variables were the regular MMPI clinical and validity scales, as well as six additional indices created from combinations of the scales.

A discriminant analysis was used to compare the overall performance of the two groups on all nine clinical scales, and a significant difference was found between the two groups. An analysis of the individual scales using the student's t test yielded a significant difference on the *Pd* and *Sc* scales. The groups were similar on the neurotic triad scales (*Hy, D,* and *Hs*); however, the aphasic group had substantial elevations relative to the nonaphasic group on the psychotic scales (*Pd, Pt,* and *Sc*); only the *Sc* scale achieved statistical significance. No significant differences between the groups were found with the six derived scales, although the scores were somewhat higher for the aphasic group on the indices for anxiety, psychosis, cognitive slippage, and acting-out impulsiveness.

From these results, one can conclude that, among those who are brain-damaged, there is considerable variation of personality patterns. Dikmen and Reitan (1974a) demonstrated with the Welsh (1956) composite profile code that the aphasic group peaked on *Sc* scales, whereas the nonaphasic group yielded a more normal profile. Furthermore, Dikmen and Reitan (1974a) concluded that, in studies of the effects of brain injury on personality, behavioral deficit identification may more efficiently define groups than locus of injury.

As noted above, the results of the Dikmen and Reitan (1974a) study suggest that the behavioral deficits of the individual may be more important to personality than is the location of the lesion that is responsible for the deficits. Osmon and Golden (1978) hypothesized that, if this is true, one would expect patients with different patterns of impairment to demonstrate different personality structures. In a study of 50 subjects with medically verified brain lesions, Osmon and Golden investigated the relationship between various neuropsychological deficits and patterns of personality variables. This study attempted to examine how behavioral deficits are related both to individual personality variables and to patterns of personality variables. Whereas the Dikmen and Reitan (1974a) study revealed that different individual personality variables, as well as profiles, exist within a brain-damaged population, the Osmon and Golden (1978) study attempted to extend this earlier research on aphasic and nonaphasic symptomatology to an investigation of the role of other major gnostic processes, such as sensory perception, concept formation, cognitive interference, concentration, planning, learning, and memory. This study also investigated the effect of behavioral deficits other than aphasia on personality variables.

The relation between the subjects' responses on the MMPI and their performance on a selected battery of tests taken from the Halstead–Reitan Neuropsychological Battery was evaluated. Although a relative lack of individual relationships was found between cognitive and personality variables, strong predictive relations between the MMPI and the presence or absence of neuropsychological deficit were obtained. Hit rates of 78%–86% were reported.

Erlandson, Osmon, and Golden (1981) investigated further the relationship between brain function and personality by extending both the Dikmen and Reitan (1977) and the Osmon and Golden (1978) studies to a psychiatric population. The neuropsychological instrument used in this study was the Luria–Nebraska Neuropsychological Battery. This instrument was chosen to validate the notion, derived from past research, that brain function plays a major role in personality variables. Using a population of 73 schizophrenic subjects with medically verified brain damage, Erlandson *et al.* found, with the exception of the *F* scale, a relative lack of individual relations between the cognitive and the personality variables. Relatively strong correlations, however, were found between neuropsychological performance and overall patterns of personality variables for 11 of the 14 neuropsychological variables. The traditional personality differences associated with lesion laterality were replicated.

These findings suggest that the relation between personality and neuropsychological functions is not a simple one-to-one relation. Instead, each neuropsychological deficit may be associated with a complex personality change that can be investigated only by use of all of the MMPI scales. One could conclude that intellectual deficits underlie the overall personality changes associated with brain damage.

The results of the Erlandson *et al.* (1981) and the Osmon and Golden studies are consistent with the discriminant analysis results in Dikmen and Reitan (1974a, 1977). Again, these results pointed out the necessity of looking at the overall personality pattern rather than the simple relation of individual neuropsychological deficits to individual personality variables, Individual neuropsychological deficits can be associated with personality profiles when the entire MMPI pattern is taken into account. A future avenue of research would be examining the relation of sets of neuropsychological variables to the set of MMPI variables.

Several limitations of these studies should be pointed out. These studies were conducted with relatively small ratios of subjects to predictors. These circumstances can result in unstable least-squares solutions, limiting the generalizability of the results. Cross-validation is a necessary precondition before reasonable conclusions can be reached. Also, because of the correlational nature of the designs, we cannot make causative, etiological statements regarding the role of the neuropsychological deficits in producing the MMPI patterns. We do not even know if the MMPI profiles represent a change or stable functioning. The use of this particular multivariate methodology limits the clinical utility of the results.

ADDENDA

As for any proposed typology, there are some exceptions. In the present case, there are least two studies that do not fit neatly into the tripartite division we have proposed. These two studies examined the amount of variance shared by MMPI information and evaluations of neuropsychological functioning. This correlational design does not fit into any of the three paradigms, but its logic pervades each of them. The logic posits a relationship between neuropsychological functioning and relatively stable patterns of behavioral functioning.

In order to investigate this premise, Wiens and Matarazzo (1977) administered the Halstead–Reitan Neuropsychological Battery, the MMPI, the Cornell Medical Index, and the Taylor Manifest Anxiety Scale to two separate samples of healthy, normal young males. Each sample contained 24 individuals, and the second sample was used as a cross-validation sample for the first. There were no significant correlations between any of the Halstead–Reitan variables and any of the personality variables. Because normal individuals were used, the lack of correlations might at first be ascribed to restriction of range. However, there was sufficient range to allow the Halstead–Reitan variables to correlate among themselves in the range of .50 with a similar pattern of results among the personality variables.

Morgan, Weitzel, Guyden, Robinson, and Hedlund (1977) examined the relation between information derived from a standardized 120-question mental status exam and items on the MMPI. The authors judged 174 of the MMPI items to overlap with the mental status exam and 48 of the mental status exam items to overlap with the MMPI items. In the cases of total overlap, there was only 50%–60% agreement in the information derived from the two sources. In the cases of partial overlap, there was more variable agreement. Unfortunately, the authors did not specify their criteria for overlap, either total or partial.

All of this calls into question the existence of robust relations between standard measures of neuropsychological functioning and MMPI results. It does not mean, however, that no relation exists between neuropsychological functioning and behavioral functioning. Because of the MMPI's origin as an instrument to perform the psychological assessment of psychiatric patients, it may be inappropriate in diagnosing organic impairment. This inappropriateness does not undermine its utility in describing psychological functioning in individuals who have been diagnosed as organically impaired by the use of standard neuropsychological assessment instruments.

CONCLUSIONS

In general, the research reviewed does not support the existence of a specific personality style or profile *per se* that is unique to brain damage. A body of research does exist, however, that indicates that the relation between personality and neuropsychological functioning is not a simple one-to-one relation. Neuropsychological deficits have been associated with certain complex personality changes.

From the literature reviewed, it can be concluded that the localization paradigm has failed to relate personality to brain function, as evidenced by the conflicting data accumulated to date. Even if brain damage is confined to an individual cerebral lobe, there is far too much variability in the resultant behavioral deficits for a consistent personality type to emerge.

Research using the second paradigm (comparing brain-damaged groups with various psychopathological and normal groups without brain damage) assumes the existence of a personality pattern common to all brain-impaired patients. In view of Reitan's findings (1955a), it seems unlikely that one personality profile is common to all types of brain damage. Reitan's findings, indicating that brain-damaged individuals exhibit numerous psychopathological symptoms, confound any comparison of a general brain-damaged group with a specific psychopathological group.

The third paradigm that was reviewed (defining the brain-damaged group by behavioral deficits) has two advantages over the other two paradigms discussed. This approach allows for a more behaviorally relevant method of separating the various brain-damaged groups and their concomitant personality characteristics. Erlandson *et al.* (1981) also maintained that this approach allows much more powerful theoretical statements to be made concerning the relation between brain functioning and personality changes than do other research designs. Although research in this area is promising, additional study appears warranted.

An alternative paradigm not discussed, but worthy of mention, is one modeled after the notion of *incremental validity* (Sechrest, 1963); it is concerned with how much knowledge of a test's outcome (an MMPI profile, for example) contributes to the prediction of a criterion (a correct diagnosis or treatment decision). Schwartz and Wiedel (1981) reported the use of the MMPI in neurological decision-making. In a review of 13 cases representing a range of different neurological and psychiatric diagnoses, it was found that knowledge of the MMPI results increased the diagnostic accuracy of a group of neurology and psychiatry residents. The actual hit rates were not reported, nor were the diagnostic groups used. The importance of this study lies in the recognition that information generated by the MMPI, as by any other psychometric instrument, should not be used in isolation. More appropriately, results from the MMPI should be integrated with other test data, as well as with information derived from clinical observation, and from a review of the patient's history.

Reliability data are lacking for neuropsychologically impaired subjects. Although interscorer reliability is moot in the case of the MMPI, test–retest and internal-consistency reliability remain important issues that have not been addressed.

The Rorschach Inkblots

with Douglas E. Robbins

The use of the Rorschach as a neuropsychological instrument remains an issue of controversy. Despite the extensive clinical and theoretical literature that has been written on the Rorschach, those most critical of this instrument maintain that the validity of the Rorschach has not been established according to strict psychometric standards. Proponents of the Rorschach maintain that the functional utility of this instrument relies on the clinical skills and sensitivities of the individual using it. Regardless of one's bias toward the use of this instrument, there is a paucity of research on its validity and reliability when it is used with the neurologically impaired client. The utility, or the potential utility, of this procedure, however, continues to be of interest (see the symposium listing for the Eighth European Conference of the International Neuropsychological Society, Costa & Rourke, 1985).

The present review of the efficacy of the Rorschach as a measure of organicity synopsizes the findings of Baker (1956), Klebanoff, Singer, and Wilensky (1954), and Goldfried, Stricker, and Weiner (1971) regarding the validity of the Rorschach test and gives an overview of the research literature since these publications. It continues to be difficult to assess the Rorschach in terms of the experimental and statistical models typically used in psychology. Similarly, the methological shortcomings discussed in the above reviews continue to cause problems.

The Rorschach is used as an indicator of brain pathology because brain damage can result in personality changes. The implied assumption is that tests of personality functions should therefore be sensitive to the existence of an ''organic'' personality. Researchers have therefore attempted to isolate Rorschach signs that are characteristic of certain brain-damaged samples, and to use these signs in predicting the presence of brain pathology. This monolithic approach has not been proven to be highly successful, however, in part because of the erroneous assumption that brain damage is a unitary concept and that the manifestation of brain pathology is consistent regardless of the etiology, the location, or the circumstances of the injury. Similarly, brain lesions are likely to produce both general and specific effects, and signs constructed from a heterogeneous group of neurologically impaired subjects can be sensitive, at most, to the general effects. The extent to which personality changes are a result of neuropsychological impairment and/or are a secondary reaction to the stress inherent in the loss of previous intellectual functioning can also be a difficult and complex distinction, as well as a confounding variable. In addition, it is important to note that the Rorschach is a complex visual-perceptual task requiring such cognitive processes as attention, recognition, integration, naming, and the ability to formulate an oral-verbal expressive response. Lesions affecting any one of the functional systems involved in the above processes may therefore be manifested on the Rorschach.

Before we discuss the various sign approaches that have been used with the Rorschach, it is important to provide a general overview of the Rorschach, as the various sign approaches are often interpreted in the context of the entire Rorschach protocol.

An evaluation of the utility of the Rorschach is complicated by the fact that a number of scoring systems have been developed for use with this instrument (e.g., Beck, Beck, Levitt, & Molish, 1961; Exner, 1974). Most of these systems share such common scoring categories as location, determinants, and content. The analysis of a Rorschach protocol is based on the relative number of responses falling into the various categories, as well as on certain ratios and interrelations among different categories (Exner, 1974).

NORMATIVE DATA

Normative data have been provided by a number of researchers on the various scoring systems for the Rorschach (see Ames, 1966; Ames, Metraux, Rodell, & Walker, 1973; Beck *et al.,* 1961; Cass & McReynolds, 1951; Klopfer & Davidson, 1962). Ames and her associates, for example, collected and published Rorschach norms on children between the ages of 2 and 10, on adolescents between the ages of 10 and 16, and on adults 70 and older (Ames, Learned, Metraux, & Walker, 1954; Ames, Metraux, Rodell, & Walker, 1974; Ames, Metraux, & Walker, 1971). Combining data from 15 studies, Levitt and Truumaa (1972) compiled a summary of the published normative data for children and adolescents up to 16 years old. The means of various quantitative Rorschach indices were provided by age and intellectual level.

Despite the above efforts, it must be concluded that, in general, adequate normative data bases have not been established for the Rorschach (Goldfried, *et al.,* 1971). Often, there has been a failure to ensure that the data base is representative of the sample on which the data are based. Similarly, a review of the literature reveals that there has been a general failure to control or assess the effects of age, sex, IQ, and educational level in the

development of these data bases. Finally, norms have not been established
to control for the effects of varying response totals on the Rorschach.

Exner (1974) began addressing many of the shortcomings noted above
in what he termed the "Comprehensive System." The Comprehensive System, which is an integration of the five major Rorschach systems, synthesizes, according to psychometric criteria, the most reliable and useful indices
from the other Rorschach scoring systems. Exner (1974, 1978) has compiled
a substantial data base for this scoring system based on a nonpatient group
(n = 325) and four psychiatric groups: a outpatient nonpsychotic group (n
= 185), an inpatient character-problems group (n = 90), inpatient depressives (n = 155), and inpatient schizophrenics (n = 210). Means and standard
deviations are provided for the following categories: responses, location
features, determinants, and ratios and derivations. According to Exner
(1978), the five samples of subjects were closely monitored to ensure that
various socioeconomic strata would be proportionally represented in accordance with the 1970 U.S. Census figures. All five of the patient samples
were reported to be essentially equivalent in terms of sex. Normative data
for older adults were not differentiated, nor was information regarding education or level of intellectual functioning provided. As noted previously,
education and intelligence have been found to be a confounding variable
with the Rorschach, especially in such variables as the number of responses
produced on a protocol (R). Awareness of this fact is important in that the
number of responses produced has a direct bearing on a number of ratios
that are derived from the patient's protocol. A low number of responses
severely limits the usefulness of many of these ratios.

It should be noted, however, that normative data (n = 1,870) have been
collected and reported for nonpatient children across 12 age groups (ages 5
through 16). Sex differences, socioeconomic differences, and geographical
differences have also been discussed (Exner, 1982).

RELIABILITY

Of the three measures of reliability—comparability of forms, internal
consistency, and temporal stability—only the latter has proved plausible
with the Rorschach. Comparability of forms, for example, has not been
possible because an alternate form of the Rorschach has not been developed.
Many clinicians maintain that, because of the variable "pull" in each of the
Rorschach designs, it would be difficult to construct an alternate set of designs equivalent in all those aspects to which the client is capable of
responding.

One would expect that measures of internal consistency for the Rorschach would be difficult to obtain because this test measures heterogeneous, not homogeneous, traits. Similarly, the limited number of stimulus cards, coupled with the variable "pull" of each card, would limit one's chances of establishing significant levels of internal consistency. However, a limited number of studies have been reported that challenge this perception. Hertz (1934), for example, reported that, in a study of 100 junior-high-school students, an "odd–even" procedure was used that resulted in reliability coefficients ranging from .66 to .97. Following essentially the same approach used by Hertz, but using records of younger children, Ford (1946) obtained comparable split-half reliabilities.

It has been research in the area of temporal stability, however, that has proved most promising for establishing the reliability of the Rorschach as a diagnostic procedure. The use of test–retest measures, however, is inherently limited to those traits that one would expect to be stable over time. For example, developmental scorings, or measures of transitory depression or anxiety, would be inappropriate, as changes *would* be expected on these measures over time.

As noted previously, in the retest reliability studies that have been reported, the findings have been relatively positive. Ford (1946) reported reliabilities for scoring determinants ranging from $+.38$ to $+.86$ for a group of young children retested after 30 days. Kerr (1936), however, reported substantially lower reliabilities for young children retested after 1 year, results that may logically be attributed, in part, to developmental issues. Using a schizophrenic sample, Holzberg and Wexsler (1950) reported significant reliabilities across most scoring variables. Kelley, Margulies, and Barrera (1941) found very little change in the "psychograms" of 12 patients retested 2 hours after having received electroconvulsive therapy. These subjects demonstrated total amnesia for the first testing, which had been completed just before treatment.

Exner (1978) assessed the temporal stability of the Comprehensive System by evaluating the performance of several different groups of subjects at varying intervals. Three nonpatient groups consisting of 25, 25, and 100 subjects were retested after 7 days, 60 days, and 3 years, respectively. Data from the following four psychiatric groups was also assessed: 30-day retest of 25 outpatients waiting for treatment assignment; 20 patients diagnosed as schizophrenic who were retested on Day 10 of a 10-day evaluation period (without treatment); 35 outpatients retested after a 90-day interval, during which brief treatment had occurred; and 30 long-term outpatients, who were retested 180 days later. The results of the above seven studies (including the study of the schizophrenic group) provide support for the temporal stability of the Rorschach. In the three studies involving nonpatients, for example, 17 of the 19 variables correlated were found to be stable over time (having correlation coefficients of .70 or higher).

VALIDITY

Content validity for the Rorschach has proved difficult to demonstrate. Goldfried *et al.* (1971) suggested that the Rorschach may not be amenable to such an evaluation because it has not been shown that the Rorschach is, indeed, representative of those personality and cognitive variables that it purports to measure. Although they involve problems, measures of criterion-related validity and construct validity appear to be more promising in terms of establishing support for the Rorschach as a psychometric procedure. Two major approaches, which are somewhat divergent but not mutually exclusive, have been used to establish the validity of the Rorschach: the empirical sign or psychometric approach and the conceptual approach. The following discussion of Exner and his colleagues' research on the Comprehensive System represents an example of the empirical sign approach.

Most validation studies of the Comprehensive System have revolved around the "four-square" interrelationships (Viglione & Exner, 1983). The four square incorporates the basic scores and ratios thought to be characteristic of one's problem-solving style, and it forms the foundations for Exner's Comprehensive System. The four indices of the four square are: (1) Erlebnistypus (EB, the ratio of human movement to weighted color responses); (2) Experience Actual (EA, the sum of human movement and weighted color responses); (3) Experience Base (eb, the ratio of nonhuman movement to shading and gray–black responses); and (4) Experience Potential (ep, the sum of nonhuman movement, shading, and gray–black responses). According to Exner and his colleagues, these four variables taken as a whole incorporate the fundamental information about the psychological habits and capacities of an individual and represent the crucial interpretive departure from previous Rorschach systems (Lerner & Lerner, 1986).

Research conducted by Exner and his colleagues involving temporal consistency data indicates that the EA:ep ratio stabilizes through development and achieves permanence by adulthood (Exner, 1982). Normative data indicate that EA increases relative to ep as children mature, and that ratios in which EA is greater than ep are associated more often with normal subjects than with patients. Collectively, the above findings demonstrate that the EA:ep relation represents a stable personality characteristic that indicates the "amount" of psychological activity organized and available for "coping purposes" as opposed to more immature experiences that impinge on the subject. Treatment studies reveal increases in EA, both alone and in relationship to ep, among patients who have shown improvement in psychotherapy (Exner, 1978). For subjects beginning treatment with ep greater than EA, a reversal has been demonstrated in most cases; that is, EA becomes greater than ep when intervention is not short-term (Exner, 1978). Exner (1978) suggested that such intervention either facilitates the organization of psychological resources or relieves stress. According to Exner, the occurrence of ep is not always disruptive or pathological; rather, ep activity in moderate amounts stimulates underlying motivational processes.

In contrast to the psychometric or sign approach to the Rorschach, the conceptual approach addresses issues of construct as opposed to criterion-related validity. Construct validity therefore addresses the extent to which a theoretical formulation can account for relations between selected aspects of a Rorschach protocol and some condition or behavior (see Lerner & Lerner, 1986).

Empirical findings have also been reported that provide support for the concept of construct validity. Hall, Hall, and Lavoie (1968), for example, reported differences between right- and left-hemisphere-damaged patients on a variety of Rorschach variables. Similarly, three studies have assessed the performance of epileptics on the Rorschach: Vagrecha and Sen Mazumadar (1974); Delay, Pichot, Lemperier, and Perse (1958); and Loveland (1961).

ORGANIC SIGNS

Although numerous sets of Rorschach signs have been developed for the purpose of assessing brain damage (see Aita, Reitan, & Ruth, 1947; Dorken & Kral, 1952; Evans & Marmorston, 1963b, 1964; Hughes, 1948; Piotrowski, 1937, 1940; Ross & Ross, 1944) it is questionable whether any system has demonstrated sufficient validity to warrant their use clinically (Goldfried *et al.,* 1971).

Piotrowski Signs

Piotrowski (1937) developed the most notable of these systems, which consists of 10 signs dealing with both the response style and the content of the response. Piotrowski's research indicates that organic patients tend to give Rorschach protocols with less than 15 responses, long latencies for each response, perseveration, perplexity (the patient demonstrates a distrust of her or his own ability and seeks reassurance), poor form, little movement, color naming, and impotency (the patient recognizes an unsatisfactory response but does not change or improve it). Piotrowski (1937, 1940) cautioned, however, that, although the presence of five signs suggests brain impairment, a qualitative analysis of the patient's performance is necessary before a diagnosis of brain damage can be made.

Criticisms of this system include: (1) that this system results in what approximates a high number of "false negatives" or nonconclusive diagnoses; (2) that the signs do not differentiate chronic schizophrenics from organic patients; and (3) that the most effective of the Piotrowski signs, unfortunately, are those that might also be elicited by many other psychometric techniques. Perplexity, impotence, perseveration, and automatic phrases are ways of dealing with a stimulus situation rather than unique Rorschach variables, such as color denomination, reduced movement, and percentage of popular responses, which are much less successful signs.

Although the Piotrowski signs have been researched more than any other system, the efficacy of these signs has yet to be proved (Birch & Diller, 1958; Goldfried *et al.*, 1971; Hertz & Loehrke, 1954). The Piotrowski signs continue, however, to be the Rorschach signs most commonly used in the assessment of brain damage.

Hughes Signs

The Hughes system (1948) consists of 14 signs derived from a factor-analytic investigation. The records of 100 patients—of whom 32 were organic (a heterogeneous group of subjects diagnosed as having traumatic head injuries, cerebral arteriosclerosis, brain tumors, and cerebral syphilis), 39 were neurotic, and 29 were schizophrenic—were scored for Piotrowski's signs, Miale and Harrower-Erickson's neurotic signs, and Klopfer's schizophrenic signs. By means of Thursone's complete centroid method, a factor analysis was performed. From this procedure, eight orthogonal factors were extracted. Factor 1 was labeled the organic factor and provided the basis for the Hughes system. Factor loadings were used in determining the weights of the various signs. Of the 14 signs that were derived, 7 are identical to Piotrowski's signs. The score on the Hughes signs can range from -7 to $+17$, with a recommended cutoff of $+7$ being used to define brain damage (Goldfried *et al.*, 1971). Research has not shown the Hughes signs to provide an appreciable advantage over the Piotrowski signs.

Dorken and Kral Signs

The Dorken and Kral (1952) system consists of seven signs, whose presence is considered contraindicative of organicity. The method by which the signs were chosen was unspecified. The signs were weighted according to their incidence in a criterion population (Goldfried *et al.*, 1971). Of all of the major systems, that of Dorken and Kral (1952) has the highest call rate, so it produces the most false positives. Unfortunately, it does this while continuing to produce the usual number of false negatives, and for this reason, it does not seem to be a particularly fruitful technique.

Aita, Reitan, and Ruth Signs

The signs suggested by Aita *et al.* (1947) for the diagnosis of organicity were not proposed as a formal sign system. No cutoff point was suggested for the nine signs as indicating the presence or absence of brain pathology.

Evans and Marmorston Signs

Evans and Marmorston's system (1963b, 1964) represents a compilation of signs suggested by other researchers. Their initial 46-item list includes the 9 signs of Aita *et al.*, as well as the 10 signs composing Piotrowski's system. A number of cutoff points have been suggested for the 46-item list, depending on the type of comparison being made. The use of this system has been restricted primarily to the authors, in research with patients with cerebral thrombosis and acute myocardial infarctions.

NORMATIVE DATA FOR THE SIGN SYSTEMS

In general, it must be concluded that adequate normative data have not been established for any of the major Rorschach sign systems. There has been a general failure to provide adequate control or assessment of such variables as age, sex, intelligence, or level of education. Sample sizes have also tended to be inadequate. For example, in a review of 24 studies in which the Piotrowski signs were used, the median sample was found to be made up of fewer than 30 subjects (Goldfried *et al.*, 1971). These samples have tended to be heterogeneous, and the method of diagnosis of brain injury in almost half the cases was unspecified.

RELIABILITY STUDIES

Aside from interscorer reliability measures, essentially no research has been conducted regarding the reliability of the various Rorschach sign systems. In a study using selected signs from Piotrowski's system (impotency, automatic phrases, perplexity, and repetition), and from the Hughes system (contamination, color shock, and shading shock), Forar, Farberow, Meyer, and Tolman (1952) reported interscorer reliability, both between independent scorers and between the same scorer on two different occasions, for the Piotrowski signs to be consistently in the 80s. In the Hughes system, the color shock sign was found to be unreliable, and the shading shock sign was found to be of questionable validity. The contamination sign was found to be consistently reliable.

Additional reliability data have been reported by Evans and Marmorston (1963a,b, 1964), using their 46-item list. Test–retest correlations of .97 (for the same evaluator) were obtained following an intertest interval of 6 months. The test–retest reliability was recorded as .77.

A review of the research literature indicates that research on test reliability is needed. There has been only a limited amount of research on interscorer or test–retest reliability, and additional research is warranted as well.

VALIDITY OF THE SIGN SYSTEMS

The majority of the validity studies reviewed have been criterion-related studies. The Piotrowski system is the only major system on which sufficient data have been published to permit an adequate assessment of its validity. These signs have proved to be able to differentiate brain-damaged and control groups about 50% of the time. The call rate (the percentage of subjects diagnosed as brain-damaged) is considered low, and as a result, few false positives are produced. In contrast, these signs are liable to produce false negatives. The impotency sign has been found to be one of the best predictors of brain impairment, whereas more traditional Rorschach variables have proved to be relatively poor predictors.

In validity studies using the Piotrowski and the Hughes systems (Fisher, Gonda, & Little, 1955; Hertz & Loehrke, 1954), the Piotrowski signs have been found to be slightly superior. Fisher *et al.* (1955) also compared the Piotrowski and Hughes systems to the Dorken and Kral signs. This study found the Piotrowski system the most effective and the Dorken and Kral system the least effective of the three systems evaluated. This is true even though the Dorken and Kral system had the highest percentage of accuracy of the three systems studied. This accuracy was due to the preponderance of organics in the sample, as well as to the tendency of the Dorken and Kral system to produce a diagnosis of brain damage. Even in their initial study, it is clear that the Dorken and Kral (1952) system had a much higher call rate than either the Piotrowski or the Hughes system; this call rate produces a great many more false positives without appreciably reducing the number of false negatives.

Construct Validity

A systematic approach to establishing the construct validity of any of the major Rorschach systems has not been reported. Independent studies have been conducted on a variety of patient populations and have provided some support for several of the Rorschach systems. For example, Allison and Allison (1954) used the Dorken and Kral signs in a study of the effect of transorbital lobotomies; Evans and Marmorston (1963a, 1965) studied the effects of Premarin therapy by randomly dividing groups of cerebral-thrombosis and myocardial-infarction patients and administering Premarin to half and a placebo to half; Grauer (1953) selected 18 improved paranoid schizophrenics and 18 unimproved paranoid schizophrenics and compared their Rorschach protocols. No differences in Piotrowski signs were found between the two groups in this last study.

As noted previously, the research methodology most used in evaluating the Rorschach's ability to assess the neuropsychological changes associated with brain damage has been the sign approach. A number of methodological problems become obvious as one reviews the research literature in this area.

A second methodological problem that is common in the research on the various sign systems is that not one of the major systems of Rorschach indicators has controlled for such variables as age, intelligence, education, sex, race, or socioeconomic class.

Third, there has been a general failure to cross-validate the signs, as well as a failure to take base rates into account when assessing the signs' ability to discriminate between different groups.

CONCLUSIONS

The value of the Rorschach in the diagnosis of organicity has yet to be established, because of significant methological problems: an adequate definition of the nature of the organic involvement of the criterion groups is usually absent, the researchers typically fail to exclude organic involvement in the control subjects, and there is a lack of adequate reliability studies.

Goldfried *et al.* (1971) concluded that, although several of the Rorschach indices surveyed have demonstrated enough validity to justify their use in research, their suitability for clinical use has not been sufficiently established. The Rorschach does not lend itself easily to split-half reliability studies, nor is there any satisfactory parallel form for the test. Rorschach reliability studies must therefore focus on the temporal stability of this instrument.

Future studies will need to define the subject groups on the basis of preestablished diagnostic guidelines. There is also a need for normative data for specific populations. Future researchers should discard the unitary concept of brain damage, given the problems with the heterogeneity of the effects of brain damage and the need to separate groups according to the characteristics of the lesion and of the affected person. It may be possible to provide multiple sets of relevant signs and norms that control for age, sex, intelligence, and level of education. All of this research should be conducted with cross-validation, and attention should be paid to base-rate information.

The Rorschach may be affected by visual-spatial difficulties or perceptual problems that suggest emotional problems that may not be present. Certain frontal disorders or disorders such as dementia may reflect the client's inability to process information cognitively rather than provide a measure of the patient's personality style.

One of the principal problems has to do with defining the term *brain damage*. Birch and Diller (1958) argued that a distinction should be made between brain damage, which is an anatomical occurrence, and organicity, which is possibly a behavioral consequence. Of necessity, the Rorschach can be expected to be sensitive only to organicity. Organicity is not, however, a necessary sequel to brain damage. Lesions can exist with no apparent sensory, motor, mental, or emotional symptoms, and lesions can produce sensory or motor symptoms without accompanying mental or emotional difficulties. Every case in which a lesion exists without a cognitive or emotional symptom—in other words, in which brain damage exists without organicity—will produce a false negative, in that it would be impossible for the Rorschach to detect the brain damage in the absence of organicity.

The Wechsler Memory Scale

The Wechsler Memory Scale (WMS) was one of the first standardized memory tests. It consists of seven subtests, which were designed to measure different aspects of memory. It exists in two forms (I and II). The first test, Personal and Current Information, is composed of six questions regarding the age and the birth date of the subject and the names of people who currently hold public office. The second subtest, Orientation, assesses the subject's knowledge of the date and location of the test situation. Mental Control, the third test, requires the subject to count backward from 20, to recite the alphabet, and to add serial 3s. In the fourth test, Logical Memory, the subject is read two short narratives and is asked to repeat as much as he or she remembers. In the fifth test, Digit Span, the subject is asked to repeat auditorily presented backward and forward digits. The sixth test, Visual Reproduction, requires the subject to draw designs from memory. The last subtest, Associate Learning, is exactly that, a verbal paired-associates learning test. These subtests are scored for the number of correct responses, which are then summed. The summed score is age-corrected and converted to a Memory Quotient, which has a mean of 100.

The WMS is still in popular use despite the criticism that it does not discriminate well between intact and brain-damaged subjects (Prigatano, 1977). Because of the criticisms raised, it is very important that a clinician interested in using the instrument be familiar with the research regarding the reliability and the validity of the WMS.

NORMATIVE DATA

The original standardization sample consisted of 200 normal subjects who ranged in age from 25 to 50. The proportion of males to females was not given in the manual (Weschler & Stone, 1973). The small size of the standardization sample and the unavailability of important descriptive statistics regarding the sample detract from the usefulness of this instrument. Ivison (1977) presented some normative data derived from a sample of Australian subjects. Using some of the same sample, des Rosiers and Ivison (1986) reported some normative data regarding the difference between performances on the high associative word pairs and on the low associative word pairs.

It is unfortunate that there are no published reports of larger standardization studies of this instrument. The original sample size was probably inadequate, and the lack of descriptive information in the manual makes it difficult to evaluate the representativeness of the sample. (Initial reports indicate that the revised version, or WMS-R, will obviate some of these criticisms.) Ivinskis, Allen, and Shaw (1971) attempted to examine performance on the WMS in younger subjects. These authors used 30 subjects in the 10- to 14-year age range and 44 subjects in the 16- to 18-year age range. The proportion of males and females was not given. Compared with the subjects used in Wechsler's original sample, the younger sample of Ivinskis *et al.* performed more poorly on each of the subtests except Associate Learning, on which they performed better than the older subjects. This sample was also too limited in size to allow confidence in generalizing the results. However, the results do point out the differences in WMS performance that may be attributed to the effects of age.

Cauthen (1977) looked at the WMS with older subjects. The subject sample included 64 people over age 60. The effects of both age and IQ were examined in this study. Although the older subjects did more poorly on all of the subtests, only Visual Reproduction showed a statistically significant decline with age.

RELIABILITY

Reliability information on the WMS is scarce. However, Ryan, Morris, Yaffa, and Peterson (1981) performed a test–retest experiment on Form I with both a normal ($n = 34$) and a mixed psychiatric-neurological inpatient sample ($n = 30$). Unfortunately, the intertest interval was not equivalent for the two groups. All of the normals were retested after 14 days, but the patients were retested after 5 days to 37 months with a mean interval of 14.2 months. Pearson product–moment correlation coefficients were calculated, relating the memory quotient (MQ) scores separately for the two groups and resulting in a value of .75 for the normals and a value of .89 for the patients. Although some subjects showed a gain in scores across the two test occasions and some showed a decrement, on the average there was a gain in MQ scores for the two groups. The normals gained an average of 7.2 points ($t = 3.95$, $p < .001$), and the patients gained an average of 4.0 points ($t = 2.32$, $p < .05$). These results suggest that, although there is adequate reliability in terms of the stability in position in group distribution, individual subjects are likely to manifest a gain in scores across time. There are no other reports of test–retest reliability, and there are no reports of alternate-forms reliability.

The closest approximation to a test–retest design can be found in Stinnett and DiGiacomo (1970), who administered Form I to 15 psychiatric inpatients before electroconvulsive therapy (ECT) and Form II sometime after ECT, with a mean interval of 18.9 days. In examining the data, Prigatano (1978) computed a correlation coefficient of .80. It should be noted that, because of the time that intervened between the two tests and the procedure that was performed (ECT), it may be that this is a lower estimate of what the test–retest reliability may actually be in this sample. However, because of the limited sample size, care should be taken in interpreting the stability of the solved coefficient.

In reviewing the unsystematic studies that have been performed on the WMS, Prigatano (1978) concluded that its test–retest reliability is fairly stable and that its alternate-forms reliability is probably adequate. However, this information should be tempered with the knowledge that, over short intervals, MQ scores will increase, and that, with longer intervals (that is, with age), the MQ scores will decrease.

The WMS produces both a single Memory Quotient score and scores for the seven subtests. A reasonable question regards the degree of internal consistency in the test as a whole as well as in the subtests. No internal consistency data are reported in the manual. Ivinskis *et al.* (1971) reported that the split-half reliability of the WMS is .75. However, this information exists only as a single statement in the conclusions section of their paper dealing with use of the WMS in younger populations. Because there are no other extant reports of split-half reliability in the literature, we can assume that Ivinskis *et al.* derived that value from their sample of 74 subjects between the ages of 10 and 18. The authors provided no information on the type of split that was used and whether or not the Spearman–Brown formula was used to correct for the length of the test.

Additionally, there is only one report of an examination of the internal consistency of the subtests. Hall and Toal (1957) reported Cronbach's coefficient alpha values for the WMS subtests. The values were low for two of the subtests: .383 for Mental Control and .368 for Associate Learning. The values for the other subtests were more moderate: .814 for Logical Memory, .647 for Digit Span, and .634 for Visual Reproduction. Cronbach's coefficient alpha for the whole test was .686. No values were reported for the Information or Orientation subtests. Hall and Toal (1957) reported low intercorrelations among the subtests, a result that Ivinskis *et al.* (1971) supported, using their sample of younger subjects. There is a report of the intercorrelations among the WMS subtests of Form I translated into French. It is worthwhile to discuss foreign-language studies of the WMS because of its seeming applicability. The Personal Information and Orientation sections seem readily translatable. Visual Reproduction can obviously transcend language problems, and the remaining subtests are also well suited to translation. Of course, once the tests are translated, the American norms are not useful. The translated instruments would need standardization in their own languages.

For example, Ivison (1977) adapted the WMS for use with Australian people. Although Australians share the English language with citizens of the United States, there are enough cultural differences to imply that restandardization is necessary. After changes were made to reflect differences in culture and language (e.g., changing "president" to "prime minister" in the Information section and "took up a collection" to "made up a purse" in the Logical Memory section), the Australian WMS was normed on 500 hospitalized subjects. Slightly different norms were obtained, underscoring the importance of restandardization for clinical interpretation.

However, it is instructional for us to examine the intercorrelations among these translated subtests in order to glean whatever useful information may be contained there. Clement (1966) administered the French WMS to 477 males and 276 females who ranged in age from 16 to 100. He did not correlate the Personal Information, the Orientation, or the Mental Control subtests with the other four subtests, and he entered the Digits Backward score separately from the Digits Forward score. The correlation coefficients ranged from $-.05$ to .41. Although the analysis was conducted on a French translation, its results agree with the English-language version, a finding lending further support to the notion of meaningful subtest interpretation. In the same study, the subtests were correlated with the total WMS score. These correlation coefficients ranged from .36 to .71, which do not support the notion of high internal consistency in the test as a whole. Pershad and Lubey (1974) calculated intercorrelations among the WMS subtests in a sample of 150 subjects in an Indian translation. They reported correlations that ranged from .31 to .73, again adding limited support to the notion of subtest interpretability over MQ interpretability.

Factor structure is an area that has been more adequately, if still somewhat sparsely, investigated. The WMS is scored separately for each of the categories (e.g., personal information, orientation, and mental control). These scale scores are often used differently to diagnose specific memory problems. However, they are also summed into the MQ. This procedure raises the question of whether the WMS is unidimensional. The question of unidimensionality can be partially addressed by a factor analysis of the instrument. The first published account of a factor analysis of the WMS was given by Davis and Swenson (1970). This study used 622 mixed psychiatric and neurological patients. The authors performed a centroid factor analysis with an oblique rotation, and they interpreted the resulting two factors as memory and freedom from distractibility. It must be remembered that the results of factor analysis are influenced by the sample as well as by the structure of the instrument.

Dujovne and Levy (1971) conducted separate factor analyses for 276 normals and 158 patients, 81 of whom had been diagnosed as organic, and the rest of whom had psychiatric diagnoses. In a preliminary examination of the data, it was determined that a large majority of all the subjects had passed all of the items in the Personal and Current Information and the Orientation scales of the WMS. The authors therefore removed these scales from further analysis. The remaining WMS items were then submitted to factor analysis, along with the WAIS Full Scale, Verbal, and Performance IQ scores and the classification of patient or normal, all of which were used as reference variables. A principal-axis solution with varimax rotation was used. The authors interpreted the three factors for the normal group as general retentiveness, simple learning, and associative flexibility. The three solved factors for the patient group were mental control, associative flexibility, and cognitive dysfunction, indicating both some similarity and some disparities in the structure of the WMS in subjects with different characteristics. There are two problems in interpreting these results as indicative strictly of the internal structure of the WMS. First, the use of the WAIS variables as references very likely modified the factor analysis results. Second, the removal of the Personal and Current Information and the Orientation variables from the analysis means that only a partial view of the structure could be afforded by the analysis.

Kear-Colwell (1973) addressed the issues at hand more directly by performing a factor analysis on all of the WMS variables, as well as a separate analysis, using the same subjects, on the WMS factor scores, the WAIS variables, and the age and the sex of the subjects as a comparison. The sample used included 161 males and 89 females. All of the subjects had been referred for neuropsychological evaluation, and 66 had organic deficits, as confirmed by neurological or neurosurgical exam. The factor analyses were performed by the principal-components method, and the scree test was used as the criterion for stopping extraction. The extracted factors were rotated by the use of oblimin. The analyses were conducted separately for the 66 confirmed organics and the 184 suspected organics. In the case of the WMS-only analysis, both groups produced highly similar factors that were not significantly different when Harmon's psi congruence coefficient was used. The two groups were combined, and the combined analysis produced an almost identical factor structure, which produced three factors. These were interpreted as learning and recall of novel material, attention and concentration, and orientation and long-established verbal information. The analyses that included the WAIS and demographic data were again similar and were again combined. The combined analysis was similar to both of the separate analyses and produced three factors, which were interpreted as intellectual ability, verbal–performance discrepancy, and age. Kear-Colwell

(1973) concluded that the factor structure of the WMS was identical in subjects with confirmed lesions and in subjects without confirmed lesions. Together, these three factors accounted for 77% of the variance in the WMS. Kear-Colwell (1977) attempted a replication, in which he again found three factors that, when compared by use of the Harmon psi coefficient, were similar to the factors in the original study.

One of the factors extracted in the analysis that used demographic data was age. This finding raises the possibility that the factor structure of the WMS is influenced by age. In order to investigate this question, Arbit and Zagar (1979) used a data set of 2,500 hospitalized and nonhospitalized patients with suspected neurological disorders. There were 1,322 males and 1,178 females. The subjects were divided into three groups on the basis of age (13–39, 40–59, and 60–88 years). In each group, both the males and females were divided into two randomly assigned groups, for a total of 16 samples. The analyses performed were principal components, with oblique rotation, and an eigenvalue criterion of .92 for factor extraction. In each analysis except for the 60- to 88-year-old group, similar solutions of two factors were obtained. The differences between the solutions in the above studies may be related to differences in the types of analyses conducted: oblique versus varimax rotation (Sawicki & Golden, 1984a) and the scree test versus the eigenvalue criterion for the extraction of factors (Franzen & Golden, 1984a).

Dye (1982) performed a factor analysis on 99 older males (average age, 63.43 years). The type of factor analysis was not reported, but the rotation method (varimax) and the factor extraction criterion (eigenvalues > 1.0) were reported. The three obtained factors were interpreted as general retentiveness, attention and concentration, and orientation. The author concluded that the factor structure of the WMS is indeed stable over age. However, several caveats must be issued before such a conclusion can be reached. First, the sample size was probably too small to allow much confidence in the stability of the solution. Second, the method of factor analysis differed from that of the earlier studies, so that comparisons are difficult, at best. Third, no similar concurrent analysis was conducted on younger age groups with which to compare these results.

Skilbeck and Woods (1980) conducted two parallel factor analyses. One was on a sample of 150 neurological inpatients, and the second was on a sample of 156 geriatric subjects. Both times, the method used was principal-factor analysis with oblimin rotation, and the scree test was used for the number of factors. The neurological patient sample yielded three factors, which were interpreted as learning–recall, attention–concentration, and information–orientation, similar to the earlier analyses of neurological patient analyses. The geriatric sample yielded three factors, which were interpreted as learning–recall, attention–concentration, and visual–short-term memory. With the use of Harmon's psi coefficient, the first two geriatric factors were congruent with the first two factors of the neurological sample; however, the third factor was not congruent. The safest conclusion in considering all of these studies together is that the factor structure of the WMS does change with age, especially after 60.

Other characteristics of the sample may also influence the factor structure of the WMS. Kear-Colwell and Heller (1978) attempted to replicate the earlier results found in neurological inpatients in a normal sample of 116 subjects. They found a three-factor solution that did not replicate the earlier solutions. When they forced a four-factor solution, they found that the first, second, and fourth factors roughly agreed with the earlier solutions. They concluded that the factor structure of the WMS was stable, a statement that is not borne out by the data. Age and neurological status are two variables that can affect the structure.

Ernst, Warner, Morgan, Townes, Eiler, and Coppel (1986) investigated the factor structure of the WMS in a sample of 70 psychiatric inpatients. They used principal-factors analysis with varimax rotation on the raw data of scores from the delayed-recall variant of the WMS. This procedure resulted in a four-factor solution. The first two factors were interpreted as attention–concentration and rote memory. The third and fourth factors were labeled minor factors and were not interpreted. The rote memory factor appeared to be similar to earlier factors labeled *retentiveness*.

VALIDITY

Just as there has been little direct research on the reliability of the WMS, there has been little direct research on the validity of the WMS. From an examination of the instrument, arguments regarding its construct validity can be raised. Although it supposedly measures memory as a whole, the WMS is seemingly weighted toward the assessment of verbal memory. Of the seven subtests, all but one (Visual Reproduction) depend heavily on verbal ability and verbal memory. There are no tests of delayed memory or of memory with interference. The existence of the MQ begs the question of whether memory is actually a unitary construct. Can there be deficits in verbal memory but not in visual memory? Is memory always impaired as a whole? These questions need to be addressed before there can be a reasonable clinical interpretation of the WMS.

Originally, Wechsler saw the WMS as a test of organic impairment when used in conjunction with the Wechsler–Bellevue (at first) and later with the Wechsler Adult Intelligence Scale. The MQ was developed to have the same meaning as the IQ. It was supposed to represent the memory ability of an individual in comparison to the memory ability of other people of roughly the same age. An individual was assumed to have roughly the same IQ as MQ. If there was a discrepancy between the two scores (e.g., if IQ was sufficiently higher than MQ) then a memory deficit was present. Additionally, it was thought that all brain damage would result in memory impairment and, as a consequence, would result in a large IQ-MQ discrepancy.

The diagnostic validity of the IQ-MQ split has not been supported by studies in the literature. MQ was found to be slightly, but not significantly lower than IQ in a group of mixed neurological patients. Additionally, the same IQ-MQ pattern was found in the normal subjects who served as controls in the study (Parker, 1957). Cohen (1950) had earlier reported similar results, but without a control group. Fields (1971) also reported a failure to support this clinical interpretation guide in a sample of 126 neurological patients. Norton (1979) examined IQ-MQ split in 95 neurologically normal and 87 abnormal patients who had been referred for neuropsychological evaluation. He found no relationship between the IQ-MQ split and the eventual finding of neurological abnormality as defined by the results of noninvasive neurodiagnostic techniques. McCara (1953) examined the MQ-IQ split in adults of average and superior intelligence and found that the size of the split was related to IQ. The subjects in the superior group (mean IQ = 134.4) had a significantly larger MQ-IQ split than did the subjects in the average IQ group (mean IQ = 105.3).

Bachrach and Mintz (1974) examined the usefulness of the WMS in separating individuals whom neurologists had diagnosed as impaired from individuals who had not been so diagnosed. These authors found that, in a discriminant function analysis, the seven subtest scores were able to discriminate between the two groups of subjects. Unfortunately, the authors did not report the percentage of correct and incorrect classifications that resulted from the application of the discriminant function, nor did they attempt a cross-validation; both kinds of information are necessary for us to judge the accuracy of the variables in discriminating between the two groups (Franzen & Golden, 1984b). An interesting result of this study is the fact that the Visual Reproduction subtest alone had a zero-order correlation that was almost identical to the multiple correlation relating all of the WMS subtest scores and group membership. This finding indicates that nearly all of the discriminatory power in the WMS is actually contained in the Visual Reproduction subtest. The limited sample size (n = 84) and the lack of cross-validation, not to mention the lack of information regarding accuracy, make it impossible for us to comment on the validity of the WMS in this study.

Kljajic (1975) examined the accuracy of detecting organicity in a sample of 19 neurologically impaired and 18 neurologically nonimpaired subjects, using two different formulas for the interpretation of WMS scale scores, and reported a 70% accuracy rate. The need for cross-validation is obvious because of the small sample. Prigatano (1977) examined the utility of the WMS in making a diagnosis of organicity when the IQ-MQ split was used, when the equations suggested by Kljajic (1975) were used, and when systems that were derived from the results of factor analysis were used. His sample contained 31 mixed brain-dysfunction patients and 26 matched controls. He concluded that there was no support for the use of the WMS in diagnosing brain impairment when any of the methods were used.

Although he did not use either the split or any of the other methods for using the WMS to detect brain dysfunction, it is useful to consider two published reports by Black. Black (1973a) found slightly lower but not statistically significant scores on the WMS for 100 subjects with penetrating missile wounds to the head when they were compared with 50 normal subjects. Black (1974a) compared the WMS scores of 50 subjects with closed-head injuries and 50 subjects with penetrating missile wounds and found that those with closed-head injuries had significantly more impaired scores on the WMS. This finding is an indication that the WMS is not sensitive to brain impairment in general but is sensitive to certain forms of brain damage. Further evidence is found in Kear-Colwell and Heller (1980) and in Brooks (1976); both reported significantly impaired WMS performance following closed-head injury.

If IQ and MQ do not actually differ much following brain damage, do they measure the same thing? Fields (1971) reported a correlation of .83 between the two Wechsler quotients, indicating a fair amount of shared variance. McCara (1953, as reported in Prigatano, 1978) found that, although IQ is highly related to MQ at normal IQ levels, the relationship deteriorates as IQ increases. Fish and Sinkel (1980) correlated IQ with MQ in 10 alcoholic subjects and 10 matched normals. Each of the subjects was administered the WMS and the WAIS twice, with a 1-month interval. For the normal group, the correlation coefficient was .87 on the first administration and .93 on the second administration. For the alcoholics, the correlation coefficient was .58 on the first administration and .61 on the second. The authors concluded that the WMS measures an ability separate from IQ in alcoholics, but not in normals.

Libb and Coleman (1971) correlated the WMS, the Quick Test, and the Revised Beta with the WAIS in a sample of 30 clients from a rehabilitation center. Sixteen of the clients were diagnosed as retarded. The WMS correlated .80, the Quick Test correlated .84, and the Revised Beta correlated .83. Because both of the other tests are used for estimates of IQ, it would seem from these results that the WMS may actually measure IQ. Similar results have been reported by other researchers (Black, 1973b; Ivinskis *et al.*, 1971; Kear-Colwell, 1973). An important point needs to be raised here: Even though the correlation between MQ and IQ may be .80, that still means that 36% of the variance in the WMS and the WAIS is not shared.

Because there is not a larger correlation between IQ and MQ, it appears that each instrument offers information that is independent of the other. Larrabee, Kane, and Schuck (1983) conducted a factor analysis of the WMS and the WAIS combined in order to address the question of unique information from each. They used a maximum-likelihood solution with orthogonally rotated factors. They found a factor structure that replicated earlier factor-analysis research into the WMS and the WAIS separately. The factors were interpreted as perceptual organization, verbal comprehension, attention and concentration (with loadings from both WAIS and WMS subtests), verbal learning and recall, and orientation and information. They concluded that the previously reported correlations between the WMS and the WAIS were the result of shared procedures (the Digit Span) and a shared factor (attention and concentration). The discrimination of IQ from MQ is important in the evaluation of construct validity. However, it is also necessary to demonstrate that the variance not shared with intelligence actually does measure memory.

THE WMS AS A MEASURE OF SHORT-TERM VERBAL MEMORY

By face validity, the WMS is a measure of short-term verbal memory. The only subtest that does not ostensibly tap verbal memory is the Visual Reproduction subtest. There is no test of memory with interference or of delayed memory. However, face validity is not sufficient to recommend the instrument for clinical use; it must demonstrate empirical manifestations of validity as well. As a test of verbal short-term memory, we would expect the WMS to be sensitive to disturbances of physiology and structure in the deep posterior left hemisphere and to be sensitive to disturbances as a whole.

Alcoholism is a disorder that is often associated with memory disorders. In a study to test the effect of alcoholism and a history of blackouts, Tarter and Schneider (1976) examined the effect of blackouts on memory function by using the WMS, consonant trigrams, the retention of temporal sequencing, and Hebb's number-recall test. There was no relation between low- and high-incidence blackout subjects and any of the measures. This study is very difficult to interpret, as it seems to suggest not only that the WMS is insensitive to memory deficits in alcoholics, but that so are several memory tests. Clearly, a replication is needed in order to facilitate an understanding of these results.

Another disorder that is associated with memory deficits is Huntington's disease. In a sample of 22 patients with advanced Huntington's, 6 patients with recently diagnosed Huntington's, and 42 normal controls, it was found that the advanced Huntington's subjects demonstrated deficits on several measures of neuropsychological functioning, but the subjects with recently diagnosed Huntington's demonstrated deficits only in memory (Butters, Sax, Montgomery, & Tarlow, 1978).

Rausch, Lieb, and Crandall (1978) correlated WAIS and WMS measures with EEG spike activity in 12 patients with intractable temporal-lobe epilepsy. Total spike activity was correlated with IQ, but lateralization of the spike activity was correlated with MQ. This finding is consistent with the hypothesis that the WMS is sensitive to dysfunctions in deep posterior dominant-hemisphere activity.

Earlier, we discussed the nonsignificant findings in the attempts to relate penetrating missile wounds to WMS scores. The lack of positive findings was probably related to the fact that the experimental group of missile-wound victims was a heterogeneous group in terms of the location of the wound. When separate groups are used for right- and left-hemisphere missile wounds, very different results ensue. Black (1973b) found significant deficits on the WMS when left-hemisphere missile-wound subjects were compared with normal controls, but not when right-hemisphere missile-wound subjects were compared with normals. Bornstein (1982a) examined the relation between location of lesion and performance on the WMS. Although there were no significant differences in MQ or IQ–MQ split between the two groups, a pattern analysis of the subtests demonstrated significant differences. The left-hemisphere subjects performed more poorly on the Logical Memory and the Paired Associates subtests, and the right-hemisphere subjects performed more poorly on the Visual Reproduction subtest. These findings once more underline the insensitivity of the MQ as compared to the sensitivity of the subtests themselves.

Another methodology with which to observe the relation between hemispheric function and WMS performance is to study the effects of unilateral and bilateral ECT. Jackson (1978) reported that ECT in general produced memory deficits. These deficits were temporary and tended to disappear in a few days. Bilateral ECT produced the largest effect on WMS performance, unilateral left ECT the next largest, and unilateral right ECT the smallest effect, although all three produced deficits in comparisons with a control group. Following ECT, the unilateral left ECT group demonstrated the best performance. Fraser and Glass (1980) reported that both unilateral right ECT and bilateral ECT eventually improved memory to the same degree. Unfortunately, there was no attempt to examine the effects of unilateral left ECT. Likewise, Stromgren (1973) and Stromgren, Christensen, and Fromholt (1976) reported that unilateral right ECT eventually improved WMS scores, without a comparison with unilateral left ECT. When memory was assessed the day following the last ECT treatment, unilateral right ECT improved MQ scores, whereas bilateral ECT decreased MQ scores. There was no information on recovery on follow-up.

ATTEMPTS AT IMPROVING THE WMS

Many criticisms have been leveled at the WMS. Many of these criticisms have been related to issues that have been discussed in this chapter. Specifically, criticisms have been directed at the adequacy of the standardization sample, the reliability of the instrument, and the validity of the scores obtained. Some of the criticisms have also been directed at the adequacy of the scoring system. For example, the manual (Wechsler & Stone, 1973) states that the Logical Memory section should be scored for each reiteration of an idea as marked on the protocol. Unfortunately, the marked ideas often contain more than one word, and confusion results when, for example, the subject correctly reiterates the first name of the story's protagonist but gives incorrectly the last name of the protagonist. Sweet and Wysocki (1982) suggested that the ideas be scored for equivalence of meaning rather than for verbatim performance. These authors presented a table of acceptable equivalents and stated that the interscorer reliability for their scoring system is .97. This is good start in the right direction, but it may be inadequate to remedy other aspects of the WMS that have been criticized.

Osborne and Davis (1978) attempted another improvement on the WMS by suggesting that the subtests be given standardized scores. By examining the standard deviation and the means of Mental Control, Logical Memory, Visual Reproduction, and Associate Learning reported in Davis and Swenson (1970), these authors gave formulas for calculating standardized scores with a mean of 10 and a standard deviation of 3 from raw scores on the subtests. Unfortunately, there are no data on the usefulness of these scores.

Russell's Revision of the WMS

Russell (1975a) identified some of the shortcomings of the WMS. These shortcomings were partly based on the assumptions underlying the construction of the battery. One of those assumptions is that memory is a unitary construct that has verbal and visual implications, but not verbal and visual components. The ramification of this assumption is that memory deficits are deficits in both verbal and visual memory, and that a deficit in one area is always associated with a deficit in the other. Second, the WMS assumes that brain damage is a unitary construct that can be determined by a single test. Citing both experimental work on memory and factor analyses of the WMS, Russell concluded that a more precise, multidimensional scoring system for the WMS would increase its utility.

After consideration of the factor analysis studies and the validity studies of the WMS, Russell (1975a) decided on two subtests for the WMS: Verbal (consisting of the Logical Memory subtest of the WMS) and Figural (consisting if the Visual Reproduction subtest of the WMS). In addition, Russell added what he termed a long-term memory factor, although it could more accurately be termed a *delayed-memory factor*. This factor is produced by asking the subjects to recall the material in the test one-half hour following the original administration. Six scores are available: short-term verbal, long-term verbal, the difference between the two, short-term figural, long-term figural, and the difference between the two.

Russell (1975a) administered his revised WMS to 30 normals and 75 brain-damaged inpatients at a VA medical center. When corrected for test length by the Spearman–Brown formula, the split-half reliability of the six scores obtained ranged from .88 for the long-term verbal score to .51 for the figural difference score. No other forms of reliability were reported in this study.

The validity of the Revised WMS (RWMS) was assessed by examining the effect of an organic diagnosis on the RWMS subtest scores. The organics had significantly worse performance on each of the subtests. Next, the subtest scores were correlated with each subject's Average Impairment Rating (AIR), which was derived from the results of an examination with the Halstead–Reitan Neuropsychological Battery. The correlation coefficients ranged from − .49 to − .76, indicating moderate relationships between memory scores and general brain impairment. When the same relations were assessed separately for brain-damaged subjects and normal subjects, it was observed that the correlations were always lower for the normal subjects (Russell, 1975a).

Using the same sample, Russell (1975a) translated the raw subtest scores on the RWMS to a 5-point scale by transforming both AIR and RWMS scores to z scores and using the AIR 5-point scale as a reference for the determination of the 5 points in the RWMS scale. Drawing the lateralized subjects from the original sample of brain-damaged individuals, Russell examined the effect of a lateralized diagnosis on the subtest scores and concluded that the subtest scores could be used, in conjunction with each other, to lateralize damage. He further concluded that long-term memory subtests were more sensitive to lateralized damage than were the short-term subtests.

This was a noble effort to improve the utility of the WMS, but it fell short of its goal for several reasons. The standardization sample of 105 subjects was even less sufficient than Wechsler's sample of 200 subjects. The fact that Russell's study was conducted in a VA setting means that only 7% of the subjects were female; thus, the applicability of the RWMS to a broad population is severely limited. Most fatally, all of the above analyses were conducted on the same sample of 105 subjects. We can have very little confidence in the generalizability of the results beyond the sample. Sound scale-construction methodology dictates that separate samples be used at each step of the study.

Further research would be needed before any conclusions regarding the utility of this instrument could be reached. Along those lines, Brinkman, Largen, Gerganoff, and Pomara (1983) provided evidence that the subtest scale scores significantly differentiated between 31 healthy elderly and 25 elderly with diagnoses of probable Alzheimer's disease.

In an attempt to provide additional evidence regarding the RWMS, McCarty, Logue, Power, Ziesat, and Rosenstiel (1980) administered two forms of the RWMS to 25 female residents of a nursing home for the elderly. The two forms of the RWMS were composed from the alternate forms of the WMS. The alternate-form reliability estimates ranged from .74 for short-term verbal scores to .40 for verbal difference scores. However, because of the differences in the level of scores for individual subjects, it appears that a comparison of the two forms should not consist of raw scores.

Following up on this study, Keesler, Schultz, Sciara, and Friedenberg (1984) administered the alternate forms of the RWMS in counterbalanced order. The subjects for these two studies were drawn from two different populations: a group of 48 inpatient alcoholics and a group of 60 normal volunteers drawn from the staff of a private psychiatric hospital. Consistent with the results of McCarty *et al.* (1980), these authors found that these subjects performed better on the Immediate Figural Recall measure of Form II than they did on the same measure on Form I. In addition, the normal subjects performed better on the Immediate Semantic Recall and the Delayed Semantic Recall measures of Form I than they did on the same measures on Form II.

These results have two implications for the RWMS. The first implication is that the use of the alternate forms of the RWMS to perform serial testing is likely to eventuate in inaccurate conclusions regarding the improvement or the deterioration of the subject's memory, depending on which form is administered first. The second implication involves the danger of making even slight changes in a test without renorming the revised form. One should not assume that the equivalence of the alternate forms of the WMS will carry over to the revised scoring system of Russell. Instead, what is needed is an evaluation of the equivalence of the two revised forms. In considering the differences in scores on the two forms, Schultz, Keesler, Friedenberg, and Sciara (1984) recommended two possible solutions. Their first suggestion was to raise the scores obtained from the form with the lower performance by the percentage by which the stimuli for the two forms were judged to be more difficult. In other words, they suggested that the score obtained on the Immediate Figural Memory scale of Form I be increased by 10%. Although such a linear transformation of scores would not affect the distribution of the scores obtained by a sample or affect the reliability of Form I, it would have effects on the validity of the interpretation of the obtained scores. Therefore, we can not recommend the practice.

The second recommendation of Schultz *et al.* (1984) was to reverse the stimuli across forms, that is, to administer Figure 1 from Form I and Figure 2 from Form II, and so on. This suggestion would result in even more undesirable effects regarding the resultant test. The consequence would be two brand new tests with unknown psychometric and clinical properties. Although it is possible that this approach might result in equivalent forms, that conclusion cannot be reached without extensive empirical investigation. Before the appearance of data in favor of this suggested revision, it is recommended that clinicians also refrain from this practice.

A more direct method of dealing with this problem would be to convert the raw scores obtained on the two forms to standardized scores by means of a linear transformation. This transformation would not affect the reliability of the instrument and would permit a comparison of the scores obtained from Form I with the scores obtained from Form II.

There is no study that examines the structure of the RWMS by itself. Russell (1982) did examine the structure in conjunction with the WAIS and the Halstead–Reitan. He interpreted the factors as immediate verbal memory, recent verbal memory, recent memory, figural learning, and verbal learning storage. It is difficult to interpret the results of this analysis because of the inclusion of the WAIS and the Halstead–Reitan, and because of the existence of a substantial loading of nonmemory tasks on factors that Russell interpreted as memory factors.

A few validation studies exist for the RWMS. Using an analysis-of-variance methodology, Logue and Wyrick (1979) reported that the RWMS discriminated between 29 normal aged and 29 demented aged. Prigatano, Parsons, Wright, Levin, and Hawryluk (1983) reported that 100 chronic obstructive-pulmonary-disease patients performed significantly worse on the RWMS than did 25 normal controls. Crosson and Trautt (1981) presented case study evidence that the RWMS is a sensitive indicator of recovery from brain-stem infarction. These are all indications that the RWMS may be a useful instrument for the assessment of memory functions. However, much more work, such as the elderly norms reported by Haaland, Linn, Hunt, and Goodwin (1981), is needed before the RWMS can be recommended for clinical use. Evidence supporting the need for further work, especially in establishing a normative base, can be found in Crosson, Hughes, Roth, and Monkowski (1984), who found that, when Russell's norms were applied to data from previous studies, a large proportion of subjects were misclassified as memory-impaired, when the Logical Memory subscale, but not the Visual Memory subscale, was used. Wallace (1984) presented normative data for the Russell revision of the WMS, but all of the data had been previously published in 10 studies. Wallace (1984) therefore represented a valuable gathering of the available data in a single location but did not address the concerns voiced above. The Logical Memory and the Visual Reproduction subtests are still based on a sample of only 66 normal subjects, who ranged in age from 10 to 94.

CONCLUSIONS

The Wechsler Memory Scale is a widely used instrument that has little empirical evidence to support its clinical application. Originally construed as a unidimensional measure of brain damage when the MQ is used in conjunction with the IQ, it has been shown to be neither a good index of brain damage in general nor a single indicator of memory impairment. Although it has failed to stand up to its initial conceptualization, there is evidence that it may be useful as a measure of particular forms of memory impairment. There is much work to be done before it can be recommended for clinical use. First, a more objective scoring system must be developed. Second, information regarding its reliability, including test–retest, alternate-forms, and internal consistency, must be obtained. Third, data on the performance of the instrument must be gathered from a large and representative normative sample. Alternately, data could be gathered on its performance in special populations. And fourth, its validity must be assessed in its intended settings.

WECHSLER MEMORY SCALE–REVISED

In 1987, the long-awaited revision of the Wechsler Memory Scale was published (Wechsler, 1987). The Wechsler Memory Scale–Revised (WMS-R) has several intended improvements over the original WMS. The WMS-R has age-related norms for nine age groups: 16–17 years, 18–19 years (estimated), 20–24 years, 25–34 years (estimated), 35–44 years, 45–54 years (estimated), 55–64 years, 65–69 years, and 70–74 years. Because of criticisms regarding the loss of information in using a single memory quotient (MQ), the WMS-R has five composite scores: General Memory, Attention/Concentration, Verbal Memory, Visual Memory, and Delayed Memory. Each of these composite scores has a mean of 100 and a standard deviation of 15. There were also new subtests added in order to obtain nonverbal information (related to figural, spatial, and visual associative memory) analogous to the verbal information obtained on the original WMS. A delayed recall procedure was added, and scoring procedures were revised in order to make them more reliable. The items related to Information and Orientation were deleted from the computation of index scores because of the controversy regarding whether they reflected memory or not.

The scorable subtests of the WMS-R consist of Mental Control, Figural Memory, Logical Memory, Visual Paired Associates, Verbal Paired Associates, Visual Reproduction, Digit Span, Visual Memory Span, and delayed procedures for the Logical Memory, Visual Paired Associates, Verbal Paired Associates, and Visual Reproduction subtests. The scores for the Digit Span and Visual Memory Span subtests can be converted to percentiles by age, separately for the forward and the backward procedures. Percentile equivalents are also available for the Logical Memory and the Visual Reproduction subtests separately by age for both the original administration and the delayed recall procedures.

Normative Information

A nationally stratified sample of 316 individuals was used to standardize the scoring system. There were approximately 50 individuals in each of the six age groups mentioned above. The sample was approximately one-half male and one-half female. The racial composition of the sample was proportionate to information derived from the 1980 census. Subjects were stratified across four geographic regions according to the 1980 census data. Subjects were also stratified across three educational groups: 0–11 years, 12 years, and 13 or more years of education. The number of subjects in each educational group was proportional within age groups, based on 1980 census data. Finally, each subject was administered all or a portion of the WAIS-R in order to help ensure that the distribution of IQ of subjects in each age group was equivalent to the distribution of IQ in the general population. Scoring weights for the arithmetic combination of subtests were decided upon by comparing the methods of simple unweighted combination, weighting the subtests proportional to the inverse of the standard deviation of each subtest, and weighting the subtests inversely proportional to the standard error of measurement of the subtests. The comparison was based on the criteria of optimal reliability and maximum discrimination between a normal sample and a clinical sample. The best overall method of combination was based on the third method (inverse proportion of standard error of measurement).

Reliability

The manual provides test–retest reliability information for the Mental Control subtest ($r = .51$) as well as for both the initial ($r = .58$) and the delayed recall ($r = .58$) procedures of the Visual Paired Associates subtest and the initial ($r = .60$) and the delayed recall ($r = .41$) procedures of the Verbal Paired Associates subtest. Internal consistency reliability estimates are provided for the Figural Memory ($r = .44$), the initial Logical Memory ($r = .74$), the delayed recall of Logical Memory ($r = .75$), the initial Visual Reproduction ($r = .59$), the delayed recall Visual Reproduction ($r = .46$), the Digit Span ($r = .88$), and the Visual Memory Span subtest ($r = .81$). The intertest period ranged from 4 to 6 weeks.

Because the scoring criteria for most of the subtests are objective, interscorer reliability was computed only for the Logical Memory and Visual Reproduction subtests. Two trained scorers rated a set of sixty protocols. The interscorer reliability coefficient was .99 for Logical Memory and .97 for Visual Reproduction.

The manual reports the standard error of measurement as ranging from 4.86 for the Attention/Concentration index to 8.47 for the Visual Memory index. In addition, the standard error of difference for three pairwise comparisons were computed and reported in the manual. For comparing General Memory with Attention/Concentration, the value is 16.38. For comparing Verbal Memory with Visual Memory, the value is 21.89. For comparing General Memory with Delayed Memory, the value is 19.75.

Validity

The manual reports the results of a principal components factor analysis conducted on the standardization sample in which two factors seemed to emerge; a General Memory and Learning factor and an Attention/Concentration factor. Principal components factor analysis of a mixed clinical sample provided similar results. Roid, Prifitera, and Ledbetter (1988) reported the results of a confirmatory factor analysis on the data from the normative sample, indicating that the two-factor solution provided the best fit to the data.

Bornstein and Chelune (1988) subsequently reported a series of principal components factor analysis of data derived from 434 patients referred for neuropsychological evaluation. When the initial administration subtest scores were included, a two factor solution similar to that obtained with the standardization sample was obtained. When WAIS-R VIQ and PIQ were included in the analysis, the factor structure of the clinical sample remained unchanged; however, in the normal sample, the two factors switched places with the attentional factor being extracted first. When the delayed recall subtests were included in the analysis with the initial administration subtests, a three-factor solution emerged; verbal memory, nonverbal memory, and attention. When PIQ and VIQ were included in the analysis, they tended to load on the third factor. Apparently, the factor structure of the WMS-R differs slightly in a normal versus a clinical sample.

Contrasted groups designs were used to evaluate the validity of the WMS-R. There were significant differences between the standardization sample and the clinical memory impaired samples of mixed psychiatric, schizophrenic, alcoholic, closed head injury, stroke, tumor, seizure disorder, multiple sclerosis, and neurotoxin exposed patients (Wechsler, 1987). Subsequent reports have focused on patients with Alzheimer's disease and Huntington's disease (Butters *et al.*, 1988), patients with multiple sclerosis (Fisher, 1988), Alcoholics (Ryan & Lewis, 1988) and patients exposed to industrial solvents (Crossom & Wiens, 1988).

Of particular note is a study by Chelune and Bornstein (1988). These researchers investigated WMS-R performance in patients with unilateral lesions. They found that although there was a significant multivariate difference between the two groups of patients, there was a significant univariate difference only for the Verbal Memory score. On the other hand, comparison among subtests in the same individuals indicated that patients with left-hemisphere lesions performed better on the subtests of verbal memory than on the subtests of visual memory, and that patients with right-hemisphere lesions performed better on the subtests of visual memory than on the subtests of verbal memory.

The one concurrent validity study published to date investigated the relation between the WMS-R and the California Verbal Learning Test

(CVLT). This study (Delis, Cullum, Butters, & Cairns, 1988) indicated that there are significant correlations between the two tests. There were a total of 460 correlations computed, of which 341 were significant at the .01 level.

Criticisms

The WMS-R is a vast improvement over its predecessor. However, there are a few shortcomings in the WMS-R. One potentially serious problem is the fact that scores bottom out at 50; therefore, there is likely to be over-estimation of memory function in individuals with marked or severe memory deficits. There is no verbal recognition test even though there is a test of visual recognition. Although the transformation of raw scores to standardized scores is stratified by age group, there are no normative data available for subjects in the age groups 18–19 years, 25–34 years, and 45–54 years, and scores for these subjects are consequently estimated. Finally, the WMS-R is not standardized for subjects older than 74 years. This last point is unfortunate because older individuals are overrepresented in the population of people with memory complaints.

Conclusions

Despite its drawbacks and its relative youth, the WMS-R is one of the best instruments available for the overall evaluation of memory functions. It has already generated a fair amount of research interest which is likely to increase multiplicatively. It may very well become the standard for the clinical evaluation of nonseverely memory impaired, nonelderly patients.

Tests of Memory

MEMORY FOR DESIGNS TEST

The Memory for Designs (MFD) Test was written in 1946 and revised in 1960 (Graham & Kendall, 1960). It is a series of designs that the subject examines and then draws from memory. It is suggested for use in subjects older than 8 years. The original derivation sample consisted of 140 subjects equally divided between brain-damaged and normal control subjects. The brain-damaged subjects had a variety of diagnoses. No information is given regarding the ages of the subjects. The two authors evaluated the test's protocols separately for each of the 140 subjects; the interscorer reliability coefficient was .99. Howard and Shoemaker (1954) reported an interscorer reliability of 93% agreement with less sophisticated scorers. Riege, Kelly, and Klane (1981) reported an interscorer reliability coefficient of .82.

In the original derivation sample, the split-half reliability was reported as .89 (Graham & Kendall, 1960). In a sample of 32 children and 180 adults, the test–retest reliability was .89 when the retest occurred after less than 24 hours. (The retest intervals varied from immediately afterward to approximately 24 hours afterward.) However, there was a consistently lower score on the second test occasion, indicating the presence of practice effects. The difference was not significant, but it was most marked in the brain-damaged sample. This issue needs to be further explored before the MFD can be recommended as a serial test instrument for a brain-impaired population.

The original validation evaluation examined the difference in scores between the 70 brain-impaired subjects and the 70 normal controls. There was a significant difference in scores between the two groups, a finding that was replicated in a sample of 168 normal controls and 33 brain-impaired subjects. There were no differences due to the type of impairment, nor were there any differences due to anterior versus posterior location of the lesion. There were no significant differences between the performance of neurologically impaired subjects and that of psychotic subjects. However, the authors recommended retesting in order to differentiate these two groups, as organic subjects can be expected to improve and psychiatric subjects can be expected to present variable performances. This recommendation is in need of empirical validation. As well as being sensitive to psychiatric diagnoses, scores on the MFD are significantly related to age (Riege *et al.*, 1981).

Grundvig, Needham, and Ajax (1970) compared different strategies of presentation and scoring. They found that the most accurate classification of 114 subjects into three groups of increasing neurological impairment occurred with the use of the original Graham–Kendall scoring system, when the stimuli were presented tachistocoptically.

Marsh and Hirsch (1982) administered the MFD and the Benton Visual Retention Test to 100 subjects who had been referred for evaluation. The Benton Visual Retention Test misclassified 29% of the impaired subjects. The MFD misclassification was much larger: 61% of the impaired subjects. The problem with false negatives in screening instruments is widespread; however, Marsh and Hirsch's data (1982) cast serious doubt on the utility of the MFD. Black (1974b) reported similar problems with false negative results in evaluating subjects with penetrating head injuries. Kljajic (1976) examined the MFD by using a sample of 15 impaired and 15 nonimpaired subjects. The impairment had been determined from the results of pneumoencephalography or EEG. The two groups showed a large amount of overlap in scores, resulting in no significant differences.

In order to assess the efficiency of the MFD in separating organically impaired psychiatric inpatients from psychiatric inpatients who were not organically impaired and from normals, Shearn, Berry, and Fitzgibbons (1974) administered the instrument to inpatients at the Institute for Living. The patients had been rated as suspected organics or not, both at admission and 4 months later. The ratings had been performed by the attending physicians for each subject and were based on clinical judgment. The MFD scores, taken at admission, did not separate the groups at admission, but did separate the suspected organics from the psychiatric patients who were not suspected of organicity and the normals after the 4-month interval. The authors concluded that the MFD was an effective predictor of organicity judgments after 4 months but not at admission. It is difficult to see the utility of being able to predict clinical judgment when the purpose of testing is to provide objective information.

Korman and Blumberg (1963) compared the MFD scores of 52 patients with those of 40 matched subjects (no mention is made of the 12 patients who were unmatched). The authors administered the Trials Test, the Spiral Aftereffect Test, the Bender–Gestalt, the MFD, and the Vocabulary subtest of the WAIS. They found that, when they used an optimum cutoff point (not the value reported in the MFD manual), they were able to achieve a 90% accuracy rate, which was the highest on all of the tests evaluated.

There is an important consideration in assessing the utility of these experimental results for clinical practice: Although some of these studies report reasonable hit rates, they do so with different cutoff points. Generally, when the cutoff points suggested by the manual are used, there are many misclassifications. However, manipulation of the cutoff points results in more accurate classifications, and each study reports a different optimum cutoff point. In order to be useful in clinical settings, there must be a standardized cutoff point with reasonable accuracy, or the MFD must remain a research instrument.

PAIRED ASSOCIATES

The use of paired associates in assessing learning and memory has a long history in laboratory research. David Wechsler included this procedure when he devised his Wechsler Memory Scales. The Randt Memory Test is another clinical instrument that uses a paired-associates procedure. This type of procedure has also been used in clinical research into memory deficits.

For example, Ottosson (1960) developed a memory test to evaluate the memory changes associated with electroconvulsive therapy (ECT). This test has three components, one of which is a paired-associates task. There are two alternate forms in the Swedish language. The Ottosson test uses both immediate recall of the pairs and a delayed recall. In a sample of 120 psychiatric subjects, Ottosson reported Kuder–Richardson (K-R) 20 values of .84 and .69 for the two forms in the immediate-recall condition and .87 and .82 in the delayed-recall condition. In a further evaluation of this instrument, Cronhom and Ottosson (1963) administered the test to 112 psychiatric patients. They found K-R 20 values equivalent to the first study but also reported significant differences between the values obtained on the two forms by the same subjects. In order to assess the concurrent validity, they calculated point biserial correlations between values on the test and membership in a group that had received ECT or in a group with a similar diagnosis that had not received ECT. The resulting values were .89 and .62 for the two forms. Apparently, the two forms are not exactly equivalent. In a modification of the Fiske–Campbell multitrait–multimethod matrix methodology, Cronham and Ottosson reported higher correlations between the immediate-recall condition of the paired associates and two other immediate-recall procedures and the relevant delayed-recall conditions of the same procedures. However, conclusions must be limited because of the modifications imposed on the method. Other types of reliability and validity must also be investigated. Sternberg and Jarvik (1976) translated the test into English and shortened it. These authors did not investigate the properties of the test, but they did find that performance on their modification of the test varied with the degree of depressive symptomatology.

The paired-associates procedure potentially gives the clinician information about the type of memory deficit manifested by a given client. Because the Wechsler version includes both pairs with high *a priori* associative value and pairs with low associative value, a difference in performance is possible. Using this idea and Tulving's concept (1972) of semantic versus episodic memory, Wilson, Bacon, Kaszniak, and Fox (1982) investigated memory in 39 senile dementia patients. They concluded that the pairs with low associative value draw on episodic memory alone, and that the pairs with high associative value draw on both episodic and semantic memory.

The construct validity of the paired-associates procedure needs to be carefully evaluated. Although this procedure is often used as a test of memory, it is important to keep in mind that it can also be conceptualized as a test of learning. Lambert (1970) found that scores on a paired-associates procedure could be used to predict scores on vocabulary achievement tests. When a stepwise multiple-regression methodology was used, the score on the paired-associates procedure was entered ahead of SES and the other achievement variables. Rohwer and Lynch (1968) found that retardates performed more poorly on the test than nonretardates, even when the mental age of the subjects was equated across the two groups. Finally, Schwinn and Postman (1967) found that prior exposure to the task improved performance even when different lists were used.

In conclusion, the paired-associates procedure has great potential as a clinical assessment device. However, a standardized form needs to be developed and evaluated in terms of the above considerations.

TRIGRAMS

The use of trigrams (nonsense "words" composed of three letters) has a long history in experimental settings. Because the three-letter combinations are largely without semantic meaning, they can be used in the evaluation of verbal stimuli without the influence of contextual meaning. Not all trigrams are without meaning because of the use in our culture of acronyms. Witmer (1935) provided estimates of the association value of various trigram combinations by asking normal subjects to rate the trigrams by the number of associations that could be made. The cultural substrate that provides meaning changes over time. Therefore, Constantini and Blackwood (1968) provided updated tables of assocative value for 343 trigrams. For example, in 1935, few people could generate associations with the trigram *JFK*. After the 1960s, there was an increase in the number of people who made associations with this trigram.

Trigrams have been used in the assessment of immediate and delayed memory. They can be useful in the evaluation of memory decay. Peterson and Peterson (1959) reported that, in an experiment with normal college students, 72% of 48 sets of trigrams were retained after 3 seconds and only 38% were retained after 9 seconds.

Trigrams have also been used in the experimental investigation of unilateral neglect. Heilman, Watson, and Schulman (1974) presented consonant trigrams to either ear of eight subjects with unilateral neglect and concluded that unilateral neglect is the result of an arousal or alerting deficit. DeLuca, Cermak, and Butters (1975) used consonant trigrams and random shapes to investigate memory deficits in patients with Korsakoff's disease. Additionally, Hannay and Malone (1976) used trigrams to assess differences in laterality associated with the sex of the subject.

There are no reliability studies for the trigram procedure, nor are there guides for the clinical interpretation of the results of an evaluation using trigrams. Milner (1972) stated that deficits in trigram performance are related to the extent of the involvement of the left hippocampus. Samuels, Butters, and Fedio (1972) reported that there were no differences between left-temporal- and right-temporal-lesioned subjects when the trigrams were presented visually. However, when the trigrams were presented auditorally, the left-temporal-lesioned subjects performed significantly worse.

These studies indicate the potential utility of the trigram procedure in clinical settings. However, more information is needed before the procedure can be recommended.

WORD SPAN

Word-span procedures have been a popular means of assessing memory. They are very similar to digit span procedures. In the word-span procedure, a list of words is presented to the subject, and the subject is then asked to repeat the list back to the examiner. Although there is no standardized word-span procedure that stands independently, there are several memory tests that use word-span procedures. These include the Wechsler Memory Scale, the Randt Memory Test, and the Luria–Nebraska Neuropsychological Battery (LNNB). The LNNB has the added twist of asking the subject to predict how many of the seven words she or he expects to remember each time.

Although there are no standardized word-span procedures, there are data to suggest the utility of such a procedure in a neuropsychological evaluation. Basso, Spinnler, Vallar, and Zanobio (1982) suggested that the word-span procedure may be useful in the evaluation of individuals with left-hemisphere damage. However, the data also suggest that a word-span procedure needs to be carefully constructed.

Although Talland (1965a) found no differences in performance on word span across age in subjects who were grouped by decades (20s, 30s, 40s, 50s, and 60s), Kausler and Puckett (1979) found that there was a significant age effect on the length of the word span. Weingartner and Silberman (1982) found that the presence of clinical depression significantly affected performance on a word-span task. Schutz and Keisler (1972) found that there was an interaction between social class and the type of words used in the word-span procedure in children. Children of lower SES performed significantly poorer than other children when the lists in the word span were composed of functors (prepositions and conjunctions), but not when the lists were composed of nouns or verbs. This result was replicated by the Laboratory of Comparative Human Cognition (1976).

Word-span procedures have also been used to investigate the memory deficits involved in certain disorders. Normal individuals remember the words at the beginning and the end of the list better than the words in the middle of the list. The words at the beginning of the list are better remembered because they are entered into long-term memory without proactive inhibition from earlier words. The words at the end of the list are better remembered because they are still in short-term memory when the recall occurs. However, the words in the middle of the list are affected by both retroactive and proactive inhibition. Miller (1971, 1973) used these ideas to investigate the memory deficits involved in Alzheimer's disease. He found that people with Alzheimer's disease remembered the words at the beginning of the list as poorly as the words in the middle of the list. He concluded that the memory deficit associated with Alzheimer's disease involves impairment in the transfer from short- to long-term storage. Oltmanns (1978) used a modified word-span procedure to study attention in schizophrenic and manic subjects and concluded that the attention problems demonstrated by schizophrenic subjects were associated with the thought disorder and not with the recognition and sensory-storage stages of processing.

Although the word-span procedure shows great promise as a clinical assessment technique, the lack of reliability and validity data on the free-standing procedure do not allow it to be recommended. However, when used in a procedure such as the Wechsler Memory Scale, the data regarding that particular instrument should be consulted.

THE REY AUDITORY-VERBAL LEARNING TEST

The Rey Auditory-Verbal Learning Test (AVLT) is a short test of auditory memory that allows the examiner to evaluate immediate recall, repetitive learning, and the influence of interference by the use of two lists of 15 words each. The test was originally normed on French-speaking subjects, but it has become somewhat popular among English-speaking neuro-psychologists. Rey (1964) presented normative data based on a sample of

25 manual laborers, 30 professionals, 47 students, 15 laborers over the age of 70, and 15 professionals over the age of 70. Especially because of the sample sizes, it is important to provide normative data based on English-speaking populations.

Lezak (1983) investigated the test–retest reliability of the AVLT in a sample of 23 young male subjects and reported statistically significant practice effects over intervals that ranged from 6 months to 1 year. Additional information is needed in order to more fully evaluate the reliability of the AVLT. In particular, it will be important to evaluate the stability of the test results in a sample of chronically impaired subjects.

There are two forms of the AVLT: Form A and Form C. Using the discrepancy between scores on the WAIS-R and the WMS, Ryan and Geisser (1986) divided a sample of VA patients into 41 subjects with intact memory and 32 subjects with impaired memory. Forms A and C of the AVLT were administered in counterbalanced order with an interval of 2½ hours. Discriminant function analyses showed similar classification rates in the use of the two forms. Only the sum of scores from Trials I–V significantly contributed to the discriminant function. However, t tests revealed significant differences between the two groups on three variables: the sum of Subtests I–V, the score on subtest VI, and the recognition score. Ryan, Geisser, Randall, and Georgemiller (1986) administered the two forms of the AVLT to a sample of 85 VA patients. Once again, there was a counterbalanced order but with an interval of 140 minutes. The correlations between equivalent subtests ranged from .60 to .71. There were significant differences between the two forms on Trials IV and V, Form A having higher scores in both cases. Clearly, more empirical work is needed before the equivalency of the two forms can be accepted or rejected.

In order to evaluate the utility of the AVLT, Mungas (1983) administered it to five groups of six subjects each: amnesiacs, head trauma victims, schizophrenics, nonpsychotic psychiatric subjects, and subjects with a diagnosis of attention deficit disorder. He found that although the delayed-recall score did not differentiate among the groups, the five-trial initial-word-list procedure did, especially as the number of trials increased. These results are intriguing but are in need of replication with a much larger sample.

There is some evidence that the results of the AVLT may overlap with the results of an intellectual evaluation. Query and Megran (1983) administered the AVLT to 677 Caucasian male VA inpatients, including 23 subjects over the age of 70. There were moderately low correlations between results on the AVLT and level of education. However, the learning score correlated .82 in the subjects between the ages of 30 and 34, and .60 in the subjects between the ages of 50 and 54. An earlier study, Query and Berger (1980), looked at this issue slightly more directly. The AVLT and the WAIS were administered to 49 acutely brain-impaired subjects (mainly victims of trauma and cardiovascular accidents), 40 chronically brain-impaired subjects (mainly alcoholics), and 143 subjects with no evidence of brain impairment. Multiple-regression methodology was used to partial out the influence of age, education, and WAIS FSIQ. The adjusted group means indicated that the acutely brain-impaired subjects performed more poorly than either the chronically impaired subjects or the nonimpaired subjects. However, no tests of statistical significance were reported, and the data in the report do not allow us to perform any tests.

Rosenberg, Ryan, and Prifitera (1984) also evaluated VA inpatients using the AVLT. Their sample consisted of 92 psychologically and neurologically impaired subjects. These subjects were divided into groups of 45 memory-impaired and 47 non-memory-impaired subjects on the basis of WAIS and Wechsler Memory Scale results. A subject was classified as memory-impaired if his Wechsler Memory Scale MQ was at least 12 points below his WAIS FSIQ, or if his MQ was less than 85. The memory-impaired subjects scored significantly worse than the nonimpaired subjects.

As a test of the construct validity of the AVLT, Ryan, Rosenberg, and Mittenberg (1984b) administered the Wechsler Memory Scale, the WAIS, and the AVLT to 108 mixed psychiatric and neurological male VA inpatients. A principal-components factor analysis was performed using the scree test to determine the number of factors to be extracted and varimax rotation. The results indicated that the AVLT scores loaded most heavily on the verbal factor. However, Moses (1986) conducted a factor analysis on the AVLT scores of VA inpatients and found that the AVLT loaded highly on the same factor, as did the Benton Visual Retention Test, a finding indicating that the scores of the AVLT may not be purely modality-specific.

Talley (1986) administered the AVLT and Digit Span to a sample of 153 children between the ages of 7 and 16. All of the children had been diagnosed as learning-disabled. The AVLT did not predict the digits-forward scores and shared only 7% of the variance with digits backward. A principal factors analysis with varimax rotation resulted in a three-factor solution that accounted for 71% of the total variance. The factors were interpreted as long-term memory, short-term memory, and short-term memory with control processes.

Lezak (1979) administered the AVLT to 24 male head-trauma patients at 1, 2, and 3 years postaccident. There were 8 left-hemisphere-damaged subjects, 8 right-hemisphere-damaged subjects, and 8 bilaterally damaged subjects. The AVLT scores tended to improve over time. However, these results must be considered in the light of Lezak's study (1982), which demonstrated significant practice effects.

In conclusion, the AVLT has potential as a useful instrument in the evaluation of memory-impaired subjects. However, much more information is needed before that potential can be realized. Specifically, normative data are needed on English-speaking subjects, reliability data need to be gathered, and validity studies using other than male VA inpatient samples need to be conducted.

DIGIT SPAN

The use of strings of numbers presented in an auditory modality for the purposes of eliciting a repetition from the subject is common in many forms of evaluation. It is generally thought of as a measure of short-term memory, attention, and concentration. The most common form is exemplified in the Digit Span subtest of the Wechsler intelligence tests and in the Wechsler Memory Scale. Those scales have standardized lists and orders of digits and have been investigated in the contexts of their respective tests.

The use of this procedure can also be found in a heterogeneity of methods and lists. Often, a report in the literature will state that the numbers were chosen at random. This approach makes replication difficult. It also clouds the interpretation of studies in which different random lists are used as pre- and postintervention measures.

Blackburn and Benton (1957) suggested an alternate method to the customary one as exemplified by the Wechsler tests. In this procedure, the subject is given both series of each length, a procedure adopted in the development of the WAIS-R and the WISC-R. Other changes include terminating the administration when three consecutive failures have been recorded, rather than after two consecutive failures, and scoring 1 point for each series that is successfully repeated rather than using the length of the last successful series as the score. Blackburn and Benton (1957) concluded that these changes result in increases in reliability. Normative data for this set of procedures are presented in Hamsher et al. (1980). Norms for aged subjects are presented in Benton, Eslinger, and Damasio (1981).

Another variation is the supraspan procedure, in which a series of either eight or nine digits is repeated until the subject is successful in two consecutive attempts or until 12 trials have occurred. Bauer (1979) reported significant differences between the performance of seven learning-disabled and seven normal children in a supraspan procedure. The description of how the learning-disabled children were identified indicates that there were multiple sources of information that had not been standardized across subjects. The fact that differences were found shows the robustness of the procedure and supports efforts to further standardize the procedure. Hamsher, Benton, and Digre (1980) presented normative data on the supraspan procedure based on 500 subjects and reported that, in a comparison study, the supraspan procedure was more sensitive to brain impairment than was the usual digit-span procedure. Similarly, Drachman and Arbit (1966) and Drachman and Hughes (1971) reported that the supraspan procedure is more sensitive to brain impairment than is the usual digit-span procedure.

Hebb (in Milner, 1971) presented a potentially useful variation on the digit-span method. He used nine digit series and repeated a certain series every third presentation. In that way, a learning curve was generated and longer term memory could also be evaluated with the same procedure.

Digit-span procedures appear to be sensitive to both brain impairment and age (Parkinson, 1980). Other research suggests that variability in digit-span performance can be attributed to the time in the diurnal cycle: morning performance was superior to afternoon performance in the same subjects (Baddeley, Hatter, Scott, & Snashall, 1970). It will be important to partial out extraneous influences on digit-span performance in order to specify its clinical meaning. Weinberg, Diller, Gerstman, and Schulman (1972) found that, although patients with left-hemisphere lesions performed more poorly than normals on digit span both forward and backward, subjects with right-hemisphere lesions performed more poorly only on the backward procedure. Black and Strub (1978) investigated the relation of the quadrant of locus of lesion to digit-span performance. They found that, for the forward procedure, right-anterior-, left-anterior-, and left-posterior-lesioned subjects performed more poorly than did normals. For the backward procedure, there were no significant differences between any of the groups.

In conclusion, there are procedures (the Wechsler tests, the Randt Memory Test, and the procedures proposed by Benton and Hebb) that have been standardized, and for which there is some knowledge of the psychometric properties. However, validation studies need to be conducted to show the clinical usefulness of the tests. In particular, research should be directed at partialing out extraneous influences, such as time of day and emotional state, and at specifying the physiological correlates.

KIMURA'S RECURRING FIGURES TEST

Kimura's Recurring Figures Test is conceptualized as a measure of visual recognition. There is only one report of its reliability: Rixecker and Hartje (1980) administered the test to 427 German subjects. They reported a Kuder–Richardson reliability coefficient of .94. They also reported that there were significant differences in level of performance due to college education. There are no other reports of any other form of reliability.

Depending on the scoring system used, right-temporal-lobectomy patients scored worse than or the same as left-temporal-lobectomy patients. Both left- and right-lobectomy patients scored worse than the 11 control subjects in this study (Kimura, 1963). In another small-sample experiment, head injury patients scored poorly long after the incidence of injury (Brooks, 1972). Brooks (1974) found that 34 head-injured patients scored more poorly than 34 orthopedic patients. The number of false positive identifications by the head-injured subjects was about equal to the number emitted by the control subjects. The number of false negative identifications emitted by the head-injured subjects was greater than the number emitted by the control subjects.

As well as investigations of the reliability of this test, there need to be investigations of its construct, concurrent, and predictive validity.

KNOX'S CUBE TEST

Knox's Cube Test (KCT) was developed by Dr. H. Knox in order to aid him in detecting cognitive impairment in adult immigrants who did not speak English. The KCT has gone through several revisions since its initial formulation in 1914. The current version consists of four standardized blocks, which are glued to a baseboard in a straight line. The administrator uses a smaller fifth block to tap out a pattern on the four stimulus blocks, and the subject is to copy the tapping pattern. There are two forms available, a Junior and a Senior version. These forms differ only in that the Junior Form, for ages 2–8, starts with a smaller series of 2 taps and ends with a series of 6 taps, whereas the Senior Form, for ages 8 and over, starts with a series of 3 taps and concludes with a series of 8 taps. The exact order of the tapping sequences is specified in the manual (Stone & Wright, 1980). Testing continues until five consecutive errors are made by the subject.

Scoring is conducted by assigning a value of 1 for each success and a value of 0 for each failure. The score for each item is then summed. Reliability values based on classical test theory are available for early versions of the KCT. The current version of the KCT was evaluated by use of the Rasch model, a set of statistical procedures that is sometimes known as *item response theory*. The test authors combined information from previous studies in order to estimate the reliability of each item. These studies covered a range of over 60 years and were derived from all of the versions. Therefore, it may be necessary to update the norms by using the current version.

The use of the Rasch model allows the examiner to calculate the best estimate of the subject's ability level and to construct boundaries around this estimate. Failures below the boundaries or successes above the boundaries cast doubt on the validity of the results. Scores are then translated into values of the KCT variable. The use of the Rasch model also allows the examiner to separate estimates of the subject's ability from the difficulty level of the item. Finally, the use of the scoring procedures suggested in the manual results in an age equivalence score.

The use of the Rasch model to evaluate the KCT represents an advance in the evaluation of the instrument. However, the psychometric properties of the KCT have not been as well evaluated by use of the methodology of classical test theory. As the Rasch model is meant as an adjunct to classical test theory rather than as a substitute for it, it is desirable to evaluate the KCT under classical test theory as well.

Using subjects drawn from a population of medical, surgical, and non-psychotic psychiatric inpatients, Sterne (1966) reported a test–retest reliability coefficient on the KCT of .64 for 56 adult male subjects with a reported interval of "not more than four days." Although Sterne did not report an evaluation of a test for the significance of differences between mean levels of performance, this evaluation was easy to perform, given the data regarding the means and the standard deviations. There were no significant differences. In order to investigate the possibilities of increasing the reliability values, Sterne then administered the KCT twice in the same day to a group of 50 male subjects drawn from the same sample as above. The test was read-ministered twice the following day. Averages were computed for each day's performance, and these averages were used as the data for the evaluation of the test's reliability. The correlation between the two averages was .82, and again, there were no significant differences. Because of the methodology of the second study, it is difficult to separate the effect of shortening the interval from the effect of averaging two test performances. However, the results indicate that the test–retest reliability may be beneficially affected by one or both of the manipulations used.

Although the KCT is thought to measure attention and short-term spatial memory, there has been little work to investigate the veracity of this assumption. There are studies of note that have attempted to evaluate the validity of the KCT.

Brooks (1976) administered the KCT to 55 Maori 4-year-olds and 55 Pakeha 4-year-olds in New Zealand. He reported that there were no significant differences due to socioeconomic status or to ethnic background. There were significant differences due to sex in the Maori sample, the females scoring higher than the males.

In an attempt to evaluate the discriminant validity of the KCT, Paletz and Hirshhoren (1972) administered both the KCT and the Visual-Sequential Memory subtest of the Illinois Test of Psycholinguistic Ability. There were 96 subjects, 12 subjects in each of the six cells formed by crossing sex with school grade level in the kindergarten, second, fourth, and sixth grades. The resulting correlation coefficients ranged from .08 for the fourth-grade subjects to .57 for the kindergarten subjects. Paletz and Hirshhoren concluded that the two tests measured different aspects of visual memory.

Horan, Ashton, and Minto (1980) compared the effects of bilateral and unilateral ECT on performance on the KCT by comparing the pre- and post-ECT performance of each subject. Performance improved significantly in the right-sided unilateral ECT subjects. Because the subjects used in this study numbered only 20, an attempt was made at replication. In the second study, there were 10 matched controls who did not receive ECT, 7 subjects who received bilateral ECT, and 7 subjects who received unilateral right

ECT. The unilateral ECT subjects manifested significant improvements in KCT performance, which were not demonstrated by either the control subjects or the bilateral ECT subjects.

None of the above studies were conducted with subjects with neuropsychological impairment. In order to remediate this deficiency (from the point of view of the clinical neuropsychologist), Bornstein (1983a) administered the KCT as well as the Halstead–Reitan Neuropsychological Battery, the WAIS, the Wechsler Memory Scale, and the Verbal Concept Attainment Test to 300 subjects who had been referred for neuropsychological evaluation. The subjects were divided into two equivalent samples. Identical statistical analyses were conducted on both samples, consisting of principal-factors factor analysis. In both analsyes, the KCT loaded most heavily on factors that were interpreted as reflecting visual and auditory attention span. The results of this study indicate the potential utility of the KCT as a neuropsychological assessment instrument. However, more work needs to be done to specify the construct underlying the KCT, as well as the sensitivity of the KCT to particular forms of brain impairment.

BLOCK TAPPING TEST

The Block Tapping Test may be seen as a spatial equivalent of the word- and digit-span tests that are sometimes used to measure aspects of memory. The test consists of nine uniformly small, white wooden blocks, which are distributed over a rectangular board. There are numbers from 1 to 9 printed on the sides of the blocks that face the examiner. The examiner taps the blocks in a pattern that is then copied by the subject. Five sequences are tapped for each series. A correct performance is scored when the subject is able to correctly copy three of the five sequences. When a correct response is given, the next sequence is given until a series of eight blocks is given or until the subject is unable to copy three of the five sequences. In order for a correct response to be scored, the subject must tap only one block at a time and must tap directly on the top of the block, not to the side. The pattern of taps is repeated for every third sequence; however, the intervening taps are not repeated. Normal subjects improve on the repeated stimuli, but not necessarily on the nonrepeated sequences.

The reliability of this instrument has not been investigated. However, some evidence has been presented in the literature that addresses the validity of the Block Tapping Test. Cantone, Orsini, Grossi, and De Michele (1978) investigated the performance of 85 subjects on the Block Tapping Test and the Digit Span subtest from the WAIS. The groups were constituted of the following subjects: 90 control subjects, 20 subjects with a diagnosis of Huntington's chorea, 25 subjects with multi-infarct dementia, 16 subjects with cerebral atrophy, 21 subjects with a diagnosis of suspected Alzheimer's, 7 subjects with senile dementia, 4 subjects with Pick's syndrome, and 2 subjects with normal-pressure hydrocephalus.

There were significant differences between the controls and the other groups on both the Digit Span and the Block Tapping Test, with the exception of the comparison between the controls and the multi-infarct dementia subjects. Cantone *et al.* (1978) also examined the ratio between the verbal span measure and the spatial span measure. Significant differences, in comparison with the control group, were found only for the senile dementia and the Alzheimer's groups. The authors concluded that verbal memory was more affected by dementia than was spatial memory.

Milner (1971) examined the performance of temporal lobectomy subjects on the Block Tapping Test. In this study, there were 12 subjects with right temporal lobectomy and minimal hippocampal removal, 13 subjects with right temporal lobectomy and radical hippocampal removal, 11 subjects with left temporal lobectomy and minimal hippocampal removal, 8 subjects with left temporal lobectomy and radical hippocampal removal, and 1 subject with bilateral temporal lobectomy and radical hippocampal removal. All of the subjects had roughly equivalent error rates on the non-repeated sequences. But the subjects with right temporal lobectomy, radical hippocampal removal, and bilateral temporal lobectomy had roughly one half the rate of correct responses of the other groups. No statistical tests of significance were performed on the data. However, it appears that radical hippocampal removal in conjunction with right temporal lobectomy impairs performance.

De Renzi, Faglioni, and Previdi (1977) reported a study in which they examined the performance of left- and right-brain-damaged subjects with and without visual field defects. The presence and laterality of the brain damage had been determined by neurological exam, brain scan, EEG, and neuroradiological findings. There were 20 subjects in each of the four experimental groups, as well as 40 control subjects. Multiple comparisons were performed, but the only significant differences found were between the experimental groups with visual field defects and the controls. None of the other pairwise comparisons were significant. The authors then allowed the subjects to learn the sequences to criterion to a maximum of 50 trials. Only 65% of the right-hemisphere-damaged subjects with visual field defects were able to learn the sequences. The authors concluded that the right occipital region was implicated in the spatial memory task. It is apparent that left-hemisphere lesions also impair performance, although to a lesser extent.

Because of its spatial components, the Block Tapping Test was originally hypothesized to be sensitive to damage to the right hemisphere. In order to test this hypothesis, De Renzi and Nichelli (1975) examined the performance of 30 control subjects and 125 brain-impaired subjects. The brain-impaired subjects included 39 left-hemisphere-injured subjects without visual field defects, 31 left-hemisphere subjects with visual field defects, 23 right-hemisphere subjects without visual field defects, and 32 right-hemisphere subjects with visual field defects. The authors found that visual field defects tended to lower performance on the Block Tapping Test regardless of the lateralization of the injury. Although the right-hemisphere subjects tended to score somewhat lower than the left-hemisphere subjects, the left-hemisphere subjects with visual field defects scored significantly lower than the controls. The authors concluded that the Block Tapping Test can be used to lateralize the site of damage only when it is used in conjunction with other tests such as the digit span, which has more specific lateralization and which can be used to rule out left-hemisphere involvement.

Orsini, Schiappa, and Grossi (1981) investigated the effects of sex and urban versus rural home environments on performance on the Block Tapping Test and on the Digits Forward subtest of the WISC-R. This study used 1,113 Italian children between the ages of 4 and 10. Four subgroups were formed by crossing the gender variable with the environment variable. Across all subjects, the Block Tapping Test correlated .53 with Digits Forward. Urban subjects performed significantly better than rural subjects on both tests. Boys performed better than girls only on the Block Tapping Test. Apparently, the Block Tapping Test is sensitive to variables other than cortical integrity, and separate norms may be necessary for an accurate interpretation of the results of an evaluation using this instrument.

One variable of interest is the length and the spatial arrangement of the paths formed by the tapping. Milner (1971) and most other clinicians and researchers have used random paths. This procedure raises the possibility that performance on the Block Tapping Test is related to characteristics of the task; that is, one randomly chosen path may be more difficult than another path, and subjects given the first path may perform more poorly without actually having more organic impairment. In order to investigate this hypothesis, Smirni, Villardita, and Zappala (1983) varied path length and sequence in a group of 83 normal subjects. In addition, the administration of the Block Tapping Test varied from the usual in that all the subjects were given the maximum number of sequences. Fifty-eight percent of the subjects passed later sequences after failing earlier, shorter sequences. This result indicates that the complexity of the path, as well as the length of the path, and possibly other characteristics are all important variables to consider in the use of this procedure. The authors then suggested a possible sequence of paths that could be used in a standardized fashion. The next step is the provision of norms for these standardized sequences. Hopefully, the authors of this study are engaged in that activity.

The Block Tapping Test would seem to be a useful addition to the armamentarium of neuropsychological assessment techniques. It has a unique set of task demands and appears to be sensitive to brain impairment. However, as Smirni *et al.* (1983) pointed out, the usefulness is limited by a lack of standardized procedures. Their suggested standardized sequences go a long way toward remediating the existing shortcomings of this procedure. Additional research is needed to better specify the psychometric properties of the test, as well as to determine the utility of the new procedures. It is particularly important to investigate the construct validity of the instrument in light of the findings that poor performance is associated with visual field defects as much as with the location of the lesion (De Renzi *et al.*, 1977).

Tests of Verbal Functions

A subject's understanding of objects and his or her ability to demonstrate the use of them has sometimes been suggested as a means of assessing the brain-impaired subject. For example, Zangwill (1966) stated that frontal lobe patients offer unconventional uses for an object and do not offer the usual use. The Use of Objects test is most often used to assess for the presence of ideational apraxia. In this case, the examiner is interested in whether the subject can correctly string together the necessary sequence of actions that together comprise the behavior associated with the use of the object in question.

De Renzi, Pieczuro, and Vignolo (1968) tested the traditional assumption that a left-posterior temporal-parietal lesion results in ideational apraxia. Their subject sample included 40 control subjects, 45 subjects with right-hemisphere lesions, and 160 subjects with left-hemisphere lesions. In the test used, four objects were presented to the subjects, who were then asked to demonstrate the objects' use. All of the right-hemisphere patients and the control subjects were able to perform without error. Errors were committed by 45 of the left-hemisphere subjects, 43 of whom showed signs of aphasia. There was no significant relation between ideational apraxia and scores on the Raven's Progressive Matrices and response latencies from a reaction-time task. The presence of ideational apraxia and the results of an aphasia examination were found to have a Spearman rank-correlation coefficient value of .579. Interestingly, the researchers found that ideational apraxia was bound to the test situation. Subjects who could not demonstrate the use of a toothbrush in the test situation were able to demonstrate its use in a bathroom with the additional cues present there.

Ettlinger (1970) suggested that ideational apraxia is associated with bi-lateral lesions. He further stated that ideational apraxia has two components: a language-dependent disorder and a disorder of skilled motor movements.

His identification of a language disorder in ideational apraxia is congruent with the results of De Renzi *et al.* (1968) discussed above. However, his suggestion of the necessity of bilateral lesions needs to be verified by data.

In general, the use of object procedures needs to be standardized and evaluated before clear clinical implications can be determined. The construction of such a test should take into consideration the previous experience of the subject with the object, as Jones and Shea (1974) demonstrated that the cultural background of a subject can influence his or her ability to demonstrate a knowledge of the use of the object.

OBJECT-NAMING TESTS

Object-naming tasks have been a popular form of evaluation of the brain-impaired individual. Some form of object naming is included in many standardized procedures, including the Luria–Nebraska Neuropsychological Battery. The use of nonstandardized procedures is risky, as several variables can influence performance on this test, including the familiarity of the subject with the object, the use of an object itself as opposed to a picture of the object, and whether the object word can also be used as a verb (Barker & Lawson, 1968). In order to subvert these potential problems, Oldfield and Wingfield (1965) developed a set of pictures that can be used in a standardized fashion. Newcombe, Oldfield, Ratcliffe, and Wingfield (1971) found this task to be sensitive to brain injury. However, the reliability and the specific validities of this procedure still need to be evaluated. Lawson and Barker (1968) administered an object-naming test to 100 individuals with organic dementia and 40 volunteers from an elderly persons' social club. They scored a failure to respond as well as the latency of response and found that both variables discriminated between the two groups significantly. They also found that demonstration facilitated naming in the impaired subjects but not in the control subjects. This information points to the possible clinical utility of the procedure.

WORD ASSOCIATION PROCEDURES

Word association procedures have a long history in psychological evaluations. Perhaps the best known context for word association procedures is the assessment of psychological dynamics. However, word association procedures have also been recommended for the assessment of organic impairment.

Bachrach (1971) administered a word association test to a group of 30 patients with cerebral impairment and a group of 60 psychiatric patients who had been judged to be free of cerebral impairment. In this particular procedure, the subjects were asked to associate to a list of words as quickly as possible. The subjects were then presented with the same list and were asked to respond with a different association. The scoring procedure used reaction time, the number of occasions when reaction time exceeded 6 seconds, the number of times the patients offered the same association across the two occasions, and the number of times the subjects offered a multiword association. There were significant differences between the two groups on each of the scoring dimensions. Brotsky and Linton (1969) administered the same list of words to subjects twice, across a 4-week interval, and found that their subjects tended to give the same associations on both occasions. It may be, therefore, that the organic subject has an impaired ability to provide alternate associations. Using a different administration and scoring system, Bartel, Grill, and Bartell (1973) found no significant differences between learning-disabled and normal children, although there were significant differences due to age and to IQ. The efficacy of the word association procedure may be limited to particular types of cerebral impairment.

Much more research is needed before word association tasks can be recommended for clinical uses. Silverman (1968) found that expectancies of the assessor can have significant effects on performance. Further, there is evidence that some of the variance in word association tasks may be explained by psychological variables other than organic impairment (Innes, 1972).

THE TOKEN TEST

The Token Test has gone through many different incarnations. As a result, there are several versions extant. De Renzi and Vignolo (1962) published what is probably the first version of the Token Test. In this version, there were no standard stimuli or instructions, although the authors did describe the stimuli and the types of instructions they had used. Needless to say, this unstandardized approach resulted in the different versions that can be found in the literature. Some of the changes have been seemingly minor. For example, Boller and Vignolo (1966) changed the commands from *take* to *touch*. Other changes were made to facilitate ruling out the influence of other impairments from the production of errors. The commands are said to increase in difficulty level; however, this claim has not been investigated empirically. In another version, the blue-colored tokens were changed to black in order to not penalize subjects who might be blue–green color-blind.

In general, reliability studies have not been a major focus of evalutions of the Token Test. Gallagher (1979) investigated test–retest reliability by administering the Token Test to 30 aphasic subjects on three occasions interspersed in an 8-day period. Although the Wilcoxin Matched Pairs Signed Ranks test was not significant, the Spearman rank-correlation coefficients were .98 for the comparison of the first administration with the second, .96 for the comparison of the second with the third, and .95 for the comparison of the first with the third administration.

McNeil and Prescott (1978) presented a Revised Token Test in which they addressed some of the traditional psychometric issues in aphasia evaluation. For example, they stated that, in their version, the intrascale homogeneity is controlled by the use of standard stimuli. Unfortunately, they did not empirically evaluate this assumption. Test–retest reliability was evaluated by administering the test twice to 10 brain-damaged subjects across a 2-week interval. The average subtest correlation was .90. Intrascorer reliability was evaluated by videotaping nine administrations of the Revised Token Test. Three judges scored three administrations twice each. The agreement of the judges with themselves was about .99 for the mean subtest scores. Interscorer reliability was evaluated by having three judges score the same three videotaped administrations. Agreement for the subtest means ranged from .98 to .97. Unfortunately, the authors did not say what the subject characteristics were. If the subjects used were normal subjects, this level of agreement is not surprising. Also, we would want to know what the agreement of diagnosis was across the judges. Norms are available for non-brain-damaged subjects, brain-damaged subjects, and aphasic subjects. Unfortunately, the manual states that the Revised Token Test discriminates between aphasic and nonaphasic brain-damaged subjects at only slightly better than chance levels (55% correct). Concurrent validity was evaluated by administering the Revised Token Test and the Porch Index of Communicative Ability to a sample of 23 aphasic subjects. The overall correlation was .67.

Another form of the Token Test involves the use of concrete objects rather than tokens. Martino, Pizzamiglio, and Razzano (1976) reported that, in a sample of 70 brain-damaged and 10 normal subjects, there was good agreement between the results of the traditional Token Test and the results of the Concrete Objects Token Test.

Orgass and Poeck (1966) attempted one of the first empirical validation studies using the Token Test. They administered the test to 66 subjects without brain damage, 49 subjects with brain damage but without aphasia, and 26 aphasics. The subjects ranged in age from 5 to over 60. The authors stated that the aphasics demonstrated clear signs of aphasia, but they did not describe what they meant by "clear signs." They found that performance was significantly related to age and that there were differences due to age. The influence of education was significant but was not judged to be important in clinical situations. Using a cutoff score of 11 errors, the authors were able to correctly classify 84% of the aphasics, 96% of the brain-damaged but not aphasic subjects, and 100% of the normals. There was no attempt at cross-validation in this report.

Because the cutoff scores were determined by an examination of the distributions against which the accuracy of classification was checked, it is especially important to attempt a cross-validation. This procedure can be seen in Hartje, Kerschensteiner, Poeck, and Orgass (1973), who found that changing the cutoff score to 23 errors resulted in an optimal correct classification rate for this sample. Apparently, although the Token Test may be sensitive to aphasic disorders, the use of a single cutoff point for diagnosis causes problems.

Lass and Golden (1975) investigated the concurrent validity of the Token Test by correlating the scores obtained by 20 normal subjects on the Token Test with their scores on the Peabody Picture Vocabulary Test (PPVT). These authors found a correlation of .71. Because the PPVT is a test of verbal intelligence, the moderately high correlation calls into question the interpretation of the Token Test as a measure of purely verbal language capacity.

Spellacy and Spreen (1969) investigated a short form of the Token Test by using two types of scoring procedures: a weighted score procedure, in which more sensitive items were given heavier weights, and a pass–fail score procedure, in which all items were given equal weight. They administered their short form to 37 nonaphasic brain-damaged subjects and 67 subjects who had been judged aphasic by medical diagnosis. The internal consistency reliability, determined by use of the weighted scoring procedure was .79. The internal consistency reliability determined by use of the pass–fail scoring procedure was .92. Using an optimal cutoff developed on the same sample resulted in 89% correct classification of the aphasic subjects and 72% classification of the nonaphasic subjects. With the use of the pass–fail scoring procedure, 79% of the aphasic subjects and 86% of the nonaphasic subjects were correctly classified. Cross-validation is likely to result in even less accurate classification rates.

De Renzi and Faglioni (1978) gave a short form of the Token Test to 215 control subjects and 280 aphasic subjects. Using a regression correction for the amount of education, they found that an optimal cutoff score correctly classified 95% of the normal subjects and 93% of the aphasic subjects. For the same reasons discussed above, this optimal cutoff score is in need of cross-validation.

Cole and Fewell (1983) investigated the use of De Renzi and Faglioni's short version of the Token Test (1978) in a sample of 90 children aged 31 months to 103 months with a mean age of 66.4 months. They also administered the Preschool Language Scale (PLS) to the same subjects. The Token Test correlated .78 with the language age derived from the PLS, .74 with the Auditory Comprehension scale of the PLS, and .76 with the Verbal Ability scale of the PLS. By choosing a cutoff score that resulted in zero false negatives, these authors obtained 11 false positives compared to diagnosis determined by the PLS.

In short, the Token Test, although often used in language disorder clinics, as well as in neuropsychological settings, is in need of standardization and basic reliability and validity research.

THE NEW WORD LEARNING TEST

The New Word Learning Test operates on the principle that organically impaired individuals will demonstrate lower levels of performance than will organically intact individuals on a task requiring them to learn the meanings of unfamiliar words. Walton and Black (1957) and Walton (1957) reported that New Word Learning Test scores do indeed discriminate organic subjects from psychotic subjects and normal subjects. These studies also found that, although intelligence, age, and size of working vocabulary were related to scores on the New Word Learning Test, these variables did not have an appreciable effect on the classification of the subjects.

Walton, White, Black, and Young (1959) revised the scoring system of the New Word Learning Test so that low scores represented poor performance and high scores represented good performance. They also penalized the subjects for each additional repetition required before adequate performance was demonstrated. They administered the test to a sample of 83 normal subjects, 66 neurotic subjects, 32 psychotic subjects, 45 mentally retarded subjects, and 78 organically impaired subjects. Using a cutoff score of 26 points resulted in perfect classification of the normal, neurotic, and psychotic subjects. Fifteen percent of the organically impaired subjects were misclassified, as were a large proportion of the mentally defective subjects. These misclassifications may have been due to the authors' inexplicable inclusion of the mentally retarded subjects in the normal classification. However, it is apparent that scores on the New Word Learning Test are affected by IQ.

White (1959) found that the New Word Learning Test classified 74% of 40 nonimpaired children (including 18 psychiatric subjects), 8 retarded subjects, and 10 brain-impaired subjects, all of whom were between the ages of 6 and 16. In a second study contained in the same report, there were no significant differences between 17 brain-impaired children and 17 matched controls. Evidently, the New Word Learning Test is not equally sensitive to brain impairment in all age groups. The limits of its applicability have yet to be defined. Additionally, Teasdale and Beaumont (1971) found that the presence of depressed mood can affect scores so that subjects may be misclassified as brain-impaired when they are not.

The New Word Learning Test is in need of research to assess both its reliability and its validity.

BOSTON NAMING TEST

The Boston Naming Test is in almost the exact opposite condition of most neuropsychological instruments. Whereas most neuropsychological instruments have been evaluated in terms of their validity but not in terms of their reliability, the Boston Naming Test has been evaluated in terms of its reliability but not in terms of its validity. Normative data are available on a sample of 78 healthy, independently living adults aged 59–80 (Van Gorp, Satz, Kiersch, & Hening, 1986).

The Boston Naming Test is a somewhat lengthy procedure that could be useful in serial examinations of the recovery of speech functions or in the documentation of decline. In order to enhance the utility of the Boston Naming Test in these contexts, Huff, Collins, Corkin, and Rosen (1986) divided its 85 items into two subtests of 42 items each and administered them to 15 healthy adults, 24 subjects with senile dementia of the Alzheimer's type, and 17 subjects with diagnosed brain lesions. Form I had an alpha coefficient of .96, as did Form II. The two alternate forms had similar means and standard deviations, and the correlation between the two forms was .97.

Goodglass and Kaplan (1983) reported the results of administering the Boston Naming Test to 242 aphasics, a remarkable feat that must have taken much patience and effort—even in just locating that many aphasics. These authors then performed multiple statistical operations on their data in order to examine the reliability and the factorial structure of the instrument.

In the original study reported in the manual (Goodglass & Kaplan, 1983), Kuder–Richardson reliability coefficients were calculated on the basis of data provided by 34 aphasics. Unfortunately, in this case, as in all subsequent cases, the authors failed to describe by what means the subjects had been classified as aphasic or whether the subjects also exhibited other forms of neuropsychological impairment. This analysis resulted in values ranging from .96 for the Word Discrimination test to .68 for the Body Parts Identification test. This sample of 34 subjects was used to generate standardized z scores. This system was replaced by the calculation of percentiles based on the later sample of 242 aphasics.

A factor analysis conducted on this sample of 242 aphasics yielded a set of 10 factors that the authors suggested can be used for interpretation. However, there is no empirical evidence linking these factors to observable referents, so that their utility is limited in a clinical setting. The authors did not specify the number-of-factors rule that they used to decide when to terminate extraction. Additionally, 44 variables were used in the factor analysis, which would require triple the number of subjects used in order to provide a stable solution. Another factor analysis conducted with the same subjects and a smaller number of variables (only the language variables) yielded a similar factor structure. This result may mean only that the language and nonlanguage variables are independent, but it also speaks to the issue of the stability of the derived language variables' structure. A third factor analysis with the same subjects, which deleted the rating scale variables, generated a similar factor structure. A fourth factor analysis used only the variables that were normally distributed and a sample of 41 aphasics from the original sample. What is needed is an attempt at cross-validation that uses a separate sample.

In another attempt to investigate the multivariate properties of the instrument, the authors performed a discriminant function analysis using 41 aphasics divided among the diagnostic groups of Broca's aphasics, Wernicke's aphasics, conduction aphasics, and anomic aphasics. Ten variables were selected to be included in the predictors on a theoretical basis. Even with this attempt to pare the number of potential predictors, the sample should have been four times the size in order to give any confidence in the generalizability of the solution. Another drawback is that the *a priori* classifications (diagnoses) were determined partly on the basis of the scores on the variables, which were then used as predictors.

Borod, Goodglass, and Kaplan (1980) reported normative data on the Boston Diagnostic Aphasia Examination (BDAE), the Parietal Lobe Battery, and the Boston Naming Test. These data were based on an evaluation of 147 normal subjects, and they go a long way toward increasing the utility of these instruments in a clinical diagnostic setting. The authors recommended the BDAE on the basis of its content and its face validity, which are considerable. However, much basic validation work needs to be conducted.

Tests of Visual Functions

The Rey–Osterreith Complex Figure Test involves the copying and recall of abstract line drawings. No information is available regarding the reliability of the test. Bennett-Levy (1984) administered the test to a sample of 107 normals and found that females performed significantly better than males. Additionally, the scores were significantly correlated with age. These data suggest the need for separate norms for sexes and age groups, which have not been provided yet.

An effort in that direction has been made by Waber and Holmes (1986), who administered the Rey–Osterreith to a sample of 454 children between the ages of 5 and 14. All of the subjects were students in a normal classroom, and there was no effort to screen the subjects for learning disability. Instructions for immediate reproduction were given to 57% of the subjects, and the rest of the subjects were asked to reproduce the design after a 20-minute delay. Relatively detailed scoring criteria were given. The interrater reliability between two judges was found to be .94 in a random sample of protocols; the interrater agreement on the clinical rating of the same protocol was 84%. There was no attempt to validate the results against an outside criterion.

Binder (1982) compared the performance of 14 normal, 14 right-hemisphere-damaged, and 14 left-hemisphere-damaged subjects. He reported that the right-hemisphere subjects demonstrated more distortions and that the left-hemisphere subjects were more likely than the normals to break the configural units into segments. King (1981) compared the performance of 71 normals, 22 left-hemisphere, 45 right-hemisphere, and 47 diffusely damaged subjects. He found that the left-hemisphere subjects were more likely to make simplification errors, and that the right-hemisphere subjects were more likely to make distortion errors, but that there was no difference between the two groups on the number of errors they made. All three of the damaged groups made significantly more errors than the normals. There were no differences due to type of injury: trauma, cerebrovascular problems, or degenerative disorders. As evidence of the construct validity of the test, King (1981) reported that the test correlated .28 with the Visual Recall subtest of the Wechsler Memory Scale when the influence of age and sex were partialed out.

Taylor (1969) investigated the construct validity of the Rey–Osterreith by administering it and a similar abstract-form-copying task to a series of patients who had received temporal lobectomies. There were 50 subjects altogether; 23 had received left temporal lobectomies, and 27 had received right temporal lobectomies. At the presurgery assessment, the two groups exhibited similar test scores. At 2 weeks postsurgery, the left-hemisphere subjects' copying scores had improved somewhat, and the right-hemisphere subjects' copying scores had declined. The delayed-recall score of the left-hemisphere subjects had improved, and that of the right-hemisphere subjects had remained about the same. These data may be interpreted as evidence of the role of an intact right temporal lobe in the successful completion of the Rey–Osterreith Complex Figure Test, although replication and further evidence are needed.

THE ISHIHARA COLOR BLIND TEST

The Ishihara Color Blind Test can be used to determine the presence of color-blindness in subjects. The determination of color-blindness is an important issue when other test stimuli may be colored. Particularly for males, in whom color-blindness can be genetic rather than acquired, the integrity of color vision may need to be documented before the possibility of a deficit in color-naming skills can be evaluated.

The Ishihara Color Blindness Test (Ishihara, 1970) contains 14 color plates composed of different-sized dots. The dots are of different hues. Same-colored dots are arranged in recognizable designs, such as numbers, or in trails. In the first case, the subject is asked to name the number outlined by the same-colored dots. In the second case, the subject is asked to trace the trails formed by the same-colored dots.

Internal consistency reliability was computed by use of the Kuder–Richardson Formula 20 in a sample of 90 mentally retarded boys aged 8–16. The reliability coefficient for the Numbers plates was .901; for the Trails plates, the coefficient was .927; and for the overall test, the coefficient was .914.

De Renzi and Spinnler (1967) reported that, in a sample of 100 control subjects, 100 left-hemisphere-injured patients, and 73 right-hemisphere-injured patients, the right-hemisphere-injured patients were more likely to produce impaired performances on the Ishihara. It was found that left-hemisphere-injured patients performed at a level commensurate with that of the control subjects.

Performance on the Ishihara is apparently insensitive to the effects of intelligence. Salvia and Ysseldyke (1972) found that, in a sample of 90 boys aged 8–16 with IQs between 40 and 75, there was little indication of impaired performance. These results were consistent with earlier reports by Wilson and Wolfensberger (1963) and Salvia (1969).

More information is needed regarding the other forms of reliability of this test, as well as regarding the validity of using the Ishihara in diagnosing right-hemisphere damage. The Ishihara may have utility in the diagnosis of color agnosia or color aphasia. However, empirical data are wanting on these points.

MEANINGFUL PICTURES

The meaningful pictures procedure has not been extensively used in research settings. However, it is an interesting procedure that uses an original methodology. The one report of the use of meaningful pictures in the literature was given by Battersby, Bender, Pollack, and Kahn (1956). This report describes the procedure as using five pictures chosen from color-magazine illustrations. These pictures were chosen for their quality of being symmetrical about the median plane. The pictures are presented to the subject one at a time for 10 seconds each. Following the presentation of each picture, the subject is asked to describe the details and to note their relative position in the picture. The pictures are then given to the subject again, and she or he is asked to describe the details while holding the pictures. The "omission, faulty recall (or description) of numerous details on one side only was taken as an index of asymmetric spatial perception" (Battersby et al., 1956, p. 74). The authors studied the performance on this task of 42 spinal cord patients, 85 patients with space-occupying lesions, and 37 patients with nonlocalizable lesions. The results indicated that poor performance on this task was not related to the location of the lesion, but that it was related to sensory impairment superimposed on a condition of cognitive impairment. No information is available regarding the reliability of this procedure or regarding the general aspects of the validity of this procedure. The procedure would also benefit from a statement of more explicit rules for scoring the results.

STICK CONSTRUCTION

A stick construction test has been reported in a few studies. The test usually involves having the subject copy a drawing of a figurative or nonfigurative organization of sticks, although the test may also involve constructing letters or figures with sticks by command rather than from a model. There have been no reports of investigation of the reliability of this test. Although right-hemisphere-lesioned subjects are more likely to exhibit impaired performance on this test than are left-hemisphere subjects (Hecaen & Assal, 1970), subjects with lateralized lesions will show impairment regardless of whether they are right- or left-hemisphere-lesioned (Benton, 1967). More research is needed before this test can be recommended for clinical use.

THE MINNESOTA PAPER FORM BOARD

The Minnesota Paper Form Board Test is purported to be a test of perceptual organization. It is a paper-and-pencil test that requires the subject to select the correct alternative depicting a figure made from a combination of the parts shown in the stimulus. For example, the stimulus may show two separate triangles, and the alternatives may be a circle, a square joined to a triangle, and two triangles connected to form a diamond. The Likert and Quashal manual (1948) provides normative data separately by sex and by occupation. No information is available regarding the reliability of this test. The construct validity of the Minnesota Paper Form Board is also in question (Lezak, 1983). Dee (1970) concluded that it was actually a measure of perceptual ability associated with contructional ability. However, Dee did not use the original form of this test but used a shorter version and increased the size of the stimuli and the allowable time limits. Gazzaniga and LeDoux (1978) demonstrated that the performance of a single patient may vary with the method of administration. Because of the variability in administration in published reports of this test, it is difficult to draw any definite conclusions regarding its reliability or validity.

FIGURE–GROUND TESTS

Brain impairment has often been associated with a disruption in the ability to discriminate figure–ground relations. Gottschaldt's Hidden Figures Test has been used in some neuropsychological settings. There have been no investigations of the reliability of this instrument, but there has been some research that points to its sensitivity to brain abnormalities. Impaired performance on the Hidden Figures Test has been associated with penetrating head wounds (Teuber, Battersby, & Bender, 1960; Weinstein, 1964). Russo and Vignolo (1967) reported that left-hemisphere patients without aphasia scored in the unimpaired range; however, Corkin (1979) reported that impairment results regardless of the laterality of the lesion. Poor performance on this test is also associated with Korsakoff's disease (Talland, 1965a) and uremic disease (Beniak, 1977). Apparently, there are many types of brain injury that will cause impaired performance. As well as reliability investigations, validation studies are needed to specify the functional systems involved. The exact construct implicated in the successful performance of the test also needs to be specified.

The Group Embedded Figures Test was designed as a measure of field dependence–independence. As such, it was originally conceptualized as a measure of cognitive style rather than of ability. However, more recent work (Widiger, Knudson, & Rorer, 1980) has indicated that, in fact, the Embedded Figures Test correlates more highly with tests of ability than with tests of cognitive style. This finding suggests its potential utility in the assessment of brain-impaired individuals. Research with undergraduate students majoring in business (DeSantis & Dunikoski, 1983) indicated that the reliability, the score distributions, and the sex differences are relatively robust in samples different from undergraduate liberal arts students, on which the test was normed. However, research evaluating the characteristics of the test in neuropsychological populations, as well as the validity of the instrument in the same population, still needs to be conducted.

HOOPER VISUAL ORGANIZATION TEST

The Hooper Visual Organization Test has been used widely in psychiatric settings. However, the reliability and the validity of the test were not well evaluated in the studies reported in the manual (Hooper, 1958). Of the two studies reported in the manual, one demonstrated acceptable accuracy in identifying normal subjects and reasonable (79%) accuracy in identifying organically impaired subjects. In the second study, the classification of the subjects into criterion groups was partly accomplished by reference to scores on the Hooper, hopelessly confounding the significant differences that were then found. There were no reports of reliability evaluation in the manual.

Lezak (1982) evaluated the test–retest reliability of the Hooper in a sample of 23 normal male subjects. The test was given on three occasions with approximate intervals of 6 months and 1 year. The report of this study is somewhat confusing, as not all subjects were given the test on each occasion, and information is not provided about which subjects took the test on which occasion. The report is further confused by the fact that, although the text refers to significant differences in level in the Hooper scores, the accompanying table presents values that are not significant. Be that as it may, the pairwise correlation coefficients ranged from .92 for the first and second occasions to .77 for the second and third occasions. Moreover, there was a significant difference in one of the comparisons of mean levels. This study represents the only attempt to investigate the reliability of the instrument.

Sterne (1973) evaluated the diagnostic validity of the Hooper in a sample of 75 VA inpatients, 25 of whom had been diagnosed as organic, 25 as psychiatric, and 25 as indeterminate. As well as the Hooper, the WAIS, the Benton Visual Retention Test, the Porteus Mazes, and Trails A and B were administered. All of these variables were entered as predictors in a multiple-regression equation, with diagnosis as the criterion. Unfortunately, the diagnosis was determined by the results of the psychological testing and the result was a confound. Even when the results of the Hooper were used to diagnose subjects, the Hooper was unable to provide significant prediction beyond that afforded by the other variables, a finding calling into serious question the validity of this instrument.

In general, the results of validation attempts have not been encouraging. Pershad and Verma (1980) found that, although scores on the Hooper were sensitive to brain impairment in an Indian sample, the use of the cutoff points suggested in the manual resulted in both false positives and false negatives. Love (1970) reported similar results in a sample of 115 New Zealand psychiatric patients.

Wang (1977) evaluated the diagnostic accuracy of the Hooper in classifying neurosurgery patients as brain-impaired. The sample included 49 brain-impaired subjects (15 left-hemisphere, 19 right-hemisphere, and 15 bilateral) and 17 non-brain-impaired subjects (largely with peripheral-nervous-system disorders). Using the cutoff points suggested in the manual eventuated in a 43% misclassification. Raising the cutoff to over double that in the manual still resulted in a 17% false-negative rate, although it did not result in any false positives. There were no differences among the right, left, or bilaterally impaired subjects.

Jackson and Culbertson (1977) evaluated the use of the Hooper in classifying children as organically impaired. This study used 20 normal children and 20 neurologically impaired children, as determined by their status in classes for the learning-impaired. There were no reports of how these children had been placed in the classes. There was overlap in the distributions of the scores in the two groups, and the cutoff points suggested in the manual resulted in many incorrect classifications. The authors then readjusted the cutoffs to maximize correct classifications. The readjustment resulted in no false positives, but it still produced a large number of false negatives. This is a problem with many screening devices. Because screening devices can usually assess the integrity of a single system, they are not sensitive to focal impairment in other systems.

Boyd (1981) described an attempt at validation using 40 brain-impaired subjects and 40 nonimpaired psychiatric subjects. The cutoff points in the manual produced 97.5% correct classifications of the control subjects but only 15% correct classifications of the brain-impaired subjects. Using cutoffs

that maximized correct classification resulted in 67.5% accuracy of classification in the brain-impaired subjects and 80.0% accuracy in the control
subjects, for an overall rate of 73.8% accuracy. There were no significant
differences due to site of lesion or acuteness of injury. Boyd also correlated
the Hooper scores with Peabody Picture Vocabulary Test (PPVT) IQs, age,
and education. He found only moderate correlations with these variables.

Boyd (1981) was subsequently criticized by Rathbun and Smith (1982)
for using the PPVT and for using a system-specific test like the Hooper as
a screen. They then cited two unpublished studies that they said supported
their points. Rathbun and Smith (1982) recommended using Smith's own
test, the Symbol Digit Modalities Test, as a screen. Boyd (1982a) replied
that the studies cited by Rathbun and Smith actually used the Benton Visual
Retention Test (BVRT) and Raven's Progressive Matrices and did not even
use the Hooper. Obviously, what is needed is a study that compares the
utility of the BVRT with the Hooper when used as screening devices.

Woodward (1982) also criticized Boyd (1981) on the grounds that there
were no workups of the controls to rule out impairment and that the even
ratio of impaired and nonimpaired subjects was artificial and may have inflated the accuracy rates. Boyd (1982b) replied that his study had been meant
to demonstrate the sensitivity of the Hooper to brain impairment, not to
evaluate its use in uncovering the incidence of brain impairment in the general population. These responses are fine, but they do not address the fact
that the use of the Hooper in the original study resulted in a misclassification
of many of the subjects.

SATZ BLOCK ROTATION TEST

The Block Rotation Test (BRT) was developed by Paul Satz as his
dissertation project. After graduation, Satz continued to provide validation
information regarding the BRT (Satz, 1966). Although the actual number of
publications evaluating the BRT is minimal, the quality of these publications
is generally good. The BRT was developed to be sensitive to brain impairment in general. However, this was done in the context of knowing the
difficulty of determining the existence of brain impairment when brain impairment is not viewed as a unitary construct.

The BRT is an interactive test that takes about an hour to administer
to normal subjects. Its administration to impaired subjects takes somewhat
longer, depending on the nature and the severity of the impairment. The
stimulus items consist of red and white colored blocks similar to those used
in the Block Design subtest of the WAIS. The object of the test is for the
subject to reproduce the designs formed by the examiner, but rotated 90
degrees, either to the left or to the right. This is accomplished by moving
the blocks one at a time. The test is divided into two parts. In the first part,

the stimuli are presented aligned with the horizontal and vertical axes. In the second part, the stimuli are presented at an angle to the axes. There are 15 designs in Part A and 7 designs in Part B. For both parts, there is an initial practice period in which the subject's understanding of the task requirements is assessed.

Six scores are obtained from the use of this instrument. Duplication errors consist of designs that merely replicate the design without the required 90-degree rotation. Angulation errors are those subject designs that, although rotated to some degree, deviate from the required rotation. Time errors are the result of a failure to complete the task within the 65-second time limit. Part A errors are the sum of the errors in Part B. Part B errors are the sum of the errors in Part B. Total errors are the total sum of errors over the entire test.

Reliability

Test–retest reliability was assessed in a sample of 18 subjects who were involved in the standardization of the instrument. The reported test–retest interval was "about four weeks." Pearson product–moment correlation coefficients between the scores obtained on the two test occasions ranged from .91 for total errors to .67 for time errors. No information has been reported regarding the assessment of change of level of scores with the use of analysis of variance. Therefore, no conclusions can be drawn regarding the existence of practice effects.

Lawriw and Sutker (1978) reported internal-consistency reliability values using data from 57 (40 male and 17 female) consecutive referrals to a neuropsychological assessment service. They reported an alpha coefficient of .94. These authors also performed various split-half analyses and reported Spearman–Brown corrected split-half reliabilities ranging from .94 for right-versus left-turning items on Part A to .77 for right- versus left-turning items on Part B.

Validity

The original standardized sample for the BRT consisted of 122 adult male subjects from VA hospitals. These subjects were divided into four groups: normals (psychiatric nursing assistants), neurotic patients, schizophrenic patients, and neurological patients (Satz, 1966). The diagnoses were obtained from case records and were performed by the respective attending physicians. A linear discriminant-function analysis was obtained from the six test scores, the Performance IQ as measured by the WAIS, and the age of the subjects as predictors. The criterion was the dichotomous division of organic or not organic. All of the variables were forced into the discriminant function regardless of the amount of discrimination provided. This fact may account for some of the later shrinkage observed in the cross-validation. The standardized beta weights are not reported, so we cannot judge the relative amounts of independent variance accounted for by the individual predictors.

The cutoff points for the values obtained from the discriminant function were determined by computing the mean of the group average discriminant function scores. This is a reasonable strategy when the distributions are normal. However, to the extent that the distributions may have been skewed toward each other, this procedure may have resulted in a less than optimum cutoff point. For example, if the nonorganic group's distribution was skewed to the right, the proposed cutoff point may not have minimized the number of false positives, as seems to have been the case in the derivation and cross-validation studies. Nevertheless, the resultant procedure eventuated in an 89% correct classification rate overall. When the results were analyzed for the effects of type and location of lesion, it was concluded that the test was sensitive to nonspecific effects of brain impairment.

An important point needs to be raised here. This original study used only male subjects. This is unfortunate, as the construct most probably measured by the BRT (visual-spatial skills) has been found to be significantly and robustly different in the two sexes (Tapley & Bryden, 1977). Therefore, any generalization of these results to female subjects is a problem.

The first cross-validation study, also reported in Satz (1966), used 100 consecutive referrals to a neuropsychological assessment service. The sex of these subjects and of the subjects in the subsequent cross-validation studies is not specified. As noted above, sex is an important variable, and this represents an unfortunate omission of information. There were 48 neurological patients, as diagnosed by history, neurological examination, EEG, brain scan (not defined, but probably not CT scan because of the date of the publication), skull films, and, in some cases, arteriogram, angiogram, or pneumoencephalogram. The comparison groups consisted of 52 psychiatric, normal, or medical patient subjects, as determined by negative history, neurological exam, and sometimes a negative EEG, a skull film, an angiogram, or a pneumoencephalogram. When the discriminant function derived in the first study was used, there was 75% correct classification overall; 71% of the nonorganic subjects were correctly classified, and 79% of the organics were correctly classified. The cross-validation subjects were then combined with the original sample, and a new discriminant function was derived by the same methodology. The result was an 82% correct-classification rate overall: 88% correct for the nonorganic subjects and 76% correct for the organic subjects.

This discriminant function was then cross-validated on the next 151 consecutive referrals to the neuropsychology service (61 organic and 90 nonorganic subjects). The result was a 79% correct-classification rate overall: 83% correct for the nonorganic and 72% correct for the organic subjects.

These subjects were then combined with the concatenated sample, and the same methodology was used. This last sample was composed of 157 organic subjects and 210 nonorganic subjects. This final procedure resulted in an 81% overall correct-classification rate: 90% correct for the nonorganic subjects and 70% correct for the organic subjects. There was no cross-validation of this last discriminant function.

Classification by subgroup was also examined in this last study. Satz (1966) reported 97% correct classification of the normal control subjects (n = 39), 90% correct classification of the psychiatric subjects (n = 120), 82% correct classification of the medical subjects (n = 51), 83% correct classification of the cerebrovascular subjects (n = 30), 81% correct classification of the arteriosclerotic subjects (n = 37), and only 50% correct classification of the convulsive disorder subjects (n = 32). These results point to the ineffectiveness of the BRT in diagnosing brain impairment in convulsive subjects.

Satz (1966) used Bayesian methodology to determine the differential utility of the BRT in populations with different base rates of organic subjects. In settings such as mental health clinics, where the base rate of organicity is low, the BRT would have only 44% accuracy. However, in inpatient medical settings, where the base rate of brain impairment is higher (Satz used an estimate of 60%), the BRT would be 91% accurate.

Satz, Fennell, and Reilly (1970) examined the relation of the BRT and neurological test procedures (EEG, brain scan, skull X ray, arteriogram, and pneumoencephalography) to the eventual diagnosis of organic impairment. Unfortunately, the diagnoses were decided by use of all of the procedures except the BRT, so the results are contaminated because of a confound of independent with dependent variables. Despite this confound, it is interesting that, when the Goodman–Kruskal test of strength of association was used, only the EEG and the BRT had strong and significant predictive associations with the criterion.

All of the above discussion relates to predictive validity. Other types of validity have not been evaluated for the BRT. Lawriw and Sutker (1978) performed a factor analysis on the BRT but did not try to relate the results to the construct validity of the instrument. With 40 male and 17 female subjects who had been referred to the neuropsychological assessment service, a principal-components analysis was performed. The variables were the BRT scores, the PIQ from the WAIS, and the age of the subjects. By use of the eigenvalue greater than 1.0 as the decision rule, three factors were extracted. Following varimax rotation, these factors were interpreted as general visual-spatial-constructional ability, psychomotor slowing, and spatial ability. The authors then performed a similar factor analysis on the data in the Satz (1966) original sample of 122 males. No tests of factor structure similarity were performed. However, from an inspection of the factor loadings, it appears that only the spatial ability factor was replicated. Most probably, the instability of the factor solution was due to the small sample sizes used in both cases. There are several areas where more information is needed on the BRT. The reliability of the test needs to be more fully evaluated. The scoring is based on examiner judgment. Therefore the most important type of reliability information missing is interscorer reliability. Additionally, a test–retest sample of 18 subjects is not adequate. The issue of the sex of the subjects in the last three cross-validation samples may obviate the issue of the sex differences in spatial abilities if it turns out that females were included. Lastly, the final derived discriminant function needs to be cross-validated.

THE MINNESOTA PERCEPTO-DIAGNOSTIC TEST

The Minnesota Percepto-Diagnostic Test (MPDT) was first described by Fuller and Laird (1963) in a monograph. The revised version was described in a subsequent monograph (Fuller, 1969). Thirteen years later, the manual was published (Fuller, 1982). Much of the information provided in the manual is available in the monograph's descriptions of identical studies, including exactly the same subject characteristics.

The MPDT consists of six Gestalt designs that are to be copied by the subject. These designs are scored on the basis of the three dimensions of rotation, separation of the components of the design, and distortion of the designs. The rotation score is obtained by use of a protractor, 25 degrees being the maximum score. The other scores are qualitative and are scored for presence or absence.

Fuller (1969) denoted four uses of the MPDT: to classify the etiology of reading and learning disorders in children; to classify behavior-problem children as having normal, emotionally disturbed, or schizophrenic perception; to assess the maturational level of normal and retarded children; and to classify adults as normal, brain-damaged, or emotionally disturbed.

The normative data on the MPDT were obtained from 4,000 students between the ages of 5 and 20. The author of the test attempted to correct for age and IQ in the test. This correction was accomplished with a methodology first used by Fuller, Sharp, and Hawkins (1967). Each of the age groups was examined for differences in test score due to age, separately for children with IQs over 88 and under 87. There were no significant differences for ages over 14 in the IQ-over-88 group, so these groups were collapsed together. For the same reason, the children with IQs under 87 were collapsed into groups of 5–9 years, 10–15 years, and 16 years and older. Then IQ was correlated with the test scores separately for each of the collapsed age groups. The solved regression formulas were used to predict the median test score for each group in the normative sample. The difference between the predicted and the obtained median test scores was then used as the correction factor. Although this seems to be a reasonable methodology, it must be pointed out that the extent to which the suggested procedure actually corrects for the influence of age and IQ has not been empirically demonstrated.

Reliability

The MPDT has a suggested alternate form, which actually consists of the same items given in a different order. The relation between these two forms was examined in a sample of 1,128 normal schoolchildren, who received both forms in counterbalanced order. The same mean rotation scores were obtained for both forms, but the standard deviations were different for the 9- and 10-year-old children. Therefore, the raw scores obtained by use of the alternate form should not be interpreted in these age groups. The alternate-form reliability coefficients for the rotation scores ranged from .34 for the 8-year-old children to .88 for the 14-year-old children. When corrected for the restricted range of the score values, the coefficients ranged from .74 for the 7-year-olds to .98 for the children older than 14.

Test–retest reliability over a 1-year interval was evaluated for 165 children. The coefficients ranged from .37 for the 7-year-old children to .60 for the 11-year-old children. When 177 children aged 9–12 were tested with a 3-month interval, the coefficients ranged from .53 to .70. The MPDT has differential temporal stability across age groups. The interpretation of gains or losses obtained on retest occasions should therefore be tempered by consideration of the age-appropriate reliability coefficients.

Split-half reliability was evaluated by comparing the rotation scores for the circle–diamond stimuli with the scores for the dot stimuli. No information was given about the subjects in this study reported in the manual (Fuller, 1982). The coefficients ranged from .40 to .73. Split-half reliability was also examined by comparing the rotation scores of the first half of the items with the second half. It was reported that the coefficients ranged from .52 to .86. All of these studies used children as subjects. There are no published reports of the reliability of the MPDT in adult subjects.

Vance, Lester, and Thatcher (1983) examined the interscorer reliability of the MPDT when one of the scorers had expert status (the author of the test) and one scorer had novice status (a testing technician with 2 hours of instruction). The subject sample used was a group of 30 children (18 males and 12 females) who had been referred for evaluation. The authors found no significant differences between the two scorers on the Separation of Circle–Diamond and Distortion of Dot scores, but they did find significant differences on the Rotation scores and the Distortion of Circle–Diamond scores. These results indicate the sensitivity of the test results to the level of training of the scorer.

In all of the above reliability studies, the values of the coefficients were moderate at best. This fact has implications for the clinical utility of the

MPDT. Without reliable scores, diagnosis conducted with the MPDT is likely to be of uncertain accuracy. Fuller (1969) argued that a more appropriate test of reliability would be to assess the stability of diagnostic decisions based on data from the MPDT. However, to date, no study has examined this facet of the instrument.

Validity

In the original description of the development of the MPDT (Fuller, 1969), the diagnostic validity of the test was evaluated on a sample of 5,552 children divided among the categories of normal, emotionally disturbed, schizophrenic, reading-disabled, brain-damaged, and good readers. The reading-disabled children were identified by scores 2 or more years below their expected scores on either the Gates–MacGinitie Reading Tests or Gray's Oral Reading Test. Similarly, good readers were identified by scores on the same reading tests that were 1 or more years ahead of expected scores. Membership in the other groups was determined by decisions made by various professionals using unspecified criteria. By examining the distribution of scores, optimal cutoff points were determined that correctly classified 84% of the normal, 80% of the emotionally disturbed, and 81% of the brain-damaged children. These rates are likely to shrink in any attempt to apply the cutoff points to subjects who were not in the derivation sample. There is no report of an examination of the diagnostic accuracy of these cutoff points in a cross-validation sample.

An evaluation of the validity of an instrument includes an assessment of the extent to which it provides data that covary with conceptually similar information and the extent to which they do not covary with conceptually dissimilar information. Helmes, Holden, and Howe (1980) reported that the MPDT does not correlate with the Smith Symbol Digits Modality Test, a test that is also supposed to tap aspects of cortical integrity. Snow, Hynd, Hartlage, and Grant (1983) reported that the MPDT does not correlate well with any of the clinical scales of the Luria–Nebraska Neuropsychological Battery–Children's Revision (LNNB-C). These authors argued that this result was due to the MPDT's being sensitive to aspects of cortical functioning that are not tapped by the LNNB-C. However, this is unlikely for two reasons. First, the LNNB-C taps a extremely wide range of cortical functioning. Second, as mentioned above, the MPDT has not been reported to correlate with other tests of cortical integrity.

Scores on the MPDT may be sensitive to other variables. For example, Fuller and Friedrich (1979) reported that, in a sample of 60 black and 60 Caucasian children, with IQ as a covariate, scores on the MPDT were sensitive to both academic achievement and race. Lin and Rennick (1973) found that relations between the rotation score of the MPDT and IQ were different by sex in a sample of 117 epileptic men and 60 epileptic women.

Many of the uses of the MPDT proposed in the manual are related to the detection of perceptual problems that would adversely affect academic achievement. A direct assessment of the validity of the instrument would involve an evaluation of the relation of scores obtained from the instrument to other measures of perception. There are no published reports of such a study. A less direct assessment of the validity of the instrument would involve an evaluation of the relation between the MPDT and some measure of academic achievement. Fuller and Wallbrown (1983) reported that, in a sample of 69 first-grade children, the scores of the MPDT were related to academic achievement as measured by the California Achievement Test. However, the largest correlation coefficient had a value of $-.59$, explaining only 35% of the variance. Wallbrown, Wallbrown, and Engin (1977) examined the relation of the MPDT to California Achievement Test scores in a sample of 153 third-grade students and found the highest correlation to be only $-.56$. Putman (1981) examined the relation of the MPDT to reading achievement scores obtained from the Woodcock Reading Mastery Test. She used a sample of 102 remedial readers, and when the influence of mental age was partialed out, there was a correlation of $-.25$, which was not statistically significant. The modest correlations reported in these studies indicate the limited utility of the MPDT in this area.

A second proposed use of the MPDT involves the discrimination of brain-damaged and non-brain-damaged children. Fuller and Hawkins (1969) reported a hit rate of 85% in discriminating brain-damaged from non-brain-damaged adolescents. Fuller and Friedrich (1974) reported that Hillow (1971), in her unpublished master's thesis, had only a 45% hit rate using their actuarial system, but a 68% hit rate using a discriminant function analysis. Fuller and Friedrich (1974) reported a 63% hit rate using Hillow's discriminant function in a sample of 241 adolescents and a 79% hit rate using Fuller and Hawkin's actuarial formula (1969). Considering there were only two groups and almost a 50% chance of correct classification, none of these hit rates are very impressive.

Several studies have examined the ability of the MPDT to discriminate between brain-damaged, non-brain-damaged, and psychiatric adult subjects. Helmes et al. (1980) reported that the MPDT was not sensitive to the presence or absence of brain damage in 82 psychiatric subjects. Holland and Wadsworth (1974) found that the MPDT was unable to discriminate between 20 brain-damaged and 20 schizophrenic subjects when the influence of IQ was partialed out. Crookes and Coleman (1973) reported that, although rotation scores alone could not discriminate brain damage from psychiatric diagnoses, there was a significant difference between the overall scores (including qualitative scores) of brain-damaged and psychiatric subjects. George (1973) found that the MPDT was sensitive to all psychiatric disturbances, and that, the more severe the disturbance, the more similar to brain-damage scores were the scores. Holland, Wadsworth, and Royer (1975b) reported that the MPDT could not discriminate between 20 brain-damaged and 20 schizophrenic subjects who were matched for age, educational level, and IQ. Crookes (1983) found that, overall, there was no significant difference between psychiatric and brain-damaged subjects on the MPDT, unless the subjects were matched for age.

This last point raises an important consideration. Although the manual (Fuller, 1982) recommends the use of the MPDT to discriminate adult brain-damaged subjects from psychiatric subjects, the scoring system is based on a normative sample whose oldest subject was 22 years old. The manual made a careful effort to partial out the effect of IQ and age in the scoring system, but only in subjects younger than 22. The inconclusiveness of the studies reviewed above may be partly the result of using an age-inappropriate scoring system.

Watson, Gasser, Schaefer, Buranen, and Wold (1981) attempted to improve the discriminative power of the MPDT by adding a background interference to the procedure. They used age-matched groups of married schizophrenics, unmarried schizophrenics, affective psychotics, alcoholics, subjects with neurotic personality disorders, and organics. There were 30 subjects in each group. Unfortunately, the basis for deciding whether or not a subject would be included in each group was not reported. The authors reported significant differences in the qualitative scores, but not in the rotation scores.

Fuller and Friedrich (1976) examined 112 subjects, 28 in each group of normal, personality disorder, psychotic, and organic subjects. When age was covaried, the test scores were significantly affected by the group membership variable. However, because the authors did not report the group distributions, it is difficult to tell whether the MPDT would be useful for diagnostic purposes in the individual case.

Another reason for the inconclusive results of the validity studies may lie in the conceptual basis of the test. Wallbrown and Fuller (1984) stated that MDPT abnormal scores may be obtained as the result of either emotional or organic factors. The MDPT is said to measure accurate perception, which is sensitive to a wide range of factors. Because the test requires the subject to draw, it is also a measure of fine-motor control and of the reproduction of spatial relations. The utility of the instrument would be enhanced if the scoring method allowed a means of separating these factors. Wallbrown and Fuller (1984) provided a five-step method of interpreting the MDPT but failed to provide adequate empirical evidence regarding the accuracy of this procedure. Additionally, the five-step method does allow one to decompose the test results into the skill areas that are described in the manual.

Reliability information is lacking for adult populations and for special populations of children, such as retarded children or brain-damaged children. There is no published research that examines the ability of the instrument to classify children's perceptions as normal, emotionally disturbed, schizophrenic, or brain-damaged. Also needed is research that demonstrates the relation between the diagnoses made by the five-step method and diagnostic decisions made from independent information. Another line of research would investigate the treatment implications of diagnoses made with the instrument. Treatments for different diagnoses are themselves different. Therefore, research is needed investigating the effectiveness of treatments prescribed on the basis of the information provided by the instrument. Wallbrown and Fuller (1984) described three different types of reading disabilities that can be identified by the MDPT, but more research is needed to evaluate the validity of the instrument in performing these diagnoses.

18

Tests of Higher Cognitive Functions

THE PORTEUS MAZE

The Porteus Maze Test is a series of increasingly difficult mazes, which the manual states are designed to examine the ability to use "planning capacity, prudence, and mental alertness in a new situation of a concrete nature" (Stoelting, undated, p. 1). The manual also asserts that performance on the test is affected by "impulsiveness, suggestibility, irresolution, and excitability" (p. 1). The user is told to expect practice effects, but not to worry about their presence because practice is built into the test. The Porteus has held fascination for clinical neuropsychologists for a long time. It has often been used as a dependent measure in experimental and clinical investigation, but its diagnostic utility is largely unknown.

Because of its reliance on successful planning, inhibition of impulsive behavior, and ability to change set, the Porteus has been used to document the behavioral effects of psychosurgery of the frontal regions. Smith and Kinder (1959) examined schizophrenics before surgery and 8 years post-surgery. There were 28 operated schizophrenics and 24 nonoperated schizophrenics. The subjects were further divided into young and old subjects, and the operated subjects were divided into orbital-topectomy subjects and superior-topectomy subjects. Both the pre- and postevaluations were actually pairs of evaluations 1 month apart in each case. The means of each of these two evaluations were taken as the pre- and postmeasures. At the 8-year follow-up, the operated schizophrenics demonstrated significantly worse performance than did the nonoperated subjects. There were no significant differences due to age or locus of surgery.

Smith (1960) also examined the impact of psychosurgery on Porteus Maze performance. With the same subjects as were used in Smith and Kinder (1959), and with the addition of 16 more operated schizophrenic subjects,

225

the analysis was conducted using only one each of the pre- and postsurgery Porteus measurements. Additionally, Porteus scores taken shortly after surgery were included in the analysis. In this analysis, there was a significant age-by-site interaction; the younger orbital-site subjects actually increased their postsurgery scores slightly. However, in general, the results were that the scores decreased both following surgery and at the 8-year follow-up. Smith interpreted the results in terms of the effects on the frontal lobe; namely, a dysfunctional frontal lobe results in decrements in certain psychological functions over time, as the brain no longer has its "executive" to direct learning. These results were at odds with earlier studies, which had reported that postoperative losses in Porteus scores were recovered over time. Riddle and Roberts (1978) reviewed several of these studies and concluded that most of the postoperative recovery was due to practice effects, which had gone unnoticed because of the lack of a control group in the design. The study reported by Smith (1960) had such a control group, which is why he was able to document the permanence of the effects.

Meier and Story (1967) studied subjects who had received subthalamotomy as a treatment for Parkinsonism. There were 12 subjects who had received left thalamotomy and 17 subjects who had received right thalamotomy. The subjects were administered the Porteus, Trails A and B, and the Wechsler–Bellevue Intelligence Scale 1 week before surgery and between 5 and 15 months after surgery. There were no changes in the Trails or Wechsler–Bellevue scores; however, there was a statistically significant average decrease of 3 years in mental age score on the Porteus in the right-subthalamotomy subjects and a nonsignificant decrease of 1 year in mental age score in the left-subthalamotomy subjects. The authors hypothesized that the decrements occurred because the surgeries had been done on areas in the fields of Forel, which have abundant innervation to the frontal lobes.

Gow and Ward (1982) administered the Porteus to 90 subjects across a range of IQ values. They divided their subjects into three groups of 30 subjects each: a group with IQs between 135 and 116, a group with IQs between 115 and 86, and a group with IQs less than 85. They found significant differences due to group membership, indicating that the Porteus is sensitive to intelligence. However, it likely that the Porteus measures a more narrowly defined skill than is usually thought of as intelligence, as might be construed from the Meier and Story (1967) study, in which there were effects for the Porteus but not for the measure of general intelligence. Research to partial out the particular constructs of the Porteus is now needed. This is particularly important, as Riddle and Roberts (1977) indicate that scores on the Porteus are partly affected by degree of impulsivity and the presence of delinquency in younger subjects.

The practice effects need to be documented clearly by test–retest reliability studies. Also other forms of reliability need to be investigated. Finally, the construct validity of the Porteus needs to be investigated.

ELITHORN'S PERCEPTUAL MAZE

Elithorn's Perceptual Maze Test (PMT) was designed to study the effects of psychosurgery (specifically prefrontal leucotomy) on intellectual functioning (Elithorn, 1955). Because at the time, the Porteus Maze was considered the most sensitive measure of frontal damage, a maze procedure was used. The PMT consists of 30 patterns that have dots superimposed on a lattice background. The subject is required to connect the dots in a way that maximizes the number of dots transversed by the line. However, the subject can draw the line only forward and is not allowed to back up in order to connect additional dots. In the original version, the paper on which the pattern was drawn was pulled through a mask via a motor that standardized the speed of movement of the piece of paper. However, the time constraints seemed to intimidate some subjects, so this procedure was discontinued in favor of a flat sheet of paper on which the pattern was printed. Performance was then timed.

Elithorn, Mornington, and Stavrou (1982) stated that the intent of the test is to adhere to the experimental tradition rather than the psychometric tradition. The test is therefore criterion-referenced rather than norm-referenced, and little has been done to investigate the statistical and psychometric properties of the test.

In the procedure used in the original report (Elithorn, 1955), 30 patterns were used. There was one best solution for each pattern. If the subject did not solve the maze in 60 seconds, the solution was shown, and the next pattern was presented. Testing was discontinued when the subject failed to solve four consecutive mazes within the 30-second time limit for each maze. The score consists of 1 point for each successful solution and 1 bonus point for each solution within the 30-second limit.

Three groups of subjects were used (Elithorn, 1955). The first group consisted of 20 individuals who had had psychosurgical procedures and who were tested pre- and postsurgery. Of the 15 subjects given a prefrontal leucotomy, 12 improved their scores on the PMT an average of 10 points. Of the 5 subjects given temporal lobectomies, all decreased their score on the PMT an average of 8 points. In the second group of subjects in this report, 22 individuals were given a full leucotomy, and 13 were given a partial leucotomy. No presurgery data are available for these subjects. The subjects who received partial leucotomies scored 5 points higher on the average; however, this difference was not statistically significant. The 85 subjects in the third group consisted of neurological and psychiatric inpatients who did not have psychosurgery. These individuals were administered the PMT and the Vocabulary subtest and Block Design subtest of the WAIS. There was a correlation of .46 with the Vocabulary subtest and .74 with the Block Design. The author concluded that the PMT was sensitive to frontal dysfunction and that the PMT tapped spatial skills (Elithorn, 1955).

There is also a group form available for the PMT. The group form consists of two parts: Part A, which has 30 patterns, and Part B, which has 20 patterns. An alternate form of these two parts exists in the form of inverted copies of the patterns. The group form is timed, and there is no feedback regarding performance as there is in the individually administered form. Subjects are allowed 10 minutes to finish each part. Elithorn, Kerr, and Mott (1960) reported the results of an investigation of these forms of the PMT. Some of the subjects in this study were administered the original form twice, and some of the subjects were administered first the original form and then the alternate form. With a 14-day test–retest interval, the correlation for the same form was .89. For the alternate form with the same interval, the correlation was .81. The difference between the two correlation values is not statistically significant. No data are available regarding alternate-form reliability when the order of administration is counterbalanced, or when no time interval separates the administration of the two forms. There is no test–retest reliability available for the individually administered form.

There is also a computerized version of the PMT that can be individually administered. Elithorn *et al.* (1982) stated that many more potential scores are available with the computerized form, such as reaction time and a record of the solution strategy. However, the characteristics of these scores have not been investigated.

There has been research investigating the validity of the PMT as a measure of spatial visual-perceptual skills and of planning. Lee (1967) reported that performance on the PMT was relatively independent of previously acquired skills and was sensitive to brain damage. Weinman and Cooper (1981) administered the PMT to a group of 817 first-year secondary-school children in the United Kingdom. The children had an average age of 11.4. The authors found that the response characteristics were related to the overall level of perceptual-problem-solving skills.

Jahoda (1969) administered the PMT to 280 male students at the University of Ghana and found that the scores were normally distributed. Sixty-six of these subjects were also administered the Block Design subtest of the WAIS, the Embedded Figures Test, and a test of algebraic ability. There was a correlation of .52 with the Block Design Test, .46 with the Embedded Figures Test, and .40 with algebraic ability. The students who came from a literate family scored significantly better than the students from an illiterate family. These results indicate that the PMT is sensitive to more than just visual-perceptual skills, consistent with the conclusion of Elithorn *et al.* (1982) that performance on the PMT is sensitive to the personality variable of introversion–extroversion, as conceptualized by Eysenck (1952).

In order to investigate the organic substrate of performance on the PMT, Elithorn, Svancara, and Weinman (1971) administered the PMT to 14 pairs of monozygotic twins and 17 pairs of dizygotic twins. When the score used was the number of trials successfully completed and the influence of age was partialed out, there was a .28 correlation between monozygotic twins and of .41 between dizygotic twins. When the score used was the total number of dots connected, there was a correlation of .70 between the monozygotic twins and of .60 between the dizygotic twins. Apparently, the degree of genetic organic substrate underlying performance on the PMT depends partially on which score is used.

Colonna and Faglioni (1966) administered the PMT to 112 subjects with unilateral hemispheric lesions as diagnosed by X rays, EEGs, and a neurological exam. There were 53 subjects with right-hemisphere lesions and 59 subjects with left-hemisphere lesions. An analysis of covariance was performed, with age and education used as the covariates. The results of this analysis indicated that the right-hemisphere subjects performed significantly worse than the left-hemisphere subjects, that subjects with visual field defects performed significantly worse than subjects without defects, and that aphasics performed significantly worse than the nonaphasics.

Archibald (1978) administered the PMT to 29 left-hemisphere-lesioned subjects (18 of whom were aphasic), to 19 right-hemisphere-lesioned subjects, and to 30 normal control subjects. There were no significant differences among the groups in age or education. All of the lesions had been caused by cardiovascular accidents (CVAs), and all subjects were tested at least 3 months post-CVA. When time limits were used, the normals scored significantly better than either the right- or left-hemisphere-lesioned subjects, and the left-hemisphere-lesioned subjects scored better than the right-hemisphere-lesioned subjects. There were no differences between the aphasic and the nonaphasic left-hemisphere-lesioned subjects. When the performance was measured without time limits, there were no differences between the left-hemisphere subjects and the normals, although the right-hemisphere subjects performed significantly worse than either.

Benton, Elithorn, Fogel, and Kerr (1963) examined performance on the PMT and on the 27 tests in Benton's assessment battery in 100 brain-damaged and 100 normal subjects. They found that the PMT was one of the most sensitive indicators of brain damage in the battery of 28 tests used. Additionally, the PMT differentiated between the right- and left-hemisphere-lesioned subjects.

The PMT appears to be a sensitive indicator of frontal lobe damage, of right-hemisphere damage, and of brain damage in general. However, research can increase the usefulness of this procedure in a clinical setting. In light of the various forms and scores available, a standardized version would be useful in evaluating individual subjects. In particular, although the original intent of the test was not psychometric, that type of evaluation can provide needed information about the characteristics of the various scores that can be derived. The theoretical meaning of poor performance on the PMT needs to be delineated; such a delineation will help provide localization information as well as an elucidation of the functional significance of performance on the PMT.

VERBAL CONCEPT ATTAINMENT TEST

The Verbal Concept Attainment Test (VCAT) is a verbal problem-solving test that can be seen as a verbal analogue of tests such as the Category Test or the Wisconsin Card Sorting Test. In the VCAT, the subject is presented with a list of 16 words arranged on a page in a 4-by-4 matrix. The subject is told that one word in each row has something in common with one word in each of the other three rows and is asked to underline those four words that form a concept. There are no reports of evaluations of any form of reliability of this test.

Bornstein (1982b) administered the VCAT and the Halstead–Reitan to 109 patients who had been referred for neuropsychological evaluation. He found that the VCAT correlated with all of the Halstead–Reitan measures except the Finger Tapping Test. The Wisconsin Card Sorting Test was administered to 92 of the subjects. There was a small but significant correlation (.31) between the VCAT and the Wisconsin Card Sorting Test. (The score from the Wisconsin Card Sorting Test was not reported, but most likely, it was the total error score.) The data were then submitted to an unspecified form of factor analysis with varimax rotation. The VCAT was found to load on the verbal reasoning factor and the nonverbal reasoning factor. Bornstein (1983a) found similar correlation patterns in a sample of 75 patients who had been referred for neuropsychological evaluation. A booklet form of this test was found to have a significant relation to the Impairment Index of the Halstead–Reitan in the same report. Bornstein and Leason (1985) administered the VCAT to 97 patients with unilateral lesions, 52 patients with right-hemisphere lesions, and 45 patients with left-hemisphere lesions. In addition, the patients were divided into frontal and nonfrontal lesions. An analysis of variance conducted on the data indicated that the left-hemisphere patients scored significantly worse than the right-hemisphere patients. The frontal lesion patients scored significantly worse than the nonfrontal lesion patients.

Bornstein (1986b) compared the Halstead Category Test, the Wisconsin Card Sorting Test, and the VCAT in their response to unilateral lesions in a sample of 53 patients who had been diagnosed with the aid of CT, EEG, and angiography. An ANOVA indicated that there were no significant effects of caudality or laterality on Halstead Category Test performance, and that there was only an effect of caudality on the Wisconsin Card Sorting Test perseverative score (frontal injuries were associated with worse performance). However, there was a significant interaction effect of caudality and laterality on VCAT performance (left-hemisphere injuries and anterior injuries were associated with worse performance). A discriminant function analysis resulted in 67.9% correct classification into the quadrant of lesion, with VCAT scores entered first into the stepwise equation. However, there was a low ratio of subjects to predictors, and the results are in need of cross-validation.

These results imply the promise of the instrument in clinical settings. However, the reliability of the instrument needs to be determined. Additionally, cutoff points and interpretation guidelines need to be developed.

WEIGL COLOR–FORM SORTING TEST

The Weigl Color–Form Sorting Test was designed by Weigl (1941) as a test sensitive to structural brain lesions. In particular, Weigl was interested in the abstraction-skills deficits demonstrated by aphasics. The test has been revised and currently consists of three subtests. In the first subtest, the subject is given nine plastic figures of three shapes (a triangle, a square, and a circle) and three colors (red, blue, and yellow). The subject is asked to sort the plastic figures on the basis of the two categories of color and shape. In the second subtest, there are 18 figures: the original 9 and 9 additional figures, which are the same as the originals except that they are one half their size. In the third subtest, there are 36 figures: the figures from the second subtest plus their replicas constructed of cardboard. In each subtest, the variable of interest is the ability of the subject to shift categories while sorting. The reliability of the Weigl has not been investigated.

There is some intriguing information that suggests the clinical usefulness of the Weigl. In an investigation of the construct validity of the Weigl Test, Tamkin and Kunce (1982) reported small correlations with WAIS Verbal IQ scores ($r = .46$), the Similarities subtest of the WAIS ($r = .42$), Bender–Gestalt recall scores ($r = .32$), and the Hooper Visual Organization Test ($r = .30$) in a sample of 38 male psychiatric inpatients. Further, there was a negative correlation with age ($r = -.33$). There was no significant correlation with education. In a stepwise multiple-regression application, there was a multiple R of .52 when the VIQ and age were used to predict Weigl scores. An earlier study had demonstrated an effect of education on Weigl scores (Tamkin, 1980). Ward (1982) investigated the Weigl in a sample of 400 children aged 8–11 and reported a significant relation with age. There is apparently a relation between Weigl scores and age and education that needs to be articulated before widespread clinical use of the instrument can be recommended.

The accuracy of the Weigl in diagnosis has been investigated. McFie and Piercy (1952) examined Weigl performance in 74 brain-damaged individuals. There was a wide variety of etiologies and of locations of lesions, so the results are difficult to interpret. The authors concluded that the Weigl is sensitive to left-hemisphere impairment and is not related to aphasia. In contrast, De Renzi, Faglioni, Savoiardo, and Vignolo (1966) examined Weigl performance in 40 control subjects, 40 right-hemisphere-impaired subjects, 22 nonaphasic left-hemisphere-impaired subjects, and 45 aphasic left-hemisphere-impaired subjects. These investigators covaried out the influence of age and education and found that only the aphasic subjects scored significantly worse that the control subjects. Additionally, the aphasic left-hemisphere subjects scored significantly worse than the nonaphasic left-hemisphere subjects. There was no significant difference between the performance of the nonaphasic left-hemisphere subjects and the right-hemisphere subjects. The authors concluded that the Weigl was sensitive to aphasia and insensitive to brain impairment in general. Although the more rigorous design of the De Renzi *et al.* study allows us to have more confidence in its results, more research is needed before strong conclusions can be reached.

WISCONSIN CARD SORTING TEST

The Wisconsin Card Sorting Test (WCST) is an old and well-known instrument in clinical neuropsychology. The test was originally designed by Berg (1948), but there have been several variations. Today, the most commonly used version is by Heaton (1981). In the WCST, the subject is asked to sort a double stack of 64 cards each into categories identified by four stimulus cards. The cards can be sorted by color, form, or number. The subject is allowed to sort, and the examiner provides feedback regarding the accuracy of each sort. Unbeknownst to the subject, the correct principle changes each time the subject performs 10 consecutive correct sortings. The test is therefore an evaluation of the subject's ability to use abstraction skills as well as an evaluation of the subject's ability to change sets. Heaton provided rules for determining several scores, but the scores that have generated the most interest are the perseverative-responses score and the perseverative-errors score. The reliability of the WCST has not been evaluated. Developmental norms for the WCST were derived from children between the ages of 6 and 12 in a sample of 103 subjects (Chelune & Baer, 1986).

The WCST has been found to be sensitive to brain impairment. Both Parsons (1977) and Tarter and Parsons (1971) found that alcoholics demonstrated impaired performance on the WCST, mainly related to perseveration. Most of the interest in the WCST has been in its ability to diagnose frontal lobe impairment. Milner (1963) examined WCST performance in 71 subjects who had been given cortical excision as a treatment for intractable epilepsy. Eighteen of these patients had been afflicted in the dorsolateral frontal regions. The remaining 53 patients had had involvement in other cerebral areas. Before the surgical intervention, the frontal subjects had more impaired scores on the total-errors and the perseverative-errors scores of the WCST. Following surgery, the frontal lobe subjects performed much worse, and the other subjects actually showed some improvement. Malmo (1974) used Milner's frontal subjects (1963) and compared their performance with that of 244 psychiatric patients divided into groups of schizophrenics, alcoholics, neurotics, and mixed diagnoses. The frontal lobe patients demonstrated statistically significantly more total errors than the other groups. Taylor (1979) found more perseverative errors associated with dorsolateral lesions of the frontal lobes; he also found that the left-frontal-lobe subjects tended to score worse than the right-frontal-lobe subjects.

Drewe (1974) examined WCST performance in 22 left-frontal-lobe subjects, 21 right-frontal-lobe subjects, 24 left-nonfrontal subjects, and 24 right-nonfrontal subjects. He reported that left-frontal subjects performed significantly worse than the other subjects in total errors, in perseverative errors, and in the number of categories completed. In general, the combined frontal groups performed more poorly than the other subjects in perseverative errors and in the number of categories completed. The right-frontal subjects performed significantly better than the other subjects in nonperseverative errors.

Robinson, Heaton, Lehman, and Stilson (1980) investigated the WCST in 123 normal control subjects and 107 subjects with structural lesions, 69 of whom had focal lesions. Following an analysis of covariance of age, education, and the Average Impairment Rating (AIR) of the Halstead–Reitan Neuropsychological Battery, these researchers found that the brain-impaired subjects performed significantly worse than the control subjects, and that the frontal lobe subjects performed significantly worse than the non-frontal-lobe subjects. These authors then performed a discriminant-function analysis using the perseverative-errors score from the WCST, age, education, and the AIR as predictors of the presence of brain impairment, with a 68% accuracy rate. When a discriminant-function analysis was performed using the perseverative-errors score of the WCST and the scores from the individual subtests of the Halstead–Reitan, there was an 85% correct classification rate.

Because the Categories test of the Halstead–Reitan is said to measure some of the same functions as the WCST, an important question is whether these two tests provide different information. King and Snow (1981) administered the WCST and the Categories test to 89 brain-impaired and 67 control subjects. The partial correlation between the number of categories completed in the WCST and the total-errors score of the Categories test, when age and education were controlled for, was − .55. A second evaluation of these subjects was conducted from which those control subjects with a suggestion of brain impairment were excluded. The number of control subjects decreased to 44. When the cutoff points suggested in the respective manuals were used, the Categories test correctly classified 85% of the brain-impaired and 80% of the control subjects. The WCST correctly classified 68% of the brain-impaired subjects and 89% of the control subjects. Apparently, the Categories test is more sensitive to brain impairment in general.

In another attempt to determine the diagnostic utility of the WCST, Pendleton and Heaton (1982) administered the same two tests to 207 subjects with structural cerebral lesions (classified among frontal, nonfrontal, and diffuse lesions) and to 150 normal controls. The dependent measures were the total number of errors on the Categories test and the number of perseverative responses on the WCST. When the cutoff points from the manuals were used, the Categories test appeared to be more sensitive to brain impairment. The two tests disagreed in 24% of the cases. In cases of disagreement, the WCST was more accurate for frontal injuries, and the Categories test was more accurate for the subjects with nonfrontal and diffuse injuries.

MacInnes, Golden, McFadden, and Wilkening (1983) investigated the relation between the WCST and the Booklet Form of the Category Test. They administered both tests in counterbalanced order to 30 brain-impaired individuals and 31 normal control subjects. They calculated all 14 scores recommended in the WCST manual and found that age correlated significantly with 12 of these variables and that education correlated significantly with 10 of the variables. When the influence of age and education was partialed out, the largest correlation between the Booklet Form of the Category Test total-errors score and the WCST scores was $-.52$. With the use of a stepwise multiple-regression methodology, with age, education, and the 14 WCST scores as possible predictors, only the number of categories completed was entered into the regression equation following age and education. Age and education accounted for 46% of the shared variance. When the various hit rates in diagnosis were compared (by use of the total number of errors score from the Booklet Form of the Category Test and the five scores that are given cutoff points in the WCST manual), the Booklet Form of the Category Test had a 59.0% hit rate overall. The WCST hit rates ranged from 59.0% to 70.5%. Significantly, the Booklet Form of the Category Test misclassified 11 of the 14 subjects over the age of 45. The authors concluded that, although the Booklet Form of the Category Test and the WCST have common properties, they provide distinctly different clinical information and should not be used interchangeably.

Bornstein (1986b) administered the Halstead Category test, the Wisconsin Card Sorting Test, and the Verbal Concept Attainment Test (VCAT) to a group of 53 patients with circumscribed lesions localized by the use of CT, EEG, and angiography. Although there were no effects of caudality or laterality on Category test performance, there was a significant effect of caudality on the Wisconsin Card Sorting Test perseverative score; the anterior-lesioned patient performing worse. It should be pointed out that all of these data are based on group studies. Heck and Bryer (1986) presented the case of an individual with 1.5 years of college education who had severe frontal atrophy and who performed in the superior range on the Wisconsin Card Sorting Test. However, the performance of this individual may have been due to a high level of premorbid functioning.

Screening Devices

THE BENDER–GESTALT VISUAL MOTOR INTEGRATION TEST

The Bender–Gestalt test has a long and varied history. It has four major scoring systems and has been used for several purposes, including the diagnosis of psychosis, the identification of learning disabilities in children, the description of personality, and the diagnosis of organicity. Because of this history of multiple usage, it is important to clarify which version of the Bender–Gestalt is under discussion at a given time. Unless otherwise noted, this chapter will confine its discussion of the Bender–Gestalt to its use as an instrument for screening for organicity in adults (using the Hutt & Briskin, 1980, scoring system) and its use to identify neurological and developmental disabilities in children (using the Koppitz, 1960, scoring system).

The Bender–Gestalt is a relatively straightforward test to administer. The test materials consist of nine stimulus cards with designs printed on them. The subject is given a pencil and some plain white $8\frac{1}{2}'' \times 11''$ paper and is shown the stimulus cards one at a time. The subject is instructed to copy the designs as best she or he can. In the Hutt–Briskin scoring method, 12 errors can be made by the subject. These errors are different ways of distorting the designs. Each type of error can be scored only once per protocol. A score of 5 errors or more is representative of organic performance. The Koppitz scoring method consists of 30 characteristics of performance that are scored on the basis of absence or presence. These items are summed for possible scores ranging from zero to 30 points.

There have been some suggested alterations in administration. There is a group administration method in which the subjects are simultaneously administered the test through the use of oversized cards. In another administration alteration, the subject is asked to reproduce the designs from memory. A third alteration presents the stimuli tachistoscopically, and a fourth version requires the subject to reproduce the design on paper on which is printed a background of interfering wavy lines.

Normative Data

Lacks (1984) presented normative data on the Hutt–Briskin method for 325 normals aged 17–59. Caucasian subjects, with a mean score of 1.58 errors, tended to perform better than black subjects, who had a mean score of 2.21 errors. Males, with a mean of 2.07 errors, tended to perform more poorly than females, who had a mean of 1.37. Normative data are also available on 334 normal adults over 60 years old. Although still scoring below the organicity cutoff of 5 errors, the older subjects tended to demonstrate more errors, with a mean of 3.45 errors, compared with the young-adult mean of 1.75 (Lacks & Storandt, 1982).

Normative data are available for the Koppitz scoring method for normal children between the ages of 5 years and 10 years, 11 months (Koppitz, 1960). Norms are also available for Puerto Rican and black children in a study that used 74 Puerto Rican and 47 black children who were tested in the first grade and again in the third grade (Marmorale & Brown, 1977). Both the black and the Puerto Rican children performed more poorly than do Caucasian children. Extreme caution should be used in interpreting these norms because of the small sample size. Norms for adult retardates were reported by Andert, Dinning, and Hustak (1976). The sample for this study was composed of 510 adult resident retardates at a state school for the retarded. Norms are available for teenaged subjects only for the Pascal and Suttell scoring method (Grow, 1980).

Reliability

Lacks (1984) reviewed the reliability studies using the Bender–Gestalt. There is no alternate form for the Bender–Gestalt, and therefore, there is no estimate of alternate-form reliability. Lacks argued that, because of the nature of the test, there have been no split-half reliability studies. Given the Hutt–Briskin scoring system, it would be difficult to decide what split would be appropriate, as each of the items is different. Because categories of errors are counted only once for each protocol, it would be difficult to interpret any split-half coefficient even if it were obtained. A potential method of assessing split-half reliability would be to score each half as if it were a whole, that is, to count each occurrence of an error in each half. Presumably, the organic deficit responsible for the error would be robust enough to cause more than one occurrence of that error. However, as noted above, the items are different and probably represent different stimulus values.

It is appropriate to evaluate test–retest reliability for the Bender–Gestalt. There are three indices on which to focus the evaluation of test–retest reliability: we can examine the stability of the total scores, the stability of the occurrence of each type of error, or the stability of the dichotomous decision of organic versus nonorganic subjects. In a study of 40 psychiatric

patients (mixed inpatients and outpatients), Lacks (1984) reported a reliability coefficient of .79 for total scores, a concordance rate of 86% for the
occurrence of particular types of errors, and a 93% agreement rate for diagnosis of organicity. There was no attempt to correct for the low number
of categories by the use of Cohen's kappa (Cohen, 1960) or some other
method of assessing agreement in nominal data as discussed in Lawlis and
Lu (1972) and Tinsley and Weiss (1975). This omission presents a minor
problem with the test score data, which have 12 possible categories, but it
is an especially important problem in the case of the dichotomous diagnosis
of organicity. Here, the existence of only two categories means that there
is a 50% concordance by chance alone. Another problem with this study is
the failure of the author to take the base rate of diagnosis into account. As
a result of these two deficiencies, the values reported are most likely inflated
over their true values.

Lacks (1984) also reported the results of a test–retest reliability study
using 25 individuals with a diagnosis of Alzheimer's disease and a test–retest
interval of 12 months. The correlation coefficient relating the test scores
was .66, the concordance of scores was 63%, and the agreement of diagnosis
was 72%. The same problems discussed for the previous study—namely,
failure to account for the number of categories in nominal data and failure
to account for base rates—also apply to this study. There are additional
problems, in that Alzheimer's disease is a progressively dementing disorder.
Test–retest reliability is most accurately assessed when there is no intervening process that would change the true value of the obtained score. This
study failed to provide adequate theoretical consideration of this fact. There
are questions left unanswered. For example, would one expect more errors
over time as a result of the progressive nature of the disorder, or would one
expect more severe manifestations of the errors already present? The Hutt–
Briskin scoring system would seem to be insufficient to document and account for changes associated with Alzheimer's disease.

Lacks and Newport (1980) examined the interscorer reliability of the
Bender–Gestalt using four scoring methods and 12 scorers (3 using each
method) at three levels of scorer expertise in a sample of 50 inpatient subjects. There were no differences between interscorer reliability coefficients
among all of the methods except the Hain method. All of the scorers were
able to distinguish the organic from the nonorganic patients in fair agreement
with the discharge diagnosis. The Hutt–Briskin method was concluded to
be the most accurate in diagnosis, with an 83% agreement with discharge
diagnosis. Because of methodological flaws in the study, it is difficult to
interpret the results. Once again, there was no attempt to correct for the
number of categories in the nominal data or for the base rate of organicity
in the sample. Diagnoses of organicity were determined by the attending
psychiatrist and not by a neurologist, and the study included no examination
of the variability engendered by having different psychiatrists perform the

diagnoses nor an indication of the level of experience of the psychiatrists. Lastly, the subjects who had diagnoses of chronic alcoholism were included in the nonorganic group, and this classification was justified on the basis of the Bender–Gestalt results of these subjects. This is a clear confound of the independent variable of Bender–Gestalt scores with the dependent variable of diagnosis.

Reliability has also been examined for the Koppitz scoring method. Test–retest and interscorer reliability were assessed in a sample of 30 second-grade, 24 fourth-grade, and 27 sixth-grade children (Ryckman, Rentfrow, Fargo, & McCartin, 1972). There was a 1-week interval between testing sessions. Two scorers were used, one with an MA in psychology and the other with an Ed.D. The test–retest reliability coefficients for total obtained score were .67 for the first scorer and .64 for the second scorer. The interscorer reliability coefficients were .85 for the first test and .83 for the retest. Because the Koppitz method results in scores with a range of 0–30 points, the problems of limited categories discussed above for the Hutt–Briskin method are not as applicable here.

Wallbrown, Wallbrown, and Engin (1976) investigated test–retest reliability in 144 first-grade children with a test–retest interval of from 9 to 14 days. The average time interval was not reported. The test–retest reliability coefficient was .66. Engin and Wallbrown (1976) reported a test–retest coefficient of .63 in a sample of 157 second-grade students when the test interval ranged from 11 to 15 days. In neither of these studies were the children tested twice by the same examiner. Wallbrown *et al.* (1976) used six examiners, and Engin and Wallbrown used five examiners. Therefore, the test–retest coefficients reported in these studies also reflect interscorer variability.

Egeland, Rice, and Penny (1967) examined the interscorer reliability of the Koppitz scoring system in a sample of 80 retarded children with an average IQ of 78 as measured by either the Stanford–Binet or the WISC. The children were students in a university day-school program. Three doctoral students in a school psychology program served as the scorers. The mean correlation between total error scores for the three scorers was .90. The data were also submitted to an analysis of variance, which determined that there was a significant difference ($p < .01$) between the scores obtained by the three scorers. Although there was sufficient reliability of the relative position of the scores of each subject in the overall distribution, there was not sufficient reliability of the absolute level of scores. This result points out the necessity for caution when comparing absolute scores across scorers by the Koppitz method. Greater reliability of absolute scores is needed before an interpretation of the scores, including a comparison with cutoff points, can be accomplished.

Wallbrown and Fremont (1980) subsequently examined the test–retest reliability of Koppitz scores in a sample of 24 reading-disabled children. The test–retest interval ranged from 12 to 24 days, but no average interval was reported. The protocols were scored by three licensed psychologists, and disagreements (the level of necessary agreement was not defined) regarding the scores were settled by discussion. The test–retest reliability coefficient was .83. This coefficient is somewhat larger than what might be expected in the usual testing situation. Because the scores were taken only when there was agreement, some of the error variability associated with an individual scorer across time may have been partialed out methodologically. This coefficient is therefore a more accurate estimate of the reliability of the test itself, separate from the reliability of the scorer. However, generalization of these results to an ordinary testing situation would cause problems.

In each of the studies investigating the test–retest reliability of the Koppitz scoring method, only the reliability of the total score was reported. There was no indication of an attempt to assess the concordance of agreement of type of error or the reliability of diagnoses based on the instrument. These issues remain to be addressed by future research.

Validity

Validity research involving the Bender–Gestalt is sadly deficient. There have been no investigations of the content validity of the test, nor of the construct validity. Lacks (1984) stated that investigations of the content validity of the Bender–Gestalt are inappropriate, but this argument begs the question of what the test is supposed to measure. The lack of such studies is very likely due to the paucity of a theoretical or rational substrate for the test. The closest description of a construct associated with the test is the notion of *organicity*. This concept has been discarded in the neuropsychological literature in favor of a multidimensional concept of *organic integrity* involving multiple, semi-independent skills. A case could be made for the construct of the test as involving visual-motor skills, as has been done in the case of children. But even here, no empirical investigations have been reported.

Investigation of the validity of the Bender–Gestalt has centered on the criterion-related validity of the instrument. The criterion usually used is a diagnosis of organicity. The major shortcoming of this criterion lies in the nature of the concept of *organicity*. If we define the construct of organicity as the skills and behaviors for which brain integrity is responsible, several problems arise. The first problem is related to the content validity of the instrument. The Bender–Gestalt does not sample adequately from the realm of the skills that are mediated by the brain. The instrument is heavily loaded toward visual-perceptive and manual fine-motor skills. Although the results of the test can be seen to be sensitive to receptive language skills, there is no systematic method of assessing the impact of such skills on the results of the test. The test is insensitive to organic deficits that give rise to specific behavioral deficits, such as deficits in reading comprehension, arithmetic ability, memory, attention, or expressive speech skills. It is possible for an individual to have deficits in these areas and still manifest a normal Bender–Gestalt score. With these points in mind, let us examine the research that has investigated the criterion-related validity of the Bender–Gestalt.

Lacks (1984) evaluated the data provided by three separate studies that she conducted over a period of 20 years. She collapsed the diagnostic information into three categories: schizophrenia, personality disorder, and organic impairment. The diagnoses were provided by a variety of clinicians, both neurologists and psychiatrists. Alcoholics were included in the personality disorder group because their Bender–Gestalt scores as a whole were not different from the scores of the nonorganic subjects. This procedure spuriously inflated the estimate of the diagnostic accuracy of the test. Decisions regarding the criterion should be made independently of the values of the independent variable. Because the diagnoses were conducted over a 20-year period, they represent at least two diagnostic systems (American Psychiatric Association, 1952, 1968). There were only two diagnostic categories used as the dependent measure: organic or not organic. Lacks found that 74% of the "nonorganic" psychiatric inpatients and 18% of the organic psychiatric inpatients had Bender–Gestalt scores in the impaired range. She stated that these results were different from what one would expect on the basis of chance or on the basis of base rates; however, she made no attempt to test this hypothesis statistically. It is therefore difficult to accept the conclusion that the Bender–Gestalt is an accurate diagnostic instrument.

Lacks et al. (1970) compared the diagnostic accuracy of the Bender–Gestalt to that of their own shortened form of the Halstead–Reitan Neuropsychological Battery. For an unexplained reason, these investigators did not administer the Trails A or B, Grip Strength, Finger Tip Writing, or Visual Field tests. In order to obtain an impairment index, they prorated the results of the tests that they did administer. The subjects were 64 Caucasian male inpatients from a VA hospital who were divided into the following groups: 19 organic, 27 schizophrenic, and 18 general medical. The modified impairment index correctly identified 84% of the organics and 62% of the nonorganics, and the Bender–Gestalt correctly identified 74% of the organics and 91% of the nonorganics. It is difficult to draw conclusions from this study because of the use of a modified version of the Halstead–Reitan battery. Because the Bender–Gestalt tended to underdiagnose "organicity" in relation to the modified Halstead–Reitan impairment index, these results may actually be seen as evidence of the relative insensitivity of the Bender–Gestalt to certain types of organic impairment.

Levine and Feirstein (1972) found significant differences between the scores of organics, medical patients, and schizophrenics but did not investigate the diagnostic accuracy of the instrument. Norton (1978) compared the diagnostic accuracy of the Bender–Gestalt against both the results of a more thorough neuropsychological examination and the results of a neu-rological examination, an EEG, a pneumoencephalogram, an arteriogram, or a CT scan in a sample of 598 inpatients. The results indicated that 21% of the subjects classified as normal by the Bender–Gestalt were classified as impaired by the neuropsychological examination; 33% of the subjects classed as normal by the Bender–Gestalt had abnormal objective neurolog-ical findings.

Because of the poor performance of the Bender–Gestalt in discrimi-nating between organically impaired individuals and schizophrenic patients, Canter (1966) suggested a background interference procedure. In this pro-cedure, the subject is first asked to perform the Bender–Gestalt under stan-dard administration procedures and then to perform the Bender–Gestalt by reproducing the designs on a sheet of paper that contains an array of wavy lines. Performance under the two conditions is compared, with the general idea that organically impaired individuals will show a greater decline in per-formance under the interference condition. Canter (1976) reported fairly good results with this procedure. However, Adams and Kenny (1982) were unable to obtain favorable diagnostic hit rates in a sample of children aged 6–16. The hit rate was 81% in the children aged 12–16 but was only 60% in the children aged 6–11. Boake and Adams (1982) found a hit rate of 61% in a sample of adults and stated that the background interference procedure was not as accurate as standard neurodiagnostic techniques such as the EEG.

Part of the reason for the diagnostic inaccuracy may be that the Bender–Gestalt appears to be sensitive to variables other than organic integrity. Adams, Boake, and Crain (1982) reported that performance in the Bender–Gestalt background interference procedure is affected by age, education, race, and IQ to the extent that misdiagnosis can occur when these variables are not taken into account. The subjects in this study were 97 brain-damaged and 62 nondamaged male inpatients. The results indicated that older, less educated, less intelligent, non-Caucasian subjects were more likely to be misdiagnosed as brain-damaged when the Bender–Gestalt was used.

Lacks (1979, 1982) and Bigler and Ehrfurth (1980, 1981) have engaged in a disagreement regarding the clinical utility of the Bender–Gestalt. Lacks has argued that the test is short and accurate and can be administered by a technician with minimal training. Bigler and Ehrfurth, on the other hand, have argued the Bender–Gestalt is inaccurate and that the interpretation of the Bender–Gestalt results in information that is naively simplistic. They presented case material on subjects who had given normal Bender–Gestalt performances in spite of massive brain damage, as demonstrated by CT scans and a more rigorous neuropsychological evaluation (Bigler & Ehrfurth, 1980, 1981). Similar evidence from case material was presented by Russell (1976).

Although this case material is certainly impressive, the issue of the diagnostic accuracy of the Bender–Gestalt is more directly addressed by data obtained from many subjects analyzed in a group design. This question cannot be answered until a well-controlled and well-designed study is conducted. However, the issue of whether the Bender–Gestalt results in useful information can be debated without such a study. At the present time, the dichotomous question of whether or not the subject is organically impaired is on the verge of becoming an extinct concern. It is more likely that a neuropsychological evaluation would be sought to provide corroborative information detailing the nature of a subject's neurological disorder, or to define a subject's limitations and strengths for the purpose of treatment planning. In either of these cases, information provided by the Bender–Gestalt would be ineffectual.

The clinical interpretation of the Bender–Gestalt by use of the Koppitz scoring system is similarly beset by problems. Although the Bender–Gestalt has been argued to be culture-fair because of its nonreliance on language skills, there is some evidence suggesting that it is, in fact, sensitive to characteristics of the subjects that are not related to neuropsychological ability.

Oakland and Feigenbaum (1979) investigated test bias on the Bender–Gestalt due to the age, sex, family size and structure, birth order, health, race, socioeconomic status, and urban versus rural residence of 436 elementary-school children. They examined the effects of these subject variables on internal consistency, item difficulty indices, item total correlations, correlations with California Ability Test (CAT) scores, and factor structure when principal-components factor analysis was conducted using Bender scores in conjunction with WISC-R data. Mexican-American children had lower internal-consistency coefficients than their Caucasian and black counterparts. Correlations with the CAT were differentiated on the basis of socioeconomic status, family size, and sex. There were no effects on factor structure due to any of the subject variables.

Sattler and Gwynne (1982a) investigated the effects of race on Bender–Gestalt performance in children when the Koppitz scoring system was used. Their study used 1,938 Caucasian, black, and Puerto Rican children between the ages of 5 and 11. These authors found that the black children performed more poorly than the Caucasian children at all age levels and more poorly than the Puerto Rican children at all ages except 8. Additionally, the Puerto Rican children performed more poorly than the Caucasian children at ages 5 and 8. Robin and Shea (1983) found that children from Papua New Guinea ($n = 245$) scored significantly worse than children from Australia ($n = 74$). Additionally, the children from Papua New Guinea tended to lag 3–4 years behind the American sample on which the Koppitz scoring system was normed.

Validity of the Koppitz Scoring System

The concurrent validity of the Bender–Gestalt as a measure of cognitive ability has been evaluated by Wallbrown, Wallbrown, and Engin (1977).

These authors found significant but modest correlations (ranging from $-.18$ to $-.27$) between the Bender–Gestalt and scores on the California Achievement Test. Giebink and Birch (1970) reported a correlation of $-.19$ between Bender–Gestalt scores and reading achievement as measured by the California Achievement Test. Schneider and Spivack (1979) found no differences in Bender–Gestalt performance between reading-disabled and normal children. Caskey and Larson (1980) correlated the scores derived from both a group and an individual administration of the Bender–Gestalt with IQ scores from the Otis–Lennon Test in a sample of 92 rural and 101 suburban kindergarten students. They found significant correlations for the rural children: $-.71$ for group administration and $-.68$ for individual administration. The corresponding correlations for the suburban children were of a lower magnitude ($-.49$ for group administration and $-.31$ for individual administration), indicating that the demographic variable may intervene in the relationship between the Bender–Gestalt and the measure of cognitive ability.

The Bender–Gestalt is often used to predict academic performance. Because the Bender–Gestalt is also considered a measure of general cognitive ability, a reasonable question is whether the Bender–Gestalt can predict academic performance beyond that associated with cognitive ability. Wright and DeMers (1982) correlated the Bender–Gestalt with Wide Range Achievement Test (WRAT) scores, partialing out the influence of WISC-R IQ values in a group of 86 elementary-school students who had been referred for psychoeducational evaluation. These authors found that the partial correlations were modest (.13–.22) and did not always attain statistical significance. The possibility remains that the Bender–Gestalt roughly measures intellectual functioning rather than a broader concept of organicity.

Tymchuk (1974) investigated the discriminative validity of the Bender–Gestalt in a sample of 16 epileptic, 27 mentally retarded, and 33 behavior-problem children. He found significant differences among the three groups. However, using the recommended cutoff scores resulted in a 50% accurate classification rate. It was because of this sort of data that, in a review of the research investigating the validity of the Bender–Gestalt in screening for brain damage in school-aged children, Eno and Deichmann (1980) concluded that, although brain-damaged children as a group tend to perform more poorly on the Bender–Gestalt, these differences are not always significant. More important, interpretation on the level of the single case results in a high rate of false positives and false negatives.

The Bender–Gestalt has different validity for different diagnostic groups. Armstrong and Knopf (1982) reported the correlations between the Bender–Gestalt and the Beery Developmental Test of Visual Motor Integration for a group of 40 learning-disabled children and 40 normal children. The correlation coefficient for the learning-disabled children was .74, and the correlation coefficient for the normal children was .36. Hartlage and

Lucas (1976) reported different correlations between the Bender–Gestalt and the WISC-R for black and Caucasian children.

CLINICAL TESTS OF THE SENSORIUM

The Clinical Tests of the Sensorium (CTS) are a collection of short procedures that have been recommended as a method of performing a mental status exam and as an instrument to aid in the discrimination between organic and psychiatric disorders. In particular, the CTS is purported to assess levels of mental efficiency. The CTS consists of the subtests Orientation, Days of the Week Reversed, Serial Sevens, Recall of Address and Telephone Number, Babcock Sentence, Logical Memory Test, General Information, Digit Span, and Story Recall. The CTS exists in three alternate forms.

Withers and Hinton (1971) examined the alternate-form reliability and the test–retest reliability of the CTS. They administered all three forms in randomized order to 24 inpatients (8 medical inpatients and 16 psychiatric inpatients). They conducted an analysis of variance and reported that few significant differences were found. However, they did not report the F ratio values or the means or standard deviations, so it is difficult to evaluate the report. For the unidentified subtests that did demonstrate significant differences, modified versions were constructed and examined for significant differences in a further sample of 24 inpatients. No significant differences were found, but again, the report of results is incomplete.

Withers and Hinton (1971) then administered the three forms of the CTS to 108 consecutive-admission psychiatric inpatients. There were 57 males and 51 females, with a mean age of 36 years and a mean WAIS Full Scale IQ of 110. The order of administration of the tests was randomized. The first two administrations occurred in the first week of hospitalization, and the third administration occurred when the subjects were judged to be at their optimal level of functioning. The criterion by which this judgment was made was not specified.

The values obtained on the three administrations were then correlated. For some unspecified reason, differences in level among the three forms were tested only for a subgroup of 88 subjects who did not have a brain lesion. Significant differences were reported for the Serial Sevens subtest of Form C and the Immediate Recall of Address subtest of Form B. Unfortunately, the authors did not state what the other form was in these significant comparisons. The correlations between the scores ranged from .50 to .80, and all were significant at the .05 level. The correlations between the first and second administrations were slightly higher than the correlations between the first and second administrations, a finding indicating that the reliability tends to decline over time. An important aspect to remember about this study is that the subjects were young and had relatively high IQs for psychiatric patients.

Using the same number of subjects with the same mean IQs and ages (and apparently the same actual subjects) as Withers and Hinton (1971), Hinton and Withers (1971) examined the validity of the CTS. They reported significant correlations between the CTS scores and age and education. There were significant differences between the psychiatric patients and patients with brain lesions. There were also significant correlations between nurses' ratings of anxiety and depression and scores on the CTS. When the symptoms of anxious subjects remitted, their scores improved on the Orientation, the Serial Sevens, and the Logical Memory subtests. When the symptoms of the depressed patients remitted, their scores on the Serial Sevens, Logical Memory, and Story subtests improved. Additionally, scores improved on repetition, a finding indicating the presence of practice effects.

Although the CTS is apparently sensitive to the presence of brain lesions, it is also affected by age, education, and the presence of anxious or depressed mood. More work is needed before this test can be recommended for clinical use. The work needed includes norming by age and education or the provision of corrections for these variables, larger and more complete examinations of reliability, and examinations of discriminant validity and predictive validity.

THE NEUROPSYCHOLOGICAL IMPAIRMENT SCREEN

The Neuropsychological Impairment Screen (O'Donnell, Reynolds, & De Soto, 1983) is a self-report questionnaire that is intended to provide an overview of the possible symptoms associated with neuropsychological impairment. There are 45 questions related to symptoms and 5 questions related to response style or, as the authors refer to it, "test taking attitude." Eleven of the items are regarded by the authors as being pathognomic; that is, a positive response to any one of them is considered indicative of impairment. In addition to the test-taking attitude scale (LIE) and the pathognomic scale (PAT), the total raw score of the 45 symptom questions is called the *global measure of impairment* (GMI); the total number of items endorsed is the TIC scale, and the ratio of the GMI value to the TIC value is the symptom-intensity measure, or SIM scale.

The manual (O'Donnell & Reynolds, 1983) reports normative data based on a sample of 1,750 adults. The subjects in the normative sample came from groups of medical patients, neuropsychiatric patients, and normal subjects. Internal-consistency reliability values (coefficient alpha) are reported based on data from the normative sample. For the PAT scale, the value is .74; for the GEN scale, the value is .82. The manual does not report values for the other scales, but it does report reliability values for two scales, the

V-L (verbal learning) and the FRU (frustration) scales, which are not referred to in the rest of the manual or in any of the research reports.

A principal-factor analysis with orthogonal varimax rotation was reported for the 1,750 normative subjects. The results and a discussion of this analysis occupy only a few sentences, but it appears that there were four factors in the solution. No recommendations are made for interpretation or clinical use of the factors.

Test–retest reliability was assessed by administering the test twice to a sample of 25 inpatient neuropsychiatric subjects over an average interval of 46.76 days. The authors stated that the diagnoses of these subjects were determined by standard current nomenclature; however, they did not state specifically what diagnostic system was used. Additionally, they did not provide a rationale for using these particular subjects. In any evaluation of the temporal stability of test scores, the subjects used should be presumed to have static conditions, a point that the authors addressed in the discussion section. Unfortunately, the researchers did not address that issue in their sample. There are doubts that the conditions of these subjects were indeed stable, for 3 of the subjects had neoplastic disease and 3 of the subjects carried a diagnosis of degenerative disorder. This fact makes it difficult to interpret the obtained correlation coefficients of .85 for the SIM, .52 for LIE, .84 for PAT, .84 for TIC, and .87 for SIM. A sample of 82 undergraduate subjects was administered the NIS on two occasions with an average interval of 12.21 days and with similar values in correlation coefficients. Other forms of reliability estimates have not been conducted.

The initial validation study (O'Donnell et al., 1983) looked at the concurrent validity of the NIS by comparing its diagnostic agreement with performance on Trails A and B and the Digit Symbol subtest of the WAIS in a sample of 22 normals, 21 psychiatric patients, and 14 neurological patients. The normals exhibited the best performance on the NIS and on the three screening measures. The psychiatric subjects performed next best, and the neurological patients performed worst. Unfortunately, the subjects differed in age and education in exactly the same order as their performance on the tests. Because neuropsychological performance is known to vary with these two demographic variables, and because the authors did not attempt to control for these variables, we cannot be sure that the obtained differences were due to diagnosis. Although the NIS measures correlated with the screening tests, we cannot be sure that these correlations reflected the influence of the demographic variables.

A second validity investigation (O'Donnell, Reynolds, & De Soto, 1984b) also examined the concurrent validity of the NIS by correlating it with the Impairment Index, the Category Test score, the Localization score of the Tactual Performance Test, and Trail B of the Halstead–Reitan in a sample of 40 patients with unspecified diagnoses. The obtained correlation coefficients were only moderate, ranging from .50 to .08.

Another study by the same researchers (O'Donnell, De Soto, & Reynolds, 1984a) investigated the sensitivity and specificity of the NIS in a sample of 41 patients. The diagnoses arrived at by the use of the NIS were compared to diagnoses arrived at by the attending physicians. It is not clear if the physicians had access to the test results. At any rate, when either the GMI or the SIM or the PAT or the TIC was used, there was a reported sensitivity rate of 91% and a reported specifity rate of 43%. Clearly, the NIS tends to overestimate the prevalence of pathology; at least, it did in this sample.

Screening instruments are much needed in neuropsychological assessment, as they can help identify those subjects who need lengthier and more costly complete evaluations. For that reason, the NIS may turn out to be a useful instrument in clinical settings. However, the methodological insufficiencies of the research reports keep us from recommending this instrument. More research needs to be conducted on larger samples and with greater methodological control.

PERSONAL ORIENTATION TEST

The Personal Orientation Test is an attempt to measure deficits in the ability to place oneself in space as well as in the ability to recognize the spatial placement of various body parts. There are no reports of investigations of the reliability of this test. This test is sensitive to brain impairment (Weinstein, Semmes, Ghent, & Teuber, 1956). Semmes, Weinstein, Ghent, and Teuber (1963) reported that patterns of scores on the test are related to whether a lesion is located in the left or the right, the anterior or the posterior portion of the brain. However, Bowen (1976) reported that performance on the test is also related to subcortical dysfunction. Therefore, more research needs to be done if we are to understand what the test measures.

THE STROOP WORD–COLOR TEST

Like many neuropsychological tests, the Stroop Word–Color Test has a long and varied history. Also, like many neuropsychological tests, the Stroop had its origins in laboratory procedures. Stroop (1935) was originally interested in a perceptual interference effect, namely, the effect of interfering perceptual information on behavior. The phenomenon of perceptual interference as measured by the Stroop has been used in cognitive, personality, psychopathology, and neuropsychology research. Because of the heterogeneous body of literature associated with the Stroop, this section limits its discussion to neuropsychological topics. Although the Stroop has existed in several forms, we consider here only the most recent standardized form as published by the Stoelting Company (Golden, 1978b).

The Stroop is an easily administered and easily scored test. It takes less than 10 minutes to administer. The necessary materials consist of three sheets of $8\frac{1}{2}'' \times 11''$ paper. On the first sheet of paper are printed five columns of words, which are color names (*red, blue,* and *green*). The subject is asked to read aloud, in order, the words on the sheet. (In the group form, the subjects are asked to read the words silently.) The subjects are prompted to correct their incorrect responses. The score is the number of correct responses obtained in 45 seconds. The second part consists of a sheet of paper on which are printed columns of Xs in three different colors (red, blue, and green), and the subjects are asked to name the color. The administration and scoring are the same as in the first part. The third part consists of the same words as those in the first part; however, they are printed in colors different from the colors named by the words. For example, the word *red* is printed in blue ink. The subjects are asked to name the color, ignoring the word. The scoring is again based on the number of correct responses in 45 seconds.

The three raw scores are translated into standardized scores in order to permit comparisons across the three parts. These scores can then be transformed into ratios (C/W, CW/C) and linear combinations (C + W, CW − C). In addition, the manual suggests age corrections; however, there is insufficient information about the appropriateness (or the size) of the sample used in the derivation of these standardized scores or in the age corrections.

Reliability

Test–retest reliability has been evaluated for the three raw scores. Jensen (1965) stated that the test–retest reliability coefficient of the Word score is .79, that of the Color score is .88, and that of the Color–Word score is .71. Jensen also stated that 50 of the subjects had had a test–retest interval of a few minutes (the exact time interval was not reported), 50 subjects had had an interval of 1 day, and 336 subjects had had an interval of 1 week. However, no characteristics of the subjects are known. It should be noted that this study did not use the standardized form. Instead, tall cards similar to those used in eye exams were used at a distance of 4 feet. Also, the scores used were based on the time it took for 100 responses to be made.

Golden (1975) examined the test–retest reliability of both the group and the individual administrations. Thirty subjects were given the individual form twice, but the interval was not specified, nor were any characteristics of the subjects described. The reliability coefficients reported were .86 for the Word score, .82 for the Color score, and .73 for the Color–Word score. The test–retest reliability was assessed for the group form. Once again, the interval and the characteristics of the subjects were not specified.

Franzen, Tishelman, Sharp, and Friedman (1987) investigated the test–retest reliability of the Stroop in a sample of 62 normal individuals. Two intervals were used: 1 week and 2 weeks. There were no significant differences between the reliability coefficients for the 1- and 2-week intervals so the data were collapsed. The coefficient values were .83 for the Word score, .738 for the Color score, and .671 for the Color–Word score. Split-plot analyses of variance indicated that there were significant increases in scores for both of the intervals. Subsequent research by Connor, Franzen, and Sharp (1988) indicated that these increases tended to become asymptotic after three administrations.

In a sense, the group and individual forms may be construed as alternate forms. Therefore, the alternate-forms reliability is a pertinent question. Golden (1975) administered both the group and the individual forms in counterbalanced order to 60 subjects whose characteristics were not described. For the Word score, the alternate-forms reliability coefficient was .85; for the Color score, the coefficient was .81; and for the Color–Word score, the coefficient was .69.

Validity

Golden (1976b) examined the validity of the Stroop in discriminating brain-impaired subjects from normal subjects. The brain-impaired subjects consisted of 30 left-hemisphere-injury patients, 43 diffuse injury patients, and 31 right-hemisphere patients. All of the subjects were diagnosed by history, results on the Halstead–Reitan Neuropsychological Battery, and neurological examination. The non-brain-impaired subjects consisted of 35 schizophrenics and 37 normals. When a discriminant-function analysis was used with the three basic scores as predictors, 88.9% of the controls and 84.6% of the brain-impaired subjects were correctly classified, for an overall rate of 87%. A second discriminant-function analysis was performed to classify the brain-impaired subjects into three groups that described the location of their injury. This procedure resulted in only a 56.7% accuracy-of-classification rate. None of these results have been replicated. The Golden manual (1978b) reports rules for the interpretation of scores, but none of these rules have been empirically validated. The Stroop has been shown to be sensitive to sex (Golden, 1974; Peritti, 1969, 1971), stress (Houston & Jones, 1967), and various personality measures (Golden, 1978b). Therefore, the discriminant validity of the Stroop with regard to the detection of brain impairment needs to be addressed.

Conclusions

The Stroop Word–Color Test is a potentially useful quick test of general organic impairment. There are several areas where research can be done to further evaluate the properties of the test. For example, the reliability of the three raw scores in terms of absolute level needs to be determined. The reliability of the combination scores also needs to be evaluated. The reliability of all of the scores in special populations is missing.

Additionally, research should address the convergent and discriminant validity of the instrument. Such research is especially important because the test has been used to measure everything from creativity and cognitive style to personality and organic impairment.

20

Tests of Achievement and Aptitude

THE GENERAL APTITUDE TEST BATTERY

The General Aptitude Test Battery (GATB) is a group of tests that are used to measure nine aptitudes. Twelve tests comprise the GATB, and its composition was determined by a series of factor analyses that were conducted on a larger number of tests. Unfortunately, the factor analyses were conducted on anywhere from 9 to 27 of the tests, and at no time were all of the tests that eventually made up the GATB used in the same factor analysis. In order to remediate this shortcoming, Watts and Everitt (1980) conducted a maximum-likelihood factor analysis on the correlation matrix as published in the GATB manual (U.S. Employment Service, 1970). Watts and Everitt failed to replicate the original factor structure, a result that is not surprising because the correlation matrix indicates that some tests correlate more highly with tests that are not in the same aptitude factor than with tests that are in the same aptitude factor.

The GATB apparently has a fair amount of utility in occupational counseling (Bemis, 1968), but its usefulness for a neuropsychologically impaired population is largely unknown. Kish (1970) reported that the General, Verbal, and Numerical aptitudes of the GATB had moderate correlations with Shipley IQ scores in a sample of 71 male inpatient alcoholics in a VA hospital. The values ranged from .71 to .12. Groff and Hubble (1981) administered the GATB and the Trail Making Test to 40 incarcerated female adult subjects who were not suspected of brain impairment. These authors concluded that the complex cognitive functions measured by the Trail Making Test are largely unrelated to the GATB.

Because of its demonstrated validity in occupational counseling, the GATB may one day be useful for a cognitive rehabilitation. However, its reliability and validity in such a population need to be evaluated before its use can be recommended.

THE McCARTHY SCALES OF CHILDREN'S ABILITIES

The McCarthy Scales of Children's Abilities is a collection of 18 subtests that are grouped into six scales on a theoretical basis. The manual (McCarthy, 1972) states that the McCarthy scales are appropriate for children between the ages of 2½ and 8½. The normative sample consisted of 1,032 children who were divided among 10 age groups, so that approximately 100 children were in each age group. The normative sample was stratified by sex, race, geography, father's occupation, and urban versus rural residence in accordance with census data.

The raw scores were weighted and summed to provide the scale scores. The weights were based on the author's judgment of the relative importance of the subtests and under the secondary principle that subtests with larger standard deviations were given larger weights. No justification is stated for the strategy used. The McCarthy scales result in a Mental Age score as well as scores for the General Cognitive, Verbal, Perceptual Performance, Quantitative, Memory, and Motor scales.

In order to evaluate the test–retest reliability of the McCarthy scales, 125 children from the normative sample were administered the tests on two occasions, with approximately 1 month's interval. The children were fairly evenly divided into groups of 3–3.5 years, 5–5.5 years, and 7.5–8.5 years. The General Cognitive index demonstrated a reliability coefficient of .90 for all ages overall. The other subtests' reliability coefficients ranged from .75 to .89 for all ages combined. Split-half reliabilities were calculated on the same sample. The largest reliability coefficient was for the General Cognitive index at .93. The lowest values were for Memory and Motor at .79. The reliability of handedness was also assessed. Reliable hand preference was demonstrated for 61% of the 3- to 3.5-year-olds, 70% of the 5- to 5.5-year-olds, and 76% of the 7.5- to 8.5-year-olds. Eye preference was demonstrated in 75% of all age groups combined. Because of our knowledge of developmental issues in laterality, this information cannot actually be used as an assessment of the reliability of the McCarthy scales.

Naglieri and Maxwell (1981) reported an evaluation of the interrater reliability of the Draw-a-Child task from the McCarthy scales. They administered the McCarthy scales to 20 mentally retarded children, 20 learning-disabled children, and 20 normal children and scored the drawings independently. The overall reliability coefficient was .93, with values of .97 for the mentally retarded, .88 for the learning-disabled, and .83 for the normal children. Analyses were conducted on the standard scores and produced no significant differences between scores assigned by the two authors.

The manual (McCarthy, 1972) also reported an attempt to evaluate the concurrent validity of the instrument in a small subsample of the normative group consisting of 35 children aged 6 years to 6 years, 7 months. The General Cognitive index correlated .81 with the IQs obtained on a Stanford–Binet. In the same group, the General Cognitive index correlated .62 with the WPPSI PIQ, .63 with the VIQ, and .71 with the FSIQ. Predictive validity was estimated by correlating the McCarthy scales with Metropolitan Achievement Test scores obtained after a 4-month interval. The values ranged from − .07 to .57. These are very disappointing correlations. The inadequacy of the McCarthy scales in predicting achievement is illustrated by a correlation of .06 between the Verbal scale and the MAT Word Knowledge subtest.

Naglieri and Maxwell (1981) compared the age equivalents obtained from the Draw-a-Child task of the McCarthy scales to WISC-R IQs and found that there were no significant differences between the two. The authors concluded that this task had adequate concurrent validity.

Tivnan and Pillemer (1978) administered the McCarthy scales to 30 female and 36 male preschool children aged 4 years, 7 months to 5 years, 7 months in order to evaluate the influence of sex on performance. The female subjects scored consistently higher on each of the subtests. The differences were significant only for the Motor scale, but the use of the binomial test resulted in a significantly different pattern of scores for the two sexes.

Several factor analyses have been conducted on the McCarthy scales. Hollenbeck (1972), Kaufmann (1975b), Kaufman and DiCuio (1975), and Kaufman and Hollenbeck (1973) each used the normative sample as their data. Although they used slightly different techniques and groupings of the subjects (e.g., separating them by race or age), the resulting factor structures were very similar. Keith and Bolen (1980) conducted a factor analysis on a separate sample of 300 children who had been referred for education evaluation. These authors used both principal-factor and principal-components factor analyses, employing the varimax rotation method each time. When they used Harman's coefficient of congruence, it appeared that only two of the factors reported in the normative sample had been replicated. This finding indicates that the factor structure of the McCarthy scales may depend, at least partly, on characteristics of the sample. Because the McCarthy scales are more often used in evaluating children who evidence learning difficulties, analyses with these subjects are likely to provide more useful information than analyses of the factor structure in normal children.

In general, despite their widespread use, the McCarthy scales are in need of further evaluation for reliability and validity.

THE PEABODY INDIVIDUAL ACHIEVEMENT TEST

The Peabody Individual Achievement Test (PIAT) is made up of five subtests that measure achievement in different areas related to school performance. Therefore, it is often used in the assessment of children who demonstrate problems in academic performance. The manual (Dunn & Markwardt, 1970) reports that the standardized sample consisted of approximately 200 children at each of 13 grade levels, for a total sample of 2,884 subjects. The sample was stratified to reflect data from the 1967 U.S. Census.

The manual reports test–retest data for groups of between 50 and 75 children in kindergarten and Grades 1, 3, 5, 8, and 12. The retest interval was about 1 month. The reliability coefficients had a median value of .78, with a low value of .42 for the Spelling test in the kindergarten sample and a high of .94 for the Reading Recognition test in the Grade 3 sample.

Using a 6-month interval, Lamanna and Ysseldyke (1973) reported test–retest reliability coefficients ranging from .44 for the Mathematics test to .81 for the Reading Recognition test in a sample of 58 first-grade children. Naglieri and Pfeiffer (1983) investigated the test–retest reliability of the PIAT in a sample of 36 children who had been referred for evaluation. With a mean interval of 12 months and a standard deviation of 8.3 months, there were no significant differences between the standardized scores obtained, and the correlation values were comparable to those obtained in the normative sample.

Wilson and Spangler (1974) investigated the internal consistency reliability of the PIAT in a sample of 83 children who had been referred for evaluation. There was high reliability, with values ranging from .95 to .97. Dean (1977a) investigated the PIAT's internal consistency reliability in a sample of 30 Mexican-American and 30 Anglo children. He found no significant differences between the two samples, and he found values that were not significantly different from the normative data.

Reynolds and Gutkin (1980) presented tables of values for determining the significance of differences between the individual scale scores and the mean of all other scale scores. These tables can be very helpful in evaluating the presence of relative strengths and weaknesses.

The manual (Dunn & Markwardt, 1970) further reports that the content validity of the initial pool of 300 items was sufficient, a value judgment at best. However, items were discarded for reasons of item difficulty and discrimination, as well as for reasons of low item-total correlation values. The resulting scales have not been evaluated for content validity or for the adequacy of their sampling of the domain of interest. Concurrent validity was measured by correlating the PIAT with Peabody Picture Vocabulary Test IQs. The correlation values ranged from a high of .68 for the General Information Test to a low of .40 for the Spelling Test.

Soethe (1972) evaluated the concurrent validity of the PIAT by comparing it with the Wide Range Achievement Test (WRAT) and the WISC. There were 40 subjects in this study: 26 males and 14 females, all of whom had been referred for evaluation. He divided the subjects into a group of 13 normal subjects (IQ > 86 and no difference of more than 10 points between WISC and WRAT scores), a group of 12 reading-disabled subjects (IQ > 86 and at least a 10-point difference between WISC and WRAT Reading scores), and 15 retarded subjects (WISC < 85). The PIAT correlated more highly with the WISC than with the WRAT, and the highest correlation was only .71. The higher values were obtained in the normal sample; the retarded sample had correlation values in the .44–.60 range. This study raises serious question about the construct validity of the PIAT, as it correlated more with a test of IQ than with another achievement test. Additionally, the PIAT has different sensitivity across different levels of intelligence, limiting its general applicability. These results are supported by the research of Simpson (1982), who concluded that the PIAT was not valid for use with retarded subjects.

In another attempt to investigate the concurrent validity of the PIAT, Sanner and McManis (1978) administered the PIAT and the Stanford Achievement tests to a sample of 21 third- and 22 sixth-grade children who were average achievers. The Spearman rank-order correlations for the two tests were in the range of .42–.88, and there were significant differences in the grade equivalents on the two tests.

Wilson and Spangler (1974) correlated grade equivalence scores obtained from the PIAT with IQ scores obtained from the Stanford–Binet, the WISC, and the Peabody Picture Vocabulary Test (PPVT), after first partialing out the influence of age. Different subjects were used in each of these analyses. For the WISC ($n = 63$), the correlation was .58; for the Stanford–Binet ($n = 17$), the correlation was .49; and for the PPVT ($n = 57$), the correlation was .48. These results are encouraging because of their moderate correlations, indicating that there is a relationship between the PIAT and IQ. The moderate size of the coefficients also indicates that the PIAT is not a measure of IQ. Further evidence is needed to demonstrate that it is a measure of achievement.

Even though intelligence tests and achievement tests are intended to measure different constructs, much of the research that attempts to investigate the concurrent validity of the PIAT compares it with the WISC. Naglieri and Pfeiffer (1983) correlated WISC-R IQ scores with scores on the PIAT subtests in a sample of 36 children who had been referred for evaluation. All of the correlations with the VIQ were significant and in the range of .57–.69. The only significant correlation for the PIQ was with the PIAT Mathematics scale (.42). All of the PIAT subtests correlated significantly with the FSIQ, ranging from .46 to .64. Beck, Lindsey, and Facziende (1979) correlated the General Information subtest of the PIAT with the Information subtest of the WISC-R in a sample of 100 children who had been referred for evaluation. The overall correlation coefficient had a value of .76; however, the correlation for a subsample of 43 children with IQs under 69 was .43, a finding indicating that the relationship between the PIAT and measures of IQ may be different for different levels of ability.

Wickoff (1978) administered both the WISC-R and the PIAT to a sample of 123 male and 57 female children who had been referred for evaluation. However, instead of stopping after correlating the two tests, he conducted factor analyses to attempt to see if the PIAT offered information beyond that gained from the use of the WISC-R. In the first factor analysis, he used both the PIAT and the WISC-R subtest scores. In a principle-factor analysis with varimax rotation, he decided that the four-factor solution was most meaningful and interpreted the factor as the three traditional WISC-R factors plus a word recognition factor formed largely by the PIAT. A separate factor analysis of only the PIAT data by means of the same methodology resulted in a two-factor solution that Wickoff interpreted as word recognition and school-related knowledge.

Dean (1977a) analyzed the PIAT and WISC-R data from 100 Mexican-American and 100 Anglo children in order to investigate the factor structure of the PIAT. However, instead of factor analysis, Dean used canonical correlation. He found that 72% of the variability in the PIAT was redundant with 45% of the variability in the WISC-R in the Anglo sample. In the Mexican-American sample, 63% of the variability in the PIAT was redundant with 43% of the variability in the WISC-R. Dean concluded that there was a substantial amount of overlap between the two tests. Although not consistent with Wickoff's conclusions, these results are consistent with Wickoff's data, as the first two factors in his four-factor solution had heavy loadings from both of the tests. If the PIAT is highly related to tests of intelligence, then the construct validity of the test is questionable. More research is needed on more varied samples than are referred to researchers for evaluation. Additionally, the concurrent validity of the test needs to be assessed by comparison with other measures of achievement rather than with tests of intelligence.

THE WIDE RANGE ACHIEVEMENT TEST

The Wide Range Achievement Test (WRAT) was originally designed to provide an estimate of children's level of functioning in the academic areas of Reading, Spelling, and Arithmetic (Jastek & Jastek, 1978). The raw scores can be translated into grade-level ratings, standard t scores, and percentiles. The manual states that, in norming the test, no attempt was made to provide national representation. The normative sample was composed of 1,800 children and 200 adults. The manual reports split-half reliability values of .94 (Arithmetic), .96 (Spelling), and .98 (Reading) for children between the ages of 5 and 11 and comparable values for subjects between the ages of 12 and 24. The sample sizes are not described. The manual also reports an overall alternate-form reliability of .90. Unfortunately, not enough information is given in any of these studies to allow a consideration of their generalizability.

Few validity studies are reported in the manual. In one of these studies, there was a correlation of .78 between WRAT Reading scores and teachers' informal evaluations on a 9-point scale. In a sample of 74 children aged 5–15, the Reading scale correlated .81, the Spelling scale correlated .74, and the Arithmetic scale correlated .84 with the California Mental Maturity Scale.

Because of the paucity of reliability information, Woodward, Santa-Barbara, and Roberts (1975) investigated the test–retest reliability in a sample of 106 children who were enrolled in special-education classes for the emotionally disturbed or for slow learners. These children were between the ages of 5 and 12. There were two test–retest intervals: 2 weeks (63 subjects) and 22 weeks (43 subjects). The correlation coefficients were reasonably high, ranging from .87 to .98. The tests for changes in absolute level of scores resulted in significant differences in Spelling scores for the 2-week period and for the Reading scores at 22 weeks. The results for the 22-week interval are problematic, as one would expect changes as a result of the special-education intervention.

Silverstein (1980) evaluated the 1976 and 1978 norms presented in the manual, looking at both scaled grade equivalents and scaled raw scores. He found that the grade equivalents were not comparable across the two sets of norms, even though they were based on the same subjects, particularly for Grades 8–11. The standard score comparisons resulted in small but systematic differences. He therefore recommended that retest situations use the same sets of norms in comparing scores. These results were in agreement with those of Sattler and Feldman (1981). Naglieri and Parks (1980) found similar results in evaluating the scores of 115 Hopi Indian children. They also conducted a 1-year test–retest study with the same subjects and reported moderate correlation coefficients ranging from .60 to .70.

Before the WRAT can be enthusiastically recommended for use with brain-impaired adults, reliability and validity studies need to be conducted on these populations.

References

Abidin, R. R. & Byrne, A. W. (1967). Quick Test validation study and examination of interform equivalency. *Psychological Reports, 20,* 735–739.

Adams, K. M. (1980a). In search of Luria's battery: A false start. *Journal of Consulting and Clinical Psychology, 48,* 511–516.

Adams, K. M. (1980b). An end of innocence for behavioral neurology? Adams replies. *Journal of Consulting and Clinical Psychology, 48,* 522–524.

Adams, J., & Kenny, T. J. (1982). Cross-validation of the Canter Background Interference Procedure in identifying children with cerebral dysfunction. *Journal of Consulting and Clinical Psychology, 50,* 307–309.

Adams, R. L., Boake, C., & Crain, C. (1982). Bias in a neuropsychological test classification related to education, age, and ethnicity. *Journal of Consulting and Clinical Psychology, 50,* 143–145.

Aita, J. A., Reitan, R. M., & Ruth, J. M. (1947). Rorschach's test as a diagnostic aid in brain injury. *American Journal of Psychiatry, 103,* 770–779.

Allison, H. W., & Allison, S. G. (1954). Personality changes following transorbital lobotomy, *Journal of Abnormal and Social Psychology, 49,* 218–223.

American Educational Research Association, American Psychological Association, & National Council on Measurement in Education. (1985). *Standards for educational and psychological testing.* Washington, DC: American Psychological Association.

American Psychiatric Association. (1950). *Diagnostic and statistical manual of mental disorders* (1st ed.). Washington, DC: Author.

American Psychiatric Association. (1968). *Diagnostic and statistical manual of mental disorders* (2nd ed.). Washington, DC: Author.

Ames, L. (1966). Changes in Rorschach responses throughout the human life span. *Genetic Psychology Monographs, 74,* 89–125.

Ames, L., Learned, J., Metraux, R. W., & Walker, R. N. (1954). *Rorschach responses in old age.* New York: Hoeber.

Ames, L., Metraux, R. W., & Walker, R. N. (1971). *Adolescent Rorschach responses: Developmental trends from ten to sixteen years* (2nd ed.). New York: Brunner/Mazel.

Ames, L., Metraux, R. W., Rodell, J. L., & Walker, R. N. (1973). *Rorschach responses in old age.* New York: Brunner/Mazel.

Ames, L., Metraux, R. W., Rodell, J. L., & Walker, R. N. (1974). *Child Rorschach responses: Developmental trends from two to ten years* (rev. ed.). New York: Brunner/Mazel.

Ammons, R. B., & Ammons, C. H. (1962). The Quick Test (QT): Provisional manual, *Psychological Reports, 11,* 111–161.

Ammons, R. B., & Ammons, C. H. (1979a). Use and evaluation of the Quick Test (QT): Partial summary through October, 1979: 1. Published papers. *Psychological Reports, 45,* 943–946.

261

Ammons, R. B., & Ammons, C. H. (1979b). Use and evaluation of the Quick Test (QT): Partial summary through October, 1979: 2. Reviews, unpublished reports, and papers. *Psychological Reports, 45,* 953–954.

Anastasi, A. (1982). *Psychological testing* (5th ed.). New York: Macmillan.

Anderson, A., & Hanvik, L. (1950). The paychometric localization of brain lesions: The differential effect of frontal and parietal lesions on MMPI profiles. *Journal of Clinical Psychology, 6,* 177–180.

Andert, J. N., Dinning, W. D., & Hustak, T. L. (1976). Koppitz errors on the Bender-Gestalt for adult retardates: Normative data. *Perceptual and Motor Skills, 42,* 451–454.

Andrich, D. (1988). *Rasch models for measurement.* Beverly Hill, CA: Sage.

Anthony, W. Z., Heaton, R. K., & Lehman, R. A. (1980). An attempt to cross-validate two actuarial systems for neuropsychological test interpretation. *Journal of Consulting and Clinical Psychology, 48,* 317–326.

Arbit, J., & Zagar, R. (1979). The effects of age and sex on the factor structure of the Wechsler Memory Scale. *The Journal of Psychology, 102,* 185–190.

Archibald, Y. M. (1978). Time as a variable in the performance of hemisphere-damaged patients on the Elithorn Perceptual Maze Test, *Cortex, 14,* 22–31.

Archibald, Y. M., Wepman, J. M., & Jones, L. V. (1967). Performance on nonverbal cognitive tests following unilateral cortical injury to the right and left hemisphere. *The Journal of Nervous and Mental Disease, 145,* 25–36.

Armstrong, B. D., & Knopf, K. F. (1982). Comparison of the Bender-Gestalt and Revised Developmental Test of Visual Motor Integration. *Perceptual and Motor Skills, 55,* 164–166.

Arrigoni, G., & DeRenzi, E. (1964). Constructional apraxia and hemispheric locus of lesion. *Cortex, 1,* 170–197.

Arthur, G. (1949). The Arthur Adaptation of the Leiter International Performance Scale. *Journal of Clinical Psychology, 5,* 345–349.

Atkinson, L., & Cyr, J. J. (1984). Factor analysis of the WAIS-R: Psychiatric and standardization samples. *Journal of Consulting and Clinical Psychology, 52,* 714–716.

Atkinson, R. C., & Shiffrin, R. M. (1968). Human memory: A proposed system and its control processes. In K. W. Spence & J. T. Spence (Eds.), *The psychology of learning and motivation: Advances in research and theory* (Vol. 2). New York: Academic Press.

Ayers, J., Templer, D. I., & Ruff, C. F. (1975). The MMPI in the differential diagnosis on organicity vs. schizophrenia: Empirical findings and a somewhat different perspective. *Journal of Clinical Psychology, 31,* 685–686.

Bach, P. J., Harowski, K., Kirby, K., Peterson, P., & Schulein, M. (1981). The interrater reliability of the Luria-Nebraska Neuropsychological Battery. *Clinical Neuropsychology, 3,* 19–21.

Bachrach, H. (1971). Studies in the expanded Word Association Test: 1. Effects of cerebral dysfunction. *Journal of Personality Assessment, 35,* 148–158.

Bachrach, H., & Mintz, J. (1974). The Wechsler Memory Scale as a tool for the detection of mild cerebral dysfunction. *Journal of Clinical Psychology, 30,* 58–60.

Baddeley, A. D., Hatter, J. E., Scott, D., & Snashall, A. (1970). Memory and time of day. *Quarterly Journal of Experimental Psychology, 22,* 605–609.

Bak, J. S., & Greene, R. L. (1980). Changes in neuropsychological functioning in an aging population. *Journal of Consulting and Clinical Psychology, 48,* 395–399.

Baker, F. B. (1985). *The basics of item response theory.* Portsmouth, NH: Heinemann.

Baker, G. (1956). Diagnosis of organic brain damage in the adult. In B. Klopfer, Ainsworth, M. D., Klopfer, G., & Holt, R. (Eds.), *Developments in the Rorschach technique: Vol. 2. Fields of application.* New York: World.

Barker, M. G., & Lawson, J. S. (1968). Nominal aphasia in dementia. *British Journal of Psychiatry, 114,* 1351–1356.

Barnes, G. W., & Lucas, G. J. (1974). Cerebral dysfunction vs. psychogenesis in Halstead-Reitan Tests. *The Journal of Nervous and Mental Disease, 158*(1), 50–60.

Bartel, N. R., Grill, J. J., & Bartel, H. W. (1973). The syntactic-paradigmatic shift in learning disabled and normal children. *Journal of Learning Disabilities, 7*, 59–64.

Bartz, W. R. (1968). Relationship of WAIS, Bets, and Shipley-Hartford scores. *Psychological Reports, 22*, 676.

Basso, A., DeRenzi, E., Faglioni, P., Scotti, G., & Spinnler, H. (1973). Neuropsychological evidence for the existence of cerebral areas critical to the performance of intelligence tasks. *Brain, 96*, 715–728.

Basso, A., Spinnler, H., Vallar, G., & Zanobio, M. E. (1982). Left hemisphere damage and selective impairment of auditory verbal short-term memory: A case study. *Neuropsychologia, 20*, 263–274.

Battersby, W. S., Bender, M. B., Pollack, M., & Kahn, R. L. (1956). Unilateral "spatial agnosia" (inattention). *Brain, 73*, 66–93.

Bauer, R. H. (1979). Recall after a short delay and acquisition in learning disabled and nondisabled children. *Journal of Learning Disabilities, 12*, 596–607.

Beck, F. W., Lindsey, J. D., & Facziende, B. (1979). A comparison of the general information subtest of the Peabody Individual Achievement Test with the Information subtest of the Wechsler Intelligence Scale for Children-Revised. *Educational and Psychological Measurement, 39*, 1073–1077.

Beck, S. J., Beck, A. G., Levitt, E. E., & Molish, H. B. (1961). *Rorschach's test: Vol. 1. Basic processes* (3rd ed.). New York: Grune & Stratton.

Bejar, I. I. (1983). Introduction to item response models and their assumptions. In R. K. Hambleton (Ed.), *Applications of item response theory*. Vancouver: Educational Research Institute of British Columbia.

Bemis, S. E. (1968). Occupational validity of the General Aptitude Test Battery. *Journal of Applied Psychology, 52*, 240–244.

Beniak, T. E. (1977). *The assessment of cognitive deficits in uremia.* Presented at the International Neuropsychological Society, Oxford, England.

Bennett-Levy, J. (1984). Determinants of performance on the Rey-Osterreith Complex Figure Test: An analysis and a new technique for single case assessment. *British Journal of Clinical Psychology, 23*, 109–119.

Bensberg, G. J. & Sloan, W. (1951). Performance of brain-injured defectives on the Arthur Adaptation of the Leiter. *Psychological Service Center Journal, 3*, 181–184.

Bentler, P. M., & Woodward, J. A. (1980). Inequalities among lower bounds to reliability: With applications to test construction and factor analysis. *Psychometrika, 45*, 249–267.

Benton, A. L. (1945). Rorschach performance of suspected malingerers. *Journal of Abnormal and Social Psychology, 40*, 94–96.

Benton, A. L. (1950). A multiple choice type version of the Visual Retention Test. *Archives of Neurology and Psychiatry, 64*, 699–707.

Benton, A. L. (1955a). Development of finger localization capacity in school children. *Child Development, 26*, 225–230.

Benton, A. L. (1955b). Right-left discrimination and finger localization in defective children. *Archives of Neurology and Psychiatry, 74*, 583–589.

Benton, A. L. (1959). *Right-left discrimination and finger localization in defective children.* New York: Hoeper-Harper.

Benton, A. L. (1967). Constructional apraxia and the minor hemisphere. *Confinia Neurologica, 29*, 1–16.

Benton, A. L. (1968). Differential behavioral effects in frontal lobe disease. *Neurophychologia, 6*, 53–60.

Benton, A. L. (1973). Visuoconstruction disability in patients with cerebral disease in relations to side of lesion and aphasic disorder. *Documents in Ophthalmology, 33*, 67–76.

Benton, A. L. (1974). *Revised Visual Retention Test* (4th ed.). New York: Psychological Corporation.

Benton, A. L., & Spreen, O. (1961). Visual Memory Test: The simulation of mental incompetence. *Archives of General Psychiatry, 4,* 79–83.

Benton, A. L., Elithorn, A., Fogel, M. L., & Kerr, M. (1963). A perceptual maze test sensitive to brain damage. *Journal of Neurology, Neurosurgery, and Psychiatry, 26,* 540–544.

Benton, A. L., Garfield, J. C., & Chorini, J. C. (1964). Motor impersistence in mental defectives. *Proceedings, the International Congress on the Scientific Study of Mental Retardation,* pp. 746–750.

Benton, A. L., Spreen, O., Fangman, M., & Carr, D. (1967). Visual Retention Test, Administration C: Norms for children. *Journal of Special Education, 1,* 151–156.

Benton, A. L., Hamsher, K., & Stone, F. (1977). *Visual Retention Test: Multiple Choice: Form I.* Iowa City: Department of Neurology, University of Iowa Hospitals.

Benton, A. L., Varney, N. R., & Hamsher, K. (1978). Visuospatial judgement: A clinical test. *Archives of Neurology, 35,* 364–367.

Benton, A. L., Eslinger, P. J., & Damasio, A. R. (1981). Normative observations on neuropsychological test performance in old age. *Journal of Clinical Neuropsychology, 3,* 33–42.

Benton, A. L., Hamsher, K. deS., Varney, N. R., & Spreen, O. (1983). *Contributions to Neuropsychological Assessment: A Clinical Manual.* New York: Oxford University Press.

Berg, E. A. (1948). A simple objective test for measuring flexibility in thinking. *Journal of General Psychology, 39,* 15–22.

Berg, R. A. & Golden, C. J. (1981). Identification of neuropsychological deficits in epilepsy using the Luria-Nebraska Neuropsychological Battery. *Journal of Consulting and Clinical Psychology, 49,* 745–747.

Berk, R. A. (1982). Verbal-performance IQ discrepancy score: A comment on reliability, abnormality, and validity. *Journal of Clinical Psychology, 38,* 638–641.

Beverly, L. & Bensberg, G. J. (1952). A comparison of the Leiter, the Cornell-Coxe, and Stanford-Binet with mental defectives. *American Journal of Mental Deficiency, 57,* 89–91.

Bigler, E. D., & Ehrfurth, J. W. (1981). The continued inappropriate use of the Bender Visual Motor Gestalt test. *Professional Psychology. 12,* 582–569.

Binder, L. M. (1982). Constructional strategies on complex figure drawings after unilateral brain damage. *Journal of Clinical Neuropsychology, 4,* 51–58.

Birch, J. R., Stuckless, E. R., & Birch, J. W. (1963). An eleven year study of predicting school achievement in young deaf children. *American Annals of the Deaf, 108,* 236–240.

Black, F. W. (1973a). Use of the Leiter International Performance Scale with aphasic children. *Journal of Speech and Hearing Research, 16,* 530–533.

Black, F. W. (1973b). Cognitive and memory performance in subjects with brain damage secondary to penetrating missile wounds and closed head injury. *Journal of Clinical Psychology, 29,* 441–442.

Black, F. W. (1973c). Memory and paired associates learning of patients with unilateral brain lesions. *Psychological Reports, 33,* 919–922.

Black, F. W. (1974a). The cognitive sequelae of penetrating missile wounds of the brain. *Military Medicine, 139,* 815–817.

Black, F. W. (1974b). The utility of Memory for Designs Test with patients with penetrating missile wounds of the brain. *Journal of Clinical Psychology, 30,* 75–77.

Black, F. W. (1975). Unilateral brain lesions and MMPI performance: A preliminary study. *Perceptual and Motor Skills, 40,* 87–93.

Black, F. W., & Strub, R. L. (1978). Digit repetition performance in patients with focal brain damage. *Cortex, 14,* 12–21.

Blackburn, H. L., & Benton, A. L. (1957). Revised administration and scoring of the digit span test. *Journal of Consulting Psychology, 21,* 139–143.

Blaha, J., & Wallbrown, F. H. (1982). Hierarchical factor structure of the Wechsler Adult

Intelligence Scale-Revised. *Journal of Consulting and Clinical Psychology, 50,* 652–660.

Blanton, P. D., & Gouvier, W. D. (1985). A systematic solution to the Benton Visual Retention Test: A caveat to examiners. *International Journal of Clinical Neuropsychology, 7,* 95–96.

Bloom, A. S., Klee, S. H., & Raskin, L. M. (1977). A comparison of the Stanford-Binet abbreviated and complete forms for developmentally disabled children. *Journal of Clinical Psychology, 33,* 447–480.

Boake, C., & Adams, R. L. (1982). Clinical utility of the Background Interference Procedure for the Bender-Gestalt Test. *Journal of Clinical Psychology, 38,* 627–631.

Bock, R. D. (1973). Word and image: Sources of the verbal and spatial factors in mental test scores. *Psychometrika, 38,* 437–457.

Bolin, B. J. (1955). A comparison of Raven's Progressive Matrices (1938) with the ACE Psychological Examination and the Otis Gamma Mental Ability Test. *Journal of Consulting Psychology, 19,* 400.

Boll, T. J. (1981). The Halstead-Reitan Neuropsychology Battery. In S. B. Filskov & T. J. Boll (Eds.), *Handbook of clinical neuropsychology.* New York: Wiley-Interscience.

Boll, T. J., Heaton, R., & Reitan, R. M. (1974). Neuropsychological and emotional correlates of Huntington's chorea. *Journal of Nervous and Mental Disease, 158,* 61–69.

Boller, F., & Vignolo, L. A. (1966). Latent sensory aphasia in hemisphere damaged patients: An experimental study with the Token Test. *Brain, 89,* 815–830.

Bonfield, R. (1972). Stability of the Pictorial Test of Intelligence with retarded children. *American Journal of Mental Deficiency, 77,* 108–110.

Bornstein, R. A. (1982a). Effects of unilateral lesions of the Wechsler Memory Scale. *Journal of Clinical Psychology, 38,* 839–392.

Bornstein, R. A. (1982b). A factor analytic study of the construct validity of the Verbal Concept Attainment Test. *Journal of Clinical Neuropsychology, 4,* 43–50.

Bornstein, R. A. (1983a). Verbal Concept Attainment Test: Cross validation and validation of a booklet form. *Journal of Clinical Psychology, 39,* 743–745.

Bornstein, R. A. (1983b). Verbal IQ–Performance IQ disprepancies on the Wechsler Adult Intelligence Scale-Revised in patients with unilateral or bilateral cerebral dysfunction. *Journal of Consulting and Clinical Psychology, 51,* 779–780.

Bornstein, R. A. (1984). Unilateral lesions and the Wechsler Adult Intelligence Scale-Revised: No sex differences. *Journal of Consulting and Clinical Psychology, 52,* 604–608.

Bornstein, R. A. (1986a). Classification rates obtained with "standard" cut-off scores on selected neuropsychological measures. *Journal of Clinical and Experimental Neuropsychology, 8,* 413–420.

Bornstein, R. A. (1986b). Contribution of various neuropsychological measures to detection of frontal lobe impairment. *International Journal of Clinical Neuropsychology, 8,* 18–22.

Bornstein, R. A. (1986c). Normative data on intermanual differences on three tests of motor performance. *Journal of Clinical and Experimental Neuropsychology, 8,* 12–20.

Bornstein, R. A. & Chelune, G. J. (1988). Factor structure of the Wechsler Memory Scale-Revised. *The Clinical Neuropsychologist, 2,* 107–115.

Bornstein, R. A., & Leason, M. (1985). Effects of localized lesions on the Verbal Concept Attainment Test. *Journal of Clinical and Experimental Neuropsychology, 7,* 421–429.

Borod, J. C., Goodglass, H., & Kaplan, E. (1980). Normative data on the Boston Diagnostic Aphasia Examination, Parietal Lobe Battery, and the Boston Naming Test. *Journal of Clinical Neuropsychology, 2,* 209–215.

Bowen, D. M. (1976). Behavioral alterations in patients with basal ganglia lesions. In M. D. Yahr (Ed.), *The basal ganglia.* New York: Raven Press.

Boyd, J. L. (1981). A validity study of the Hooper Visual Organization Test. *Journal of Consulting and Clinical Psychology, 49,* 15–19.

Boyd, T. A., & Tramontana, M. G. (1986). Cross-validation of a psychometric system for screening for neuropsychological abnormalities in older children. *Archives of Clinical Neuropsychology, 1,* 387–391.

Bracken, B. A., & Prassee, D. P. (1981). Alternate form reliability of the PPVT-R for white and black educable mentally retarded students. *Educational and Psychological Research, 1,* 151–155.

Bradley, F. O., Hanna, G. S., & Lucas, B. A. (1980). The reliability of scoring the WISC-R. *Journal of Consulting and Clinical Psychology, 48,* 530–531.

Brannigan, G. G., & Ash, T. (1977). Cognitive tempo and WISC-R performance. *Journal of Clinical Psychology, 48,* 530–531.

Breidt, R. (1970). Moglichkeiten des Benton-Tests in der Untersuchung psychoorgaischer Storungen nach Hirneverletzungen. *Archives Psychologishe, 122,* 314–326.

Brinkman, S. D., Largen, J. W., Gerganoff, S., & Pomara, N. (1983). Russell's Revised Wechsler Memory Scale in the evaluation of dementia. *Journal of Clinical Psychology, 39,* 989–993.

Brooks, C. R. (1977). WISC, WISC-R, S-B L & M, WRAT: Relationships and trends among children six to ten referred for psychological evaluation. *Psychology in the Schools, 14,* 30–33.

Brooks, D. N. (1972). Memory and head injury. *Journal of Nervous and Mental Disease, 155,* 350–355.

Brooks, D. N. (1974). Recognition memory and head injury. *Journal of Neurology, Neurosurgery, and Psychiatry, 37,* 794–801.

Brooks, I. R. (1976). Cognitive ability assessment with two New Zealand ethnic groups. *Journal of Cross-Cultural Psychology, 7,* 347–356.

Brossard, M. D., Reynolds, C. R., & Gutkin, T. B. (1980). A regression analysis of test bias on the Stanford-Binet Intelligence Scale for black and white children referred for psychological services. *Journal of Child Clinical Psychology, 9,* 52–54.

Brotsky, S. J., & Linton, M. L. (1969). The test-retest reliability of free associations following successive associations. *Psychonomic Science, 16,* 98–99.

Brown, F. G. (1970). *Principles of educational and psychological testing.* Hinsdale, IL: Dryden Press.

Brown, L. F., & Rice, J. A. (1967). Form equivalence of the Benton Visual Retention Test in low IQ children. *Perceptual and Motor Skills, 24,* 737–738.

Brown, R. J., & McMullen, P. (1982). An unbiased response mode for assessing intellectual ability in normal and physically disabled children. *Clinical Neuropsychology, 4,* 51–56.

Burke, H. R. & Bingham, W. C. (1969). Raven's Progressive Matrices: More on construct validity. *Journal of Psychology, 72,* 247–251.

Butters, N., Salmon, D. P., Cullum, C. M., Cairns, P., Troster, A. I., Jacobs, D., Moss, M., & Cermak, L. S. (1988). Differentiation of amnesic and demented patients with the Wechsler Memory Scale-Revised. *The Clinical Neuropsychologist, 2,* 133–148.

Campbell, D. C., & Oxbury, J. M. (1976). Recovery from unilateral visuospatial neglect? *Cortex, 12,* 303–312.

Campbell, D. T., & Fiske, D. W. (1959). Convergent and discriminant validation by the multitrait-multimethod matrix. *Psychological Bulletin, 56,* 81–105.

Campbell, D. T., & Stanley, J. C. (1963). *Experimental and quasi-experimental designs for research.* Chicago: Rand McNally College Publishing Company.

Canter, A. (1966). A background interference procedure to increase sensitivity of the Bender-Gestalt test to organic brain disorders. *Journal of Consulting Psychology, 30,* 91–97.

Canter, A. (1976). *The Canter Interference Procedure for the Bender-Gestalt test: Manual for administration, scoring, and interpretation.* Nashville, TN: Counselor Recordings and Tests.

Cantone, G., Orsini, A., Grossi, D., & De Michele, G. (1978). Verbal and spatial memory in dementia. *Acta Neurologica, 33,* 175–183.

Carmichael, J. A., & MacDonald, J. W. (1984). Developmental norms for the Sentence Repetition Test. *Journal of Consulting and Clinical Psychology, 52,* 476–477.

Carmines, E. G., & Zeller, R. A. (1979). *Reliability and reliability assessment.* Beverly Hills, CA: Sage.

Carroll, J. B. (1961). The nature of the data, or how to choose a correlation coefficient. *Psychometrika, 26,* 347–372.

Cartan, S. (1971). Use of the Queensland Test in the subnormal population. *Australian Journal of Mental Retardation, 1,* 231–234.

Casey, V. A., & Fennell, E. B. (1981). *Emotional consequences of brain injury: Effect of litigation, sex, and laterality of lesion.* Presented at the ninth annual meeting of the International Neuropsychological Society, Atlanta.

Caskey, W. E., & Larson, G. L. (1980). Scores on group and individually administered Bender-Gestalt test and Otis-Lennon IQ's of kindergarten children. *Perceptual and Motor Skills, 50,* 387–390.

Cass, W. A., Jr., & McReynolds, P. (1951). A contribution to Rorschach norms. *Journal of Consulting Psychology, 15,* 178–184.

Catron, D. W., & Thompson, C. C. (1979). Test-retest gains in WAIS scores after four retest intervals. *Journal of Clinical Psychology, 35,* 352–357.

Cattell, R. B., Balcar, K. R., Horn, J. L., & Nesselroade, J. R. (1969). Factor matching procedures: An improvement of the *s* index; with tables. *Educational and Psychological Measurement, 29,* 781–792.

Cauthen, N. R. (1977). Extension of the Wechsler Memory Scale norms to older age groups. *Journal of Clinical Psychology, 33,* 208–211.

Chaney, E. F., Erickson, R. C., & O'Leary, M. R. (1977). Brain damage and five MMPI items with alcoholic patients. *Journal of Clinical Psychology, 33,* 307–308.

Chapman, L. F., & Wolff, H. G. (1959). The cerebral hemisphere and the highest integrative functions of man. *Archives of Neurology, 1,* 357–424.

Chelune, G. (1982). A reexamination of the relationship between the Luria-Nebraska and Halstead-Reitan Batteries: Overlap with the WAIS. *Journal of Consulting and Clinical Psychology, 50,* 578–580.

Chelune, G. J., & Baer, R. A. (1986). Developmental norms for the Wisconsin Card Sorting Test. *Journal of Experimental and Clinical Neuropsychology, 8,* 219–228.

Chelune, G. J. & Bornstein, R. A. (1988). WMS-R patterns among patients with unilateral brain lesions. *The Clinical Neuropsychologist, 2,* 121–132.

Chmielewski, C. & Golden, C. J. (1980). Alcoholism and brain damage: An investigation using the Luria-Nebraska Neuropsychological Battery. *International Journal of Neuroscience, 10,* 99–105.

Christensen, A. L. (1975). *Luria's neuropsychological investigation.* New York: Spectrum.

Christensen, A. L. (1979). *Luria's Neuropsychological Investigation* (2nd ed.) Copenhagen: Monksgaard.

Ciula, B. A., & Cody, J. J. (1978). Comparative study of validity of the WAIS and Quick Test as predictors of functioning in a psychiatric facility. *Psychological Reports, 42,* 971–974.

Clement, P. (1966). Analyse de l'echelle de memoire de Wechsler. *Revue de Psychologie, 16,* 197–244.

Cohen, J. (1950). Wechsler memory Scale performance on psychoneurotic, organic, and schizophrenic groups. *Journal of Consulting Psychology, 14,* 371–375.

Cohen, J. (1960). A coefficient of agreement for nominal scales. *Educational and Psychological Measurement, 20,* 37–46.

Cohen, J. (1968). Weighted kappa: Nominal scale agreement with provision for scaled disagreement or partial credit. *Psychological Bulletin, 70,* 213–220.

Cole, D. A. (1987). Utility of confirmatory factor analysis in test validation research. *Journal of Consulting and Clinical Psychology, 55,* 584–594.

Cole, D. A., Howard, G. S., & Maxwell, S. E. (1981). Effects of mono- versus multiple-operationalization in construct validation efforts. *Journal of Consulting and Clinical Psychology, 49,* 395–405.

Cole, K. N., & Fewell, R. R. (1983). A quick language screening test for young children: The Token Test. *Journal of Psychoeducational Assessment, 1,* 149–153.

Colombo, A., DeRenzi, E., & Faglioni, P. (1976). The occurrence of visual neglect in patients with unilateral cerebral disease. *Cortex, 12,* 221–231.

Colonna, A., & Faglioni, P. (1966). The performance of hemisphere-damaged patients on spatial intelligence tests. *Cortex, 2,* 291–307.

Conger, A. J. (1974). Estimating profile reliability and maximally reliable composites. *Multivariate Behavioral Research, 9,* 85–104.

Conger, A. J. (1980). Integration and generalization of kappas for multiple raters. *Psychological Bulletin, 88,* 322–328.

Conger, A. J., & Lipshita, R. (1973). Measures of reliability for profiles and test batteries. *Psychometrika, 38,* 411–427.

Conger, A. J., Conger, J. C., Farrell, A. D., & Ward, D. (1979). What can the WISC-R measure? *Applied Psychological Measurement, 3,* 421–436.

Connor, A., Franzen, M. D., & Sharp, B. (1988). Effects of practice and differential instructions on Stroop performance. *International Journal of Clinical Neuropsychology, 10,* 1–4.

Constantini, A. F., & Blackwood, R. O. (1968). CCC trigrams of low association value: A reevaluation. *Psychonomic Science, 12,* 67–68.

Cook, T. D., & Campbell, D. T. (1979). *Quasi-experimentation: Design and analysis issues for field settings.* Chicago: Rand McNally.

Coop, R. H., Eckel, E., & Stuck, G. B. (1975). An assessment of the Pictorial Test of Intelligence with young cerebral-palsied children. *Developmental Medicine and Child Neurology, 17,* 287–292.

Corkin, S. (1979). Hidden-Figures-Test performance: Lasting effects of unilateral penetrating head injury and transient effects of bilateral cingulotomy. *Neuropsychologia, 17,* 585–605.

Costa, L., & Rourke, B. (Eds.). (1985). Abstracts of symposia: Symposium 7. *Journal of Clinical and Experimental Neuropsychology, 7*(2), 178.

Costa, L. D. (1976). Interset variability on the Raven Colored Progressive Matrices as an indicator of specific deficit in brain lesioned patients. *Cortex, 12,* 31–40.

Costa, L. D., & Vaughan, H. G. (1962). Performance of patients with lateralized cerebral lesions: 1. Verbal and perceptual tests. *Journal of Nervous and Mental Disease, 132,* 162–168.

Cottle, W. C. (1950). Card versus booklet forms of the MMPI. *Journal of Applied Psychology, 34,* 255–259.

Covin, T. M. (1977). Comparison of SIT and WISC-R IQ's among special education candidates. *Psychology in the Schools, 15,* 19–23.

Crockett, B. K., Rardin, M. W., & Pasework, R. A. (1975). Relationship between WPPSI and Stanford-Binet IQ's and subsequent WISC IQ's in headstart children. *Journal of Consulting and Clinical Psychology, 43,* 922.

Crockett, D. J., Clark, C., Browning, J., & MacDonald, J. (1983). An application of the background interference procedure to the Benton Visual Retention Test. *Journal of Clinical Neuropsychology, 5,* 181–185.

Cronbach, L. J. (1951). Coefficient alpha and the internal structure of tests. *Psychometrika, 16,* 297–334.

Cronbach, L. J. (1984). *Essentials of psychological testing.* New York: Harper & Row.

Cronbach, L. J. (1988). Internal consistency of tests: Analyses old and new. *Psychometrika, 53,* 63–70.

Cronbach, L. J., & Gleser, G. C. (1965). *Psychological tests and personal decisions.* Urbana: University of Illinois Press.

Cronbach, L. J., & Meehl, P. E. (1955). Construct validity in psychological tests. *Psychological Bulletin, 52,* 281–302.

Cronbach, L. J., Rajaratnam, N., & Gleser, G. C. (1963). Theory of generalizability: A liberalization of reliability theory. *The British Journal of Statistical Psychology, 16*(2), 137–163.

Cronbach, L. J., Gleser, G. C., Nanda, H., & Rajaratnam, N. (1972). *The dependability of behavioral measurement: Theory of generalizability theory for scores and profiles.* New York: Wiley.

Cronholm, B., & Ottosson, J. (1963). Reliability and validity of a memory test battery. *Acta Psychiatrica Scandinavica, 39,* 218–234.

Cronholm, B., & Schalling, D. (1963). Intellectual deterioration after focal brain injury. *Archives of Surgery, 86,* 670–687.

Crookes, T. G. (1983). The Minnesota Percepto-Diagnostic Test and presenile dementia. *Journal of Clinical Neuropsychology, 5,* 187–190.

Crookes, T. G., & Coleman, J. A. (1973). The Minnesota Percepto-Diagnostic Test (MPD) in adult psychiatric practice. *Journal of Clinical Psychology, 29,* 204–206.

Crosson, B., & Trautt, G. M. (1981). Cortical functioning during recovery from brain stem infarctions: A case report. *Clinical Neuropsychology, 3,* 3–7.

Crosson, B., & Warren, L. A. (1982). Use of the Luria-Nebraska Neuropsychological Battery in aphasia: A conceptual critique. *Journal of Consulting and Clinical Neuropsychology, 50,* 22–31.

Crosson, B., Hughes, C. W., Roth, D. L., & Monkowski, P. G. (1984). Review of Russell's (1975) norms for the Logical Memory and Visual Memory Reproduction subtests of the Wechsler Memory Scale. *Journal of Consulting and Clinical Psychology, 52,* 635–641.

Crosson, J. R., & Wiens, A. N. (1988). Wechsler Memory Scale—Revised: Deficits in performance associated with neurotoxic solvent exposure. *The Clinical Neuropsychologist, 2,* 181–187.

Dahlstrom, W., & Welsh, G. (1960). *An MMPI handbook—A guide to use in clinical practice and research.* Minneapolis: University of Minnesota Press.

Dahlstrom, W. G., Welsh, G. S., & Dahlstrom, L. E. (1975). *An MMPI Handbook, Volume II: Research Applications.* Minneapolis: University of Minnesota Press.

Davis, L. J., & Swenson, W. M. (1970). Factor analysis of the Wechsler Memory Scale. *Journal of Consulting and Clinical Psychology, 35,* 430.

Davis, L., Foldi, N. S., Gardner, H., & Zurif, E. B. (1978). Repetition in the transcortical aphasias. *Brain and Language, 6,* 226–238.

Dean, R. S. (1977). Patterns of emotional disturbance of the WISC-R. *Journal of Clinical Psychology, 33,* 486–490.

Dee, H. L. (1970). Visuoconstructive and visuoperceptive deficit in patients with unilateral cerebral lesions. *Neuropsychologia, 8,* 305–314.

DeFilippis, N. A., & Fulmer, K. (1980). Effects of age and IQ level on the validity of one short intelligence test used for screening purposes. *Educational and Psychological Measurement, 40,* 543–545.

Delay, J., Pichot, P., Lemperier, J., & Perse, J. (1958). *The Rorschach and the epileptic personality.* New York: Logos Press.

Delis, D., & Kaplan, E. (1982). Assessment of aphasia with the Luria-Nebraska Neuropsychological Battery: A case critique. *Journal of Consulting and Clinical Psychology, 51,* 32–39.

Delis, D. C., Cullum, C. M., Butters, N., & Cairns, P. (1988). Wechsler Memory Scale-Revised and California Verbal Learning Test: Convergence and divergence. *The Clinical Neuropsychologist, 2,* 188–196.

DeLuca, D., Cermak, L. S., & Butters, N. (1975). An analysis of Korsakoff patients recall following varying types of distractor activity. *Neuropsychologia, 13,* 271–279.

Denes, F., Semenza, C. Stoppa, E., & Gradenigo, G. (1978). Selective improvement by unilateral brain damaged patients on Raven Coloured Progressive Matrices. *Neuropsychologia, 16,* 749–752.

De Renzi, E., & Faglioni, P. (1965). The comparative efficiency of intelligence and viglance tests in detecting hemispheric cerebral damage. *Cortex, 1,* 410–433.

De Renzi, E., & Faglioni, P. (1978). Normative data and screening power of a shortened version of the Token Test. *Cortex, 14,* 41–49.

De Renzi, E., & Nichelli, P. (1975). Verbal and non-verbal short-term memory impairment following hemispheric damage. *Cortex, 11,* 341–354.

De Renzi, E., & Spinnler, H. (1967). Impaired performance on color tasks in patients with hemispheric damage. *Cortex, 3,* 194–217.

De Renzi, E., & Vignolo, L. A. (1962). The Token Test: A sensitive test to detect receptive disturbances in aphasics. *Brain, 85,* 665–678.

De Renzi, E., Faglioni, P., Savoiardo, M., & Vignolo, L. A. (1966). The influence of aphasia and of the hemispheric side of the cerebral lesion on abstract thinking. *Cortex, 2,* 399–420.

De Renzi, E., Pieczuro, A., & Vignolo, L. A. (1968). Ideational apraxia: A quantitative study. *Neuropsychologia, 6,* 41–52.

De Renzi, E., Faglioni, P., & Previdi, P. (1977). Spatial memory and hemispheric locus of lesion. *Cortex, 13,* 424–433.

DeSantis, G., & Dunikoski, R. (1983). Group Embedded Figures test: Psychometric data for a sample of business students. *Perceptual and Motor Skills, 56,* 707–710.

des Rosiers, G., & Ivison, D. (1986). Paired associates learning: Normative data for differences between high and low associate word pairs. *Journal of Clinical and Experimental Neuropsychology, 8,* 637–642.

Diamant, J. J. (1981). Similarities and differences in the approach of R. M. Reitan and A. R. Luria. *Acta Psychiatrica Scanidavica, 63,* 441–443.

Dikmen, S., & Reitan, R. M. (1974a). Minnesota Multiphasic Personality Inventory correlates of dysphasic language disturbances. *Journal of Abnormal Psychology, 83,* 675–679.

Dikmen, S., & Reitan, R. M. (1974b). MMPI correlates of localized cerebral lesions. *Perceptual and Motor Skills, 39,* 831–840.

Dikmen, S., & Reitan, R. M. (1977). MMPI correlates of adaptive ability deficits in patients with brain lesions. *Journal of Nervous and Mental Disease, 165,* 247–254.

Dillon, R. F., Pohlmann, J. T., & Lohman, D. F. (1981). A factor analysis of Raven's advanced progressive matrices freed of difficulty factors. *Educational and Psychological Measurement, 41,* 1295–1302.

Dodge, G. R., & Kolstoe, R. H. (1971). The MMPI in differentiating early Multiple Sclerosis and conversion hysteria. *Psychological Reports, 29,* 155–159.

Dodrill, C. B. (1978). A neuropsychological battery for epilepsy. *Epilepsia, 19,* 611–623.

Dodrill, C. B. (1979). Sex differences on the Halstead-Reitan Neuropsychological Battery and on other neuropsychological measures. *Journal of Clinical Psychology, 35,* 236–241.

Dodrill, C. B., & Troupin, A. S. (1975). Effects of repeated administrations of a comprehensive neuropsychological battery among chronic epileptics. *Journal of Nervous and Mental Disease, 161,* 185–190.

Doehring, D., & Reitan, R. M. (1960). MMPI performances of aphasic and non-aphasic brain-damaged patients. *Journal of Clinical Psychology, 16,* 307–309.

Doehring, D. G., & Reitan, R. M. (1962). Concept attainment of human adults with lateralized cerebral lesions. *Perceptual and Motor Skills, 14,* 27–33.

Dolke, A. M. (1976). Investigation into certain properties of Raven's Standard Progressive Matrices Test. *Indian Journal of Psychology, 51,* 225–236.

Domrath, R. P. (1966). Motor impersistence in schizophrenia. *Cortex, 2,* 474–483.

Dorken, H., & Kral, V. A. (1952). The psychological differentiation of organic brain lesions and their localization by means of the Rorschach test. *American Journal of Psychiatry, 108,* 764–771.

Drachman, D. A., & Arbit, J. (1966). Memory and the hippocampal complex. *Archives of Neurology, 15,* 52–61.

Drachman, D. A., & Hughes, J. R. (1971). Memory and the hippocampal complexes. *Neurology, 21,* 1–14.

Drewe, E. A. (1974). The effect of type and area of brain lesion of Wisconsin Card Sorting Test performance. *Cortex, 10,* 159–170.

Dudek, S. Z., Goldeberg, J. S., Lester, E. P., & Harris, B. R. (1969). The validity of cognitive, perceptual-motor, and personality variables for prediction of achievement in Grade 1 and Grade 2. *Journal of Clinical Psychology, 25,* 165–170.

Dujovne, B. E., & Levy, B. I. (1971). The psychometric structure of the Wechsler Memory Scale. *Journal of Clinical Psychology, 27,* 351–354.

Dunn, J. A. (1967). Inter- and intra-scorer reliability of the New Goodenough-Harris Draw-a-Man Test. *Perceptual and Motor Skills, 24,* 269–270.

Dunn, L. M., & Dunn, L. M. (1981). *Peabody Picture Vocabulary Test-Revised Manual.* Circle Pines, MN: American Guidance Service.

Dunn, L. M., & Markwardt, F. C. (1970). *Manual for the Peabody Individual Achievement Test.* Circle Pines, MN: American Guidance Service.

Dye, C. (1982). Factor structure of the Wechsler Memory Scale in an older population. *Journal of Clinical Psychology, 38,* 163–166.

Eckardt, M. J., & Matarazzo, J. D. (1981). Test-retest reliability of the Halstead impairment index in hospitalized alcoholic and non-alcoholic males with mild to moderate neuropsychological impairment. *Journal of Clinical Neuropsychology, 3,* 257–269.

Egeland, B., Rice, J., & Penny, S. (1967). Interscorer reliability on the Bender Gestalt test and Revised Visual Retention Test. *American Journal of Mental Deficiency, 72,* 96–99.

Ehrfurth, J. W., & Lezak, M. (1982). *The battering of neuropsychology by the "hit rate": An appeal for peace and reason.* Presented at the 10th annual meeting of the International Neuropsychological Society, Pittsburgh.

Elithorn, A. (1955). A preliminary report on a perceptual maze test sensitive to brain damage. *Journal of Neurology, Neurosurgery, and Psychiatry, 18,* 287–292.

Elithorn, A., Kerr, M., & Mott, J. (1960). A group version of a perceptual maze test. *British Journal of Psychology, 51,* 19–26.

Elithorn, A., Svancara, J., & Weinman, J. (1971). A twin study with the perceptual maze test. *Psychologia a Patopsychologia Dieteta, 6,* 105–112.

Elithorn, A., Mornington, S., & Stavrou, A. (1982). Automated psychological testing: Some principles and practices. *International Journal of Man-Machine Studies, 17,* 247–263.

Elliott, R. N. (1969). Comparative study of the Pictorial Test of Intelligence and the Peabody Picture Vocabulary Test. *Psychological Reports, 25,* 528–530.

Elliott, S. N., & Bretzing, B. H. (1980). Using and updating local norms. *Psychology in the Schools, 17,* 196–201.

Engin, A. W., & Wallbrown, F. H. (1976). The stability of four kinds of perceptual errors on the Bender Gestalt. *Journal of Psychology, 84,* 123–126.

Eno, L., & Deichmann, J. (1980). A review of the Bender Gestalt test as a screening instrument for brain damage with school-aged children of normal intelligence since 1970. *The Journal of Special Education, 14,* 37–45.

Erlandson, G. L., Osmon, D. C., & Golden, C. J. (1981). Minnesota Multiphasic Personality Inventory correlates of the Luria Nebraska Neuropsychological Battery in a psychiatric population. *International Journal of Neuroscience, 13,* 143–154.

Ernst, J., Warner, M. H., Morgan, A., Townes, B. D., Eiler, J., & Coppel, D. B. (1986). Factor analysis of the Wechsler Memory Scale: Is the Associate Learning subtest an unclear measure? *Archives of Clinical Neuropsychology, 8,* 637–642.

Ettlinger, G. (1970). Apraxia considered as a disorder of movements that are language-dependent: Evidence from cases of brain bisection. *Cortex, 5,* 285–289.

Evans, R. B., & Marmorston, J. (1963a). Improved mental functioning with Premarin therapy in atherosclerosis. *Proceedings of the Society for Experimental Biology and Medicine, 113,* 698–703.

Evans, R. B., & Marmorston, J. (1963b). Psychological test signs of brain damage in cerebral thrombosis. *Psychological Reports, 12,* 915–930.

Evans, R. B., & Marmorston, J. (1964). Rorschach signs of brain damage in cerebral thrombosis. *Perceptual and Motor Skills, 18,* 977–988.

Evans, R. B., & Marmorston, J. (1965). Mental functioning and Premarin therapy in cardio-vascular and cerebrovascular disease. *Proceedings of the Society for Experimental Biology and Medicine, 118,* 529–533.

Exner, J. E. (1974). *The Rorschach: A comprehensive system.* New York: Wiley.

Exner, J. E. (1978). *The Rorschach: A comprehensive system* (Vol. 2). New York: Wiley.

Exner, J. E. (1982). *The Rorschach: A comprehensive system* (Vol. 3). New York: Wiley.

Eysenck, H. J. (1952). *The Scientific Study of Personality.* London: Routledge and Kegan Paul.

Farley, F. H. (1969). Further data on multiple choice versus open-ended estimates of vocab-ulary. *British Journal of Social and Clinical Psychology, 8,* 67–68.

Fields, F. R. (1971). Relative effects of brain damage on Wechsler memory and intelligence quotients. *Diseases of the Nervous System, 32,* 673–675.

Filley, C. M., Kobayashi, J., & Heaton, R. K. (1987). Wechsler Intelligence Scale profiles, the cholinergic system, and Alzheimer's disease. *Journal of Clinical and Experimental Neu-ropsychology, 5,* 180–186.

Filskov, S. B., & Goldstein, S. G. (1974). Diagnostic validity of the Halstead-Reitan neuro-psychological battery. *Journal of Consulting and Clinical Psychology, 42,* 382–388.

Filskov, S. B., & Leli, D. (1981). Assessment of the individual in neuropsychological practice. In S. B. Filskov & T. J. Boll (Eds.), *Handbook of clinical neuropsychology.* New York: Wiley-Interscience.

Finger, S., & Stein, D. G. (1982). *Brain damage and recovery: Research and clinical per-spectives.* New York: Academic.

Finlayson, M. A. J., Johnson, K. A., & Reitan, R. M. (1977). Relationship of level of education to neuropsychological measures in brain-damaged and non-brain-damaged adults. *Journal of Consulting and Clinical Psychology, 45,* 536–542.

Fish, J. M., & Sinkel, P. (1980). Correlation of scores on Wechsler Memory Scale and Wechsler Adult Intelligence Scale for chronic alcoholics and normals. *Psychological Reports, 47,* 940–942.

Fisher, J. S. (1988). Using the Wechsler Memory Scale-Revised to detect and characterize memory deficits in multiple sclerosis. *The Clinical Neuropsychologist, 2,* 149–172.

Fisher, J., Gonda, T., & Little, K. B. (1955). The Rorschach and central nervous system pa-thology. *American Journal of Psychiatry, 111,* 486–492.

Fiske, D. W. (1971). *Measuring the concepts of personality.* Chicago: Aldine.

Fiske, D. W. (1976). Can a personality construct have a singular validational pattern? Rejoinder to Huba and Hamilton. *Psychological Bulletin, 83,* 87.

Fiske, D. W. (1978). *Strategies for personality research.* San Francisco: Jossey-Bass.

Fitzhugh, K. B., Fitzhugh, L. C., & Reitan, R. M. (1961). Psychological deficits in relation to acuteness of brain dysfunction. *Journal of Consulting Psychology, 25,* 61–66.

Fitzhugh, K. B., Fitzhugh, L. C., & Reitan, R. M. (1964). Influence of age upon measures of problem solving and experimental background in subjects with longstanding cerebral dys-function. *Journal of Gerontology, 19,* 132–134.

Flick, G. L., & Edwards, K. R. (1971). Prediction of organic brain dysfunction with the MMPI. *Newsletter for Research in Psychology, 13,* 18–19.

Forar, B. R., Farberow, N. L., Meyer, M. N., & Tolman, R. S. (1952). Consistency and agreement in the judgement of Rorschach signs. *Journal of Projective Techniques, 16,* 346–351.

Ford, M. (1946). The application of the Rorschach test to young children. *University of Min-nesota Child Welfare Monograph,* No. 23.

Franzen, M. D., & Golden, C. J. (1984a). Multivariate techniques in neuropsychology: 2. Com-parison of number of factors rules. *International Journal of Clinical Neuropsychology, 6,* 165–171.

Franzen, M. D., & Golden, C. J. (1984b). Multivariate techniques in neuropsychology: 3. Discriminant function analysis. *International Journal of Clinical Neuropsychology, 6,* 80–87.

Franzen, M. D., Tishelman, A. C., Sharp, B. H., & Friedman, A. G. (1987). Test-retest reliability of the Stroop Word Color Test across two intervals. *Archives of Clinical Neuropsychology, 2,* 265–272.

Fraser, R. M., & Glass, I. B. (1980). Unilateral and bilateral ECT in elderly patients. *Acta Psychiatrica Scandinavica, 62,* 13–31.

French, J. L. (1964). *Pictorial Test of Intelligence Manual.* Boston: Houghton Mifflin.

Friedman, S. H. (1950). *Psychometric effects of frontal and parietal lobe brain damage.* Unpublished doctoral dissertation, University of Minnesota.

Fromm-Auch, D., & Yeudall, L. T. (1983). Normative data for the Halstead-Reitan Neuropsychological Tests. *Journal of Clinical and Experimental Neuropsychology, 9,* 221–238.

Fuld, P. A. (1983). Psychometric differentiation of the dementias: An overview. In B. Reisberg (Ed.) *Alzheimer's Disease* (pp. 201–210). New York: Free Press.

Fuller, G. B. (1969). The Minnesota Percepto-Diagnostic Test (Revised). *Journal of Clinical Psychology* (Monograph Supplement), Whole No. 28.

Fuller, G. B. (1982). *The Minnesota Percepto-Diagnostic Test (Revised) Manual.* Brandon, VT: Clinical Psychology Publications.

Fuller, G. B., & Friedrich, D. (1976). Differential diagnosis of psychiatric patients with the Minnesota Percepto-Diagnostic Test. *Journal of Clinical Psychology, 32,* 335–337.

Fuller, G. B., & Friedrich, D. (1979). Visual-motor test performance: Race and achievement variables. *Journal of Clinical Psychology, 35,* 621–623.

Fuller, G. B., & Hawkins, W. F. (1969). Differentiation of organic from non-organic retarded children. *American Journal of Mental Deficiency, 74,* 104–110.

Fuller, G. B., & Laird, J. (1963). The Minnesota Percepto-Diagnostic Test. *Journal of Clinical Psychology* (Monograph Supplement), Whole No. 16.

Fuller, G. B., & Wallbrown, F. H. (1983). Comparison of the Minnesota Percepto-Diagnostic Test and Bender Gestalt: Relationship with achievement criteria. *Journal of Clinical Psychology, 39,* 985–988.

Fuller, G. B., Sharp, H., & Hawkins, W. F. (1967). Minnesota Percepto-Diagnostic Test (MPD): Age norms and IQ adjustments. *Journal of Clinical Psychology, 23,* 456–461.

Gainotti, G., D'Erme, P., Villa, G., & Caltagirone, C. (1986). Focal brain lesions and intelligence: A study of a new version. *Journal of Clinical and Experimental Neuropsychology, 8,* 37–50.

Gallagher, A. J. (1979). Temporal reliability of aphasic performance on the Token Test. *Brain and Language, 7,* 34–41.

Garfield, J. C. (1964). Motor impersistence in normal and brain-damaged children. *Neurology, 14,* 623–630.

Garfield, J. C., Benton, A. L., & McQueen, J. C. (1966). Motor impersistence in brain-damaged and cultural-familial defectives. *Journal of Nervous and Mental Disease, 142,* 434–440.

Gazzaniga, M. D., & LeDoux, J. E. (1978). *The integrated mind.* New York: Plenum Press.

George, J. (1973). Differentiating clinical groups by means of the Minnesota Percepto-Diagnostic Test. *Journal of Clinical Psychology, 29,* 210–212.

Giebink, J. W., & Birch, R. (1970). The Bender Gestalt test as an ineffective predictor of reading achievement. *Journal of Clinical Psychology, 26,* 484–465.

Gilberstadt, H., & Farkas, E. (1961). Another look at MMPI profile types in multiple sclerosis. *Journal of Consulting Psychology, 25,* 440–444.

Gillen, R. W., Ginn, C., Strider, M. A., Kreuch, T. J., & Golden, C. J. (1983). The Luria-Nebraska Neuropsychological Battery and the Peabody Individual Achievement Test: A correlational analysis. *International Journal of Neuroscience, 21,* 51–62.

Goebel, R. A. (1983). Detection of faking of the Halstead-Reitan Neuropsychological Test Battery. *Journal of Clinical Psychology, 39,* 731–742.

Golden, C. J. (1974). Sex differences in performance on the Stroop Color and Word Test. *Perceptual and Motor Skills, 39,* 1067–1070.

Golden, C. J. (1975). A group form of the Stroop Color and Word Test. *Journal of Personality Assessment, 39,* 386–388.

Golden, C. J. (1976a). The diagnosis of brain damage by the Stroop test. *Journal of Clinical Psychology, 32,* 652–658.

Golden, C. J. (1976b). The identification of brain damage by an abbreviated form of the Halstead-Reitan Neuropsychological Battery. *Journal of Clinical Psychology, 32*(4), 821–826.

Golden, C. J. (1977). Validity of the Halstead-Reitan Neuropsychological Battery in a mixed psychiatric and brain-injured population. *Journal of Consulting and Clinical Psychology, 45*(6), 1043–1051.

Golden, C. J. (1978a). *Diagnosis and rehabilitation in clinical neuropsychology.* Springfield, IL: Charles C Thomas.

Golden, C. J. (1978b). *Stroop Color and Word Test: A manual for clinical and experimental use.* Chicago: Stoelting.

Golden, C. J. (1980). In reply to Adams' "In search of Luria's battery: A false start." *Journal of Consulting and Clinical Psychology, 48,* 517–521.

Golden, C. J., & Schlutter, L. C. (1978). The interaction of age and diagnosis in neuropsychological test results. *International Journal of Neurosciences, 8,* 61–63.

Golden, C. J., Sweet, J. J., & Osmon, D. C. (1979). The diagnosis of brain-damage by the MMPI: A comprehensive evaluation. *Journal of Personality Assessment, 2,* 138–142.

Golden, C. J., Graber, B., Moses, J. A., & Zatz, L. M. (1980a). Differentiation of chronic schizophrenics with and without ventricular enlargement by the Luria-Nebraska Neuropsychological Battery. *International Journal of Neuroscience, 11,* 131–138.

Golden, C. J., Hammeke, T. A., & Purish, A. D. (1980b). *Luria-Nebraska Neuropsychological Battery manual.* Los Angeles: Western Psychological Services.

Golden, C. J., Fross, K. H., & Graber, B. (1981a). Split-half reliability of the Luria-Nebraska Neuropsychological Battery. *Journal of Consulting and Clinical Psychology, 49,* 304–305.

Golden, C. J., Kane, R. K., Sweet, J., Moses, J. A., Cardellino, J. P., Templeton, R., Vicente, P., & Graber, B. (1981b). Relationship of the Halstead-Reitan Neuropsychological Battery to the Luria-Nebraska Neuropsychological Battery. *Journal of Consulting and Clinical Psychology, 49*(3), 410–417.

Golden, C. J., Moses, J. A., Fishburne, F. J., Engum, E., Lewis, G. P., Wisniewski, A. M., Conley, F. K., Berg, R. A., & Graber, B. (1981c). Cross-validation of the Luria-Nebraska Neuropsychological Battery of the presence, lateralization, and localization of brain damage, *Journal of Consulting and Clinical Psychology, 49,* 491–507.

Golden, C. J., Berg, R. A., & Graber, B. (1982a). Test-retest reliability of the Luria-Nebraska Neuropsychological Battery in stable, chronically impaired patients. *Journal of Consulting and Clinical Psychology, 50,* 452–454.

Golden, C. J., Gustavson, J. L., & Ariel, R. (1982b). Correlations between the Luria-Nebraska and Halstead-Reitan batteries: Effects of partialling out education and post-morbid I.Q. *Journal of Consulting and Clinical Psychology, 50,* 770–771.

Golden, C. J., Ariel, R. J., Wilkening, G. N., McKay, S. E., & MacInnes, W. D. (1982c). Analytic techniques in the interpretation of the Luria-Nebraska Neuropsychological Battery. *Journal of Consulting and Clinical Psychology, 50,* 40–48.

Golden, C. J., Hammeke, T. A., Purisch, A. D., Berg, R. A., Moses, J. A., Newlin, D. B., Wilkening, G. N., & Puente, A. E. (1982d). *Item interpretation of the Luria-Nebraska Neuropsychological Battery.* Lincoln: University of Nebraska Press.

Golden, C. J., MacInnes, W. D., Ariel, R. N., Ruedrich, S. L., Chu, C., Coffman, J. A., Graber, B., & Bloch, S. (1982e). Cross-validation of the Luria Nebraska Neuropsychological Battery to discriminate chronic schizophrenics with and without ventricular enlargement. *Journal of Consulting and Clinical Psychology, 50,* 87–95.

Golden, C. J., Purish, A. D., & Hammeke, T. A. (1985). *Luria-Nebraska Neuropsychological Battery: Forms I and II.* Los Angeles: Western Psychological Services.

Golden, C. J., Hammeke, T. A., & Purisch, A. D. (1987). Diagnostic validity of a standardized neuropsychological battery derived from Luria's neuropsychological tests. *Journal of Consulting and Clinical Psychology, 46*, 1258–1265.

Goldfried, M. R., Stricker, G., & Weiner, I. B. (1971). *Rorschach handbook of clinical and research applications.* Englewood Cliffs, NJ: Prentice-Hall.

Goldstein, G., & Shelly, C. (1973). Univariate vs. multivariate analysis in neuropsychological test assessment: A critical review. *Clinical Neuropsychology, 2*, 49–51.

Goldstein, G., & Shelly, C. (1984). Discriminative validity of various intelligence and neuropsychological tests. *Journal of Consulting and Clinical Psychology, 52*, 383–389.

Goldstein, S. G., Deysach, R. E., & Kleinknecht, R. A. (1973). Effects of experience and amount of information on identification of cerebral impairment. *Journal of Consulting and Clinical Psychology, 41*, 30–34.

Goodglass, H., & Kaplan, E. (1983). *The assessment of aphasia and related disorders.* Philadelphia: Lea & Febiger.

Gorsuch, R. L. (1974). *Factor analysis.* Philadelphia: W. B. Saunders.

Gow, L., & Ward J. (1982). The Porteus Maze Test in the measurement of reflection/impulsivity. *Perceptual and Motor Skills, 54*, 1043–1053.

Graham, F. K., & Kendall, B. S. (1960). Memory for Designs Test: Revised general manual. *Perceptual and Motor Skills, 11*, 147–188.

Grauer, D. (1953). Prognosis in paranoid schizophrenia on the basis of the Rorschach. *Journal of Consulting Psychology, 17*, 199–205.

Gravitz, M. A., & Gerton, M. I. (1976). An empirical study of internal consistency in the MMPI. *Journal of Clinical Psychology, 32*, 567–568.

Greene, V., & Carmines, E. (1980). Assessing the reliability of linear composites. In K. F. Schuessler (Ed.), *Sociological methodology 1980.* San Francisco: Jossey-Bass.

Groff, M. G., & Hubble, I. M. (1981). A factor analytic investigation of the Trial Making Test. *Clinical Neuropsychology, 3*, 11–13.

Groff, M., & Hubble, L. (1982). WISC-R Factor structures of younger and older youths with low IQs. *Journal of Consulting and Clinical Psychology, 50*, 148–149.

Grossman, F. M. (1983). Percentage of WAIS-R standardization sample obtaining verbal-performance discrepancies. *Journal of Consulting and Clinical Psychology, 50*, 641–642.

Grossman, F. M., & Johnson, K. M. (1982). WISC-R factor scores as predictors of WRAT performance: A multivariate analysis. *Psychology in the Schools, 19*, 465–468.

Grow, R. T. (1980). Junior high norms for the Bender Gestalt. *Journal of School Psychology, 18*, 395–398.

Grundvig, J. L., Needham, W. E., & Ajax, E. T. (1970). Comparison of different scoring and administration procedures for the Memory for Designs Test. *Journal of Clinical Psychology, 26*, 353–367.

Gutkin, T. B. (1978). Some useful statistics for the interpretation of the WISC-R. *Journal of Consulting and Clinical Psychology, 46*, 1561–1563.

Gutkin, T. B. (1979). The WISC-R Verbal Comprehension, Perceptual Organization, and Freedom from Distractibility deviation quotients: Data for practitioners. *Psychology in the Schools, 16*, 359–360.

Hale, R. L. (1978). The WISC-R as a predictor of WRAT performance. *Psychology in the Schools, 15*, 172–175.

Hall, J. C. (1957). Correlation of a modified form of Raven's Progressive Matrices (1938) with the Wechsler Adult Intelligence Test. *Journal of Consulting Psychology, 21*, 23–26.

Hall, J. C., & Toal, R. (1957). Reliability (internal consistency) of the Wechsler Memory Scale and correlation with the Wechsler-Bellevue Intelligence Scale. *Journal of Consulting Psychology, 21*, 131–135.

Hall, M. M., Hall, G. C., & Lavoie, P. (1968). Ideation in patients with unilateral or bilateral midline brain lesions. *Journal of Abnormal Psychology, 73*, 526–531.

Halperin, K. M., Neuringer, C., Davies, P. S., & Goldstein, G. (1977). Validation of the schizophrenia-organicity scale with brain-damaged and non-brain-damaged schizophrenics. *Journal of Consulting and Clinical Psychology, 45,* 949–950.

Halstead, W. C. (1947). *Brain and intelligence: A quantitative study of the frontal lobes.* Chicago: University of Chicago Press.

Hambleton, R. K. (Ed.). (1983). *Applications of item response theory.* Vancouver: Educational Research Institute of British Columbia.

Hambleton, R. K., & Cook, L. L. (1977). Latent trait models and their use in the analysis of educational test data. *Journal of Educational Measurement, 14,* 75–95.

Hamsher, K., Levin, H. S., & Benton, A. L. (1979). Facial recognition in patients with focal brain lesions. *Archives of Neurology, 36,* 837–839.

Hamsher, K., Benton, A. L., & Digre, K. (1980). Serial Digit Learning: Normative and clinical aspects. *Journal of Clinical Neuropsychology, 2,* 39–50.

Hannay, H. J., & Malone, D. R. (1976). Visual field effects and short-term memory for verbal material. *Neuropsychologia, 14,* 203–209.

Harley, J. P., Leuthold, C. A., Matthews, C. G., & Bergs, L. (1980). *Wisconsin Neuropsychological Test Battery T-score norms for older Veterans Administration Medical Center patients.* Madison, WI: C. G. Matthews.

Harper, D. C., & Tanners, H. (1972). The French Pictorial Test of Intelligence and the Stanford-Binet, L-M: A concurrent validity study with physically impaired children. *Journal of Clinical Psychology, 28,* 178–181.

Harris, D. B. (1963). *Children's Drawings as Measures of Intellectual Maturity.* New York: Harcourt Brace Jovanovich.

Harrison, K. A., & Wiebe, M. J. (1977). Correlation study of McCarthy, WISC, and Stanford-Binet Scales. *Perceptual and Motor Skills, 14,* 10–14.

Hartje, W., Kerschensteiner, M., Poeck, K., & Orgass, B. (1973). A cross-validation study on the Token Test. *Neuropsychologia, 11,* 119–121.

Hartlage, L. C., & Lucas, T. L. (1976). Differential correlation of Bender-Gestalt and Beery Visual-Motor Integration test for Black and for White children. *Journal of Clinical Psychology, 34,* 1039–1042.

Hartlage, L. C., & Steele, C. T. (1977). WISC and WISC-R correlates of academic achievement. *Psychology in the Schools, 14,* 15–18.

Hathaway, S. R., & McKinley, J. C. (1942). A multiphasic personality schedule (Minnesota): 3. The measurement of symptomatic depression. *Journal of Psychology, 14,* 73–84.

Hathaway, S. R., & Meehl, P. E. (1951). *An atlas for the clinical use of the MMPI.* Minneapolis: University of Minnesota Press.

Havlicek, L. L., & Peterson, N. L. (1977). Effect of the violation of assumptions upon significance levels of the Pearson. *Psychological Bulletin, 84,* 373–377.

Hays, W. L. (1973). *Statistics for the social sciences.* New York: Holt, Rinehart, & Winston.

Heaton, R. K. (1981). *A manual for the Wisconsin Card Sorting Test.* Odessa, FL: Psychological Assessment Resources.

Heaton, R. K., Smith, H. H., Jr., Lehman, R. A., & Vogt, A. T. (1978). Prospects for faking believable deficits on neuropsychological testing. *Journal of Consulting and Clinical Psychology, 46,* 892–900.

Heaton, R. K., Grant, I., Anthony, W. Z., & Lehman, R. A. W. (1981). A comparison of clinical and automated interpretation of the Halstead-Reitan Battery. *Journal of Consulting and Clinical Psychology, 3,* 121–141.

Hecaen, H., & Assal, G. (1970). A comparison of constructive deficits following right and left hemisphere lesions. *Neuropsychologia, 8,* 289–303.

Heck, E. T., & Bryer, J. B. (1986). Superior sorting and categorizing ability in a case of bilateral frontal atrophy: An exception to the rule. *Journal of Clinical and Experimental Neuropsychology, 8,* 313–316.

Heilman, K. M., Watson, R. T., & Schulman, H. M. (1974). A unilateral memory defect. *Journal of Neurology, Neurosurgery, and Psychiatry, 37,* 790–793.

Heinricks, R. W., & Celinski, M. J. (1987). Frequency of occurrence of a WAIS dementia profile in male head trauma patients. *Journal of Clinical and Experimental Neuropsychology, 9,* 187–190.

Heise, D. R. (1969). Separating reliability and stability in test-retest correlation. *American Sociology Review, 34,* 93–101.

Helmes, E., Holden, R. R., & Howe, M. G. (1980). An attempt at validation of the Minnesota Percepto-Diagnosistic Test in a psychiatric setting. *Journal of Clinical Neuropsychology, 2,* 231–236.

Herman, B. P., & Melyn, M. (1985). Identification of neuropsychological deficits in epilepsy using the Luria-Nebraska Neuropsychological Battery: A replication attempt. *Journal of Clinical and Experiment Neuropsychology, 7,* 305–313.

Hertz, M. R. (1934). The reliability of the Rorschach ink-blot test. *Journal of Applied Psychology, 18,* 461–477.

Hertz, M. R., & Loehrke, L. M. (1954). The application of the Piotrowski and Hughes signs of organic defect to a group of patients suffering from post-traumatic encephalopathy. *Journal of Genetic Psychology, 62,* 189–215.

Hevern, V. W. (1980). Recent validity studies of the Halstead-Reitan approach to clinical neuropsychological assessment of lateralized brain damage. *Cortex, 9,* 204–216.

Hillow, P. (1971). *Comparison of brain-damaged and non-brain-damaged retarded children on two visual-motor tasks.* Unpublished master's thesis, North Carolina State University.

Hinshaw, S. P., Carte, E. T., & Morrison, D. C. (1986). Concurrent prediction of academic achievement in reading disabled children: The role of neuropsychological and intellectual measures at different ages. *International Journal of Clinical Neuropsychology, 8,* 3–8.

Hinton, J., & Withers, E. (1971). The usefulness of the Clinical Tests of the Sensorium. *British Journal of Psychiatry, 119,* 9–18.

Holland, T. R., & Wadsworth, H. M. (1974). Incidence vs. degree of rotation on the Minnesota Percepto-Diagnostic Test in brain damaged and schizophrenic patients, *Perceptual and Motor Skills, 38,* 131–134.

Holland, T. R., Lowenfeld, J., & Wadsworth, H. M. (1975a). MMPI indices in the discrimination of brain-damaged and schizophrenic groups. *Journal of Consulting and Clinical Psychology, 43,* 426.

Holland, T. R., Wadsworth, H. M., & Royer, F. L. (1975b). The performance of brain-damaged and schizophrenic patients on the Minnesota Percepto-Diagnostic test under standard and BIP conditions of administration, *Journal of Clinical Psychology, 31,* 21–25.

Hollenbeck, G. P. (1972). A comparison of analyses using the first and second generation Little Jiffy's. *Educational and Psychological Measurement, 32,* 45–51.

Holzberg, J. D., & Alessi, S. (1949). Reliability of the shortened MMPI. *Journal of Consulting Psychology, 13,* 288–292.

Holzberg, J. D., & Wexler, M. (1950). The predictability of schizophrenic performance on the Rorschach test. *Journal of Consulting Psychology, 14,* 395–399.

Hooper, H. E. (1958). *The Hooper Visual Organization Test: Manual.* Los Angeles: Western Psychological Services.

Hopkins, C. D., & Antes, R. L. (1978). *Classroom measurement and evaluation.* Itasca, IL: F. E. Peacock.

Horan, M., Ashton, R., & Minto, J. (1980). Using ECT to study hemispheric specialization for sequential processes. *British Journal of Psychology, 137,* 119–125.

Horn, J. L., Wanberg, K. W., & Appel, M. (1973). On the internal structure of the MMPI. *Multivariate Behavioral Research, 8,* 131–171.

Houston, B. K. & Jones, T. H. (1967). Distraction and Stroop color word performance. *Journal of Experimental Psychology, 74,* 54–56.

Hovey, H. B. (1964). Brain lesions and five MMPI items. *Journal of Consulting Psychology, 28,* 78–79.

Howard, A., & Shoemaker, D. J. (1954). An evaluation of the Memory for Designs Test. *Journal of Consulting Psychology, 18,* 266.

Huba, G. J., & Hamilton, D. L. (1976). On the generality of trait relationships: Some analyses based on Fiske's paper. *Psychological Bulletin, 83,* 868–876.

Huff, F. J., Collins, C., Corkin, S., & Rosen, T. J. (1986). Equivalent forms of the Boston Naming Test. *Journal of Clinical and Experimental Neuropsychology, 8,* 556–562.

Hughes, R. M. (1948). Rorschach signs for the diagnosis of organic pathology. *Rorschach Research Exchange and Journal of Projective Techniques, 12,* 165–167.

Husband, S. D., & DeCato, D. M. (1982). The Quick Test compared with the Wechsler Adult Intelligence Scale-Revised. *Psychological Reports, 40,* 523–526.

Hutchinson, G. L. (1984). The Luria-Nebraska controversy: A reply to Spiers. *Journal of Consulting and Clinical Psychology, 52,* 539–545.

Incagnoli, T., Goldstein, G., & Golden, C. (Eds.). (1985). *Clinical application of neuropsychological test batteries.* New York: Plenum.

Inglis, J., & Lawson, J. (1981). Sex differences in the effects of unilateral brain damage on intelligence. *Science, 212,* 693–695.

Innes, J. M. (1972). The relationship of word-association commonality response set to cognitive and personality variables. *British Journal of Psychology, 83,* 421–428.

Ishihara, S. (1970). *Ishihara Color Blind Test book.* Tokyo: Kanehara Shuppan.

Ivinskis, A., Allen, S., & Shaw, E. (1971). An extension of Wechsler Memory Scale norms to lower age groups. *Journal of Clinical Psychology, 27,* 354–357.

Ivison, D. J. (1977). The Wechsler Memory Scale: Preliminary findings toward an Australian standardisation. *Australian Psychologist, 12,* 303–312.

Jackson, B. (1978). The effects of unilateral and bilateral ECT on verbal and visual spatial memory. *Journal of Clinical Psychology, 34,* 4–13.

Jackson, D. N. (1969). Multimethod factor analysis in the evaluation of convergent and discriminant validity. *Psychological Bulletin, 72,* 30–49.

Jackson, R. E., & Culbertson, W. C. (1977). The Elizur Test of Psycho-Organicity and the Hooper Visual Organization Test as measures of childhood neurological impairment. *Journal of Clinical Psychology, 33,* 213–214.

Jahoda, G. (1969). Cross-cultural use of the perceptual maze test. *British Journal of Educational Psychology, 39,* 82–86.

Jastek, J. F., & Jastek, S. (1978). *Wide Range Achievement Test manual.* Wilmington, DE: Jastek.

Jensen, A. (1965). Scoring the Stroop test. *Acta Psychologica, 24,* 398–408.

Joesting, J., & Joesting, R. (1972). Children's Quick Test, Picture Interpretation, and Goodenough Draw-A-Person scores. *Psychological Reports, 30,* 941–942.

Johnson, J. E., & Oziel, L. J. (1970). An item analysis of the Raven Colored Progressive Matrices Test for paranoid and nonparanoid schizophrenic patients. *Journal of Clinical Psychology, 26,* 357–359.

Johnson, J. H., Klingler, D. E., & Williams, T. A. (1977). An external criterion study of the MMPI validity indices. *Journal of Clinical Psychology, 33*(1), 154–156.

Jones, J., & Shea, J. (1974). Some problems in the comparison of divergent thinking scores across cultures. *Australian Psychologist, 9,* 47–51.

Jortner, S. (1965). A test of Hovey's MMPI scale for CNS disorder. *Journal of Clinical Psychology, 21,* 285–287.

Kane, R. L., Sweet, J. J., Golden, C. J., Parsons, O. A., & Moses, J. A. (1981). Comparative diagnostic accuracy of the Halstead-Reitan and standardized Luria-Nebraska Neuropsychological Batteries in a mixed psychiatric and brain-damaged population. *Journal of Consulting and Clinical Psychology, 49*(3), 484–485.

Kane, R. L., Parsons, O. A., & Goldstein, G. (1985). Statistical relationships and discrimination accuracy of the Halstead-Reitan, Luria-Nebraska, and Wechsler IQ scores in the identification of brain damage. *Journal of Clinical and Experimental Neuropsychology, 7,* 211–223.

Kaplan, E. (1983). Achievement and process revisited. In S. Wapner & B. Kaplan (Eds.), *Toward a holistic developmental psychology.* Hillsdale, NJ: Erlbaum.

Kaufman, A. S. (1975a). Factor analysis of the WISC-R at 11 age levels between 6½ and 16½ years. *Journal of Consulting and Clinical Psychology, 43,* 135–147.

Kaufman, A. S. (1975b). Factor structure of the McCarthy Scales at five age levels between 2½ and 8½. *Educational and Psychological Measurement, 35,* 641–656.

Kaufman, A. S. (1979). *Intelligence testing with the WISC-R.* New York: Wiley.

Kaufman, A. S., & DiCuio, R. F. (1975). Separate factor analyses for groups of black and white children. *Journal of School Psychology, 13,* 11–18.

Kaufman, A. S., & Hollenbeck, G. P. (1973). Factor analysis of the standardization edition of the McCarthy Scales. *Journal of Clinical Psychology, 29,* 519–532.

Kaufman, A. S., & Van Hagen, J. (1977). Investigation of the WISC-R for use with retarded children: Correlation with the 1972 Standford-Binet and comparison of WISC and WISC-R profiles. *Psychology in the Schools, 14,* 10–14.

Kausler, D. H., & Puckett, J. M. (1979). Effects of word frequency on adult age differences in word memory span. *Experimental Aging Research, 5,* 161–169.

Kear-Colwell, J. J. (1973). The structure of the Wechsler Memory Scale and its relationship to brain damage. *British Journal of Social and Clinical Psychology, 12,* 384–392.

Kear-Colwell, J. J. (1977). The structure of the Wechsler Memory Scale: A replication. *Journal of Clinical Psychology, 33,* 483–485.

Kear-Colwell, J. J., & Heller, M. (1978). A normative study of the Wechsler Memory Scale. *Journal of Clinical Psychology, 34,* 437–442.

Kear-Colwell, J. J., & Heller, M. (1980). The Wechsler Memory Scale and closed head injury. *Journal of Clinical Psychology, 36,* 782–787.

Keesler, T. Y., Schultz, E. E., Sciara, A. D., & Friedenberg, L. (1984). Equivalence of alternate subtests for the Russell revision of the Wechsler Memory Scale. *Journal of Clinical Neuropsychology, 6,* 215–219.

Keith, T. Z., & Bolen, L. M. (1980). Factor structure of the McCarthy scales for children experiencing problems in school. *Psychology in the School, 17,* 320–328.

Keller, W. K. (1971). *A comparison of two procedures for assessing constructional praxis in patients with unilateral cerebral disease.* Ph.D. dissertation, University of Iowa.

Kelley, D. M., Margulies, H., & Barrera, S. E. (1941). The stability of the Rorschach method as demonstrated in electric convulsive therapy cases. *Rorschach Research Exchange, 5,* 35–43.

Kerr, M. (1936). Temperamental differences in twins. *British Journal of Psychology, 27,* 51–59.

Kimura, D. (1963). Right temporal lobe damage. *Archives of Neurology, 8,* 264–271.

King, G. D., Hannay, H. J., Masek, B. J., & Burns, J. W. (1978). Effects of anxiety and sex on neuropsychological tests. *Journal of Consulting and Clinical Psychology, 46,* 375–376.

King, M. C. (1981). Effects of non-focal brain dysfunction on visual memory. *Journal of Clinical Psychology, 37,* 638–643.

King, M. C., & Snow, W. G. (1981). Problem-solving task performance in brain damaged subjects. *Journal of Clinical Psychology, 37,* 400–404.

Kish, G. B. (1970). Alcoholics' GATB and Shipley profiles and their interrelationships. *Journal of Clinical Psychology, 26,* 482–483.

Kljajic, I. (1975). Wechsler Memory Scale indices of brain pathology. *Journal of Clinical Psychology, 31,* 698–701.

Kljajic, I. (1976). The MFD and brain pathology. *Journal of Clinical Psychology, 32,* 91–93.

Klebanoff, S. G., Singer, J. L., & Wilensky, H. (1954). Psychological consequences of brain lesions and ablations. *Psychological Bulletin, 51,* 1–41.

Klesges, R. C., Fisher, L., Pheley, A., Boschee, P., & Vasey, M. (1984). A major validation study of the Halstead-Reitan in the prediction of CAT-Scan assessed brain damage in adults. *International Journal of Clinical Neuropsychology, 6*, 29–34.

Klonoff, H., Fibiger, C. H., & Hutton, G. (1970). Neuropsychological patterns in chronic schizophrenia. *The Journal of Nervous and Mental Disease, 150*(4), 291–300.

Klopfer, B., & Davidson, H. (1962). *The Rorschach technique: An introductory manual.* New York: Harcourt.

Klove, H. (1959). Relationship of differential electroencephalographic patterns to distributions of Wechsler-Bellevue scores. *Neurology, 9*, 871–876.

Klove, H. (1963). Clinical neuropsychology. In F. M. Forster (Ed.), *The medical clinics of North America.* New York: Saunders.

Klove, H. (1974). Validation studies in adult clinical neuropsychology. In R. M. Reitan & L. A. Davison (Eds.), *Clinical neuropsychology: Current status and applications.* Washington, DC: Winston.

Klove, H., & Doehring, D. G. (1962). MMPI in epileptic groups with differential etiology. *Journal of Clinical Psychology, 18*, 149–153.

Knight, R. G. (1983). On interpreting the several standard errors of the WAIS-R: Some further tables. *Journal of Consulting and Clinical Psychology, 51*, 671–673.

Koppitz, E. (1960). The Bender-Gestalt test for children: A normative study. *Journal of Clinical Psychology, 16*, 432–435.

Korman, M., & Blumberg, S. (1963). Comparative efficiency of some tests of cerebral damage. *Journal of Consulting Psychology, 27*, 303–304.

Kristianson, P. (1974). A comparison between the personality changes in certain forms of psychomotor and grand mal epilepsy. *British Journal of Psychiatry, 125*, 34–35.

Kroger, R. O., & Turnbull, W. (1975). Invalidity of validity scales: The case of the MMPI. *Journal of Consulting and Clinical Psychology, 43*(1), 48–55.

Kronfol, Z., Hamsher, K., Digre, K., & Waziri, R. (1978). Depression and hemispheric functions: Changes associated with ECT. *British Journal of Psychiatry, 132*, 580–567.

Kuder, G. F., & Richardson, M. W. (1937). The theory of estimation of test reliabilities. *Psychometrika, 2*, 151–160.

Laboratory of Comparative Human Cognition. (1976). Memory span for nouns, verbs, and function words in low SES children: A replication and critique of Schutz and Keisler. *Journal of Verbal Learning and Verbal Behavior, 15*, 431–435.

Lacks, P. (1982). Continued clinical popularity of the Bender-Gestalt test: Response to Bigler and Ehrfurth. *Professional Psychology, 13*, 677–680.

Lacks, P. (1984). *Bender Gestalt screening for brain dysfunction,* New York: Wiley.

Lacks, P., & Storandt, M. (1982). Bender Gestalt performance of normal older adults. *Journal of Clinical Psychology, 38*, 624–627.

Lacks, P. B. (1979). The use of the Bender Gestalt test in clinical neuropsychology. *Clinical Neuropsychology, 1*, 29–34.

Lacks, P. B., & Newport, K. (1980). A comparison of scoring systems and level of scorer experience on the Bender-Gestalt test. *Journal of Personality Assessment, 44*, 351–357.

Lacks, P. B., Colbert, J., Harrow, M., & Levine, J. (1970). Further evidence concerning the diagnostic accuracy of the Halstead organic test battery. *Journal of Clinical Psychology, 26*, 480–481.

Lamanna, J. A., & Ysseldyke, J. E. (1973). Reliability of the Peabody Individual Achievement Test with first grade children. *Psychology in the Schools, 10*, 473–479.

Lambert, N. M. (1970). Paired associates learning, social status, and tests of logical concrete behavior as univariate and multivariate predictors of first grade reading achievement. *American Educational Research Journal, 7*, 511–528.

Lamp, R. E., & Barclay, A. (1967). The Quick Test as a screening device for intellectually subnormal children. *Psychological Reports, 20*, 763–766.

Landy, F. J. (1986). Stamp collecting versus science. *American Psychologist, 41*, 1183–1192.

Larrabee, G. J., Kane, R. L., & Schuck, J. R. (1983). Factor analysis of the WAIS and Wechsler Memory Scale: An analysis of the construct validity of the Wechsler Memory Scale. *Journal of Clinical Psychology, 5*, 159–168.

Larrabee, G. J., Kane, R. L., Shuck, J. R., & Francis, D. J. (1985). Construct validity of various memory testing procedures. *Journal of Clinical and Experimental Neuropsychology, 7*, 239–250.

Lass, N. J., & Golden, S. S. (1975). A comparative study of children's performance on three tasks for receptive language abilities. *Journal of Auditory Research, 15*, 177–182.

Law, J. G., Price, D. R., & Herbert, D. A. (1981). Study of Quick Test, WAIS, and premorbid estimates of intelligence for neuropsychiatric patients. *Psychological Reports, 52*, 919–922.

Lawlis, G. F., & Lu, E. (1972). Judgement of counseling process: Reliability, agreement, and error. *Psychological Bulletin, 78*, 17–20.

Lawriw, I., & Sutker, L. W. (1978). A further analysis of the Block Rotation Test. *Journal of Clinical Psychology, 34*, 930–934.

Lawson, J. S., & Barker, M. G. (1968). The assessment of nominal aphasia in dementia: the use of reaction-time measures. *British Journal of Medical Psychology, 41*, 411–414.

Lawson, J. S., Inglis, J., & Stroud, T. W. F. (1983). A laterality index of cognitive impairment derived from a principal components analysis of the WAIS-R. *Journal of Consulting and Clinical Psychology, 51*, 841–847.

Lee, D. (1967). Graph-theoretical properties of Elithorn's Maze. *Journal of Mathematical Psychology, 4*, 341–347.

Lerner, H. L., & Lerner, P. M. (1986). Rorschach inkblot test. In D. J. Keyser & R. C. Sweetland (Eds.), *Test critiques* (Vol. 4). Kansas City: Test Corporation of America.

Levin, H. (1973). Motor impersistence in patients with unilateral cerebral disease: A cross-validational study. *Journal of Consulting and Clinical Psychology, 41*, 287–290.

Levin, H. S., & Benton, A. L. (1977). Facial recognition in "pseudoneurological" patients. *Journal of Nervous and Mental Disease, 164*, 135–138.

Levin, H. S., Grossman, R. G., & Kelly, P. J. (1977). Impairment of facial recognition after closed head injuries of varying severity. *Cortex, 13*, 119–130.

Levine, J., & Feirstein, A. (1972). Differences in test performances between brain damaged, schizophrenic, and medical patients. *Journal of Consulting and Clinical Psychology, 39*, 508–511.

Levine, M. S. (1977). *Canonical analysis and factor comparison.* Beverly Hills, CA: Sage.

Levine, N. R. (1971). Validation of the Quick Test for intelligence screening of the elderly. *Psychological Reports, 29*, 167–172.

Levitt, E. E., & Truumaa, A. (1972). *The Rorschach technique with children and adolescents: Application and norms.* New York: Grune & Stratton.

Levy, I. S. (1971). The Goodenough-Harris Drawing Test and educable mentally retarded adolescents. *Journal of Mental Deficiency, 75*, 760–761.

Lewinsohn, P. M. (1973). *Psychological assessment of patients with brain injury.* Unpublished manuscript, University of Oregon, Eugene.

Lezak, M. D. (1979). Recovery of memory and learning functions following traumatic brain injury. *Cortex, 15*, 63–72.

Lezak, M. D. (1982). *The test-retest stability and reliability of some tests commonly used in neuropsychological assessment.* Presented at fifth European Conference of the International Neuropsychological Society, Deauville, France.

Lezak, M. D. (1983). *Neuropsychological assessment* (2nd ed.). New York: Oxford University Press.

Lezak, M. D., & Glaudin, V. (1969). Differential effects of physical illness on MMPI profiles. *Newsletter for Research in Psychology, 11*, 27–28.

Libb, J. W., & Coleman, J. M. (1971). Correlations between the WAIS and Revised Beta,

Wechsler Memory Scale, and Quick Test in a vocational rehabilitation center. *Psychological Reports, 29,* 863–865.

Liebetrau, A. M. (1983). *Measures of association.* Beverly Hills, CA: Sage.

Likert, R., & Quasha, W. H. (1948). *The revised Minnesota Paper Form Board Test.* New York: Psychological Corporation.

Lin, Y., & Rennick, P. M. (1973). WAIS correlates of the Minnesota Percepto-Diagnostic Test in a sample of epileptic patients: Differential patterns for men and women. *Perceptual and Motor Skills, 37,* 643–646.

Lindgren, S. D., & Benton, A. L. (1980). Developmental patterns of visuospatial judgement. *Journal of Pediatric Psychology, 5,* 217–225.

Lippold, S., & Claiborn, J. M. (1983). Comparison of the Wechsler Adult Intelligence Scale and the Wechsler Adult Intelligence Scale-Revised. *Journal of Consulting and Clinical Psychology, 51,* 315.

Logue, P., & Wyrick, L. (1979). Initial validation of Russell's Revised Wechsler Memory Scale: A comparison of normal aging versus dementia. *Journal of Consulting and Clinical Psychology, 47,* 176–178.

Lord, F. (1952). A theory of test scores. *Psychometrika,* Monograph No. 7.

Lord, F. M. (1980). *Applications of item response theory to practical testing problems.* Hillsdale, NJ: Erlbaum.

Love, H. G. I. (1970). Validation of the Hooper Visual Organization Test on a New Zealand psychiatric hospital population. *Psychological Reports, 27,* 915–917.

Loveland, N. T. (1961). Epileptic personality and cognitive functioning. *Journal of Projective Techniques, 25,* 54–68.

Lowrance, D., & Anderson, H. N. (1979). A comparison of the Slosson Intelligence Test and the WISC-R with elementary school children. *Psychology in the Schools, 16,* 361–364.

Luria, A. R. (1966). *Higher cortical functions in man* (1st ed.; B. Heigh, Trans.). New York: Basic Books and Plenum Press.

McCallum, R. S., & Bracken, B. A. (1981). Alternate forms reliability of the PPVT-R for black and white preschool children. *Psychology in the Schools, 18,* 422–425.

McCara, E. (1953). The Wechsler Memory Scale with average and superior normal adults. *Bulletin of the Maritime Psychology Association,* 30–33.

McCarthy, D. (1972). *McCarthy Scales of Children's Abilities manual.* New York: Psychological Corporation.

McCarty, S. M., Logue, P. E., Power, D. G., Ziesat, H. A., & Rosenstiel, A. K. (1980). Alternate-form reliability and age related scores of Russell's Revised Wechsler Memory Scale. *Journal of Consulting and Clinical Psychology, 48,* 296–298.

McElwain, D. W., Kearney, G. E., & Ord, I. G. (n.d.). *The Queensland Test.* Brisbane, Australia: Craftsman Press.

McGilligan, R. P., Yater, A. C., & Hulsing, R. (1971). Goodenough-Harris Drawing Test reliabilities. *Psychology in the Schools, 8,* 359–362.

MacInnes, W. D., Golden, C. J., McFadden, J. E., & Wilkening, G. N. (1983). Relationship between the Booklet Category Test and the Wisconsin Card Sorting Test. *International Journal of Neuroscience, 21,* 257–264.

Mack, J. L. (1979). The MMPI and neurological dysfunction. In C. S. Newmark (Ed.), *MMPI: Current clinical and research trends.* New York: Praeger.

McKinley, J. C., & Hathaway, S. R. (1942). A multiphasic personality schedule (Minnesota): 4. Psychasthenia. *Journal of Applied Psychology, 26,* 614–624.

McKinley, J. C., & Hathaway, S. R. (1944). The MMPI: 5. Hysteria, hypomania, and psychopathic deviate. *Journal of Applied Psychology, 28,* 153–174.

McNeil, M. R., & Prescott, T. E. (1978). *Revised Token Test.* Baltimore: University Park Press.

McSweeny, A. J., Grant, I., Heaton, R. K., Prigatano, G. P., & Adams, K. M. (1985). Relationship of neuropsychological status to everyday functioning in healthy and chronically ill persons. *Journal of Clinical and Experimental Neuropsychology, 7,* 281–291.

Maier, L. R., & Abidin, R. (1967). Validation attempt of Hovey's five-item MMPI index for central nervous system disorders. *Journal of Consulting Psychology, 31,* 542.

Malec, J. (1978). Neuropsychological assessment of schizophrenia versus brain damage: A review. *The Journal of Nervous and Mental Disease, 166*(7), 507–516.

Malloy, P. F., & Webster, J. S. (1981). Detecting mild brain impairment using the Luria-Nebraska Neuropsychological Battery, *Journal of Consulting and Clinical Psychology, 49,* 768–770.

Malmo, H. P. (1974). On frontal lobe functions: Psychiatric patient controls. *Cortex, 10,* 231–237.

Markowitz, H. J. (1973). *The differential diagnosis of acute schizophrenia and organic brain damage.* Doctoral dissertation, West Virginia University.

Marmorale, A. M., & Brown, F. (1977). Bender-Gestalt performance of Puerto Rican, white, and black children. *Journal of Clinical Psychology, 33,* 224–228.

Marsh, G. C., & Hirsch, S. H. (1982). Effectiveness of two tests of visual retention. *Journal of Clinical Psychology, 38,* 115–118.

Martin, J. D., Blair, G. E., & Vickers, D. M. (1979). Correlation of the Slosson Intelligence Test with the California Short-Form Test of Mental Maturity and the Shipley Institute of Living Scale. *Educational and Psychological Measurement, 39,* 193–196.

Martino, A. A., Pizzamiglio, L., & Razzano, C. (1976). A new version of the "Token Test" for aphasics: A concrete objects form. *Journal of Communication Disorders, 9,* 1–5.

Maruish, M. E., Sawicki, R. F., Franzen, M. D., & Golden, C. J. (1985). Alpha coefficient reliabilities for the Luria-Nebraska summary and localization scales by diagnostic category. *International Journal of Clinical Neuropsychology, 7,* 10–12.

Matarazzo, J. D., Wiens, A. N., Matarazzo, R. G., & Goldstein, S. (1974). Psychometric and clinical test-retest reliability of the Halstead-Reitan Impairment Index in a sample of healthy, young, normal men. *The Journal of Nervous and Mental Disease, 158* (1), 37–49.

Matarazzo, J. D., Matarazzo, R. G., Wiens, A. N., Gallo, A. E., & Klonoff, H. (1976). Retest reliability of the Halstead Impairment Index in a normal, a schizophrenic, and two samples of organic patients. *Journal of Clinical Psychology, 32*(2), 338–349.

Matarazzo, J. D., Carmody, T. P., & Jacobs, L. D. (1980). Test-retest reliability and stability of the WAIS: A literature review with implications for clinical practice. *Journal of Clinical Neuropsychology, 2,* 89–105.

Matthews, C. G., & Booker, H. E. (1972). Pneumonecephalographic measurements and neuro-psychological test performance in human adults. *Cortex, 8,* 69–92.

Matthews, C. G., & Haaland, K. Y. (1979). The effect of symptom duration on cognitive and motor performance in Parkinsonism. *Neurology, 29,* 951–956.

Matthews, C. G., Shaw, D. J., & Klove, H. (1966). Psychological test performance in neurologic and "pseudoneurologic" subtests. *Cortex, 2,* 244–253.

Matthews, C. G., Dikmen, S., & Harley, J. P. (1977). Age of onset and psychometric correlates of MMPI profiles in major epilepsy. *Diseases of the Nervous System, 38*(3), 173–176.

Mehlman, B., & Rand, M. E. (1960). Face validity on the MMPI. *Journal of General Psychology, 63,* 171–178.

Meier, M. J. (1969). The regional localization hypothesis and personality changes associated with focal cerebral lesions and ablations. In J. N. Butcher (Ed.), *MMPI: Research developments and clinical applications.* New York: McGraw-Hill.

Meier, M. J., & French, L. A. (1965). Some personality correlates of unilateral and bilateral EEG abnormalities in psychomotor epileptics. *Journal of Clinical Psychology, 21,* 3–9.

Meier, M. J., & Story, J. L. (1967). Selective impairment of Porteus Maze performance after right subthalamotomy. *Neuropsychologia, 5,* 181–189.

Miceli, G., Caltagirone, C., Gainotti, G., Masullo, C., & Silveri, M. C. (1981). Neuropsychological correlates of localized cerebral lesions in non-aphasic brain damaged patients. *Journal of Clinical Neuropsychology, 3,* 53–63.

Michell, J. (1986). Measurement scales and statistics: A clock of paradigms. *Psychological Bulletin, 100,* 398–407.

Miller, E. (1971). On the nature of the memory disorder in presenile dementia. *Neuropsychologia, 9,* 75–81.

Miller, E. (1973). Short and long term memory in patients with presenile dementia (Alzheimer's disease). *Psychological Medicine, 3,* 221–224.

Milner, B. (1963). Effects of different brain lesions on card sorting. *Archives of Neurology, 9,* 90–100.

Milner, B. (1971). Interhemispheric differences in the localization of psychological processes in man. *British Medical Bulletin, 27,* 272–277.

Milner, B. (1972). Disorders of learning and memory after temporal lobe lesions in man. *Clinical Neurosurgery, 19,* 421–446.

Mishra, S. P. (1982). The WISC-R and evidence of item bias for Native-American Navajos. *Psychology in the Schools, 19,* 458–464.

Mishra, S. P. (1983). Validity of WISC-R IQ's and factor scores in predicting achievement for Mexican-American children. *Psychology in the Schools, 20,* 442–444.

Moses, J. A. (1984a). Performance as a function of sensorimotor impairment in a brain damaged sample. *International Journal of Clinical Neuropsychology, 6,* 123–126.

Moses, J. A. (1984b). The relative effects of cognitive and sensorimotor deficits in Luria Nebraska Neuropsychological Battery performance in a brain damaged population. *International Journal of Clinical Neuropsychology, 6,* 8–12.

Moses, J. A. (1985). Relationship of the profile elevation and impairment scales of the Luria Nebraska Neuropsychological Battery in neurological examination. *International Journal of Clinical Neuropsychology, 7,* 183–190.

Moses, J. A. (1986). Factor structure of Benton's tests of Visual Retention, Visual Construction, and Visual Form Discrimination. *Archives of Clinical Neuropsychology, 1,* 147–156.

Moses, J. A., & Schrefft, B. K. (1985). Interrater reliability analyses of the Luria-Nebraska Neuropsychological Battery. *International Journal of Clinical Neuropsychology, 7,* 31–38.

Moses, J. A., Golden, C. J., Ariel, R. N., & Gustavson, J. L. (1983a). *Interpretation of the Luria-Nebraska Neuropsychological Battery* (Vol. 1). New York: Grune & Stratton.

Moses, J. A., Johnson, G. L., & Lewis, G. P. (1983b). Reliability analyses of the Luria-Nebraska Neuropsychological Battery summary, localization and factor scales. *International Journal of Neuroscience, 20,* 149–154.

Munford, P. R., Meyerowitz, B. E., & Munford, A. M. (1980). A Comparison of black and white children's WISC/WISC-R differences. *Journal of Clinical Psychology, 36,* 471–475.

Mungas, D. (1983). Differential clinical sensitivity of specific parameters of the Rey Auditory-Verbal Learning Test. *Journal of Consulting and Clinical Psychology, 51,* 848–855.

Naglieri, J. A. (1982). Two types of tables for use with the WAIS-R. *Journal of Consulting and Clinical Psychology, 50,* 319–321.

Naglieri, J. A., & Maxwell, S. (1981). Inter-rater reliability and concurrent validity of the Goodenough-Harris and McCarthy Draw-a-Child scoring systems. *Perceptual and Motor Skills, 53,* 343–348.

Naglieri, J. A., & Parks, J. C. (1980). Wide Range Achievement Test: A one year stability study. *Psychological Reports, 47,* 1028–1030.

Naglieri, J. A., & Pfeiffer, S.I. (1983). Stability and concurrent validity of the Peabody Individual Achievement Test. *Psychological Reports, 52,* 672–674.

Nehil, J., Agathon, M., Greif, J. L., Delagrange, G., & Rondepierre, J. P. (1965). Contribution a l'étude comparative des tests psychometriques de détérioration et des traces EEG. *Review of Neurology, 112,* 293–296.

Nesselroade, J. R., Stigler, S. M., & Baltes, P. B. (1980). Regression toward the mean and the study of change. *Psychological Bulletin, 88,* 622–637.

Neuringer, C., Dombrowski, P. S., & Goldstein, G. (1975). Cross-validation of an MMPI scale of differential diagnosis of brain damage from schizophrenia. *Journal of Clinical Psychology, 31,* 268–271.

Newby, R. F., Hallenback, C. E., & Embretson, S. (1983). Confirmatory factor analysis of four general models with a modified Halstead-Reitan Battery. *Journal of Clinical Neuropsychology, 5,* 115–133.

Newcombe, F., Oldfield, R. C., Ratcliffe, G. G., & Wingfield, A. (1971). Recognition and naming of object drawings by men with focal brain wounds. *Journal of Neurology, Neurosurgery, and Psychiatry, 34,* 329–340.

Nicholson, C. L. (1977). Correlations between the Quick Test and the Wechsler Intelligence Scale for Children-Revised. *Psychological Reports, 40,* 523–526.

Norton, J. C. (1975). Patterns of neuropsychological test performance in Huntington's disease. *Journal of Nervous and Mental Disease, 161*(4), 276–279.

Norton, J. C. (1978). The Trial Making Test and Bender Gestalt background interference procedure as screening devices. *Journal of Clinical Psychology, 34,* 916–922.

Norton, J. C. (1979). Wechsler variables as a function of age and neurologic status. *Journal of Clinical Psychiatry, 219,* 21–23.

Norton, J. C., & Romano, P. O. (1977). Validation of the Watson-Thomas rules for MMPI diagnosis. *Diseases of the Nervous System, 38,* 773–775.

Novick, M., & Lewis, M. (1967). Coefficient alpha and the reliability of composite measurements. *Psychometrika, 32,* 1–13.

Nunnally, J. C. (1978). *Psychometric theory.* New York: McGraw-Hill.

Oakland, T., & Feigenbaum, D. (1979). Multiple sources of test bias on the WISC-R and Bender Gestalt test. *Journal of Consulting and Clinical Psychology, 47,* 968–974.

O'Donnell, W. E., & Reynolds, D. McQ. (1983). *Neuropsychological Impairment Scale manual.* Annapolis, MD: Annapolis Neuropsychological Services.

O'Donnell, W. E., Reynolds, D. McQ., & De Soto, C. B. (1983). Neuropsychological Impairment Scale (NIS): Initial validation study using Trailmaking Test (A&B) and WAIS Digit Symbol (Scaled Score) in a mixed grouping of psychiatric, neuropsychological, and normal patients. *Journal of Clinical Psychology, 39,* 746–748.

O'Donnell, W. E., De Soto, C. B., & McReynolds, D. McQ. (1984a). Sensitivity and specificity of the Neuropsychological Impairment Scale (NIS). *Journal of Clinical Psychology, 40,* 553–555.

O'Donnell, W. E., Reynolds, D. McQ., & De Soto, C. B. (1984b). Validity and reliability of the Neuropsychological Impairment Scale (NIS). *Journal of Clinical Psychology, 40,* 549–553.

O'Grady, K. E. (1983). A confirmatory maximum likelihood factor analysis of the WAIS-R. *Journal of Consulting and Clinical Psychology, 51,* 826–831.

Oldfield, R. C., & Wingfield, A. (1965). Response latencies in naming objects. *The Quarterly Journal of Experimental Psychology, 17,* 273–281.

Oltmanns, T. (1978). Selective attention in schizophrenia and manic psychoses: The effect of distraction on information processing. *Journal of Abnormal Psychology, 87,* 212–225.

O'Malley, P. M., & Bachman, J. G. (1976). Longitudinal evidence for the validity of the Quick Test. *Psychological Reports, 38,* 1247–1252.

Orgass, B., & Poeck, K. (1966). Clinical validation of a new test for aphasia: An experimental study on the Token Test. *Cortex, 2,* 222–243.

Orpen, C. (1974). The susceptibility of the Quick Test to instructional sets. *Journal of Clinical Psychology, 30,* 507–509.

Orsini, A., Schiappa, O., & Grossi, D. (1981). Sex and cultural differences in children's spatial and verbal memory span. *Perceptual and Motor Skills, 53,* 39–42.

Osborne, D., & Davis, L. J. (1978). Standard scores for Wechsler Memory Scale subtests. *Journal of Clinical Psychology, 34,* 115–116.

Osmon, D. C., & Golden, C. J. (1978). Minnesota Multiphasic Personality Inventory correlates of neuropsychological deficits. *International Journal of Neurosciences, 3,* 113–122.

Ottosson, J. (1960). Experimental studies of memory impairment after electroconvulsive therapy. *Acta Psychiatrica et Neurologica, 145* (Supplement 35), 103–132.

Paletz, M. D., & Hirshhoren, A. (1972). A comparison of two tests of visual-sequential memory ability. *Journal of Learning Disabilities, 5,* 46–47.

Pantano, L. T., & Schwartz, M. (1978). Differentiation of neurologic and pseudo-neurologic patients with combined MMPI mini-mult and pseudo-neurologic scale. *Journal of Clinical Psychology, 34,* 55–60.

Paramesh, C. R. (1982). Relationship between the Quick Test and WISC-R and reading ability as used in a juvenile setting. *Perceptual and Motor Skills, 55,* 881–882.

Parker, J. W. (1957). The validity of some current tests for organicity. *Journal of Consulting Psychology, 21,* 425–428.

Parker, K. (1983). Factor analysis of the WAIS-R at nine age levels between 16 and 74 years. *Journal of Consulting and Clinical Psychology, 51,* 302–308.

Parkinson, S. R. (1980). Aging and amnesia: A running span analysis. *Bulletin of the Psychonomic Society, 15,* 215–217.

Parsons, O. A. (1970). Clinical neuropsychology. In C. D. Spielberger (Ed.), *Current topics in clinical and community psychology* (Vol. 2). New York: Academic Press.

Parsons, O. A. (1977). Neuropsychological deficits in alcoholics: Facts and fancies. *Alcoholism: Clinical and Experimental Research, 1,* 51–56.

Parsons, O. A., & Prigatano, G. P. (1978). Methodological consideration in clinical neuropsychological research. *Journal of Consulting and Clinical Psychology, 46,* 608–619.

Pauker, J. D. (1977). *Adult norms for the Halsteid-Reitan Neuropsychological Test Battery: Preliminary data.* Paper presented at the fifth annual meeting of the International Neuropsychological Society, Santa Fe.

Peck, D. F. (1970). The conversion of Progressive Matrices and Mill Hill Vocabulary raw scores into deviation IQs. *Journal of Clinical Psychology, 26,* 67–70.

Pendleton, M. G., & Heaton, R. K. (1982). A comparison of the Wisconsin Card Sorting Test and the Category Test. *Journal of Clinical Psychology, 38,* 392–396.

Peritti, P. (1969). Cross sex and cross educational performance in a color word interference test. *Psychonomic Science, 16,* 321–323.

Peritti, P. (1971). Effects of non-competitive, competitive instructions and sex on performance in color word interference test. *Journal of Psychology, 79,* 67–70.

Pershad, D., & Lubey, B. L. (1974). Some experience with a memory test in the aged cases. *Indian Journal of Psychology, 49,* 305–312.

Pershad, D., & Verma, S. K. (1980). Clinical utility of Hooper's Visual Organization test (VOT): A preliminary investigation. *Indian Journal of Clinical Psychology, 7,* 67–70.

Peterson, L. R., & Peterson, M. J. (1959). Short term retention of individual verbal items. *Journal of Experimental Psychology, 58,* 193–198.

Pheley, A. M. & Klesges, R. C. (1986). The relationship between experimental and neuropsychological measures of memory. *Archives of Clinical Neuropsychology, 1,* 231–241.

Piercy, M., & Smith, V. O. G. (1962). Right hemisphere dominance for certain non-verbal intellectual skills. *Brain, 85,* 775–790.

Pihl, R. O. & Nimrod, G. (1976). The reliability and validity of the Draw-A-Person test in IQ and personality assessment. *Journal of Clinical Psychology, 32,* 470–472.

Piotrowski, Z. (1937). The Rorschach inkblot method in organic disturbances of the central nervous system. *Journal of Nervous and Mental Disease, 86,* 525–537.

Piotrowski, Z. (1940). Positive and negative Rorschach organic reactions. *Rorschach Research Exchange, 4,* 147–151.

Plaisted, J. R., & Golden, C. J. (1982). Test-retest reliability of the clinical, factor, and localization scales of the Luria-Nebraska Neuropsychological Battery, *International Journal of Neuroscience, 17,* 163–167.

Poitrenaud, J., & Barrere, H. (1972). Étude sur la signification diagnostique des certaines erreurs de reproduction au V.R.T. de Benton. *Review of Applied Psychology, 22,* 43–56.

Pollock, B. (1942). The validity of the Shipley-Hartford Retreat Test for "deterioration." *Psychiatric Quarterly, 16,* 119–131.

Prado, W. M., & Taub, D. V. (1966). Accurate prediction of individual intellectual functioning by the Shipley-Hartford. *Journal of Clinical Psychology, 22,* 294–296.

Price, L. J., Fein, G., & Feinberg, I. (1979). *Cognitive and neuropsychological variables in the normal elderly.* Paper presented at the American Psychological Association convention, New York City.

Prifitera, A., & Ryan, J. J. (1981). Validity of the Luria-Nebraska Neuropsychological Battery Intellectual Processes scale as a measure of adult intelligence. *Journal of Consulting and Clinical Psychology, 49,* 755–756.

Prifitera, A., & Ryan, J. J. (1982). Concurrent validity of the Luria-Nebraska Neuropsychological Battery Memory scale. *Journal of Clinical Psychology, 38,* 378–379.

Prigatano, G. F. (1978). Wechsler Memory Scale: A selective review of the literature (monograph). *Journal of Clinical Psychology, 34,* 816–832.

Prigatano, G. P., & Parsons, O. A. (1976). Relationship of age and education to Halstead Test performance in different patient populations. *Journal of Consulting and Clinical Psychology, 44,* 527–533.

Prigatano, G. P., Parsons, D., Wright, E., Levin, D. C., & Hawryluk, G. (1983). Neuropsychological test performance in mildly hypoxic patients with chronic obstructive pulmonary disease. *Journal of Consulting and Clinical Psychology, 51,* 108–116.

Puente, A. E., Heidelberg-Sanders, C., & Lund, N. L. (1982). Discrimination of schizophrenia with and without nervous system damage using the Luria-Nebraska Neuropsychological Battery. *International Journal of Neuroscience, 16,* 59–62.

Putman, L. R. (1981). Minnesota Percepto-Diagnostic Test and reading achievement. *Perceptual and Motor Skills, 53,* 235–238.

Quattrochi, M. M., & Golden, C. J. (1983). Peabody Picture Vocabulary Test-Revised and Luria-Nebraska Neuropsychlogical Battery for Children: Intercorrelations for normal youngsters. *Perceptual and Motor Skills, 56,* 632–634.

Query, W. T., & Berger, R. A. (1980). AVLT memory scores as a function of age among general, medical, neurologic, and alcoholic patients. *Journal of Clinical Psychology, 36,* 1009–1012.

Query, W. T., & Megran, J. (1983). Age related norms for a AVLT in a male patient population. *Journal of Clinical Psychology, 39,* 136–138.

Ratcliffe, K. J. & Ratcliffe, M. W. (1979). The Leiter Scales: A review of validity findings. *American Annals of the Deaf, 124,* 38–44.

Rathbun, J., & Smith, A. (1982). Comment on the validity of Boyd's validation study of the Hooper Visual Organization Test. *Journal of Consulting and Clinical Psychology, 50,* 281–283.

Rausch, R., Lieb, J. P., & Crandall, P. H. (1978). Neuropsychological correlates of depth spike activity in epileptics. *Archives of Neurology, 35,* 699–705.

Raven, J. C., Court, J. H., & Raven, J. (1977). *Manual for Raven's Progressive Matrices and Vocabulary Scales.* London: H. K. Lewis.

Reed, H. B. C., & Reitan, R. M. (1963). Changes in psychological test performance associated with the normal aging process. *Journal of Gerontology, 18,* 271–274.

Reeve, R. R., French, J. L., & Hunter, M. (1983). A validation of the Leiter International Performance Scale with kindergarten children. *Journal of Consulting and Clinical Psychology, 51,* 458–459.

Reitan, R. M. (1955a). Affective disturbances in brain-damaged patients. *Archives of Neurology and Psychiatry, 73,* 530–532.

Reitan, R. M. (1955b). Certain differential effects of left and right cerebral lesions in human adults. *Journal of Comparative and Physiological Psychology, 48,* 474–477.

Reitan, R. M. (1955c). An investigation of the validity of Halstead's measures of biological intelligence. *Archives of Neurology and Psychiatry, 73,* 28–35.

Reitan, R. M. (1959). The comparative effects of brain damage on the Halstead Impairment Index and the Wechsler-Bellevue Scale. *Journal of Clinical Psychology, 15*, 281–285.

Reitan, R. M. (1966). A research program on the psychological effects of brain lesions in human beings. In N. R. Ellis (Ed.)., *International review of research in mental retardation* (Vol. 1). New York: Academic Press.

Reitan, R. M. (1976). Neurological and physiological bases of psychopathology. *Annual Review of Psychology, 27*, 189–216.

Reitan, R. M., & Davison, L. A. (1974). *Clinical neuropsychology: Current status and applications.* Washington, DC: Winston.

Reitan, R. M., & Wolfson, D. (1985). *The Halstead-Reitan Neuropsychological Battery: Theory and clinical interpretation.* Tucson, AZ: Neuropsychology Press.

Rey, A. (1964). *L'examen clinique en psychologie.* Paris: Presses Universitaires de France.

Reynolds, C. R., & Gutkin, T. B. (1980). Statistics related to profile interpretation of the Peabody Individual Achievement Test. *Psychology in the Schools, 17*, 316–319.

Richards, H. C., Fowler, P. C., Berent, S., & Boll, T. J. (1980). Comparison of WISC-R factor patterns for younger and older epileptic children. *Journal of Clinical Neuropsychology, 2*, 333–341.

Riddle, M., & Roberts, A. H. (1977). Delinquency, delay of gratification, recividism, and the Porteus Maze Tests. *Psychological Bulletin, 84*, 417–425.

Riddle, M., & Roberts, A. H. (1978). Psychosurgery and the Porteus Maze Tests. *Archives of General Psychiatry, 35*, 493–497.

Riege, W. H., Kelly, K., & Klane, L. T. (1981). Age and error differences on Memory for Designs. *Perceptual and Motor Skills, 52*, 507–513.

Ritter, D. R. (1974). Concurrence of psychiatric diagnosis and psychological diagnosis based on the MMPI. *Journal of Personality Assessment, 38*, 52–54.

Rixecker, H., & Hartje, W. (1980). Kimura's Recurring-Figures-Test: A normative study. *Journal of Clinical Psychology, 36*, 465–467.

Robin, R. W., & Shea, J. D. C. (1983). The Bender Gestalt Visual Motor Test in Papua New Guinea. *International Journal of Psychology, 18*, 263–270.

Robinson, A. L., Heaton, R. K., Lehman, R. A. W., & Stilson, D. W. (1980). The utility of the Wisconsin Card Sorting Test in detecting and localizing frontal lobe lesions. *Journal of Consulting and Clinical Psychology, 48*, 605–614.

Rogers, D. A. (1972). Review of the MMPI. In Oscar Burros (Ed.), *The seventh mental measurements yearbook.* Lincoln, NE: Burros Institute.

Rohwer, W. D., & Lynch, S. (1968). Retardation, school strata, and learning efficiency. *American Journal of Mental Deficiency, 73*, 91–96.

Roid, G. H., Prifitera, A., & Ledbetter, M. (1988). Confirmatory analysis of the factor structure of the Wechsler Memory Scale- Revised. *The Clinical Neuropsychologist, 2*, 116–120.

Rosenberg, S. J., Ryan, J. J., & Prifitera, A. (1984). Rey Auditory-Verbal Learning Test performance of patients with and without memory impairment. *Journal of Clinical Psychology, 40*, 785–787.

Ross, W. D., & Ross, S. (1944). Some Rorschach ratings of clinical value. *Rorschach Research Exchange, 8*, 1–9.

Rotatori, A. F. (1978). Test-retest reliability of the Quick Test for mentally retarded children. *Psychological Reports, 46*, 162.

Royce, J. R., Yeudall, L. T., & Bock, C. (1976). Factor analytic studies of human brain damage: 1. 1st and 2nd order factors and their brain correlates. *Multivariate Behavioral Research, 11*, 381–418.

Ruff, C. F., Ayers, J. L., & Templer, D. I. (1977). The Watson and Hovey MMPI scales: Do they measure organicity or "functional" psychopathology? *Journal of Clinical Psychology, 33*, 732–734.

Russell, E. W. (1975a). A multiple scoring system for the assessment of complex memory functions. *Journal of Consulting and Clinical Psychology, 43*, 800–809.

Russell, E. W. (1975b). Validation of a brain-damage vs. schizophrenia MMPI key. *Journal of Clinical Psychology, 31,* 659–661.

Russell, E. W. (1976). The Bender Gestalt and the Halstead Reitan battery: A case study. *Journal of Clinical Psychology, 32,* 355–361.

Russell, E. W. (1977). MMPI profiles of brain-damaged and schizophrenic subjects. *Journal of Clinical Psychology, 33,* 190–193.

Russell, E. W. (1980). *Theoretical bases of Luria-Nebraska and Halstead-Reitan batteries.* Paper presented at the American Psychological Association Convention, Montreal.

Russell, E. W. (1982). Factor analysis of the Revised Wechsler Memory Scale tests in a neuropsychological battery. *Perceptual and Motor Skills, 54,* 971–974.

Russell, E. W. (1987). Neuropsychological interpretation of the WAIS. *Neuropsychology, 1,* 2–6.

Russell, E. W., Neuringer, C., & Goldstein, G. (1970). *Assessment of brain damage: A neuropsychological key approach.* New York: Wiley.

Russo, M. & Vignolo, L. A. (1967). Visual figure-ground discrimination in patients with unilateral cerebral disease. *Cortex, 3,* 118–127.

Rutter, M., Graham, P., & Yule W. (1970). *A neuropsychiatric study in childhood.* London: Spastics International Medical Publication.

Ryan, J. J. (1984). Abnormality of subtest score and verbal-performance IQ differences on the WAIS-R. *International Journal of Clinical Neuropsychology, 6,* 97–98.

Ryan, J. J., & Geisser, M. E. (1986). Validity and diagnostic accuracy of an alternate form of the Rey Auditory Verbal Learning Test. *Archives of Clinical Neuropsychology, 1,* 209–217.

Ryan, J. J. & Lewis, C. V. (1988). Comparison of normal controls and recently detoxified alcoholics on the Wechsler Memory Scale-Revised. *The Clinical Neuropsychologist, 2,* 173–180.

Ryan, J. J., Prifitera, A., & Powers, L. (1983). Scoring reliability of the WAIS-R. *Journal of Consulting and Clinical Psychology, 51,* 149–150.

Ryan, J. J., Rosenberg, S. J., & DeWolfe, A. S. (1984a). Generalization of the WAIS-R factor structure with a vocational rehabilitation sample. *Journal of Consulting and Clinical Psychology, 52,* 311–312.

Ryan, J. J., Rosenberg, S. J., & Mittenberg, W. (1984b). Factor analysis of the Rey Auditory-Verbal Learning Test. *International Journal of Clinical Neuropsychology, 8,* 239–241.

Ryan, J. J., Geisser, M. E., Randail, D. M., & Georgemiller, R. J. (1986). Alternate form reliability and equivalence of the Rey Auditory Verbal Learning Test. *Journal of Clinical and Experimental Neuropsychology, 8,* 611–616.

Ryan, J. R., Morris, J., Yaffa, S., & Peterson, L. (1981). Test-retest reliability of the Wechsler Memory Scale, Form 1. *Journal of Clinical Psychology, 37,* 847–848.

Ryckman, D. B., Rentfrow, R., Fargo, G., & McCartin, R. (1972). Reliabilities of three tests of form copying. *Perceptual and Motor Skills, 34,* 917–918.

Salvia, J. (1969). Four tests of color vision: A study of diagnostic accuracy with the mentally retarded. *American Journal of Mental Deficiency, 74,* 421–427.

Salvia, J., & Ysseldyke, J. (1972). Criterion validity of four tests for red-green color blindness. *American Journal of Mental Deficiency, 76,* 418–422.

Samuels, I., Butters, N., & Fedio, P. (1972). Short term memory disorders following temporal lobe removals in humans. *Cortex, 8,* 283–298.

Sand, P. L. (1973). Performance of medical patient groups with and without brain-damage on the Hovey (0) and Watson (SC-0) MMPI scales. *Journal of Clinical Psychology, 29,* 235–237.

Sanner, R., & McManis, D. L. (1978). Concurrent validity of the Peabody Individual Achievement Test and the Wide Range Achievement Test for middle-class elementary school children. *Psychological Reports, 42,* 19–24.

Sattler, J. M., & Feldman, G. I. (1981). Comparisons of 1965, 1976, and 1978 norms for the Wide Range Achievement Test. *Psychological Reports, 49,* 115–118.

Sattler, J., & Gwynne, J. (1982a). Ethnicity and Bender Visual Motor Gestalt test performance. *Journal of School Psychology, 20,* 69–71.

Sattler, J. M., & Gwynne, J. (1982b). White examiners do not impede the intelligence test performance of black children: To debunk a myth. *Journal of Consulting and Clinical Psychology, 50,* 196–208.

Satz, P. (1966). A block rotation task: The application of multivariate and decision theory analysis for the prediction of organic brain damage. *Psychological Monographs: General and Applied, 80* (Whole No. 269).

Satz, P., Fennell, E., & Reilly, C. (1970). Predictive validity of six neurodiagnostic tests: A decision theory analysis. *Journal of Consulting and Clinical Psychology, 34,* 375–381.

Sawicki, R. F., & Golden, C. J. (1984a). Multivariate techniques in neuropsychology: 1. Comparison of orthogonal rotation methods with the receptive scale of the Luria Nebraska Neuropsychological Battery. *International Journal of Clinical Neuropsychology, 6,* 126–134.

Sawicki, R. F., & Golden, C. J. (1984b). The profile elevation scale and impairment scale: Two new summary scales for the Luria-Nebraska Neuropsychological Battery. *International Journal of Neuroscience, 23,* 81–90.

Sawyer, R. N., Stanley, G. E., & Watson, T. E. (1979). A factor analytic study of the construct validity of the Pictorial Test of Intelligence. *Educational and Psychological Measurement, 39,* 613–623.

Schludermann, E. H., Schludermann, S. M., Merryman, P. W., & Brown, B. W. (1983). Halstead's studies in the neuropsychology of aging. *Archives of Gerontology and Geriatrics, 2,* 49–172.

Schneider, M. A., & Spivack, G. (1979). An investigative study of the Bender-Gestalt: Clinical validation of its use in a reading disabled population. *Journal of Clinical Psychology, 35,* 346–351.

Schreiber, D. J., Goldman, H., Kleinman, K. M., Goldfader, P. R., & Snow, M. Y. (1976). The relationship between independent neuropsychological and neurological detection and localization of cerebral impairment. *Journal of Nervous and Mental Disease, 162,* 360–365.

Schultz, E. E., Keesler, T. Y., Friedenberg, L., & Sciara, A. D. (1984). Limitations inequivalence of alternate subtests for Russell's revision of the Wechsler Memory Scale: Causes and solutions. *Journal of Clinical Neuropsychology, 6,* 220–223.

Schutz, S. R., & Keisler, E. R. (1972). Young children's immediate memory of word classes in relation to social class. *Journal of Verbal Learning and Verbal Behavior, 11,* 13–17.

Schwarting, F. G., & Schwarting, K. R. (1977). The relationship of the WISC-R and WRAT: A study based upon a selected population. *Psychology in the Schools, 14,* 431–433.

Schwartz, M. S. (1969). "Organicity" and the MMPI 1-3-9 and 2-9 codes. *Proceedings, 77th Annual Convention, American Psychological Association.*

Schwartz, M. S., & Brown, J. R. (1973). MMPI differentiation on multiple sclerosis vs. pseudoneurologic patients. *Journal of Clinical Psychology, 29*(4), 471–474.

Schwartz, S., & Wiedel, T. C. (1981). Incremental validity of the MMPI in neurological decision-making. *Journal of Personality Assessment, 45,* 424–426.

Schwenn, E., & Postman, L. (1967). Studies of learning to learn. *Journal of Verbal Learning and Verbal Behavior, 6,* 566–573.

Scott, L. H. (1981). Measuring intelligence with the Goodenough-Harris Drawing Test. *Psychological Bulletin, 89,* 483–505.

Scott, W. A. (1955). Reliability of content analysis: The case of nominal scale coding. *Public Opinion Quarterly, 19,* 321–325.

Scruggs, T. E., Mastropieri, M. A., & Argulewicz, E. D. (1983). Stability of performance on the PPVT-R for three ethnic groups attending a bilingual kindergarten. *Psychology in the Schools, 20,* 433–435.

Sechrest, L. (1963). Incremental validity: A recommendation. *Educational and Psychological Measurement, 23,* 153–158.

Semmes, J., Weinstein, S., Ghent, L., & Teuber, H. L. (1963). Correlates of impaired orientation in personal and extrapersonal space. *Brain, 86,* 747–772.

Sewell, T. E. (1977). A comparison of the WPPSI and Stanford-Binet Intelligence Scale (1972) among lower SES black children. *Psychology in the Schools, 14,* 158–161.

Shaw, D. J. (1966). The reliability and validity of the Halstead Category Test. *Journal of Clinical Psychology, 20,* 176–180.

Shaw, F. J., & Matthews, C. G. (1965). Differential MMPI performance of brain-damaged versus pseudo-neurologic groups. *Journal of Clinical Psychology, 21,* 405–408.

Shearn, C. R., Berry, D. F., & Fitzgibbons, D. J. (1974). Usefulness of the Memory For Designs Test in assessing mild organic complications in psychiatric patients. *Perceptual and Motor Skills, 38,* 1099–1104.

Shelley, C., & Goldstein, G. (1982). Psychometric relations between the Luria-Nebraska and Halstead-Reitan Neuropsychological Batteries in a neuropsychiatric setting. *Clinical Neuropsychology, 4,* 128–133.

Shelley, C., & Goldstein, G. (1983). Discrimination of chronic schizophrenia and brain damage with the Luria-Nebraska Neuropsychological Battery: A partially successful replication. *Clinical Neuropsychology, 5,* 82–85.

Sigmon, S. B. (1983). Performance of American schoolchildren on Raven's Progressive Matrices scale. *Perceptual and Motor Skills, 56,* 484–486.

Silverstein, A. B. (1962). Perceptual, motor, and memory functions in the Visual Retention Test. *American Journal of Mental Deficiency, 66,* 613–617.

Silverstein, A. B. (1963). Qualitative aspects of performance on the Visual Retention Test. *American Journal of Mental Deficiency, 68,* 109–113.

Silverstein, A. B. (1980). A comparison of the 1976 and 1978 norms for the WRAT. *Psychology in the Schools, 17,* 313–315.

Silverstein, A. B. (1982a). Pattern analysis as simultaneous statistical inference. *Journal of Consulting and Clinical Psychology, 50,* 234–240.

Silverstein, A. B. (1982b). Factor structure of the Wechsler Adult Intelligence Scale-Revised. *Journal of Consulting and Clinical Psychology, 50,* 661–664.

Simpson, R. G. (1982). Correlation between the General Information Subtest of the Peabody Individual Achievement Test and the Full Scale Intelligence Quotient of the WISC-R. *Educational and Psychological Measurement, 42,* 685–699.

Siskind, G. (1976). Hovey's 5-item MMPI scale and psychiatric patients. *Journal of Clinical Psychology, 32,* 50.

Skillbeck, C. E., & Woods, R. T. (1980). The factorial structure of the Wechsler Memory Scale: Samples of neuropsychological and psychogeriatric patients. *Journal of Clinical Neuropsychology, 2,* 293–300.

Slosson, R. L. (1963). Slosson Intelligence Test for Children and Adults. East Aurora, NY: Slosson Publications.

Small, J. G., Milstein, V., & Stevens, J. R. (1962). Are psychomotor epileptics different? A controlled study. *Archives of Neurology, 7,* 187–194.

Smith, A. (1960). Changes in Porteus Maze scores of brain operated schizophrenics after an eight year interval. *The Journal of Mental Science, 106,* 967–978.

Smith, A., & Kinder, E. F. (1959). Changes in psychological test performances of brain-operated schizophrenics after eight years. *Science, 129,* 149–150.

Smith, R. S. (1983). A comparison of the Wechsler Adult Intelligence Scale and the Wechsler Adult Intelligence Scale-Revised in a college population. *Journal of Consulting and Clinical Psychology, 51,* 414–419.

Smrini, P., Villardita, C., & Zappala, G. (1983). Influence of different paths on spatial memory performance in the Block Tapping Test. *Journal of Clinical Neuropsychology, 5,* 355–359.

Snow, J. H., Hynd, G. W., Hartlage, L. C., & Grant, D. H. (1983). The relationship between the Luria-Nebraska Neuropsychological Battery-Children's Revision and the Minnesota Percepto-Diagnostic Test with learning disabled students. *Psychology in the Schools, 20,* 415–419.

Snow, W. G., Freedman, L., & Ford, L. (1986). Lateralized brain damage, sex differences, and the Wechsler Scales: A reexamination of the literature. *Journal of Clinical and Experimental Neuropsychology, 8,* 179–189.

Sobotka, K. R., & Black, F. W. (1978). A procedure for the rapid computation of WISC-R factor scores. *Journal of Clinical Psychology, 34,* 117–119.

Soethe, J. W. (1972). Concurrent validity of the Peabody Individual Achievement Test. *Journal of Learning Disabilities, 5,* 47–49.

Spellacy, F. J., & Spreen, O. (1969). A short form of the Token Test. *Cortex, 5,* 390–397.

Spiers, P. A. (1981). Have they come to praise Luria or to bury him? The Luria-Nebraska Neurological Battery controversy. *Journal of Consulting and Clinical Psychology, 49,* 331–341.

Spiers, P. A. (1982). The Luria-Nebraska Neuropsychological Battery revisited: A theory in practice or just practicing? *Journal of Consulting and Clinical Psychology, 50,* 301–306.

Spiers, P. A. (1984). What more can I say? In reply to Hutchinson, one last comment from Spiers. *Journal of Consulting and Clinical Psychology, 52,* 546–552.

Spreen, O., & Benton, A. L. (1963a). *Sentence Repetition Test: Administration, scoring, and preliminary norms.* Unpublished manuscript, University of Iowa.

Spreen, O., & Gaddes, W. H. (1969). Developmental norms for 15 neuropsychological tests, ages 6 to 15. *Cortex, 5,* 171–191.

Sptizform, M. (1982). Normative data in the elderly on Luria-Nebraska Neuropsychological Battery. *Clinical Neuropsychology, 4,* 103–105.

Stambrook, M. S. (1983). The Luria-Nebraska Neuropsychological Battery: A promise that may be only partly fulfilled. *Journal of Clinical Neuropsychology, 5,* 247–269.

Stein, S. (1972). Psychometric test performance in relation to the psychopathology of epilepsy. *Archives of General Psychiatry, 26,* 532–538.

Steinmeyer, C. H. (1986). A meta-analysis of Halstead-Reitan test performance of non-brain damaged subjects. *Archives of Clinical Neuropsychology, 1,* 301–308.

Sternberg, D. E., & Jarvik, M. E. (1976). Memory functions in depression: Improvement with antidepressant medication. *Archives of General Psychiatry, 33,* 219–224.

Sterne, D. M. (1966). The Knox Cube Test as a test of memory and intelligence with male adults. *Journal of Clinical Psychology, 22,* 191–193.

Sterne, D. M. (1973). The Hooper Visual Organization Test and the Trail Making Test as discriminants of brain injury. *Journal of Clinical Psychology, 29,* 212–213.

Stewart, K. D., & Jones, E. C. (1976). Validity of the Slosson Intelligence Test: A ten year review. *Psychology in the Schools, 13,* 372–380.

Stinnett, J. L. & DiGiacomo, J. N. (1970). Daily administered unilateral ECT. *Biological Psychiatry, 3,* 303–306.

Stone, M. H., & Wright, B. D. (1980). *Knox's Cube Test (manual).* Chicago: Stoelting.

Stoner, S. B. (1981). Alternate form reliability of the Revised Peabody Picture Vocabulary Test for Head Start children. *Psychological Reports, 49,* 628.

Strauss, M. E., & Brandt, J. (1986). Attempt at preclinical identification of Huntington's Disease using the WAIS. *Journal of Clinical and Experimental Neuropsychology, 8,* 210–218.

Stromgren, L. (1973). Unilateral versus bilateral electroconvulsive therapy: Investigations into the therapeutic effect in endogenous depression. *Acta Psychiatrica Scandinavica,* Suppl., 240.

Stromgren, L. S., Christensen, A. L., & Fromholt, P. (1976). The effects of unilateral brief-interval ECT on memory. *Acta Psychiatrica Scandanavia, 54,* 336–346.

Stroop, J. R. (1935). The basis of Ligon's theory. *Journal of Psychology, 47,* 499–504.

Struempfer, D. J. (1971). Validation of two quality scales for children's figure drawings. *Preceptual and Motor Skills, 32*, 887–893.

Sundet, K. (1986). Sex differences in cognitive impairment following unilateral brain damage. *Journal of Clinical and Experimental Neuropsychology, 8*, 51–61.

Sweet, J. J., & Wysocki, J. J. (1982). Improving scorer reliability of the Wechsler Memory Scale: A pilot study. *Clinical Neuropsychology, 4*, 159–161.

Sweet, J. J., Carr, M. A., Rosini, E., & Kaspar, C. (1986). Relationship between the Luria-Nebraska Neuropsychological Battery-Children's Revision and the WISC-R. *International Journal of Clinical Neuropsychology, 8*, 177–180.

Swiercinsky, D. P., & Leigh, G. (1979). Comparison of neuropsychological data in the diagnosis of brain impairment with computerized tomography and other neurological procedures. *Journal of Clinical Psychology, 35*, 242–246.

Swiercinsky, D. P., & Warnock, J. K. (1977). Comparison of the neuropsychological key and discriminant analysis approaches in predicting cerebral damage and localization. *Journal of Consulting and Clinical Psychology, 45*, 808–814.

Talland, G. A. (1965a). *Deranged memory*. New York: Academic Press.

Talley, J. L. (1986). Memory span in learning disabled children: Digit Span and the Rey Auditory Verbal Learning Test, *Archives of Clinical Neuropsychology, 1*, 315–322.

Tamkin, A. S. (1980). The Weigl Color-Form Sorting Test as an index of cortical function. *Journal of Clinical Psychology, 36*, 778–781.

Tapley, S. M., & Bryden, M. P. (1977). An investigation of sex differences in spatial ability: Mental rotation of three-dimensional objects. *Canadian Journal of Psychology, 31*, 122–130.

Tarter, R. E., & Parsons, O. A. (1971). Conceptual shifting in chronic alcoholics. *Journal of Abnormal Psychology, 77*, 71–75.

Tarter, R. E., & Schneider, D. U. (1976). Blackouts: Relationship with memory capacity and alcoholism history. *Archives of General Psychiatry, 33*, 1492–1496.

Taylor, H. C., & Russell, J. T. (1939). The relationship of validity coefficients to the practical effectiveness of tests in selection: Discussion and tables. *Journal of Applied Psychology, 23*, 565–578.

Taylor, L. B. (1969). Localization of cerebral lesions by psychological testing. *Clinical Neurosurgery, 16*, 269–282.

Taylor, L. B. (1979). Psychological assessment of neurosurgical patients. In T. Rasmussen & R. Mareno (Eds.), *Functional neurosurgery*. New York: Raven Press.

Teasdale, J. D., & Beaumont, J. G. (1971). The effect of mood on performance on the Modified New Word Learning Test. *British Journal of Social and Clinical Psychology, 10*, 342–345.

Templer, D. I., & Connolly, W. (1976). Affective vs. thinking disturbance related to left- vs. right-brain functioning. *Psychological Reports, 3*(1), 141–142.

Templer, O. I., & Tarter, R. E. (1973). Incremental validity of the Quick Test. *Psychological Reports, 32*, 568.

Terman, L. M., & Merrill, M. A. (1972). *Stanford-Binet Intelligence Scale Manual for the Third Revision, Form L-M*. Boston: Houghton-Mifflin.

Teuber, H. L., Battersby, W. S., & Bender, M. B. (1960). *Visual field defects after penetrating missile wounds of the brain*. Cambridge: Harvard University Press.

Tillinghast, B. S., Morrow, J. E., & Uhlig, G. E. (1983). Retest and alternate from reliability of the PPVT-R with fourth, fifth, and sixth grade pupils. *Journal of Educational Research, 76*, 243–244.

Tinsley, H. E., & Weiss, D. J. (1975). Interrater reliability and agreement of subjective judgements. *Journal of Counseling Psychology, 22*, 368–376.

Tivnan, T., & Pillemer, D. B. (1978). The importance of small but consistent group differences on standardized tests: The case of sex differences on the McCarthy Scales of Children's Abilities. *Journal of Clinical Psychology, 34*, 443–445.

Tramontana, M. G. & Boyd, T. A. (1986). Psychometric screening of neuropsychological abnormalities in older children. *International Journal of Clinical Neuropsychology, 8,* 53–59.

Traub, G. S., & Spruill, J. (1982). Correlations between the Quick Test and Wechsler Adult Intelligence Scale-Revised. *Psychological Reports, 51,* 309–310.

Trifiletti, R. J. (1982). Differentiating brain damage from schizophrenia: A further test of Russell's MMPI key. *Journal of Clinical Psychology, 38*(1), 39–44.

Tsushima, W. T., & Wedding, D. A. (1979). A comparison of the Halstead-Reitan Neuropsychological Battery and computerized tomography in the identification of brain disorder. *Journal of Nervous and Mental Disease, 167,* 704–707.

Tulving, E. (1972). Episodic and semantic memory. In E. Tulving & W. Donaldson (Eds.), *Organization of memory* (pp. 381–403). New York: Academic.

Tuokko, H., & Crockett, D. (1987). Central cholinergic deficiency WAIS profiles in a nondemented sample. *Journal of Clinical and Experimental Neuropsychology, 9,* 224–227.

Tymchuk, A. J. (1974). Comparison of Bender error and time scores for groups of epileptic, retarded, and behavior-problem children. *Perceptual and Motor Skills, 38,* 71–74.

Upper, D., & Seeman, W. (1966). Brain-damage, schizophrenia, and five MMPI items. *Journal of Clinical Psychology, 24,* 444.

Urmer, A. H., Morris, A. B., & Wendland, L. V. (1960). The effect of brain damage on Raven's Progressive Matrices. *Journal of Clinical Psychology, 16,* 182–185.

U.S. Employment Service (1970). *Manual for the General Aptitude Test Battery.* Washington, DC: U.S. Department of Labor.

Vagrecha, Y. S., & Sen Mazumadar, D. P. (1974). Relevance of Piotrowski's signs in relation to intellectual deficit in organic (epileptic) and normal subjects. *Indian Journal of Clinical Psychology, 1*(2), 64–68.

Vance, H., Blizt, S., & Ellis, C. R. (1980). Equivalence of Forms One and Three of the Quick Test. *Psychological Reports, 46,* 1184–1186.

Vance, H. B., & Engin, A. (1978). Analysis of cognitive abilities of black children's performance on WISC-R. *Journal of Clinical Psychology, 34,* 452–456.

Vance, H. B., Blixt, S., Ellis, R., & Bebell, S. (1981). Stability of the WISC-R for a sample of exceptional children. *Journal of Clinical Psychology, 37,* 397–399.

Vance, B., Lester, M. L., & Thatcher, R. W. (1983). Interscorer reliability of the Minnesota Percepto-Diagnostic Test-Revised. *Psychology in the Schools, 20,* 420–423.

Van Gorp, W. G., Satz, P., Kiersch, M. E., & Henry, R. (1986). Normative data on the Boston Naming Test for a group of normal older adults. *Journal of Clinical and Experimental Neuropsychology, 8,* 702–709.

Varney, N. R. (1981). Letter recognition and visual form discrimination in aphasic alexia. *Neuropsychologia, 19,* 795–800.

Varney, N. R., & Benton, A. L. (1982). Qualitative aspects of pantomine recognition in aphasia. *Brain and Cognition, 1,* 132–139.

Vega, A., Jr., & Parsons, O. A. (1967). Cross-validation of the Halstead-Reitan tests for brain damage. *Journal of Consulting Psychology, 31,* 619–625.

Velborsky, J. (1964). Der Benton-Test in der klinischen Praxis. *Diagnostica, 10,* 91–102.

Viglione, D., & Exner, J. (1983). Current research in the comprehensive Rorschach systems. In J. Butcher & C. Speilberger (Eds.), *Advances in personality assessment* (Vol. 1). Hillsdale, NJ: Erlbaum.

Vogel, W. (1962). Some effects of brain lesions on MMPI profiles. *Journal of Consulting Psychology, 26,* 412.

Waber, D. P., & Holmes, J. M. (1986). Assessing children's memory production of the Rey-Ostereith Complex Figures. *Journal of Clinical and Experimental Neuropsychology, 8,* 563–580.

Wahler, C. (1956). A comparison of reproductive errors made by brain-damaged and control patients on a memory-for-designs test. *Journal of Abnormal and Social Psychology, 52,* 251–255.

Wake, F. R. (1956). *Finger localization in Canadian school children.* Presented at Annual Meeting of the Canadian Psychological Association, June, Ottawa.

Wake, F. R. (1957). *Finger localization scores in defective children.* Presented at Annual Meeting of the Canadian Psychological Association, June, Toronto.

Wallace, J. L. (1984). Wechsler Memory Scale. *International Journal of Clinical Neuropsychology, 6* (suppl.), 216–226.

Wallbrown, F. H., & Fremont, T. (1980). The stability of Koppitz scores on the Bender Gestalt for reading disabled children. *Psychology in the Schools, 17,* 181–184.

Wallbrown, F. H., & Fuller, G. B. (1984). A five step procedure for the clinical use of the MPD in neuropsychological assessment of children, *Journal of Clinical Psychology, 40,* 220–229.

Wallbrown, F. H., Blaha, J., Wallbrown, I. D., & Englis, H. (1975). The hierarchical factor structure of the Wechsler Intelligence Scale for Children-Revised. *Journal of Psychology,* 223–235.

Wallbrown, F. H., Wallbrown, J. D., & Engin, A. W. (1976). Test-retest reliability of the Bender Gestalt for first grade children. *Perceptual and Motor Skills, 42,* 743–746.

Wallbrown, J. D., Wallbrown, F. H., & Engin, A. W. (1977). The validity of two clinical tests of visual-motor perception. *Journal of Clinical Psychology, 33,* 491–495.

Walton, D. (1957). The validity of a psychological test of brain damage. *Bulletin of the British Psychological Society, No. 34.*

Walton, D., & Black, D. A. (1957). The validity of a psychological test of brain damage. *British Journal of Medical Psychology, 30,* 270–279.

Walton, D., White, J. G., Black, D. A., & Young, A. J. (1959). The Modified New Word Learning Test: A cross-validation study. *The British Journal of Medical Psychology, 32,* 213–220.

Wang, P. L. (1977). Visual organization ability in brain-damaged adults. *Perceptual and Motor Skills, 45,* 723–728.

Ward, L. O. (1982). Variables influencing children's formulation of criteria of classification as measured by a modification of the Weigl Sorting Test. *Journal of Psychology, 111,* 211–216.

Watson, C. G. (1968). The separation of NP hospital organics from schizophrenics with three visual motor screening tests. *Journal of Clinical Psychology, 24,* 412–414.

Watson, C. G. (1971). An MMPI scale to separate brain-damaged patients from schizophrenics. *Journal of Consulting and Clinical Psychology, 36,* 121–125.

Watson, C. G. (1973). A simple bivariate screening technique to separate NP hospital organics from other psychiatric groups. *Journal of Clinical Psychology, 29,* 448–450.

Watson, C. G., & Plemel, D. (1978). An MMPI scale to separate brain-damaged from functional psychiatric patients in neuropsychiatric settings. *Journal of Consulting and Clinical Psychology, 46,* 1127–1132.

Watson, C. G., & Thomas, R. W. (1968). MMPI profiles of brain-damaged and schizophrenic patients. *Perceptual and Motor Skills, 27,* 567–573.

Watson, C. G., Felling, J., & Maceachern, D. G. (1967). Objective Draw-A-Person scales: An attempted cross-validation. *Journal of Clinical Psychology, 23,* 382–386.

Watson, C. G., Thomas, R. W., Felling, J., & Anderson, D. (1969). Differentiation of organics from schizophrenics with the Trail Making Dynamometer, Critical Flicker Fusion, and Light-Intensity Matching Tests. *Journal of Clinical Psychology, 25,* 130–133.

Watson, C. G., Gasser, B., Schaefer, A., Buranen, C., & Wold, J. (1981). Separation of brain-damaged from psychiatric patients with ability and personality measures. *Journal of Clinical Psychology, 37,* 347–353.

Watts, F. N., & Everitt, B. S. (1980). The factorial structure of the General Aptitude Test Battery. *Journal of Clinical Psychology, 36,* 763–767.

Wechsler, D. (1974). *Manual for the Wechsler Intelligence Scale for Children-Revised*. New York: Psychological Corporation.

Wechsler, D. (1981). *WAIS-R manual*. New York: Psychological Corporation.

Wechsler, D. (1987). *Wechsler Memory Scale-Revised Manual*. San Antonio: The Psychological Corporation-Harcourt Brace Jovanovich.

Wechsler, D., & Stone, C. P. (1973). *Wechsler Memory Scale Manual*. New York: Psychological Corporation.

Wedding, D. (1983). Comparison of statistical and actuarial models for predicting lateralization of brain damage. *Clinical Neuropsychology, 5,* 15–20.

Weigl, E. (1941). On the psychology of so-called processes of abstraction. *Journal of Abnormal and Social Psychology, 36,* 3–33.

Weinberg, J., Diller, L., Gerstman, L., & Schulman, P. (1972). Digit span in left and right hemiplegics. *Journal of Clinical Psychology, 28,* 361.

Weingartner, H., & Silberman, E. (1982). Models of cognitive impairment: Cognitive changes in depression. *Psychopharmacology Bulletin, 18*(2), 27–42.

Weingold, H. P., Dawson, J. G., & Kael, H. C. (1965). Further examination of Hovey's "Index" for identification of brain lesions: Validation study. *Psychological Reports, 16,* 1098.

Weinman, J., & Cooper, R. L. (1981). Individual differences in perceptual problem solving ability: A response analysis approach. *Intelligence, 5,* 165–178.

Weinstein, S. (1964). Deficits concomitant with aphasia or lesions of either cerebral hemisphere. *Cortex, 1,* 154–169.

Weinstein, S., Semmes, J., Ghent, L., & Teuber, H. L. (1956). Spatial orientation in man after cerebral injury: 2. Analysis according to concomitant defects. *Journal of Psychology, 42,* 249–263.

Weiss, D. J. (1985). Adaptive testing by computer. *Journal of Consulting and Clinical Psychology, 53,* 774–789.

Welsh, G. S. (1956). Factor dimensions A and R. In G. S. Welsh & W. G. Dahlstrom (Eds.), *Basic readings on the MMPI in psychology and medicine*. Minneapolis: University of Minnesota Press.

Wheeler, L., & Reitan, R. M. (1963). Discriminant functions applied to the problem of predicting cerebral damage from behavioral tests: A cross validation study. *Perceptual and Motor Skills, 16,* 681–701.

Wheeler, L., Burke, C. J., & Reitan, R. M. (1963). An application of discriminant functions to the problem of predicting brain damage using behavioral variables. *Perceptual and Motor Skills, 16,* 417–440.

White, F., Lynch, J. I., & Hayden, M. E. (1978). Use of the Leiter International Performance Scale with adult aphasics. *Journal of Clinical Psychology, 38,* 667–671.

White, J. G. (1959). Walton's Modified Word Learning Test with children. *British Journal of Medical Psychology, 32,* 221–225.

White, T. H. (1979). Correlations among the WISC-R, PIAT, and DAM. *Psychology in the Schools, 16,* 497–501.

Wickoff, R. L. (1978). Correlational and factor analysis of the Peabody Individual Achievement Test and the WISC-R. *Journal of Consulting and Clinical Psychology, 46,* 322–325.

Wickoff, R. L. (1979). The WISC-R as a predictor of achievement. *Psychology in the Schools, 16,* 364–366.

Widiger, T. A., Knudson, R. M., & Rorer, L. G. (1980). Convergent and discriminant validity of measures of cognitive styles and abilities. *Journal of Personality and Social Psychology, 39,* 116–129.

Wiens, A. N., & Matarazzo, J. D. (1977). WAIS and MMPI correlates of the Halstead-Reitan Neuropsychological Battery in normal male subjects. *The Journal of Nervous and Mental Disease, 164,* 112–121.

Williams, H. L. (1952). The development of a caudality scale for the MMPI. *Journal of Clinical Psychology, 8,* 293–297.

Willis, W. G. (1984). Reanalysis of an actuarial approach to neuropsychological diagnosis in consideration of base rates. *Journal of Consulting and Clinical Psychology, 52,* 567–569.

Wilson, J. D., & Spangler, P. F. (1974). The Peabody Individual Achievement Test as a clinical tool. *Journal of Learning Disabilities, 7,* 60–63.

Wilson, J. M., & Wolfensberger, W. (1963). Color-blindness testing as an aid in the etiological diagnosis of mental retardation. *American Journal of Mental Deficiency, 67,* 914–915.

Wilson, R. S., Bacon, L. D. Kaszniak, A. W., & Fox, J. H. (1982). The episodic-semantic distinction and paired associate learning. *Journal of Consulting and Clinical Psychology, 50,* 154–155.

Withers, E., & Hinton, J. (1971). Three forms of the Clinical Tests of the Senorium and their reliability. *British Journal of Psychiatry, 119,* 1–8.

Witmer, L. R. (1935). The association value of three-place consonant syllables. *Journal of Genetic Psychology, 47,* 337–359.

Woodward, C. A. (1982). The Hooper Visual Organization Test: A case against its use in neuropsychological assessment. *Journal of Consulting and Clinical Psychology, 50,* 286–288.

Woodward, C. A., Santa-Barbara, J., & Roberts, R. (1975). Test-retest reliability of the Wide Range Achievement Test. *Journal of Clinical Psychology, 31,* 81–84.

Wright, B. D. (1977). Solving measurement problems with the Rasch model. *Journal of Eductional Measurement, 14,* 97–114.

Wright, D., & DeMers, S. T. (1982). Comparison of the relationship between two measures of visual-motor coordination and academic achievement. *Psychology in the Schools, 19,* 473–477.

Yater, A. C., Barclay, A. G., & McGilligan, R. (1969). Interrater reliability of scoring Goodenough-Harris drawings by disadvantaged preschool children. *Perceptual and Motor Skills, 28,* 281–282.

Zaidel, D., & Sperry, R. W. (1973). Performance on the Raven's Colored Progressive Matrices Test by subjects with cerebral commissurotomy. *Cortex, 9,* 34–39.

Zaidel, E., Zaidel, D. W., & Sperry, R. W. (1981). Left and right intelligence: Case study of Raven's Progressive Matrices following brain bisection and hemidecortication. *Cortex, 17,* 167–186.

Zangwill, O. L. (1966). Psychological deficits associated with frontal lobe lesions. *International Journal of Neurology, 5,* 395–402.

Zimmerman, I. L. (1965). Residual effects of brain-damage and five MMPI items. *Journal of Consulting Psychology, 29,* 394.

Zwick, R. (1988). Another look at interrater agreement. *Psychological Bulletin, 103,* 374–378.

Index

Abstraction, level of, 32–33
Achievement and aptitude tests, 253–259
  General Aptitude Test Battery, 253–254
  McCarthy Scales of Children's Abilities, 254–255
Peabody Individual Achievement Test, 255–258
Wide Range Achievement Test, 258–259
Age level
  Facial Recognition Test, 124
  Halstead–Reitan Battery, 93, 94–95
  memory tests, 190
  Rorschach inkblots, 154
  Wechsler Memory Scale, 166, 170–171
  See also Elderly
Aita signs, 159
Alcoholism
  Halstead–Reitan Battery, 96–97
  Luria–Nebraska Battery, 114
Alternate-forms reliability, 15, 22
Alzheimer's disease, 60. *See also* Elderly
American Psychological Association, 45
Aphasia. *See* Language impairment
Apraxia
  Three-Dimensional Block Construction Test, 131
  Use of Objects Test, 201–202
Aptitude tests. *See* Achievement and aptitude tests
Assessment. *See* Neuropsychological assessment
Auditory memory, 190–193. *See also* Memory
Automated interpretation, 103

Behavioral observation. *See* Observation
Bender–Gestalt Visual Motor Integration Test, 237–246
  normative data, 238
  organic/nonorganic differentiation, 101
  overview of, 237
  reliability, 238–241
  validity, 241–246
Benton assessment, 121–138
  Benton Visual Retention Test, 134–137
  Facial Recognition Test, 123–125
  Finger Localization Test, 130–131
  Judgment of Line Orientation Test, 125–126
  Motor Impersistence Test, 133–134
  overview of, 121–122
  Pantomime Recognition Test, 128–129
  Phoneme Discrimination Test, 131
  Right–left orientation, 122–123
  Sentence Repetition Test, 138
  Serial Digit Learning Test, 123
  Tactile Form Perception Test, 129–130
  Three-Dimensional Block Construction Test, 131–133
  Visual Form Discrimination Test, 126–128
Benton Visual Retention Test, 3, 134–137
  Hooper Visual Organization Test and, 215
  Memory for Designs Test and, 186
  overview of, 134–135
  reliability, 135–136
  validity, 136–137
Block Rotation Test (Satz), 215–219
Block Tapping Test, 197–200
Body Parts Identification Test, 207

Boston Diagnostic Aphasia Examination, 208
Boston Naming Test, 207–208
Brain–behavior relation, 45–46
Brain impairment
  construct validity, 46
  neuropsychology and, 2
  personality and, 141–150
  validity, 29

Classical test theory, 4
  generalizability theory and, 10–11
  item response theory and, 8–9
  reliability, 15
Classification analysis, 43
Clinical Tests of the Sensorium, 246–247
Coefficient omega, 25
Coefficient theta, 24–25
Coefficients of equivalence, 22
Coefficients of stability, 21
Cognitive function tests, 225–235
  Elithorn's Perceptual Maze, 227–230
  Porteus Maze Test, 225–226
  Verbal Concept Attainment Test, 230–231
  Weigl Color–Form Sorting Test, 231–232
  Wisconsin Card Sorting Test, 232–235
Computed tomography, 44
Computer interpretation, 103
Concurrent validity
  criterion validity, 44
  Halstead–Reitan Battery, 98–99
Construct validity, 31, 32, 33
  described, 45–49
  Wechsler Intelligence Scale for Children–Revised, 67–72
Content sampling, 23
Content validity, 31–32, 38–41
Correlation coefficients, 17–20
Criterion validity, 31–32, 41–45
Cronbach's alpha, 24

Degenerative disorders, 10
Delayed-memory factor, Wechsler Memory Scale, 176
Depression, 146
Design methodology, 20–25
Digit-span procedures, 193–194
Discriminant function analysis, 43
Discriminative validity, Halstead–Reitan, 99–101

Dorken signs, 159, 161
Draw-a-Man Test. See Goodenough–Harris Drawing Test

Educational differences, 95
Elderly
  Luria–Nebraska Battery, 113
  Wechsler Memory Scale, 166, 170–171, 179
  See also Age level; Alzheimer's disease
Electroconvulsive therapy, 187
Electroencephalography, 44
Elithorn's Perceptual Maze, 227–230
Epilepsy, 114
Error component, 15–16
Ethics, 45
Evans signs, 159–160
External validity, 50

Face validity, 40
Facial Recognition Test, 123–125
Figure–ground tests, 212–213
Finger Localization Test, 130–131
Four-square interrelationships, 157

General Aptitude Test Battery, 253–254
General intelligence tests. See Intelligence tests; Wechsler Adult Intelligence Scale–Revised; Wechsler Intelligence Scale for Children–Revised
Generalizability theory
  benefits of, 14
  reliability, 10–13
Goodenough–Harris Drawing Test
  described, 73–74
  Wechsler Intelligence Scale for Children–Revised and, 65–66

Halstead–Reitan Neuropsychological Battery, 91–107
  age effects, 94–95
  education effect, 95
  Luria–Nebraska compared, 114–115
  normative data, 93–95
  overview of, 91–93
  psychiatric/neurological differentiation, 101–107
  reliability, 95–98
  sex differences, 95
  validity, 98–101
  Verbal Concept Attainment Test and, 230

Halstead–Reitan Neuropsychological
  Battery (*Cont.*)
  Wechsler Intelligence Scale for Children–
    Revised and, 71–72
  Wisconsin Card Sorting Test and, 233–234
Head injury. *See* Brain impairment
Higher cognitive function tests. *See*
  Cognitive function tests
Homogeneity of construct, 23–24
Hooper Visual Organization Test, 213–215
Hughes signs, 159, 161

Individual differences
  skills, 13
  validity, 35
Intelligence tests, 73–89
  Goodenough–Harris Drawing Test, 73–74
  Leiter International Performance Scale,
    75–76
  Mill Hill Vocabulary Test, 76
  Peabody Picture Vocabulary Test–
    Revised, 77–78
  Pictorial Test of Intelligence, 76
  Queensland Test, 78–79
  Quick Test, 79–81
  Raven's Progressive Matrices, 81–86
  Shipley–Hartford Scale, 88–89
  Slosson Intelligence Test, 87–88
  Stanford–Binet Intelligence Scale, 86–87
  See also Wechsler Adult Intelligence
    Scale–Revised; Wechsler Intelligence
    Scale for Children–Revised
Internal consistency
  Halstead–Reitan Battery, 97–98
  methodology, 23–24
Internal validity, 50
Invariance of the item parameters, 9
Ishihara Color Blind Test, 210–211
Item characteristic curve, 9
Item response theory
  benefits of, 13–14
  Knox Cube Test, 195
  methodology, 27–28
  reliability, 8–10
Internal consistency
  Halstead–Reitan Battery, 97–98
  methodology, 23–24
Internal validity, 50

Judgment of Line Orientation Test, 125–126

Kendall's tau, 19–20
Kimura's Recurring Figures Test, 194–195
Knox Cube Test, 2, 195–197
Koppitz Scoring System, 244–246
Kral signs, 159, 161

Language impairment
  Minnesota Multiphasic Personality
    Inventory, 148
  Pantomime Recognition Test, 128–129
  Phoneme Discrimination Test, 131
  Right–Left Orientation, 122
  Sentence Repetition Test, 138
  Use of Objects Tests, 201–202
  Visual Form Discrimination Test, 127–128
  See also Verbal function tests
Latent trait model. *See* Item response
  theory
Leiter International Performance Scale, 75–
  76
Length of test, 23
Localization
  Luria–Nebraska Battery, 115–116
  Minnesota Multiphasic Personality
    Inventory, 141–142
Luria–Nebraska Neuropsychological
  Battery, 3, 4, 109–120
  content validity, 39
  criticism of, 116–118
  Form II, 118–120
  Halstead–Reitan Battery and, 103–104
  overview, 109–112
  reliability, 112–113
  validity, 113–118
  Wechsler Intelligence Scale for Children–
    Revised and, 71–72
  word-span procedures, 189

McCarthy Scales of Children's Abilities,
  254–255
Magnetic resonance imaging, 44
Marmorston signs, 159–160
Meaningful pictures procedure, 211
Measurement considerations, 1–6
Medical procedures, 99
Memory
  Luria–Nebraska Battery, 115
  Luria–Nebraska Form II, 119
  Wechsler Memory Scale, 165–183
Memory for Designs Test, 185–187

Memory tests, 185–200
    Block Tapping Test, 197–200
    digit span, 193–194
    Kimura's Recurring Figures Test, 194–195
    Knox Cube Test, 195–197
    Memory for Designs Test, 185–187
    paired associates, 187–188
    Rey Auditory-Verbal Learning Test, 190–193
    trigrams, 188–189
    word-span procedures, 189–190
Mental retardation, 133
Method of contrasted groups, 43
Mill Hill Vocabulary Test, 76
Minnesota Multiphasic Personality
        Inventory, 6, 139–152
    differential performance paradigm, 142–147
    Halstead–Reitan Battery, 92–93
    neuropsychological functioning for group
        inclusion, 147–150
    overview, 139–140
    reliability, 140
    validity, 141–150
    variance, 150–151
Minnesota Paper Form Board Test, 212
Minnesota Percepto-Diagnostic Test, 219–224
Monotonicity, 19
Motor Impersistence Test, 133–134
Multitrait–multimethod matrix, 46–48

Neuropsychological assessment, 1–6
Neuropsychological Impairment Screen,
        247–249
New Word Learning Test, 206
Nonrandom error, 16
Numbers (digit-span procedures), 193–194

Object-naming tests, 202
Observation
    generalizability theory, 11
    validity, 30
Operational theory, 4

Paired associates, 187–188
Pantomime Recognition Test, 128–129
Peabody Individual Achievement Test, 66,
        255–258
Peabody Picture Vocabulary Test–Revised
    described, 77–78
    Hooper Visual Organization Test and, 215
    Token Test and, 205

Pearson product–moment correlation
        coefficient, 17–18
Personal Orientation Test, 249
Personality, 139–140
Phi coefficient, 19
Phoneme Discrimination Test, 131
Pictorial Test of Intelligence, 76
Piotrowski signs, 158–159, 161
Point-biserial coefficient, 19
Porteus Maze Test, 225–226
Prediction
    construct validity, 46
    Wechsler Intelligence Scale for Children–
        Revised, 66
Product–moment coefficient, 17–18
Psychology, 1–2
Psychopathology. See entries under names
        of specific tests
Psychosurgery, 225–226, 227

Queensland Test, 78–79
Quick Test
    described, 79–81
    Wechsler Memory Scale and, 173

Race differences
    Bender–Gestalt Visual Motor Integration
        Test, 238
    Knox Cube Test, 196
    Stanford–Binet Intelligence Scale, 87
    Wechsler Intelligence Scale for Children–
        Revised, 69–70
Random error, 16
Randt Memory Test
    described, 187
    word-span procedures, 189
Rasch model. See Item response theory
Rater agreement, 25
Rater reliability, 25
Raven's Progressive Matrices, 81–86
Reitan signs, 159
Reliability
    Bender–Gestalt Visual Motor Integration
        Test, 238–241
    Benton Visual Retention Test, 135–136
    Block Rotation Test, 216
    definitions, 7, 13, 15, 16–17, 20, 27
    design methodology, 20–25
    generalizability theory, 10–13
    general/theoretical considerations, 7–14
    Halstead–Reitan Battery, 95–98
    interpretation of information, 25–27

Reliability (*Cont.*)
  item response theory, 8–10, 27–28
  Luria–Nebraska Battery, 112–113
  Minnesota Multiphasic Personality
    Inventory, 140
  Minnesota Percepto-Diagnostic Test, 220–
    221
  practical/methodological considerations,
    15–28
  Rorschach inkblots, 155–156
  statistical methodology, 17–20
  Stroop Word–Color Test, 250–251
  Wechsler Adult Intelligence Scale–
    Revised, 54–58
  Wechsler Intelligence Scale for Children–
    Revised, 61–65
  Wechsler Memory Scales, 166–171, 181
Representational theory, 4
Rey Auditory-Verbal Learning Test, 190–
  193
Rey–Osterreith Complex Figure Test, 209–
  210
Right–left orientation, 122–123
Rorschach inkblots, 2, 153–163
  normative data, 154–155
  organic signs, 158–160
  overview, 153–154
  reliability, 155–156
  sign system normative data, 160
  sign system reliability studies, 160
  sign system validity, 161–162
  validity, 156–158
Ruth signs, 159

Satz Block Rotation Test, 215–219
Schizophrenia
  Facial Recognition Test, 125
  Halstead–Reitan Battery, 101–107
  Minnesota Multiphasic Personality
    Inventory, 143, 145, 146
  Motor Impersistence Test, 133–134
Screening devices, 237–252
  Bender–Gestalt Visual Motor Integration
    Test, 237–246
  Clinical Tests of the Sensorium, 246–247
  Neuropsychological Impairment Screen,
    247–249
  Personal Orientation Test, 249
  Stroop Word–Color Test, 249–252
Sensory impairment, 129–130

Sentence Repetition Test, 138
Serial Digit Learning Test, 123
Sex differences
  Bender–Gestalt Visual Motor Integration
    Test, 238
  Block Rotation Test, 217
  Goodenough–Harris Drawing Test, 73
  Halstead–Reitan Battery, 95
  Wechsler Adult Intelligence Scale–
    Revised, 56–57
Shipley–Hartford Scale, 88–89
Short-term verbal memory, 174–175. *See
  also* Memory; Memory tests
Skills
  assessment instruments, 3
  individual differences, 13, 35
  validity, 31
Slosson Intelligence Test, 87–88
Socioeconomic class
  Knox Cube Test, 196
  memory tests, 190
  Stanford–Binet Intelligence Scale, 87
Spatial impairment, 122
Spearman's rank coefficient, 19–20
Split-half reliability, 15
  methodology, 22–23
  Wechsler Adult Intelligence Scale–
    Revised, 54
  See also Reliability
Stanford–Binet Intelligence Scale
  described, 86–87
  Wechsler Intelligence Scale for Children–
    Revised and, 65
Statistical methodology, 17–20
Stick Construction Test, 211–212
Stroop Word–Color Test, 23, 249–252
Symbol Digit Modalities Test, 215

Tactile Form Perception Test, 129–130
Tactual Performance Test, 23
Test–retest reliability, 15
  generalizability theory, 11
  Halstead–Reitan Battery, 95–98
  methodology, 20–21
  Wechsler Adult Intelligence Scale–
    Revised, 55
  See also Reliability
Three-Dimensional Block Construction Test,
  131–133
Token Test, 203–206
Trail Making Test, 92
Trigrams, 188–189

Use of Objects Test, 201–202

Validity
  Bender–Gestalt Visual Motor Integration
    Test, 241–246
  Benton Visual Retention Test, 136–137
  Block Rotation Test, 216–219
  construct measurement, 30–31
  construct validity, 45–49
  content validity, 38–41
  criterion validity, 41–45
  definitions, 29, 38–49
  elemental considerations in, 29–36
  Halstead–Reitan Battery, 98–101
  Luria–Nebraska Battery, 113–118
  Minnesota Multiphasic Personality
    Inventory, 141–150
  Minnesota Percepto-Diagnostic Test, 221–
    224
  nature of, 31–34
  neuropsychological assessment
    applications, 37–51
  nonneurological variables and, 34–35
  observation, 30
  Rorschach inkblots, 156–158
  Rorschach inkblots sign system, 161–162
  Stroop Word–Color Test, 251
  threats to, 49–50
  types of, 37–38
  Wechsler Adult Intelligence Scale–
    Revised, 58–59
  Wechsler Intelligence Scale for Children–
    Revised, 65–72
  Wechsler Memory Scales, 171–174, 182–
    183
Verbal Concept Attainment Test
  described, 230–231
  Wisconsin Card Sorting Test and, 234–235
Verbal function tests, 201–208
  Boston Naming Test, 207–208
  New Word Learning Test, 206
  object-naming tests, 202
  Token Test, 203–206
  Use of Objects Test, 201–202
  word association procedures, 202–203
  See also Language impairment
Visual Form Discrimination Test, 126–128
Visual function tests, 209–224
  figure–ground tests, 212–213
  Hooper Visual Organization Test, 213–
    215
  Ishihara Color Blind Test, 210–211

Visual function tests (Cont.)
  meaningful pictures procedure, 211
  Minnesota Paper Form Board Test, 212
  Minnesota Percepto-Diagnostic Test, 219–
    224
  Rey–Osterreith Complex Figure Test,
    209–210
  Satz Block Rotation Test, 215–219
  Stick Construction Test, 211–212

Wechsler Adult Intelligence Scale–Revised,
    53–60
  content validity, 41
  error, 16
  Halstead–Reitan Battery and, 92
  overview, 53–54
  reliability, 54–58
  validity, 58–59
  Wechsler Intelligence Scale for Children–
    Revised and, 65
  Wechsler Memory Scale and, 171–172,
    173–174
Wechsler Intelligence Scale for Children–
    Revised, 25, 61–72
  Goodenough–Harris Drawing Test and, 74
  overview, 61
  reliability, 61–65
  validity, 65–72
Wechsler Memory Scale, 165–183
  criticism, 176–176
  improvement efforts, 175–179
  normative data, 165–166
  overview, 165
  paired associates, 187
  reliability, 166–171
  short-term verbal memory measurement,
    174–175
  validity, 171–174
  word-span procedures, 189
Wechsler Memory Scale–Revised, 180–
    183
Wechsler Preschool and Primary Scale of
    Intelligence, 65
Weigl Color–Form Sorting Test, 231–232
Wide Range Achievement Test
  described, 258–259
  Wechsler Intelligence Scale for Children–
    Revised and, 65–66
Wisconsin Card Sorting Test, 232–235
Word association procedures, 202–203
Word Discrimination Test, 207
Word-span procedures, 189–190
World War II, 1–2